AFTER D-DAY

AFTER D-DAY

THE U.S. ARMY ENCOUNTERS THE FRENCH

ROBERT LYNN FULLER

Louisiana State University Press

Baton Rouge

Published with the assistance of the V. Ray Cardozier Fund

Published by Louisiana State University Press
www.lsupress.org

Manufactured in the United States of America
First printing

Designer: Michelle A. Neustrom
Typeface: Whitman
Printer and binder: Sheridan Books, Inc.

Cover photo: American officer and French partisan crouch behind an auto during a street fight
in a French city, 1944. National Archives and Records Administration, RG 111.

Cataloging-in-Publication Data are available from the Library of Congress.

ISBN 978-0-8071-7495-1 (cloth: alk. paper) — ISBN 978-0-8071-7514-9 (pdf) —
ISBN 978-0-8071-7515-6 (epub)

In memory of Hans A. Schmitt, 1921–2006,
professor of modern European history at the University of Virginia

In 1945 Hans served as a lieutenant in the U.S. Army in Paris;
he was there.

CONTENTS

ACKNOWLEDGMENTS

A s always, the staff at all the French departmental archives that I visited to research this book were helpful, friendly, and eager to accommodate. The staffs at the departmental archives of Aube, Bouches-du-Rhône, Meurthe-et-Moselle, and Yonne all went out of their way to assist me, especially Arnoud Fouanon in Auxerre. I particularly want to thank Jérôme Leclerc of the Archives départementales de Meurthe-et-Moselle for the friendliness he extended to me. The late professor Jean-Louis Etienne in Nancy also took an interest in my work and offered sage advice. I thank the late Charlotte Goldberg for sharing with me her memories of the German occupation and liberation of Nancy. The staff of the Archives nationales in Pierrefitte-sur-Seine was welcoming, helpful, and made my research not only fruitful but enjoyable. My visit to France was made more pleasurable by the good company and friendship of Dominique and Maryline Beuret. I thank Joëlle Prim for her hospitality in Saint-Denis, Christian Darmon in Auxerre, and Patrick Thierry in Troyes. Rich Noble and Eric Van Slander of the National Archives and Records Administration in College Park, Maryland, proved helpful; Rich went out of his way to make my visit more enjoyable. Dr. Richard Sommers and the staff of the U.S. Army Heritage and Education Center of the War College in Carlisle, Pennsylvania, provided valuable assistance at the Military History Institute, as well as a General and Mrs. Matthew B. Ridgway Military History Research Grant to help defray costs of research at the MHI. The staff of the Microforms Department of the Library of Congress were friendly and helpful. Charles Robertson offered helpful counsel and good company. Anonymous reviewers offered helpful advice. I thank the many people in the United States who aided me in ways big and small: Phil Berger, Emily and Deborah Best, the late Jane Clark, Leslie Derr and the late Kurt Eigner, Tricia Fleck, Vince Giannini, Susan and Walter Haydel, and Tim Souweine and Lisa Reichenbach. My family provided lodging, food, and welcome distraction: Rick and Sue Fuller, my mother Marjorie

Huntsberger Fuller, Michael Fuller, Jeff and Rebecca Fuller, Chris and Yvonne Fuller, and Alyssa Wilson and her brood. My sister-in-law, Kathryn Ragsdale, offered valuable editorial suggestions for this work, which is better for her red pencil. Above all, I owe a debt of gratitude to my wife, Lynda Fuller Clendenning, who always provided counsel and support when I needed it. Thank you, Lynda.

ABBREVIATIONS

ADSEC/COMZ	Advanced Section, Communications Zone
AFA	Aide aux Forces alliées (Aid to Allied Forces, French office supervising the material needs of Allied armies)
AG	Adjutant General (personnel office in the U.S. Army)
AMGOT	Allied Military Government for Occupied Territories
BCRA	Bureau Central de Renseignements et d'Action (Gaullist intelligence and special operations office)
CA	Civil Affairs (Allied army officers who liaisoned with French civilian administrators)
CIC	Counter Intelligence Corps
CFLN	Comité français de Libération nationale (French Committee of National Liberation, formed by de Gaulle in 1943 to unite pro-Allied French)
CGT	Confédération générale du travail (labor union federation)
COMZ	Communications Zone (zone through which military supplies must pass to reach the front)
CRS	Compagnies républicaines de sécurité (Interior Ministry troops)
DPs	Displaced persons
FFI	Forces français de l'Intérieure (French Forces of the Interior, resistance fighters)
FTP	Francs-tireurs et partisans (Communist dominated resistance fighters)
G-5	Army designation for Civil Affairs
GPRF	Gouvernement provisoire de la République française (Provisional government of Charles de Gaulle, 1944–1945)
KIA	Killed in Action
LST	Landing Ship, Tank

LVF	Légion des voluntaires français contre le bolchevisme (unit of the German Army made up of French who volunteered to fight the Soviets)
MMLA	Mission militaire de liaison administrative (French liaison officers to Allied armies)
MP	Military Police
NCO	Noncommissioned officer
OSS	Office of Strategic Services (American intelligence agency)
PC	Ponts-et-Chaussées (department of Bridges and Roads)
PCF	Parti communiste français (French Communist Party)
PPF	Parti populaire français (a French fascist party)
PSF	Parti social français (conservative French party formed in 1936 to counter the Popular Front)
PTT	Postes, Télégraphes et Téléphones (French phone company and post office)
PX	Post Exchange (Army store)
R&R	Rest and Recreation or Rest and Recuperation
SAS	Special Air Service (a British commando force)
SD	Siecherheit Dienst (SS intelligence service)
SFIO	Section française de l'Internationale ouvrière (the main French Socialist party from 1905)
SHAEF	Supreme Headquarters Allied Expeditionary Force
SNCF	Société national des chemins de fer français (French national railroad company)
SOE	Special Operations Executive (British intelligence and special operations organization)
STO	Service du travail obligatoire (labor conscription instituted by Vichy)
USAAF	U.S. Army Air Force
WAC	Women's Army Corps

AFTER D-DAY

INTRODUCTION

Six days after American soldiers fought their way onto the beaches of Normandy and clawed their way inland, Major John J. Maginnis drove his Army jeep into the shattered and still-burning Norman town of Carentan. He did not stay long. First, constant German shelling and then a determined German counterattack made the smoldering heap too dangerous for Maginnis and his staff of five Civil Affairs officers to remain. They returned two days later, on 14 June 1944, to set up an office in the town even though it remained a target for German gunners. The relentless drizzle of German shells made it pointless for Maginnis to organize teams to put out fires in burning buildings. Nevertheless, Major Maginnis, who spoke French and had some life experience in France between the wars, was tasked with making Carentan livable again and seeing what he could do for the civilians in the immediate area. He had access to only limited supplies and no power to claim them from the Quartermaster Corps, which released only small quantities of some materials when requested by Civil Affairs. Maginnis was able to deliver medical supplies to the director of the local hospital, who agreed to supervise the disposal of the dead farm animals that presented a health hazard to soldiers and civilians alike. But first, Major Maginnis had to find Army sappers to remove mines and unexploded shells that made local farm fields treacherous. Maginnis hired local men to help clear the animals and debris that littered the area and promised to pay them with "liberation francs." Printed in England, this money had already been declared "counterfeit" by Free French leader Charles de Gaulle, who ordered no French to accept them. However, Major Maginnis of the U.S. Army had ultimate authority in Carentan and took control of decision making in consultation with the local authorities that remained. That was true until former French diplomat François Coulet set up an office in nearby Bayeux and proclaimed that the government of General de Gaulle was now in charge of Normandy. Coulet initially had no car and no phone for weeks; he had no mail, no newspapers, and no way to contact his superiors in London except by dispatches carried by British warships. Maginnis held the better hand.

Major Maginnis thus embarked on a project that illustrated some of the many complications of the American involvement in wartime France, an experience echoed throughout the country. Like many other liberating American soldiers, Major Maginnis was greeted by the French with smiles and warm welcomes. The image of the smiling GI in his jeep being greeted by jubilant French civilians with kisses and bottles of wine is well known and undergirds the usual American understanding of both the liberation of France and the relations between American soldiers and French civilians. And, no doubt, such scenes of jubilation were widespread and sincere in late 1944. However, they were only one of many different kinds of encounters between the U.S. military and the French. French civilians usually make only brief appearances in English-language histories of the war in western Europe as grateful men and women tossing flowers and apples at bedraggled GIs whizzing by in halftracks, jeeps, and tanks. A typical example is offered by Rick Atkinson in his best-selling *The Guns at Last Light: The War in Western Europe, 1944–1945,* where the French briefly enter the stage from time to time to offer glasses of wine or calvados to weary GIs, spit on German POWs, or vengefully urinate on a German corpse. Peasant men plead for cigarettes from GIs with pantomime and children beg for chocolate. Atkinson refers to the horrendous toll the liberation inflicted on the French: towns reduced to smoking rubble, massacres by the SS, and tens of thousands of French lives claimed by bombs and artillery rounds. But such asides rarely take more than a few sentences on a few pages. Of course, Atkinson's subject is not the fate of the French, but the titanic fight to evict the Nazis from France and then to crush Germany. That is the purpose of most books about the war in the west by superb historians such as John Keegan, Max Hastings, and Charles MacDonald: to present the military history of the Allied armies and their German foes, and to explain why and how the Allies prevailed. French civilians played only a small role in that story, appearing mostly—as in Atkinson's version—in the liberation of Paris, where French civilians did much of the fighting and dying to evict the German occupiers.[1]

American soldiers met French civilians in many settings and circumstances. The outcome of those meetings varied widely depending on the situations and individuals involved. Contingency loomed large in the Franco-American interchange of 1944 and 1945. Thus, this work examines diverse interactions to expose the variety, complexity, and nuances of the Franco-American junction. Most fighting by Americans occurred in Normandy and in Lorraine; thus, the Franco-American interactions in those locales necessarily produced stories warped by the violence of war. Yet, the French and Americans also met in areas relatively unscathed by violence, such as two overlooked departments in north-central France, the Yonne and the Aube, which were liberated by General George Patton's Third Army during the rapid sweep south of Paris in August. Soldiers from many countries—Britain, Canada, Poland, France, and French North Africa—fought in France in 1944, yet the United States provided nearly two-thirds of the forces that battled the Germans in northern France. While interactions between the French and members of the various Allied armies occurred throughout France, the scope of this inquiry is limited to produce a more focused examination of the intersection of French civilians with the American military in a few departments in northern France. This work occasionally compares the conduct of the German Army with that of the American and the relative impacts on French civilians in 1944. Likewise, it sometimes offers comparisons of French reactions to American troops to their responses to British soldiers to offer both similarities and contrasts as context. However, while such comparisons offer useful insights, they are included only to help answer the larger question: how did the French experience the Americans in the liberation of their country? French civilians who suffered through the fighting in 1944 had to accommodate their liberators in the wake of the liberation. Their story is less well known to English-language readers. Inevitably, interactions between armed soldiers, who spoke little or no French, and anxious civilians, who rarely spoke English, were not always smooth. In the heat and confusion of battle, the meetings could be very scary and even deadly.

Before the Americans landed in France on D-Day with the intent to drive Nazi forces out of France, various French claiming to speak for France competed for American recognition as the only reliable partner to help liberate France and ultimately Europe. The Free French led by General Charles de Gaulle eventually won the contest, but only after President Franklin D. Roosevelt exhausted every alternative. The president's plan to impose a military government (Allied Military Government for Occupied Territories, or AMGOT) upon France until it was completely free of German soldiers was fiercely opposed not only by General de Gaulle but also by General Dwight D. Eisenhower, who Roosevelt imagined would be responsible for the regime. Eisenhower wanted nothing to do with it and was happy to turn responsibility for the French population over to de Gaulle at the earliest possible moment. On the other hand, de Gaulle believed paranoid rumors that the Americans wanted to keep the Nazi puppet regime of Marshal Philippe Pétain in power after the invasion of June 1944. There was not even a remote possibility of that happening. Nevertheless, a question remains: how did Eisenhower's officers manage to cooperate with French officials of a provisional government that remained unrecognized by the United States until late October 1944? To explain how France escaped AMGOT is not difficult or complicated, but to clarify how what took its place came into being is a little more complex. De Gaulle rushed to implant his government in the sliver of liberated Normandy in order to forestall AMGOT, much to the relief of General Eisenhower. Chapter 4 examines and explains how the Gaullist regime installed in Normandy took root and flourished with Allied assistance. Both the French and the Americans then had to improvise in finding ways to get along and accommodate each other. With the U.S. military improvising in a foreign land where the rules were vague and the provisional government of Charles de Gaulle still trying to find its feet and affirm its authority, the outcome of the challenge was not assured. Nevertheless, both sides agreed that there was a war to win and victory took priority. The French and the Americans needed to arrive at rules on how to share limited resources required by both. Scarcity pitted Americans and French in a contest over supplies both parties claimed to be essential for their survival.[2]

General Eisenhower recognized the importance of reviving civilian life behind his lines, but most policy decisions and actions taken by the U.S. Army within France were dictated by practical considerations: there was a war to win. To avoid military government, Eisenhower wanted to limit U.S. Army Civil Affairs officers' role to cooperating closely with whatever French leaders happened to be in place to take care of civilians so that he could concentrate on winning the war. While the Allies—principally the Americans—effectively took control of the Norman port city of Cherbourg, they relied on French officials and leading citizens to look after the affairs of less important towns, such as Carentan. Fortunately, the Civil Affairs officer given responsibility for Carentan, Major Maginnis, left detailed accounts of daily life in that Norman town. Similarly, many American soldiers, including women of the Women's Army Corps, left lively accounts of their experiences in wartime Paris, which filled up with tens of thousands of American service troops and GIs on leave from the front. While appreciating what the French capital had to offer, most Americans stationed there would rather have been back home. Wartime Paris was not the rich and vibrant city of peacetime, and Americans stationed there recognized the sacrifices Parisians had to endure in order to win the war. The battle zone of Lorraine saw extensive contact between GIs and civilians and revealed the complexities of the two sides getting along while the war raged. GIs in Lorraine not only lacked knowledge of the French language, they failed to grasp that local friendliness toward deserters from the German Army was not bred of sympathy for Nazism or the German cause but rather by sympathy for their kinsmen drafted against their will into the Wehrmacht. Many GIs did not see Lorrainers who spoke a German dialect as French at all, but as the enemy, leading to a marked deterioration of GI consideration for the welfare of French civilians. By late 1944, many French throughout France had developed their own doubts about the Americans

While most histories of the Western Front in 1944 barely mention the French, some historians have recently shown more interest in how the French experienced their liberation. Hilary Footitt has detailed the Allied interaction with the French, which, to some extent, overlaps with the work presented here. She examined the Franco-American interaction in Cherbourg (as I do here), Marseille, and the Marne. She relied on British archival material and the French holdings in Caen, in Calvados, Normandy, for her research on Normandy. Because the British and Canadian armies liberated Calvados, the archives in Caen yield material mostly related to those armies, and not the American. This leads her to concentrate on the French reaction to the British and Canadian soldiers. Remarkably, the British and American archives hold much of the same documents about Cherbourg, so Footitt's rendition of the Cherbourg experience overlaps with mine. She also examined interactions in Marseille and the giant U.S. installations around Reims, in the Marne, where, the Americans had a larger presence, prodding Footitt to say more about friction between the French and Americans. Overall, we reach similar conclusions. An American historian, William Hitchcock, also used the archives in Caen to examine the French experience in Normandy. The explanation for the focus on the British experienced exposed in the archives in Caen is simple: the archives in Saint-Lô, which would hold documents related to the American invasion in the department of the Manche, were completely razed by the American bombings of 1944 and have taken many years to rebuild their collections. Only now are they becoming available to researchers, but not soon enough for this work The best works in French on the subject—those led by Jean Quellien, of the University of Caen—also rely heavily on the archives in Caen. The extensive studies by Quellien and his colleagues remain untranslated into English, and like most of the English-language studies of the war they focus on the war in Normandy. Mary Louise Roberts has made available in English some vivid and revealing recollections of Normans who experienced the war. Like most works focusing on French civilians living through the liberation, Roberts's collection of oral histories is also limited to Normandy, while the Allies advanced through much of northern and eastern France. Considerable combat by Americans occurred in Lorraine, where, unfortunately, the archives in Metz suffered the same fate as those in Saint-Lô, and records of the war era are still unavailable to historians. Happily, the archives in the ancient capital of Lorraine, Nancy, in the department of the Meurthe-et-Moselle, not only remained intact, but also hold rich records of the war years that reveal the Franco-American experience in eastern France. The archives in Troyes and Auxerre have much to tell about the liberation era south of Paris in the Aube and the Yonne, respectively.[3] David Reynolds produced a similar work on the Anglo-American experience in Britain, and Peter Schrijvers wrote an excellent book on the Belgian experience of liberation by the British and Americans, which resembled in many ways what the French endured.[4]

Numerous historians have turned their attention recently to various aspects of the liberation discussed in this book. Régine Torrent turned her excellent dissertation on the complications introduced by the Americans in the liberation of France into a book in 2004, which looks beyond Normandy and, like some of the works cited below, considers the effects of Allied bombing on French morale. She devotes much attention to Allied proposals to provide liberated France with a working civil administration and the complications that ensued. Claudia Baldoli, Andrew Knapp, and Richard Overy have released excellent and insightful works—often in collaboration—on the Allied air war over France, as pointed out by Overy, a subject too often neglected by English-speaking historians. Such neglect appears to be coming to an end: Stephen A. Bourque has recently produced a history devoted to the destructive Allied air war against France in preparation for Operation Overlord. This work covers some of the same ground as Bourque's book, with the addition of the Allied tactical air campaign in the east and center of France. Together, these studies add to the untranslated pathbreaking work of French historian and journalist Eddy Florentin on the Allied bombing of France. A consensus appears to be near on the nature of the internal French resistance to the German occupation with recently released studies of the French resistance movement by Olivier Wieviorka and Robert Gildea. Both historians pay close attention to the movement's internal dynamics and the evolving relations of the diverse groups that made up the resistance in occupied France. They also dwell on the efforts by the Allies—especially Gaullists—to guide or control the groups from outside of France. Benjamin Jones has contributed a specialized work that studies Allied soldiers parachuted into France to help arm, organize, and train French guerrilla fighters behind the German lines in 1944. All of these studies add to our understanding of interactions between the Allied powers and the French in their efforts to defeat Nazi Germany and help to inform this work.[5]

This book inserts the French population back into the history of the liberation, as it is their story as much as it is that of the liberating armies. It offers a corrective to the common view of the liberation of France as the rapturous meeting of GIs and French civilians after some hard fighting on the beaches and *bocage* country of Normandy. That version reflects only a small portion of the liberation saga that avoids the complicated reactions of GIs and French in 1944 and 1945. Even this work does not pretend to tell the whole story, which would require many volumes to relate. In fact, French historians have produced scores—perhaps hundreds—of books recounting the events of the liberation. This work presents a sampling of the different kinds of representative encounters experienced by the French and GIs during the war, hoping that they present a more accurate and complete version of what unfolded in the months of liberation. It offers context for those engagements with the intent to better explain why different locales and times occasioned different reactions from both sides of the encounters. It pulls the variety of encounters together into one history, not to tell the *whole* story of the liberation, but to present its variety to fill one corner of a vast canvas.

1

THE AMERICANS, THE FRENCH, AND CHARLES DE GAULLE BEFORE D-DAY

I n the wake of a heated dispute over lines of authority for French troops fighting in Italy, General Dwight D. Eisenhower met with the president of the French Committee of National Liberation, General Charles de Gaulle, in Algiers in December 1943 to discuss future military plans and the part to be played by the French. To his great relief, Eisenhower found de Gaulle to be uncharacteristically agreeable and reasonable. At the end of their meeting, he told de Gaulle, "for the approaching campaign in France, I will need your help, the cooperation of your officials, and the support of French opinion. I don't know what theoretical position my government will insist that I take in my relations with you. But . . . I will not recognize any other authority in France than yours." General de Gaulle had waited a long time to hear those words. However, General Eisenhower was stating clearly the policy of the U.S. Army toward their difficult ally, France, and not the position of the U.S. government in Washington, D.C., which had mulishly resisted recognizing de Gaulle as anything other than one of numerous leaders of the French resistance. Eisenhower had cooperated with de Gaulle since his own arrival in London in 1942 and found him preferable to President Franklin Roosevelt's French favorite, General Henri Giraud, who would amply demonstrate his incompetence on many levels in Algiers and the Mediterranean Theater. General de Gaulle had struggled unsuccessfully to win recognition from Washington since 1940, when France collapsed under the Axis onslaught. The battle for acceptance was more important for de Gaulle than for the Americans. Nevertheless, General Eisenhower rightfully acknowledged that his forces would need the cooperation of the French people to win the war against Germany, and it was that need for French cooperation that ultimately forced the Americans' hands. Initially, the struggle to win American approval of the Free French involved a small number of competing French appealing to the American public and their leaders. The contest between representatives of competing French authorities ultimately turned on the American requirement for bases and supplies, and neither Washington nor the U.S. Army cared much about who provided them. The competition among the French to be the sole authority to cooperate with the Allies was eventually won by parties loyal to Charles de Gaulle because of dynamics among the French and not because Washington particularly chose de Gaulle to be the one to help the Allies liberate France from Nazi rule.[1]

Americans watched with dismay as France suddenly collapsed before the German military in 1940. They wanted France to win the contest, but, despite the revulsion provoked by the Axis powers, most did not want it enough to embroil the United States in another European war. Desperate appeals by French premier Paul Reynaud for American planes, ships, and even troops to prevent the French catastrophe elicited only American bromides and best wishes for ultimate victory. When General Charles de Gaulle established his Free French committee in London in June 1940 to keep the war alive for the French beyond France, he did not bother appealing to Americans for help. He would not have received any had he done so. President Franklin D. Roosevelt's administration firmly believed it could accomplish more good by maintaining friendly relations with the regime of Marshal Philippe Pétain in Vichy than by breaking relations and siding with the quixotic General de Gaulle in London. The supremely proud and cantankerous de Gaulle spent the next four years waiting for the United States to realize that he alone embodied true France. He expended little energy attempting to win over Secretary of State Cordell Hull and President Roosevelt like a common itinerant salesman. He, or rather, in his mind, France, was too proud to stoop to salesmanship, even if many talented and intelligent French did strive to convert American thinking about war-devastated France. While de Gaulle believed it would be necessary to rely on American soldiers to liberate France from Nazi occupation, he never thought that American acceptance of his leadership was crucial. He would lead with or without the blessing of the president. Roosevelt likewise thought the United States would crush Nazi rule in Europe with or without the cooperation of de Gaulle.[2]

Charles de Gaulle was a graduate of the French war colleges, Saint Cyr and l'École supérieure de guerre—the French war college for staff officers. After service in the First World War under General Pétain, he wrote books and articles on "the lessons of the war" that differed dramatically from most orthodox thinking. He argued that France should organize its conscripted military around a core of highly trained professional soldiers adept at utilizing the modern machines of war—especially tanks. Some journalists, politicians, and military professionals saw the merits of de Gaulle's arguments, but most did not. Paul Reynaud, a center-right deputy from Paris and future premier, was one of the few men of public affairs to endorse and argue the merits of de Gaulle's plea for a reformed French military. Unfortunately, de Gaulle's patron Pétain retained his faith in the power of artillery and fixed defense, and vigorously disputed de Gaulle's conclusions. Dismissed by high-ranking officialdom, de Gaulle pushed all the harder to mobilize support for his ideas. In doing so he made many enemies. His haughty manner, dismissive tone, and narcissistic sense of righteousness served him poorly in his quest. His classmates at Saint Cyr mockingly dubbed him "the constable"—in medieval France, the head of the king's armies—in honor of his pretensions and inflated self-regard. As future British ambassador to France Duff Cooper put it, "[he] had no gift for acquiring friends." Again and again his personal faults proved to be handicaps in winning friends, supporters, and allies, and guaranteed that the road to the reestablishment of Free France after 1940 would be rough. His prickly personality and bloated ego alienated many Britons, Americans, and Frenchmen and women whose help he would need in setting France upon her feet again.[3]

The day after his arrival in London, de Gaulle broadcast his appeal over the BBC for Frenchmen and women everywhere to rally to his standard of defiance, not just against the Germans, but against the Vichy regime of Marshal Pétain. The following day, 19 June, de Gaulle broadcast again "in the name of France" calling on all French military personnel everywhere to continue the fight and not accept the armistice, "a crime against our country." He entreated the French governors of North Africa in particular to keep up the fight. Most French who wanted to continue the war from the empire looked to General Auguste Noguès, governor-general of Morocco, for leadership. He, however, was unwilling to commit in public until he knew not only which way the wind was blowing, but how hard. De Gaulle's radio appeals and letters to French military and political leaders in French North Africa elicited no positive response. On 27 June, Britain's Prime Minister Winston Churchill officially accepted de Gaulle as the leader of "Free France" in London and recognized him as the leader of all French who chose to continue the fight alongside Great Britain. De Gaulle proclaimed that the French Republic lived on in him a bit prematurely. Pétain, with the blessing of the National Assembly, did not declare it dead until 10 July.

In mid-July, de Gaulle received a notice from the French embassy in London that he was under arrest and should turn himself in to a prison in Toulouse, France. When he failed to arrive in Toulouse in August, de Gaulle's sentence was changed to death.[4]

A diffident Gaullist diplomat, Raoul Aglion, pointed out in his memoirs that had de Gaulle not declared himself the incarnation of France, but instead announced he would lead a "French Legion" to fight alongside the British, he would have avoided many problems and been more easily accepted by not only Frenchmen and women, but by foreign leaders. Jean Monnet, who had served as a procurement liaison for both Britain and France within the United States, decided to stay in the fight as a supply expert working for the British as a Frenchman, but he served what remained of "the Allies" and not France. De Gaulle's presumptuousness and willingness to arrogate to himself authority that few were willing to recognize annoyed and repulsed many (probably most) French outside of France. The highest-ranking diplomat in the French embassy in London, counselor and chargé d'affaires Roger Cambon, resigned rather than serve Vichy, but he was aghast at the prospect of aligning himself with de Gaulle. Cambon had warm relations with many other diplomats in London and waged a campaign to convince them—especially the Americans— that de Gaulle was simply a fascist who wanted to set himself up as an alternate dictator to Pétain. By claiming to be the government of "Free France" de Gaulle had carried out a bloodless coup, placing a brigadier general at the head of an unelected government that answered to no one. Thus, it is easy to understand why so many, especially in the American press, insisted that de Gaulle was a "fascist" or a "dictator." Many of his political ideas indeed ran close to fascism, though he was never a fascist. His father was an overt royalist with no affection for the Republic. He loyally read the neo-royalist newspaper, *L'Action Française,* which was obsessively anti-British, anti-Semitic, and accused by many of being a fascist mouthpiece. De Gaulle himself imbibed the social-Catholicism popular among the bourgeois of Lille, where he grew up, and he absorbed the Anglophobia normal to French nationalism that informed his worldview. There was little to recommend him as the embodiment of republican France.[5]

After de Gaulle repeatedly took to the airwaves on the BBC, Vichy labeled him a traitor and began a concerted propaganda effort to counter his radio appeals. Paradoxically, Vichy's attempts to denigrate de Gaulle and shout him down brought him only more attention. In the minds of many—not least the

British government—de Gaulle increasingly became the symbol of anti-Vichy resistance. Thus, Churchill agreed on 7 August to recognize his French National Committee as the sole representative of fighting France, and to supply de Gaulle with armaments and money to keep his campaign alive. The Treasury extended credit to the committee, and any French ship that might fall into British hands was to be handed over to them. However, French soldiers and sailors that rallied to de Gaulle would ultimately be under British command. In return, Churchill agreed to do all in his power to restore France to the position of power and prestige she had known before 1940. By 14 July, when the Free French staged a small military parade in London, de Gaulle had adopted the Cross of Lorraine (the symbol of Joan of Arc) as the symbol of the Free French and his small force was received in review by King George VI. De Gaulle insisted that any monies advanced to his committee by the British government were simply loans to be repaid when possible. Churchill had given up hope of finding anyone more prestigious or influential to take the place of de Gaulle, and thus accepted de Gaulle as the best he could get—for the moment.[6]

From mid-July de Gaulle had temporary quarters in London on Carleton Gardens—not even the French embassy in Knightsbridge. The Free French committee was denounced by Vichy authorities as "a handful of mercenaries grouped around a [British] microphone." He claimed to speak "for France" and yet he exercised control over only rented accommodations on The Mall across from Saint James Park. No government can claim to be a state without exercising sovereignty over real territory. The New Hebrides Islands in the Pacific Ocean were the first French possessions to rally to de Gaulle on 23 July, soon followed by the French ports in India (completely surrounded by British India), Tahiti, and New Caledonia. Baron Louis de Benoist, the head of the Anglo-French Suez Company that owned and operated the Suez Canal, saw that the canal was entirely hostage to British indulgence and thus opted for General de Gaulle despite the pro-Vichy sentiments of almost the entire French community in Egypt. The military commander of French forces in Indochina, General Georges Catroux, refused to accept the armistice, but it cost him his post. The governor-general of Chad, Félix Eboué, opted to align with de Gaulle in late July, but declined to do so publicly until Free French agents in Africa were ready to spring into action.[7]

De Gaulle's overtures in Africa paid dividends quickly. French Cameroon rallied to de Gaulle early and easily for several reasons: it was closely linked to

British Nigeria through trade and colonial officials there were inclined to align with the British colony. More importantly, French Cameroon had been German just 22 years earlier and most residents of Cameroon assumed if Germany won the war, it soon would be German Cameroon once again. Much of French Equatorial Africa was seized by Gaullists in a series of coordinated bloodless coups at the end of August. Gaullists operating from Nigeria and the Belgian Congo, which remained outside of the German orbit, and coordinating with Governor Eboué, struck at French colonial administrative centers throughout the region and gained cooperation—sometimes reluctantly—at most posts. A Free French coup failed at Gabon due to the presence of French naval units in Libreville; French naval officers proved the least susceptible to Gaullist blandishments and most loyal to Vichy. Dakar remained outside Free French control and was assumed by all to be the key to dominating not only the region but the Atlantic sea lanes off Africa. Thus, Churchill determined to use de Gaulle and his modest Free French forces to seize Dakar for the Allies. When the attack was met with resistance and failed miserably, many assumed the plan had been leaked by de Gaulle's people, who talked too much. The fiasco at Dakar and the seeming hostility that met de Gaulle's forces convinced Roosevelt and many American editorialists that de Gaulle had poor judgment and was a potential liability to the Allied cause.[8]

Early moves by de Gaulle may have repulsed some Americans and their leaders, but actions taken by the Vichy regime within France were equally repellent to most Americans. The Vichy State taking shape in France looked a lot like many such regimes forming in imitation of Fascist Italy and Nazi Germany. That might have pleased Mussolini—Hitler probably did not care—but it disgusted the overwhelming majority of citizens of Britain and the United States. In Britain, as Vichy repelled, de Gaulle appeared more attractive, regardless of his faults. That was true for much of the public in the United States as well, who were offered increasingly flattering views of de Gaulle in much of the press. While many columnists came to admire de Gaulle and his movement, the U.S. government retained its commitment to Pétain and Vichy. President Roosevelt retained a good deal of sympathy for Marshal Pétain, whom he had met and liked, while de Gaulle continued to be dismissed by the president and Secretary of State Cordell Hull as a presumptuous and arrogant nobody. Nevertheless, from June 1940 until November 1942, Vichy and de Gaulle's London committee waged propaganda warfare to win the support of the American public and the cooperation of the U.S. government. As Vichy drifted toward fascism, de Gaulle made positive moves to convince the world that he was committed to freedom and democracy. While on an inspection tour of Free French territories in Africa, de Gaulle laid out the organization of the Free French regime and proclaimed in the Brazzaville Manifesto (in October) the "organic charter," which declared the movement's purpose and goals. It denounced the Vichy regime as unconstitutional and under the control of the Germans, and asserted that the Gaullist regime was the only legitimate French government. The charter also affirmed France as a "Republic" that would freely choose its legislative representatives as soon as proved possible.[9]

After Chad, Cameroon, and other African territories opted to join the Free French, the Vichy regime became more concerned about the security of French possessions in West and North Africa. Thus, on 9 September Pétain dispatched General Maxime Weygand to buttress Vichy's hold on North Africa. His mission was to appoint officials that could be relied on to support Pétain and not rally to de Gaulle as well as to fortify the French military in North Africa so that it could repel incursions, whether by the British, Germans, Italians, or Free French. Weygand vowed to oppose any attack regardless of its source, but of course his principal concerns were the Free French and British. When Mussolini's troops in North Africa found themselves pushed deep into Libya by the British in the winter of 1940–1941, Hitler responded by promising the Italian dictator crack German troops to expel the British. He dispatched General Erwin Rommel to Tripoli in February 1941 to take command of a small German corps intended to prevent an Italian disaster rather than conquer Egypt. A successful quick push by Rommel to the Egyptian border placed enormous strains on Axis supply lines in Libya, persuading Hitler to look to French Tunisia as a solution to such problems. At first, the Axis resorted only to buying limited food supplies from the French in North Africa, but in the spring of 1941 that expanded to buying gasoline and renting trucks, and then to using ports in Tunisia to bring in gasoline, food, and mechanical parts, all to be used by the German and Italian armies in Libya and Egypt. Although the precarious British position in Egypt concerned the United States, it failed to excite as strong a reaction as did the German infiltration into French North Africa, which Roosevelt viewed as vital to American interests.[10]

When leaders in the Vichy cabinet agreed that French premier Pierre Laval's promises of Franco-German military action against the British and Gaullists in Africa placed France in a dangerous position, Marshal Pétain dismissed the pro-German and Anglophobic Laval. The dismissal of Laval was rightfully perceived by both the British and the Americans as showing that Vichy had opted not to collaborate militarily with the Nazis. His replacement as premier in February 1941, Admiral François Darlan, favored closer ties to the United States, as did the old marshal, who generally held a high opinion of the United States based largely on his experiences during the First World War. Sensing a change in Vichy policy and hoping to maintain close ties between Vichy and Washington, Roosevelt decided to appoint an ambassador to Vichy, his close friend Admiral William Leahy. Leahy, who barely spoke French and knew little about France or the French, arrived at his new post in Vichy in January 1941, just as Hitler decided to intervene in the flagging Italian campaign in North Africa. Having an admiral to deal with an admiral might have been a good idea, but ultimately Leahy and Roosevelt concluded they could work cooperatively with Darlan because he was, above all, an opportunist who wanted France to align with the winner of the war. For that reason, both Leahy and Roosevelt believed that Darlan could be manipulated into accepting American policies. The Americans judged that he would adjust French policy as the wind blew, and ultimately he did.[11]

With German troops filtering into North Africa, the United States became more interested in strengthening relations with Vichy in order to keep Axis forces out of French North Africa. Thus, Roosevelt dispatched special envoy Robert Murphy to undertake discrete talks with General Weygand, now governor-general of French North Africa, to facilitate the expansion of trade between French North Africa and the United States. When Hitler invaded Russia in June 1941, Weygand became convinced that Germany would lose the war and grew more cooperative with the United States. Weygand accepted the "Murphy-Weygand accord" that provided for American goods to reach the civilian population of North Africa. This served several purposes: it eased the plight of the civilian population, increased American prestige among the populace, and allowed the stationing of American "inspectors" to see that imports were not diverted to the Axis powers. Vichy agreed to grant the 12 "vice-consuls" in North Africa diplomatic status—which allowed them to send encrypted cables—with the understanding that these "consuls" would serve as intelligence agents. These inspectors not only saw that American goods did not fall into the wrong hands, they gathered intelligence of interest to the United States and kept close eyes on German agents also operating in French North Africa. Robert Murphy stayed on in Algiers to serve as Roosevelt's personal representative to Weygand. During his stay in North Africa, Murphy had extensive dealings with Vichy officials and came to know, like, and trust many of them, with Weygand high on the list. This disposed Murphy to favor a continuation of Vichy control of North Africa even after the Allied landings there. However, many in North Africa were wary of the Vichy regime and reacted badly to crowds of unqualified and often unscrupulous personnel inserted into offices by Vichy. People shoved aside by Vichy as "unreliable" often proved easy recruits for de Gaulle or were happy to cooperate with Murphy's "vice-consuls." Thus, an anti-Vichy underground of the discontented took shape in North Africa that kept in close touch with Murphy.[12]

DE GAULLE WOOS WASHINGTON IN 1941

The summer of 1940 witnessed a concerted campaign by the two competing French camps within the United States: one trying to convince Americans that Vichy was the illegitimate machine of a fascist cabal within France; the other trying to persuade public opinion that the Vichy regime was still France of old, which needed and deserved American help. American public opinion was divided between those who most feared war and those who most feared a Nazi victory in Europe. The Vichy announcement that the leaders of Third Republic would be tried for their responsibility for the war and defeat was received very badly and roundly condemned in the press. Vichy persecution of Jews, Spanish Republicans, and German refugees also aroused widespread indignation. To counter this obviously unfavorable drift in public opinion, Vichy dispatched a new ambassador, Gaston Henry-Haye, who, despite arriving in Washington with warm recommendations from Ambassador William C. Bullitt and Robert Murphy, was denounced by most everyone as Laval's man. He was especially poorly received by French citizens in the United States and rejected as a fascist. After he arrived, a wave of resignations by embassy and consular staff unhappy with the new regime in Vichy followed. Vichy also dispatched former Premier Camille Chautemps on a speaking tour of the United States to explain Vichy positions and to lobby Washington for better relations. While touring the United States, Chautemps denounced de Gaulle as a fascist, which confirmed for some what they already suspected. However, his own close association with the unhappiest years of the Third Republic and the surrender of 1940 made Chautemps a feeble salesman; he was poorly received and proved ineffective. He was soon recalled to France, but he took the prudent path and chose not to go.[13]

Thus, the United States served as a propaganda battleground for competing forces claiming to represent France. When Vichy mounted a pro-French propaganda campaign that stressed sentimental attachments to France and things French, like fashion, wine, and cheese, Raoul de Roussy de Sales, head of the *Havas* press agency in New York and an advocate for de Gaulle, condemned it as "the stupidest kind of propaganda imaginable." In fact, it was somewhat effective in influencing American attitudes toward France. In a move to improve relations with the United States in June 1941, de Gaulle dispatched to Washington as his personal representative 40-year-old René Pleven, who had been the European agent of a Chicago-based phone company and had many friendly contacts in the United States. But these business friends did not help him in his mission: neither Hull nor Roosevelt consented to receive him. Still, he was able to meet with many other administration figures—Henry Wallace, Harry Hopkins, Henry Stimson, Henry Morgenthau, among others—on an unofficial basis. These friendly discussions paid off: Pleven was invited to attend a meeting to discuss the extension of Lend-Lease aid to the Free French as part of the British program. In his usual maladroit manner, de Gaulle refused to allow Pleven's participation unless he were received as an official representative of Free France, which, of course, Washington would not allow. The talks did not occur. Nevertheless, the State Department agreed to recognize the Free French committee in the United States as a "delegation," and Pleven remained in contact with administration officials. The State Department instructed the U.S. consul in Léopoldville—in the Belgian Congo (just across the river from French Brazzaville, loyal to de Gaulle)—to have no dealings with de Gaulle's government that might be interpreted as recognition of its legitimacy; however, he was allowed to treat de Gaulle's officials as "local authorities," the *de facto* authorities if not *de jure*. Under this doctrine, U.S. officials dealt with whomever seemed to be in charge in any locale so long as they did not interfere with U.S. goals and served American interests. This remained U.S. policy toward the Free French and Vichy authorities until October 1944.[14]

American interest in airbases on Free French islands in the Pacific persuaded Washington to adopt a friendlier attitude toward de Gaulle's committee in September 1941, when Pleven was invited to meet with Under Secretary of State Sumner Welles to discuss an arrangement for the State Department and the London committee to keep in touch. Pleven continued to work among French expatriates, seeking out respected Frenchmen to build a firm base for de Gaulle's campaign in the United States. Most French within the United States, such as Jean Monnet, remained aloof from de Gaulle and his London committee, or antagonistic. That so many French expatriates, some highly regarded by members of the Roosevelt administration, disliked and distrusted de Gaulle continued to hinder him into 1944. Pleven did succeed in recruiting Adrien Tixier while in Washington. Tixier had been a rough and rude professional labor union organizer in France who had become an official of the International Labor Organization, which was put together by the League of Nations after the First World War. According to Raoul Aglion, Tixier "was difficult to deal with, sometimes unpleasant, suspicious of everyone and everything. Many of these qualities must have appealed to de Gaulle." He also recruited Raoul de Roussy de Sales, of the *Havas* news agency, who joined the cause with reluctance. Pleven assembled a committee of five, including Aglion, to represent Free France in the United States and perform different functions intended to influence American and expatriate opinion, and U.S. government policy. Pleven persuaded the State Department to recognize his committee and grant them limited diplomatic status, but not recognize Free France. When Pleven left the United States to undertake other missions for de Gaulle, Adrien Tixier was left in charge of the committee in the United States and acted as the principal contact with the State Department. Tixier's personality replicated de Gaulle's: "sarcastic, rude, irascible." Having him in the United States representing the Free French caused almost as much irritation as de Gaulle himself would have.[15]

When the Vichy regime allowed the Japanese to establish military bases in French Indochina, Washington worried that Vichy would extend the same privileges to Nazi Germany in Dakar and Morocco. Murphy was convinced that General Weygand was pro-American, but he also knew that he was loyal to Pétain and would not buck orders from Vichy. Despite his loyalty to the marshal, Pétain recalled Weygand from North Africa in November, most likely due to pressure from Germany. Weygand's removal from North Africa startled the Americans, who worried about both German and Vichy intentions. Although the United States still did not recognize de Gaulle's committee as a legitimate government, in November 1941 the United States extended Lend-Lease aid directly to the Free French, rather than routing it through British intermediaries, as had been the arrangement beforehand. Nevertheless, it still extended aid according to the "local authorities" doctrine: Free French forces in control of areas vital to U.S. interests received Lend-Lease aid. On 8 December, the United States entered the war against the Axis as an ally of Britain. That did not make much difference to American relations with Vichy; however, it did make the presence of U.S. agents in North Africa and unoccupied France more important. It also made little difference to American relations with de Gaulle's Free French. In the United States, only Fiorello La Guardia's New York City and the British consulate officially recognized Free France.[16]

As Weygand no longer offered a rampart for U.S. policy in North Africa, Charles de Gaulle barged into American considerations on Christmas Eve, 1941, by launching a complicating takeover of two tiny French islands off the coast of Canada, Saint-Pierre and Miquelon. With much else to worry about in December 1941, Roosevelt resented having to bother with this distraction and Secretary of State Hull became obsessively irate at de Gaulle. The coup complicated American relations with its new allies, Canada and Britain. Moreover, Gaullists were not the only *résistants* among the French, and they had almost no presence in French North Africa, the focus of U.S. interest in early 1942. Marshal Pétain was personally very popular in North Africa, and Germany was not; thus, many influential French there joined informal groups and sought American help in opposing the Axis in Africa. Robert Murphy, American consul Kenneth Pendar, and the American "inspectors" in North Africa remained in close contact with the non-Gaullist French underground, collecting maps and useful information channeled to them by helpful French patriots. While resident Americans prepared for the coming Allied invasion in the summer 1942, there was only a tiny isolated cell of Gaullist agents in North Africa, and de Gaulle was personally loathed by most French there.[17]

Fully engulfed in the Pacific war by that point, the United States was forced to treat de Gaulle and the Free French with greater seriousness because Washington required their help in that war. Some sort of agreement about American bases on French islands became urgent and the committee acceded to American requests to establish military bases on New Caledonia in order to prevent the Japanese from doing so. Even as President Roosevelt infuriated de Gaulle with his snubs and public statements, the United States was developing closer relations with broad elements of the Free French. In March 1942, the United States invited a member of the committee to join the Pacific War Council to coordinate policies in the war against Japan. In July 1942, General Eisenhower attended the Bastille Day parade staged by the Free French in London. By saluting the Free French flag, Eisenhower began implementing his own policy toward de Gaulle's movement. The American intelligence agency, the Office of Strategic Services (OSS), worked easily with the Free French and established links to receive valuable intelligence from them. The State Department established a consulate in Free French Brazzaville (Congo), even if still under the "local authorities" doctrine. When Vichy protested, Under Secretary of State Sumner Welles explained the doctrine to Ambassador Henry-Haye and made explicit that the policy applied to Vichy as well. In late July, Generals George Marshall, Eisenhower, and Mark Clark and Admiral Ernest King met de Gaulle in London in a meeting without an agenda or substance. De Gaulle had hoped to discover Allied plans for an invasion of France and insert himself and the Free French into the center of discussions. In the brief meeting, he learned nothing and left the Americans with an unfavorable impression of him as an irritable and officious Frenchman.[18]

De Gaulle was right to believe something was afoot—an invasion was indeed in the works, but not of France. Because of British reverses in North Africa and a renewed powerful offensive by the Axis in Russia, Roosevelt and Chief of Staff George C. Marshall decided that the United States needed to start fighting the Axis as soon as possible. As the greatest threat appeared to be against the oil fields of the Middle East, the Western Allies agreed that an attack against North Africa would serve to draw the Germans away from Egypt and thwart any German plans to open submarine bases in French Africa. Roosevelt believed that the invasion of North Africa should be an entirely American affair because the inclusion of British or Free French forces would likely provoke stiff resistance by French troops stationed there. General de Gaulle was kept entirely out of the operation and not even informed of it because no one trusted the Free French to keep the plan secret and both Murphy and Leahy assured Roosevelt that Frenchmen hated de Gaulle. Regardless of their attitudes, Allied planners expected resistance from the French military just to show they could not be shoved aside as inconsequential. With General Weygand out of the picture and de Gaulle still out of favor, the Americans cast about for someone who could assume the mantel, especially the military leadership, of French North Africa. The U.S. embassy in Vichy suggested General Henri Giraud, who had escaped from a German POW camp and made his way to unoccupied

France via Switzerland in April 1942. Giraud's bustling about Vichy attracted the attention of many hostile to collaboration and favorably impressed the U.S. embassy staff. When Roosevelt was told about General Giraud, he was delighted that at last there was someone who could supplant de Gaulle. With little time and not a lot of choice, the Americans decided to include Giraud in their plans for North Africa: he would be placed in charge of the French military there, and if need be, political administration as well.[19]

Murphy sounded out the head of all French troops in North Africa, General Alphonse Juin, about the attitude of French forces in the event of an Axis invasion of North Africa. Juin replied that in such an event, he would call upon the United States right away for assistance in resisting them. General Charles Mast, chief of staff for the military region around Algiers, assured Murphy that he would be happy to help facilitate an American landing in North Africa even without an Axis invasion. Mast further recommended General Giraud to Murphy as the man who could command the loyalty of the French military in North Africa and lead it alongside the Allies. Mast and Murphy both believed that de Gaulle had no following in North Africa—indeed, that he was so widely reviled by the military there that they would refuse to join any cause that included him. When contacted in France by Murphy through an intermediary, General Giraud agreed to support an American (but not British) invasion of North Africa if a French general were placed in command. Eisenhower, through Murphy, would not commit to this, but did not rule it out either. General Mark Clark and others arrived by submarine in late October to meet Mast and his staff in a secret meeting at Cherchell, west of Algiers, where Mast argued forcefully that Giraud had to be in charge of the invasion. Clark could not reveal many details about the invasion, such as its date, to Mast and made only vague assurances about Giraud's role, yet General Mast enthusiastically agreed to cooperate. He assured Clark that the Americans coming ashore would be greeted by French troops as friends.[20]

Despite U.S. efforts to keep de Gaulle in the dark about invasion plans, he got wind of them and complained bitterly to the U.S. military liaison in Beirut. He argued—not very convincingly—that excluding him personally would outage the French in North Africa and actually *provoke* resistance out of resentment. Although the French populace was growing increasingly skeptical of Vichy, that did not mean they were transferring their faith to de Gaulle. However, the OSS began receiving reports from France that summer claiming shifts in popular opinion, with more people accepting de Gaulle as the leader of French resistance both within and outside of France. The OSS had a higher opinion of de Gaulle than most Americans possibly because their agents had established close working relations with de Gaulle's agents inside France. Nevertheless, U.S. interest in late 1942 focused on opinion in North Africa and not in France, and de Gaulle was indeed not at all popular in French North Africa.[21]

The invasion was already underway when Giraud arrived at Gibraltar and met Generals Eisenhower and Clark for the first time and declared his willingness to assume command of the Allied invasion of North Africa. He was as shocked to learn that he was not to have overall command as they were surprised to hear that he expected it. Eisenhower disabused him of his claim to a role in the venture and offered to place him in charge of French civil and military authority in North Africa. Both American generals strove for hours—through an interpreter—to convince Giraud that his demand was outlandish and illogical. Clark fumed to Giraud after three hours of arguing, "the time of your usefulness to the Americans and for the restoration of the glory that was once France is *now!*" and insisted he should accept the role being offered of command of all French forces in the theater as soon as practically possible. Ultimately, Giraud agreed. But then, at the last minute, all the negotiating with Giraud and fretting about de Gaulle was—perhaps—rendered moot: the commander in chief of all French military forces, Admiral François Darlan, arrived in Algiers to visit his son, Alain, who lay in a hospital bed, stricken with polio. Darlan's presence in Algiers threw any question of Giraud taking charge into very grave doubt.[22]

OPERATION TORCH: NORTH AFRICA, 8–25 NOVEMBER 1942

Operation Torch called for three American landings on the Atlantic coast of Morocco (Port Lyautey, Casablanca, and Safi) and Anglo-American landings flanking both Oran and Algiers on the Mediterranean coast of Algeria. Allied planners were painfully aware that landings further east—as far as Tunisia—would have been ideal, however they judged that the invaders would be overextended and too vulnerable to Axis counterattack. The Allies could not extend air cover that far to the east, where the landings would have been exposed to certain Axis air attacks. They planned to seize airfields outside of Algiers and Oran by airborne assaults, but not in time to cover landings in Tunisia. The

French defended North Africa with a sizeable force of 135,000 troops—mostly native Muslims under French officers—about 350 obsolete military aircraft, strategically placed coastal artillery, tanks, and a handful of naval craft to protect the coasts.

At their Algiers headquarters Admiral Darlan and General Juin received reports that Allied soldiers were landing at beaches in Algeria and Morocco. Juin quickly realized that great events were now in motion and that his reactions were of tremendous importance. He knew the Germans would not remain passive and would probably act swiftly to intervene. Juin decided not to oppose the landings, but until ordered otherwise, not to accept them either. He ordered his troops to "maintain elastic contact [with the invaders] without aggression," and told his artillery not to fire and his tanks not to attack. He also recognized the restraint of the American forces. There was no real battle for Algiers because Juin decided there would not be one. Darlan delayed making any decisions until he had a clearer picture of the size of the invading force. As General Weygand had said to Churchill in 1940, if the British sent six divisions to North Africa, he would fight them; if they sent 20, he would join them. Darlan thought along similar lines in 1942: if the invasion were serious, he would join the Allies; if not, he would oppose them. While the French Army responded to the Allied invasion phlegmatically or not at all, the navy and air force put up real fights wherever they met the invaders. Despite the keenness of some to fight, General Juin agreed to a cease-fire to start at 7 P.M. for Algiers and its region. It stipulated that the port would be opened to Allied ships and that French soldiers and police would retain their arms and duties. Civil administration would remain in place. It was not a surrender and it applied only to the region around Algiers; fighting continued in Morocco and in Algeria around Oran.[23]

After the landings began and the first reports were favorable, the British convinced Giraud, still in Gibraltar, to see reason. He agreed to Eisenhower's original proposal: he would be commander of all French civil and military personnel in North Africa. No one had planned on Darlan being in Algiers, and Clark was determined to set into place the agreement worked out between Eisenhower and Giraud: Giraud would be in charge and not Darlan. However, Darlan could be reconciled to the Allied presence; in fact, he had already accommodated himself to the new situation and was locked into frustrating negotiations with Murphy and General Clark about what was to happen next. Unfortunately, on 9 November there were two different and irreconcilable agreements between the Americans and the French. One placed Darlan in charge and the other recognized Giraud. Giraud was initially furious that Clark was negotiating with Darlan as commander of French forces, when he believed he was the commander! Pétain took to the airwaves denouncing the treachery occurring in North Africa and pronounced Giraud a traitor. It took only a few hours in Algiers for Giraud to realize that the French military in North Africa pledged its loyalty to Darlan and, to his great surprise, considered Giraud a "rebel"—no better than de Gaulle! Any authority Giraud might claim in North Africa would have to be imposed by American arms. The Americans were understandably disappointed to discover that Giraud carried no weight with the French military in North Africa, who looked to Darlan for directions. Even Giraud recognized this and told Clark that only Darlan could order a cease-fire that would be obeyed. When Clark threatened Darlan that he would replace him with Giraud if he did not order an immediate cease-fire, Darlan was not impressed. Similarly, General Mast was renounced by most French officers, who refused to serve under him. Giraud came to Juin's house at 3 A.M. on 10 November, to be greeted by Juin on his front steps with "Well general, what is all this bullshit?"[24] They discussed what was to be done and both agreed that it was of paramount importance that the French Army of Africa remain united and that it turn all of its might against, not the Allies, but the Axis forces then landing in Tunisia. They also agreed that only Darlan had the respect and authority in North Africa to see that occur. Darlan, however, still looked to the marshal for an order to cease fire, a position forcefully opposed by Juin, who urged Darlan to order a stop to the fighting and to inform Vichy after the fact. Juin ultimately convinced Darlan that any order from Vichy would have the stamp of Germany on it and that the marshal was not free to choose what was best for France. Darlan ordered a general armistice for the morning of 11 November without authorization from Vichy.[25]

The "Darlan deal" forced the United States into an awkward position. President Roosevelt's policy stated that the United States would recognize any local government the Allied invaders happened to find in place, and if it proved too difficult to deal with, it would be replaced by another more amenable to Allied policy. He wanted to exclude General de Gaulle if possible, to not give his London committee the American imprimatur of legitimacy, or seem to impose de Gaulle upon the French as the Allies' choice for them. When the Allies reached a cease-fire with the Vichy-installed regime of North Africa, the United States found itself in the uncomfortable position of accepting the Vichy authorities on the spot in exchange for a cease-fire and interacting in a friendly manner with men loyal to a reprehensible regime, something the United States had done without hesitation in Vichy until 8 November. The man at the top, Admiral Darlan, had been widely and repeatedly denounced by the American press and administration as one of the most reprehensible of the lot, and yet the United States dealt cooperatively with him within a few days of the first landings on North African beaches. Having already decided not to recognize de Gaulle, the United States recognized Darlan instead.[26]

In response to the end of French resistance in and around Algiers ordered by Admiral Darlan, Hitler ordered the occupation of all of France by Axis troops on 11 November. A swath of southern France abutting Italy was turned over to Italian occupation and administration. Pétain spoke to the French on the radio, protesting the German invasion and declaring that the Armistice Convention of 1940 had been breached. The French navy scuttled its fleet at Toulon to keep it out of Axis hands, just as the French had promised Churchill and Roosevelt in 1940. Darlan interpreted this as his cue to side with the Allies and order resistance to the Axis in Tunisia. When Laval preached dire consequences for France if they turned against Germany, Pétain disavowed Darlan and ordered the army in North Africa to resist the Allies and not the Axis. Despite Pétain's loyalty to Hitler, when Laval demanded a declaration of war against the Allies, most of the cabinet in Vichy resigned. Pétain continued to serve as *chef* of the French government and, despite the Axis occupation, the French government still handled day-to-day affairs until Vichy functionaries were forcibly displaced or coopted by the Allied invaders in the summer of 1944. Even though Axis troops occupied all of France and Vichy government officials resigned *en masse*, Pétain dispatched Admiral Charles Platon to Tunisia to see that French authorities there remained loyal to Vichy and the Axis.[27]

The occupation of all of France gave the French military and civil administration in North Africa loyal to the marshal the pretext they needed to join the Allied cause. General George Patton was planning to assault Casablanca with his tanks and artillery when word of the cease-fire arrived. The French governor-general of Morocco, Auguste Noguès, agreed to a cease-fire in Morocco after receiving a message supposedly from Vichy stating that Pétain was a prisoner of the Germans and thus not free to govern. An arrangement was soon worked out about who ran North Africa without reference to Vichy, even

though Darlan insisted he still acted in the name of Pétain With a general armistice in place, Eisenhower flew from Gibraltar to Algiers to work out a *modus
vivendi* with the French authorities. He met with Darlan, Giraud, Noguès, Juin,
Clark, Murphy, and others on 12 November and agreed to the arrangement
struck by Clark and Murphy. Eisenhower thus recognized Darlan as the civil
authority in North Africa, Giraud as the head of all French military in the theater, Juin as the head the French Army, and Noguès as governor-general of Morocco (Patton had taken a liking to Noguès and insisted he be retained). What
remained of the French fleet was reserved for Admiral Darlan. Giraud, with
no taste for politics and no desire to cross Darlan, readily agreed to cede civil
authority to him. The Frenchmen sent a cable to Pétain asking him to confirm
the agreement struck with Eisenhower. When this was announced on French
radio, the British and de Gaulle were outraged and many in Washington were
not pleased. This was the "Darlan deal," which was to anger so many people in
so many capitals. Eisenhower was just following orders—the "local authorities"
doctrine—to treat with whatever authority he found in charge, and Darlan was
unquestionably in charge. But Eisenhower had further incentive to come to
a quick settlement with Darlan: he needed to disengage Allied soldiers from
fighting the French in order to rush as many as possible to Tunisia to prevent an
Axis build-up there. Unfortunately, 12 November was already too late for that.
German and Italian troops were rushing into Tunisia and the troops in eastern
Algeria under British general Kenneth Anderson were too few in number and
too far away to stop them.[28]

When reports first reached the United States and Britain that Darlan was
negotiating with the Allies as "a guest" of the American commander, press reaction was neither friendly nor hostile toward Darlan. However, the press response in the United States and Britain to keeping Darlan as the French authority in North Africa was mostly negative. Two years of drum beats denouncing
him as a fascist and pro-Nazi had an effect that was hard to counter, and British
papers reacted bitterly toward the "Darlan deal." When de Gaulle learned of the
Allied invasion on the morning of 8 November, he told his aide, "I hope those
men in Vichy throw them back into the sea! One does not get into France by
breaking in." Nevertheless, de Gaulle broadcast a speech on the evening of 8
November giving full-throated approval of Operation Torch: "French leaders,
soldiers, sailors, airmen, civil servants, and colonists—arise every one of you!
Help our Allies, Join them without reserve. The France which fights on calls

upon you to do so!" De Gaulle recognized the delicacy of the situation and thus agreed to serve with Giraud, the candidate preferred by Washington, and made plans to fly to Algiers. The "Darlan deal," however, caused de Gaulle to cancel his plans to go to Algiers; he would have nothing to do with any regime linked to Darlan. After the "deal" he had nothing positive to say about Torch or the Americans, questioning their motives, wisdom, and judgment.[29]

If this put the United States in the position of having to choose Darlan or de Gaulle, the choice was easy. Hull gloated that Darlan's acceptance of the Allies in North Africa vindicated his Vichy policy. Still, all parties—the United States, Britain, and the Free French—wanted to avoid the existence of two rival French governments independent of Vichy. On 14 November, André Philip—a former socialist deputy in the Third Republic who had by then signed on with de Gaulle—and Adrien Tixier, representing de Gaulle's committee in the United States, met with Secretary Hull to express their satisfaction with Operation Torch and their hope that the United States would not accept Darlan as the legitimate authority in French Africa. Hull reminded them that until Vichy broke relations with Washington in protest of the invasion, the United States had recognized Vichy as the legitimate government of France. While that situation had not changed, in view of the German occupation of all of France, U.S. policy was now subject to review. In response to adverse public reaction to the "Darlan deal" and to protests from Churchill, Roosevelt released a public statement calling the acceptance of Darlan's authority in North Africa a "temporary arrangement" and a "temporary expedient." This was accepted by Darlan with comparatively good grace. He was reassured by Clark and Murphy that he was the recognized authority in North Africa until a permanent French government said otherwise. Despite de Gaulle's having been frozen out of the agreement reached in Algiers, Roosevelt agreed to meet with Tixier and Philip on 20 November. In this meeting, Roosevelt stressed that the U.S. Army would be the final authority in North Africa, as if to reassure them that Darlan was not the real sovereign at all: Eisenhower was. This failed to mollify the two men and the conversation became heated, strengthening Roosevelt's resolve to keep the Free French at arm's length.[30]

On 22 November, General Mark Clark, representing Eisenhower, signed an agreement with Darlan accepting the existing French authorities in North Africa as the legitimate government with which the Allies would cooperate to achieve their mutual goal of expelling the Axis from Africa. Marshall and Leahy both urged Roosevelt to accept Eisenhower's arrangements in North Africa as a necessary adjustment to reality. The invasion of North Africa cost the French around 3,000 casualties, about the same as the Allies. The Americans lost 70 planes shot down or crashed. The battleship *Massachusetts*, two cruisers, and two destroyers were severely damaged, and around 100 smaller craft were lost on the beaches or offshore. The invasion had achieved its minimum objectives in seizing the major ports and placing Allied soldiers in a position to threaten the Axis in the rear of the British Middle-Eastern armies, but no more. The Allies had hoped to sweep into Tunisia and deprive the Axis of an important base of operations; however, they failed to do that because of the four days of resistance by the French. They had hoped to install a friendly government under General Giraud and failed to do that, too. Instead, they agreed to accept the Darlan government, which continued to favor Vichy, forcing the Americans to continue their awkward balancing act between Vichy and the committee in London. The British managed to deal with the Darlan government by deferring to Eisenhower in all things. It was an American show, despite the important British military contribution, and the British pretended to be simply adjuncts to the Americans. De Gaulle was frozen out of all decisions regarding North Africa; however, he was tenacious and relentless, so that posture was certain not to last forever.[31]

To govern French North Africa, Darlan organized an Imperial Council consisting of Noguès, Giraud, Governor-General of West Africa Pierre Boisson, Darlan's security chief, Jean Bergeret, and Governor-General of Algiers Yves Châtel to act "in the name of Marshal Pétain," even if the captive marshal was unable to exercise any real authority.[32] Darlan headed the council and served as the marshal's viceroy. Juin encouraged him to make contact with de Gaulle in London and establish a unified "France" outside of Vichy. But Darlan was aware that many in the administration, the military, and the population never viewed him as a legitimate authority. He thus felt his position in North Africa was insecure. He suggested to Murphy that he would prefer to hand responsibility to someone else and go with his son, Alain, to America, where he could be treated for his polio. On Christmas Day 1944 Admiral Darlan was gunned down by an assassin as he arrived at his office; Giraud reluctantly agreed to take up the position of the murdered admiral. After Darlan's murder, Roosevelt assumed that the United States was fully in control of all military and civil affairs in "former French territory" in Africa and wrote to Murphy that the "local French" had to defer to Allied wishes or be replaced. Seventeen U.S. Army Civil Affairs officers presented themselves to Murphy expecting to be assigned positions as civil governors of "occupied" North Africa. A few spoke French and none spoke Arabic. Murphy was surprised at their arrival and had no idea what to do with them, so he referred them to Eisenhower's headquarters in Algiers and never heard of them again. Eisenhower was depressed at the prospect of having to impose American authority upon the French in North Africa and knew there was no serious prospect of effectively doing so. He later wrote that "General Giraud was no help" in ironing out any of the political difficulties presented by the continuance of the Vichy regime in North Africa. The Allies were far from pleased with how civil authority in North Africa was functioning: 8,000 political prisoners still languished in Vichy prisons or internment camps, including General Emile Béthouart, who had aided the Allies in their landings, along with many others who had helped the Allies on 8 November. Two members of the Lafayette Squadron, equipped with new British Spitfires, flew off to Marseille at the first opportunity, and under the Vichy hold-over General Jean Mendigal the French investigation into the incident went nowhere. When Eisenhower looked for alternatives to the Vichy officials running affairs, Giraud had no counsel to offer.[33]

In January 1943, President Roosevelt met Prime Minister Churchill in Casablanca to plot the Allies' next move and to close a number of open issues. There Churchill persuaded Roosevelt to accept the invasion of Sicily—in order to safeguard shipping lanes across the Mediterranean Sea—after the expulsion of the Axis from North Africa. Although Roosevelt and Churchill agreed that the Casablanca Conference was to address military questions only, the problem of who was to represent France and, thus, control North Africa needed to be settled urgently. Roosevelt spoke as if the United States controlled every aspect of decision making in North Africa, much to the exasperation of Murphy, who knew he would be unable to implement many of Roosevelt's proposals. Fortunately, Murphy realized, most of these ideas were spontaneous utterances, never committed to paper, and soon to be forgotten. Churchill was ready to support de Gaulle's claims to political authority in Africa and persuaded Roosevelt that de Gaulle should be part of the solution to the civil authority quandary in French Africa. Roosevelt joked repeatedly about a "shotgun wedding" of the two French generals to produce a united Free French movement. Churchill got into the spirit and referred to de Gaulle as "the bride" and mused that he might get cold feet. As Giraud constantly disavowed any interest in political questions, the subordination of General Giraud, the military man, to General de Gaulle, the politician, made complete sense. Murphy and Churchill's envoy to Algiers, Harold Macmillan, agreed that de Gaulle could be inserted into the North African government by reorganizing the Imperial Council in Algiers to include representatives of de Gaulle's London committee, but not necessarily de Gaulle himself. De Gaulle could be invited by the council to come to Algiers to meet with Giraud and plan the future. Churchill sent a cable to London inviting de Gaulle to come to Casablanca to meet Giraud, to which de Gaulle snappishly responded, rather predictably, that he did not require an invitation from the British prime minister to come to French territory to discuss purely French affairs with another Frenchman. He did, of course, need British transportation and protection to get there. Churchill did not mention that Roosevelt would be in attendance because he feared that the persistent leaks of information from de Gaulle's London office would reveal Roosevelt's secret presence in Casablanca.[34]

After de Gaulle arrived in Casablanca, Murphy tried to explain the American position on France, French North Africa, and recognition of a French government without offending de Gaulle. He suggested gently that if de Gaulle did not press too hard on the question of who was to lead Free France, Giraud would cede the position to de Gaulle in short order and without any fuss. De Gaulle replied that he was unable to enter into any kind of formal agreements with anyone without the prior approval of the committee in London. Throughout his two days of meetings in Casablanca, de Gaulle kept to that position, refused to agree to anything with anyone, and constantly objected to the presence of the uninvited Anglo-Saxon guests on French soil. At least Giraud did agree to receive a representative of de Gaulle's London committee at Algiers. Close to the end of the Casablanca Conference, when de Gaulle proved mulish about agreeing to anything, both Murphy and Roosevelt proposed dropping him from further discussions, much to Macmillan's alarm. Harry Hopkins persuaded the president to keep trying to find some formula to which de Gaulle would agree. Before Roosevelt and the prime minister left on 24 January, they asked Murphy and Macmillan to get the two French generals to at least release some kind joint declaration for the press. At the press conference, with Roosevelt, Churchill, Giraud, and de Gaulle in attendance, de Gaulle agreed to pose for photographs shaking hands with Giraud in the company of Churchill and Roosevelt, but no more. Both Churchill and Roosevelt then fell for their own propaganda and assumed the photograph meant the two French generals had reached some kind of accord, which they had not.[35]

Throughout April, General Georges Catroux, shuttling between Giraud in Algiers and de Gaulle in London, negotiated over what a provisional government should be and their places within it. Robert Murphy deeply suspected de Gaulle and favored Giraud, and as Roosevelt's representative in North Africa, Murphy's opinions carried weight. Jean Monnet, who showed up from Washington with only a vague purpose, was convinced that Giraud was not up to the task of heading a civilian government and also deeply distrusted the Vichy remnants clinging to offices in North Africa. Churchill's representative Harold Macmillan pulled for de Gaulle as strongly as Murphy pushed against him. Algiers steadily filled up with de Gaulle loyalists who drifted in from Egypt, Central Africa, Britain, and even France. The members of de Gaulle's committee somehow found money to pay a growing contingent of Gaullists who formed a parallel army and administration in Algeria. On 30 May 1943, de Gaulle moved his headquarters from London to Algiers, and four days later he and Giraud reached an agreement to form a seven-member French Committee of National Liberation (CFLN), with the two generals serving as co-chairmen. The Imperial Council, which had served as the governing body for French North Africa, was then dissolved and all involved with the new committee assumed it would serve as the French government in exile. De Gaulle steadfastly refused to sit on the new committee with the leftover Vichyists, who were forced off. Even though Monnet was nominated to the CFLN by Giraud—each general appointed half the council's members—Monnet was more anti-Vichy than he was partisan of either general, and when Gaullists pushed to evict Vichy appointees from all government posts, Monnet invariably sided with the Gaullists. Noguès was ousted as governor-general of Morocco, and Marcel Peyrouton was forced to resign as governor-general of Algeria; Darlan's security chief General Bergeret was retired. Boisson was forced out of his post in Dakar a few weeks later. De Gaulle imposed his stamp on French Africa quickly and definitively by purging officials who had sworn fidelity to the marshal and had vigorously and sometimes violently opposed Gaullists. That they had also previously opposed the Allies was incidental to de Gaulle and of little concern to Churchill or Roosevelt.[36]

De Gaulle steadily undermined Giraud's position in Algiers as he maneuvered within the CFLN to expand his authority and reduce that of Giraud. That de Gaulle proved much more adept at such scheming than Giraud revealed to all involved Giraud's inadequacy in committee politics and de Gaulle's skill, convincing most French personnel to edge away from Giraud and into de Gaulle's orbit. It did not take long for de Gaulle to command the loyalty and respect of the majority of the CFLN in Algiers, which, at the suggestion of the Gaullists, expanded from seven members to 14 a week after its creation. Giraud agreed to stay away from politics and concentrate solely on leading the French military. He resigned from the CFLN in August 1943 and remained as a figurehead commander of the French army in North Africa. Despite the integration of the French North African Army and the Free French force that had accompanied the British Eighth Army across Libya, in Monnet's view the French army in North Africa remained thoroughly Pétainist and never really gave its loyalty to Giraud. The unified army nevertheless gladly followed General Juin, despite his enthusiastic embrace of the Allied cause and break with Pétain. In any event, it did not please General de Gaulle to keep Giraud in charge of the Free French Army, and he was soon relegated to irrelevance as an inspector of troops. He was forcibly retired from the French Army in April 1944 and the object of an assassination attempt in Algiers in August. When Giraud was nominated by de Gaulle to the Legion of Honor after the liberation of France, Giraud declined the honor.[37]

With de Gaulle firmly in place in Algiers and the CFLN unquestionably in charge, de Gaulle happily acceded to left-wing demands that former Vichy officials be arrested and put on trial. Boisson, Peyrouton, and Edouard Flandin were arrested on de Gaulle's orders in late December 1943. A warrant was issued for Noguès, who had wisely "retired" to Portugal and was out of reach. Roosevelt saw subterfuge, bad faith, and double dealing in these maneuvers in Algiers and refused to recognize the CFLN as the *de facto* government for France. Orders to arrest the two governors, Noguès and Boisson, who had swung to the Allied cause with assurances from Roosevelt and Churchill, angered Roosevelt, who instructed Eisenhower to order de Gaulle to release Boisson, Peyrouton, and Flandin immediately. Despite public statements welcoming the formation of the CFLN, Roosevelt still erroneously believed that the United States controlled events in North Africa and could impose its will. Eisenhower knew otherwise and asked Murphy to see what he could do. Murphy met with de Gaulle, who was surprisingly amiable and agreeable except when it came to the release of the Frenchmen; he categorically refused to admit foreign intervention into a strictly French affair. At the end of the war the prisoners remained in French prisons awaiting trial for treason. Former Vichy Interior Minister Pierre Pucheu, who made his way to North Africa in May 1943 with a safe conduct guarantee from General Giraud, was tried in Algeria after a violent Communist press campaign for his head and, despite a personal plea from Giraud for mercy, placed before a French firing squad in March 1944.[38]

PREPARING FOR THE INVASION OF FRANCE

Shortly after its formation in June 1943, the CFLN expanded to 14 commissioners to serve as government ministers responsible for all the functions of government. Despite Roosevelt's refusal to recognize de Gaulle's committee as a "government," it had assumed all the powers and responsibilities of a government in the French empire, nearly all of which had rallied to the Free French cause by the spring of 1943. In August both the United States and the United Kingdom announced recognition of the CFLN as the legitimate authority wherever it was accepted by the governed. It had an executive committee that included politicians of all colors of the moribund Third Republic and a council of commissioners to serve as ministers. It was then in a position to negotiate "agreements"—treaties being reserved for states—with all the Allied powers to define the place of France within the coalition. De Gaulle's committee was not recognized by the United States as a government in exile, but rather as a rebel group that had managed to seize French colonial territory and did not merit a treaty. This stance assumed large importance in 1943 as the Allies planned to invade France in 1944.[39]

The French in Algiers were unsettled that their allies had agreed to abide by the Hague Convention of 1899 on the treatment of civilians in wartime, which addressed in some detail what "occupying powers" were allowed to do in occupied *enemy territory* but was silent on the rights of civilians in friendly countries. In September 1943 the Allies presented a document to the CFLN outlining an agreement on the administration of France after an Allied invasion. The British and Americans had signed similar treaties with the governments-in-exile of Norway, Belgium, and the Netherlands. The proposal sought the committee's acceptance that Allied Civil Affairs officers should be the ultimate civil authorities in liberated France in consultation with whatever authority they should happen to find in place until the French could freely choose a new government for themselves. The CFLN was invited to attach a *military* committee to Eisenhower's Headquarters (SHAEF—Supreme Headquarters Allied Expeditionary Force) to advise Civil Affairs, but it would have no recognized civil authority in liberated France. In return, the Allies promised not to recognize the authority of the Vichy regime and to seek to liquidate its rule wherever encountered—something they had made no effort to do in Africa. Not surprisingly, de Gaulle and the committee rejected the proposal out of hand. This proffered accord was less generous than one previously agreed to by Anthony Eden and Charles de Gaulle concerning the islands of Reunion and Madagascar, that recognized British military authority in Reunion and Madagascar until a Free French army could be reconstituted in those territories. The Free French agreed to place delegates on the islands to exercise sovereignty over the territories, which the CFLN placed at the disposal of British military authorities while a state of war continued to exist against the Axis. That meant the British were free to take the measures they thought necessary—after consulting with and gaining the permission of the French—to conduct the war, but sovereignty remained with the French. That the Allies proposed an agreement that offered less to the French in their own country raised alarms among all the Free French and not just de Gaulle. It compelled the committee to recognize that seizing control of the interior administration of France at the moment of liberation would be their primary concern. They had to worry about the Allies, especially the Americans, as much as they did about the Germans. In February 1944, the Consultative Assembly in Algiers reaffirmed the state of siege declared by the Republic on 3 September 1939 and maintained by the Vichy regime since 1940. It granted all police powers in France to Commissioner of the Interior Emmanuel d'Astier de la Vigerie, who could call upon the services of the French Army to maintain order if needed.[40]

Roosevelt remained adamant that the United States would treat with de Gaulle on a military level as an ally, but refused to consider him or his committee as a provisional government. Eisenhower, encouraged by his chief of staff, Walter Bedell-Smith, saw the wisdom of recognizing *some* French entity to represent legitimate authority in France upon the German withdrawal, and the Gaullists presented the most obvious candidate. SHAEF also believed that de Gaulle commanded wide popularity and loyalty among the occupied French, making him the preferred option. Neither Eisenhower nor Bedell-Smith had any interest in imposing any government—American military or French—on liberated France. Roosevelt insisted on the formula that SHAEF should treat with *any* French entity that offered to aid the Allies, which at least did not exclude the CFLN. However, orders from Washington forbade SHAEF from dealing with any French entity unless it guaranteed that it favored the restoration of traditional French liberties, had no intention of retaining power indefinitely, and would seek a constitutional mandate from the French people. The CFLN satisfied all these criteria, but arguably the PCF (Communists) did not, so this directive could have been seen as anti-Communist rather than pro-Gaullist. In March and again in April 1944, the Consultative Assembly in Algiers voted that an election for a constitutional convention using universal adult suffrage (including women, who had never before voted in France) would be held within one year of the Germans being evicted from the majority of French departments and that, once convened, the Consultative Assembly would dissolve and hand over all authority to the constitutional convention.[41]

Both the French and Eisenhower realized the importance of an agreement between SHAEF and the CFLN about civil authority—who would be in charge—*before* invading France. To SHAEF this was a practicality, but for de Gaulle and the CFLN it was a matter of vital importance. To Jean Monnet, entangling the Allies in the details of cooperation posed the best way to wrest *de facto* recognition of the CFLN from them without pushing for *de jure* recognition that would almost surely be denied. To that end the committee proposed and Eisenhower accepted an accord on mutual aid in time of war; it would establish the office of the Aide aux Forces Alliées (Aid to Allied Forces, or AFA) to ensure not so much that the Allied armies received the local assistance in France they would require to win the fight, but that such assistance would be provided only by the permission of the CFLN. The committee resolved to appoint an official in every department and region (a grouping of three or four related departments) to receive requests for aid and to see that it was provided. In all cases, where possible, requisitions would be made through French authorities and under French law. This was similar to the frantic efforts of Vichy to control the assistance rendered to the Nazis, such as arrests or confiscation of Jewish property, so that the French could assert their own control over the process rather than cede it to foreigners. According to the agreement on the AFA, Gaullist prefects would appoint people to receive military requests for billeting or goods, such as fresh meat or vegetables, and the French official would find the housing or food and establish a price. Price schedules for almost every kind of exchange were to be worked out by French officials and delivered to appropriate Allied officers, and payment was to be rendered to the AFA and not to the vendor, except under special circumstances agreed to by the French. In active war zones, Allied units could request from mayors supplies and billeting to meet only their immediate and temporary circumstances, and not long-term. Regional and department financial officers were to be appointed by the committee to deal with all financial transactions and questions. Some transactions were to be applied as "reciprocal aid"—that is, no payment was to be made by the Allies, but the amount due was to be subtracted from the French debts incurred under Lend-Lease. A metaphorical gigantic ledger was to be kept by both sides, adding bills for American aid to the French and subtracting French aid to the Americans. With luck, at the end of the war the ledger would balance at zero.[42]

The CFLN also recognized that military necessity would demand *de facto* Allied authority over some parts of France while fighting continued. Thus, the accords allowed the Allied military to retain substantial control over some port facilities and communication lines within France to win the war against Germany. In all cases, French liaison officers would be attached to Allied military staff at various levels to act as intermediaries between French and Allied authorities. Once French civil and justice administration had been reestablished, Allied military Civil Affairs officers would operate through French officials rather than deal directly with French civilians or low-level French public servants. Accords signed in April 1944 required the Allies to cede authority to French civilians as soon as the military situation permitted. Delegates of the CFLN would assume functions until such time as a popularly elected republican government could be restored. This came very close to recognizing de Gaulle's committee as the provisional government of France. The accords certainly acknowledged that de Gaulle's committee would be the most likely authority to prevail within liberated France and seemingly was the preferred sovereign to treat with the Allies. In any event, the U.S. State Department was determined to keep any agreements on authority in liberated France between the CFLN and SHAEF, or a matter for the Department of War and *not* the Department of State. Agreements signed by SHAEF were military matters and *not* matters of state. All of these agreed-upon measures would be just castles built in the sky until France was liberated from Nazi rule.[43]

2

THE AIR WAR IN FRANCE

The first contact between the French populace on the Continent and the American military came from above. Britain-based bombers from the U.S. Eighth Air Force and fighters and medium bombers of the Ninth Air Force began to range over targets in France in 1942. Their purpose would have been easily understood by almost all French on the ground who saw them: to defeat Germany. Paradoxically, many of the targets were not German at all, but French, as the Germans placed increasingly large orders for military equipment with French manufacturing firms. The German air force especially relied on French factories for parts for its planes. Around 21 percent of all bombs dropped on Europe by western Allied planes during the Second World War landed in France: 570,730 tons out of a 2,770,540-ton total. U.S. bombers struck rail yards, factories, and warehouses that served the Germans in some fashion, even if no German soldier was anywhere nearby. The inexperienced pilots and technicians aboard the American four-engine bombers—B-17s and B-24s—thus learned their crafts and honed their skills over targets potentially teeming with French civilians. Often the bombs landed far from their intended targets, sometimes miles away. In lucky cases, errant bombs landed on farmers' fields—unlucky for any cows that happened to be grazing there, but doing little damage otherwise. In too many cases, however, luck deserted both the American bombers and the French below, and mistargeted bombs landed in populated areas with tragic results. The German and Vichy propaganda machines attempted to use damage inflicted by American bombs to turn the public against the Allies. Axis propagandists had little influence until errant Allied bombs in 1943—too often American—hit too many houses and killed too many French while bringing liberation no closer. The Allies tried to influence French public opinion with propaganda of their own, which they dropped from the sky by the ton, usually to be accepted gratefully by the news-starved French. Despite suffering under Allied attacks from the air, the French public, for the most part, favored the Allied cause and regarded the Americans as their friends.[1]

AN UNEASY BEGINNING

The first American strategic bombing foray on the Continent occurred on 17 August 1942. It is unfortunate that General Spaatz chose an urban site in Normandy—Sotteville-les-Rouen, an industrial suburb of Rouen—as the best place for American B-17 crews to practice their skills. It was fortunate for Sotteville that only 12 bombers undertook this initial raid that targeted the extensive railroad marshaling yards situated between the town's commercial center and the Seine River. Because few German fighter planes rose to challenge the attackers and the yards were only lightly defended by antiaircraft cannons (FLAK), the American bombing was relatively accurate and almost nine out of 18 tons of bombs found the rail yards. "Relatively accurate" thus meant that half the bombs missed their target, finding instead houses, workshops, and stores on streets nearby. Some bombers mistook barracks in southern Rouen, dating back to the reign of Louis XIV, for engine sheds and loosed their loads prematurely. Fifty-two French were killed and 120 injured. The massive rail yards at Sotteville were targeted again in September 1942 with a raid three times as large as the August attack. Many bombs fell wide of their targets and destroyed houses and a school; the headmaster and his 72 students had to be dug out of their shelter. None of the students and teachers was harmed; however, 103 other civilians were killed and 120 injured. The *rouennais* learned their lesson and organized a serious civil defense service, identified suitable shelters, and set into place plans to deal with emergencies. They were going to need them.[2]

The Allies avoided bombing Paris—doing so would have been too fraught with symbolic complications—but the Germans had put the city's industrial suburbs to work for their war effort, attracting the attention of American and British bombers, which sometimes crashed into Paris. On Sunday, 4 April 1943, stray bombs seeking the Renault plants in Boulogne-Billancourt instead found the horserace track at Longchamps while a race was underway. The races were interrupted for an hour and a half—time enough to remove the wounded and seven dead, and to repair the craters in the track—before racing resumed. Rumors quickly spread that the Germans ordered the races to continue as if nothing happened; others said it was a phone call from Vichy that demanded the races resume. The inaccurate raid killed 403 French and injured 600 more. Among the dead were around 100 killed when a bomb penetrated the Metro station at Pont-de-Sèvres. Parisian newspapers under the supervision of the Germans exaggerated the number of dead and wounded in the region and decried the criminals responsible for such massacres. In fact, some Parisians did not think the trivial damage inflicted on the factories serving the German war effort was worth the price in French blood. Gaullist intelligence received reports from Paris that people were shocked by the inaccuracy of the American bombs, which was roundly resented. De Gaulle's representative in London, René Massigli, lodged a protest with the British Foreign Ministry, which influenced subsequent targeting.[3]

The fall and winter of 1942–1943 witnessed a growing air campaign against targets in France. In anticipation of the invasion of North Africa, the Americans were especially anxious to disrupt the German U-boat bases along the French Atlantic coast. Raids against the sub pens posed challenges for the American Army Air Force; the British had not even bothered to bomb them after initial efforts against those in Lorient had disappointing results, instead mistakenly unloading 400 tons on the town during a series of night raids. American raids launched in October against sub pens in Saint-Nazaire, Brest, Lorient, Bordeaux, and La Pallice were not very effective in destroying any submarines or the huge concrete shelters built by the Germans to protect them. None of the 31 tons of bombs dropped by B-17s on 21 October 1942 penetrated any of the sub pens. Only five bombs, dropped from 17,000 feet—which was 5,000 to 10,000 feet lower than normal—actually hit the pens. This was admittedly an early raid, when the crews of American bombers were still honing their skills, but accuracy was not good and crews had to learn with many innocent French civilians living and working in or near their targets. It probably did not help that many French stood in their streets and watched the spectacle unfold with fascination. Two weeks later, B-17s tried to improve their accuracy and effectiveness, and reduce civilian casualties, by bombing from 7,500 to 10,000 feet above Saint-Nazaire, with disastrous results for the B-17s, which ran into accurate and deadly FLAK fire. The German antiaircraft fire also disrupted bomber flight paths so that bomb accuracy was even worse than from higher altitudes. The experiment was not repeated. The 350 tons of bombs dropped on Saint-Nazaire during five raids in November caused extensive damage to the town and little to the sub pens. Local French informants told the Americans that one raid killed 200 apprentices in a workshop and, because most local workers had fled the raids and refused to return, their bodies had to be left under the rubble as there was no one to retrieve them. By February 1943, 60 percent of the buildings in Saint-Nazaire were damaged or destroyed and the bulk of its population had fled. The number of U-boats prowling the Atlantic only increased.[4]

Saint-Nazaire was hit repeatedly in November and February 1943, causing enormous damage not only to the factories serving the Germans, but also to much of the small city that served and housed the civilian population. Warnings were broadcast over the BBC French-language service, telling people of Saint-Nazaire to seek shelter. Despite earlier raids and warnings, few residents of Lorient had evacuated the city before January 1943. With the new BBC broadcasts, 40,000 people (75 percent of the population) took heed and left the city beforehand. Because the sub pens were the only really safe shelters in Saint-Nazaire, the Germans consented to sheltering civilians in them during raids—it was where all the Germans took shelter even though the pens were the target of the raids. After the devastating raids in February 1943—mostly by the RAF—the town was 60 percent destroyed. There was no gas, no water, little electricity, no shops, no services, no food coming in, no public offices, or any other sort of offices to manage services. Nevertheless, about 4,200 families remained in town. When the RAF let up on Lorient and Saint-Nazaire, the U.S. Eighth Air Force took on these targets with no better results. On the last day in February, American strategic bombers raided the town from high altitude with tragic consequences: three-quarters of the town was razed, over 300 people lost their lives—including 150 young shipyard apprentices—and most of the remaining population fled to the surrounding countryside. Prefect Lecornu called it "a night in Hell"; a veteran of the Battle of Verdun, he declared he "had never witnessed anything equal to this." A similar attack a month later effectively destroyed the town and ended its usefulness as an industrial center. Saint-Nazaire and its submarine base remained in German hands until 8 May 1945 and surrendered only when the whole German Army surrendered. Of 8,000 houses counted in the prewar census, only 100 remained intact in June 1945. Perhaps it is surprising that only 475 French lost their lives in Saint-Nazaire after 52 aerial raids and a siege from August 1944 to May 1945.[5]

Marshal Arthur "Bomber" Harris of the British RAF had been agitating for a sustained offensive against German industry from the start, but the British Navy and merchant marine had insisted on continuing to target sub bases regardless of the ineffectiveness of such attacks. French agent "Rémy" had been sending British intelligence unrequested figures on French civilian casualties caused by Allied bombing for many months as addenda to his reports on the military effectiveness of the air raids, helping to convince Harris that port bombings accomplished only the needless deaths of a lot of French civilians and nothing more. Nevertheless, with the Battle of the Atlantic taking an enormous toll on crucial Allied ships and their precious cargos, Allied leaders—especially American—argued for the importance of the air campaign against the German sub pens.[6]

A 16 September 1943 raid by 131 American bombers aiming for the ship-yards and an aircraft factory in Nantes was especially inaccurate and destroyed much of the center of the city. The population of Nantes tended to be loyal to Marshal Pétain, but the shooting of hostages after the assassination of Colonel Karl Hotz in October 1941 had turned many against the Germans, and attitudes toward Vichy notably cooled. Nevertheless, the people of Nantes were extremely dismayed by the inaccuracy of American bombers, especially when compared to previous raids undertaken by the British. The 16 September attack was unexpected, as Nantes had not been the target before and the town was packed with shoppers from area farms and villages at 3:00 P.M. when the bombers struck. People saw the bombers and watched them with fascination, not believing they would bomb Nantes: they were too high in the sky and must be heading for another site. But then the bombs began to fall and people in the streets had little time to seek shelter even though the sirens had sounded a full half-hour before. Forty patients in the hospital were killed in the raid; the remaining patients were evacuated through holes in the roof and walls only with difficulty by the sisters. Medical teams turned the seminary into a temporary hospital. An elementary school, Sainte Thérèse, was leveled, but fortunately its pupils were on dinner break. The post office burned; the elegant ancient houses on the Place Royale went up in flames. The stained glass windows in the Basilica of Saint Nicholas were turned to shards. The busy commercial center with its full shops and department stores was left in flames, and shoppers staggered bloody, covered in dust, and dazed down smoking streets according to one young witness searching for his mother. The targets were the port and the German airbase, but two of every three bombs hit the city center. When the list of dead was posted three days later at city hall, it covered eight pages, and almost half the victims, still buried in the ruins, were not yet listed. Ultimately, the list grew to include over 1,300 names, with another 1,700 injured. Another attack on 23 September left over 240 dead, 600 injured, and enormous damage inflicted on the town. With electrical power and water cut off, firefighters resorted to attaching their hoses to cisterns of wine to fight fires. When the population fled the city after the raid, the sub-prefect had to use gendarmes to retrieve those considered essential to the functioning of the city. But the city was effectively dead after 325 air-raid alerts, 1,732 dead, 2,946 injured, 2,000 houses destroyed, and another 6,000 rendered uninhabitable, leaving close to 20,000 people homeless; 70,000 left to make their lives elsewhere. Despite such horrific numbers, Vichy agents reported that much of the populace accepted the attacks as legitimate, even if wildly inaccurate.[7]

The German authorities assumed that these raids that killed innocent French men and women would turn the populace against the British and Americans, and forge a bond with their fellow sufferers, the Germans. There were probably some exceptions, but despite the efforts of Vichy propagandists that did not happen. For the most part the French were pleased to see the factories that served the German military bombed—especially if the bombings were highly accurate—and accepted French casualties as the unfortunate price for eventual liberation. An RAF raid in the spring of 1942 targeted the giant Renault plant in Boulogne-Billancourt—a Paris suburb—that turned out 13,600 trucks per year for the Wehrmacht and reconditioned tanks. With 40 percent of the factory destroyed, the British judged the operation a grand success. However, it came at a steep price for the French: 391 killed, 254 badly injured, and 200 houses and a hospital destroyed. Vichy Cabinet Secretary Jacques Benoit-Méchin exploited the event for a propaganda spectacle by displaying 300 coffins of the victims in the Place de la Concorde and inviting the French to pay their respects. French fascists and collaborators used the occasion to launch anti-British tirades; newsreels of the damage and dead were shown in every French town with a screen. Such propaganda evidently had little impact on the population: the people of Boulogne-Billancourt turned their anger not against the British, but against the Germans who "exposed the population to massacres." The Parisian populace was generally pleased by the attack, evidenced by a fashion fad that soon followed: women and young girls wore franc pieces around their necks with a hole between the R and F of République Française, signifying "RAF." During the raid, people in Montmartre were seen watching from their windows applauding. In London, the Gaullists accepted the raid as part of the price of liberation. When bombers raided the locomotive works out-side Nantes in March 1943, the largely working-class crowd that attended the subsequent mass funeral vented their anger at the factory management that failed to offer them any kind of shelter against the air raids, rather than against the Allies that carried them out. Local fury intensified when a July raid heavily damaged a plant that produced parts for Heinkel warplanes and the Luftwaffe decided to move its machinery to a safer site. When the French management objected that the machinery was theirs and force would be necessary to take it away, the Germans obligingly sent soldiers to seize it. They also seized the newly unemployed workers and shipped them off to help build coastal fortifi-cations. An English journalist working for British intelligence in Switzerland during the war, Elizabeth Wiskemann, wrote after the war, "I often heard both French and Italians applaud RAF raids on their own countries under German occupation." When the U.S. Army Air Force bombed Schaffhausen, Switzer-land, by mistake in April 1944, the Basel newspapers called the Americans "air-gangsters"—a term favored by the Nazi press—but according to Wiske-mann, the slur found no echo among the Swiss population. Even though 37 were killed and 60 injured, the Swiss showed "astonishingly little indignation" about the bombing. Forty-year-old Denise Petit and her mother, bombed out of both Saint-Nazaire and Nantes, did not come to hate the Americans but did wonder what the Americans thought they were achieving by all this useless bombing.[8]

While many French regarded the civilian deaths and destruction wrought by Allied bombing as the inevitable product of war for which they held the Germans responsible, it nonetheless was difficult for people to reconcile them-selves to deaths caused by the notoriously inaccurate bombing by high-flying American heavy bombers. Early U.S. raids on marshalling yards in Lille, Rouen, and sub pens at Lorient all proved wildly imprecise, causing hundreds of need-less deaths and injuries. The bombers on a November 1942 raid on Lille failed to find their main target—the marshalling yards—but destroyed some factories and 81 houses; mercifully, only five civilians lost their lives. The bombers re-turned a month later and this time leveled the train workshops at the cost of 25 workers killed. Sixty-six houses were razed and 281 damaged. A January 1943 raid on Lorient by B-17s was initially greeted by townspeople with excitement, "oh, they're beautiful . . . quick, come see—they're really impressive!" yelled one woman to her neighbor when she saw the formation in the sky. The bombers missed the sub yards completely and hit the town instead, destroying 500 houses and many stores; 25 civilians were killed. The inhabitants were shocked: "how could they make such a mistake and bomb the town?" the woman asked. "In their hearts, bitterness was greater than anger," she commented later on. A second wave of British bombers arrived the same evening, hitting their targets dead-on. British bombers were more accurate, and the people on the ground knew it; they greeted RAF bombers with relief. About half of the 150 killed in a fall 1942 raid on Lorient were German; most of the rest were Dutch and Belgian workers laboring on the sub pens. That large numbers of foreigners worked at the pens may have contributed to some French feeling that those who worked for the Germans got what they deserved. After the devastating fall attacks, close to 40,000 French were evacuated from Lorient, which continued to be targeted by massive raids in January and February that reduced much of the town to rubble. On 29 June 1943, 84 B-17s targeted the engine works in Le Mans from 23,000 feet with 726 bombs and missed the target entirely. Fortunately, the imprecise bombing killed only two French civilians. On 4 July, 105 B-17s returned and repeated their effort at 26,000 feet. This time, 5 percent of their 500-pound bombs actually hit the engine works, with most bombs falling 10 miles south of the target. Of 1,764 bombs dropped, only seven hit the engine works in Le Mans using Norden bombsights, which the Air Force claimed was astonishingly accurate.[9]

The inaccuracy of the bombing raids proved especially bewildering and maddening to the French. Most historians who consider the question found that French popular opinion began to turn against the Western Allies in late 1943 when seemingly senseless and wildly inaccurate Allied bombing raids brought liberation no closer. French Air Force officers with little else to do during the German occupation studied Allied air force tactics and the results of their raids. They were mystified by Allied intentions. Could the wild inaccuracy of the bombing patterns be the result of some intentional but unfathomable plan? In early 1944, French censors reported many more complaints about raids in letters, telegrams, and intercepted phone calls. Vichy intelligence agents noted growing resentment of the Americans and a general weariness of the war by the populace as raids grew more common and increasingly destructive. Vichy propaganda evidently had more impact than it had earlier in the air campaign after raids grew more frequent, destructive, and deadly. Even if people were not directly targeted by Allied bombers, life became more difficult and complicated because of the bombings, and more people in France knew someone killed, injured, or rendered homeless by Allied raids. Sadness and anguish at the damage wrought to ancient French monuments by Allied bombing proved understandably common. Armand Idrac's family who lived outside of Caen, in Normandy, remained upset for years by the damage done to Rouen by Allied bombers before the invasion. André Maurois, who spent the war years in the United States drumming up support for France—outside the Gaullist sphere—wrote a book sadly musing on the destruction wrought upon Rouen by the bombings.[10]

THE FRENCH AND THE ALLIED AVIATORS

Whether the French accepted the inevitability of deaths and damage or resented Allied mistakes, many of them risked terrible retribution to aid Allied airmen in need of help. On 3 September 1943, the RAF unleashed 100 bombers on the German airfield at Romilly-sur-Seine, Aube, badly damaging the base and its facilities and destroying about 20 German planes on the ground. The raid also struck the hamlet of Maizière-la-Grande-Paroisse, flattening 12 houses, killing six people, and injuring about 20, some of them very badly. Three days later, about 100 "Anglo-American" bombers flew over Troyes but dropped no bombs. However, they attracted the attention of the Germans, who let loose a barrage of antiaircraft fire and squadrons of fighter aircraft to bring down the bombers. Allied bombers defending themselves with heavy-caliber machine guns added to all the lead and splinters of steel arching through the skies, which had to come back to earth somewhere. A deadly hail fell from the sky and struck civilians on the streets watching the drama overhead, killing one man and injuring 18—two seriously. When German troops buried 15 American aviators killed in the battle in the local cemetery, French citizens were kept away to prevent any pro-Allied demonstrations. When five French citizens attempted to put bouquets of flowers on the wreckage of the planes, they were arrested by German police. Despite the arrests and the German ban on honoring the Allied dead, French citizens continued to place bouquets on the American graves in the cemetery. French police posted there failed to prevent growing crowds of French from visiting the American graves and what the German authorities dubbed "demonstrations" in the cemetery. *Sturmführer* Hellenthal demanded that the ineffective police be punished and the cemetery closed on weekends. These sorts of demonstrations became commonplace in France as the Germans continued to bury Allied airmen in French cemeteries. German authorities fined three people who placed bouquets on an American aviator's grave in Villiers-sous-Prény, Meurthe-et-Moselle, in February 1944. They also fined the mayor who failed to prevent them from doing it. Despite the damage and death brought by Allied bombers, and unrelenting German and Vichy propaganda intended to depict the Allied airmen as murderers, and a detectable souring of many French on Allied air raids, many French continued to honor Allied aircrews.[11]

On 14 October 1943, an American bomber returning from a raid over Germany crashed northwest of Nancy after its crew bailed out. Eight of them were found by some local farmers, who showed them a path through the woods to avoid German patrols. One of the aviators was unable to walk, so the farmers flagged down a passing truck that took him to a nearby hospital. All of the aviators evaded the Germans. Another downed aviator, James Becker, was hidden for a week by a farmer, who then passed him to a local teacher. The teacher gave him civilian clothes and passed him to the French Forces of the Interior (FFI) to spirit him out of France. On the night of 1 November 1943, Gordon Lee of San Fernando, California, fell on the house of M. and Mme. Henri Revol, café-owners in Laneuveville-devant-Nancy. They took him to another house that they believed was safer than theirs, where he stayed for three nights. The Revols gave him civilian clothes, food, and ration tickets, and Mme. Revol took him into Nancy to be photographed for a fake identity card. She then arranged for Lee to meet members of the FFI, who smuggled him to Britain. All of these French were just ordinary citizens reacting to their situations as they saw best in the face of extreme danger from the Germans if caught. Despite the damage done by Allied bombers and the French lives lost, they still knew who their friends were and who the enemy was, and were willing to take great risks to help their friends. However, such sentiments were not universal among the French; some French farmers in Morbihan alerted German authorities when they found downed flyers.[12]

Starting with British soldiers stranded on the Continent in June 1940, French citizens took the initiative to help Allied soldiers get back to England and the fight. Teams quickly coalesced to pass soldiers and, soon, downed aviators from house to house to get them back to England. Aiding stranded British soldiers and downed airmen was for many French their first act of resistance.

An art historian at the Musée National des Arts et Traditions Populaire, Agnès Humbert, was one of the few who actually heard de Gaulle's radio appeal of 20 June, took heart from its message of defiance, and gladly accepted the risk and responsibility to hide a British airman (who turned out to be Polish) in her Paris apartment in November 1940. She joined a group that slowly gathered like-minded people in Paris to produce an underground newspaper and help Allied fighters and French needing to escape to get out of the country. Her career as a clandestine editor and "helper" of airmen was cut short when she was arrested by the Gestapo in April 1941. Aiding Allied airmen or escaped prisoners gave French men and women the opportunity not only to defy the occupiers, but to actively support the Allies in the war. It was also for many their first contact with American servicemen. The "Zéro France" network, one of many helping downed aviators, relied on 1,000 people to operate. Agnès Humbert's Musée group relied on around 300 full-fledged conspirators and helpers. Humbert and many others found out how dangerous the work was as both Vichy security forces and the Nazis worked assiduously to root them out. Many, including Humbert, were captured by the Gestapo and sent to concentration camps in Germany; around 500 were shot by the Nazis.[13]

Like Agnès Humbert, many "helpers" of Allied airmen performed other underground resistance work as well. Eugene François d'Hallendre and his wife, Lucienne, from La Madeleine, adjacent to Lille, began working in the resistance shortly after the catastrophe of 1940 when they helped stranded British and French soldiers reach England. Eugene held the important post of inspector for the national railway line, SNCF, and used his valuable information about train movements. He became a leader in a branch of an early important resistance group, l'Organization Civile et Militaire (OCM), in the Nord soon after. The d'Hallendres also gathered intelligence and passed clandestine publications before joining the Comet group, which funneled downed Allied airmen back to England, in June 1941. Like so many others, Eugene was betrayed to the Gestapo in July 1943, and he, his wife, and their 21-year-old son were arrested. Eugene was shot by the Germans in December 1943. Shortly afterward, Lucienne was shipped to a concentration camp in the east, where she remained until her liberation by the Russians in May 1945; their son was liberated from a Belgian prison in September 1944. Resisters helping Allied airmen escape the Continent were active all over France. Mathurin Branchoux lived on the north coast of Brittany and entered into resistance work in 1941 by recruiting and directing a number of French in gathering intelligence for the Allies. Branchoux secured clothing, shelter, false papers, rail tickets, and, when needed, medical aid for evaders he routinely met in groups arriving by train from Paris. He personally drove his charges to their rendezvous on the Channel more than 40 times, mostly avoiding German patrols but bluffing his way through checkpoints when necessary. Armed with incredible self-control and sangfroid, he never lost an airman. Branchoux aided 90 fliers, and his organization in Brittany returned 150 airmen to the battle. As the Americans came closer in 1944, he took up arms with the FFI.[14]

Because Paris was the central railroad hub for northern France, helpers in Paris were crucial to the system. One line running through Paris was taken over by Paul Campinchi, a civil servant at the Prefecture de Police (police headquarters for all of Paris). He set up escape routes for flyers, passing them along to helpers in Brittany until that line was shut down by the Gestapo. British Special Operations agents who parachuted into France convinced Campinchi to take over the remnants of escape organizations devastated in 1943 by betrayals and German infiltrators. While in charge of the Paris hub of the Shelburne Line, Campinchi personally helped 119 flyers reach safety and was instrumental in facilitating the escapes of many more. As Campinchi's responsibilities increased, he came to rely more and more on one of his helpers, Marie Rose Zerling, who had attended Wellesley College in Massachusetts and knew American English well. Zerling was originally from Alsace, so she also spoke German fluently. Campinchi put her language skills to good use to sniff out fakes planted by the Gestapo to infiltrate the lines. A school teacher in the Paris suburb of Valenciennes, Zerling began resistance action as a writer and courier for an underground newspaper. As Campinchi's responsibilities mounted, he relied more on Zerling, until she was the number two person in the ring, undertaking most actions that kept the operation going. Zerling escorted flyers, found them safe houses, clothing, food, and fake documents. Despite her skills with English, she was fooled by a fake Norwegian flyer and arrested by the Gestapo in February 1944. Although condemned to death, she was sent to Auschwitz along with her parents. Marie Rose Zerling and her mother survived, but her father did not, for which she blamed herself. With Zerling in the hands of the Gestapo, Campinchi came to rely on a Belgian-born Frenchwoman, Marie Wiame, who started helping when she received a Canadian flyer in June 1942. Like Zerling, Wiame was central to unmasking traitors—two pretending to be downed flyers and one Frenchman—and attended their ultimately fatal disposition. She was forced to flee Paris in March 1944 but continued from another hideout in the suburbs until the liberation of Paris. Marie Wiame helped over 100 Allied aviators, including 69 Americans.[15]

The frequency of aid offered to downed aviators testifies to pervasive support for the Allied cause among common French people. Around 12,000 people (French and Belgian) were active members of such underground networks, and perhaps as many as a dozen others helped each member in some way. After the war, the French government recognized 266 such underground networks involving 150,000 members and helpers who by the summer of 1944 had helped over 5,000 Allied airmen escape the Continent.[16]

THE AIR WAR IN PREPARATION FOR
THE NORMANDY LANDINGS

After Allied strategists decided on a massive invasion of Normandy, they planned to isolate the invasion area from the rest of France in order to prevent the Germans from rushing in reinforcements. The commanders settled on a plan to concentrate air attacks against railroad targets in western Germany, the Low Countries, and France in order to hamper German abilities to move troops and supplies in response to the invasion. As part of that campaign, Allied strategists decided to destroy all 12 railway bridges and 14 highway bridges crossing the Seine River, hoping to cut off the Normandy invasion beaches from the main concentration of German troops in northeastern France. Such was the plan anyway. In the event, German engineers proved just as effective at improvising temporary bridges and arranging ferries as the Allies did when they, too, faced the Seine River denuded of bridges. This sustained air campaign to disrupt rail transportation in northern France was assigned to the U.S. Ninth Air Force, composed entirely of fighters and light and medium bombers, which were used for tactical rather than strategic strikes. Tactical bombers dropped their bombs from lower altitudes than strategic bombers (the two-engine B-26 Marauder typically bombed from 6,000 to 12,000 feet), and when properly trained their crews achieved greater accuracy and hopefully fewer civilian casualties.[17]

When informed of the plan, Winston Churchill had great reservations because of the estimated 20,000 dead civilians it would cause in a friendly nation.

An early study by the R AF had put the number of French civilian dead at 40,000 and another 160,000 injured. Those figures raised great alarms and were later reduced. Even so, Eisenhower had to argue with Churchill and Bomber Command to convince them that the cost in French civilian lives would be worth the price if the Continent could be liberated. Eisenhower admitted it would be a heavy burden, but he assumed full responsibility for the decision and the cost. When the British War Cabinet also objected that the railroad bombing campaign would be too costly in French lives, the United States agreed to drop leaflets warning the civilian population to stay off the trains. Even the War Cabinet—"unanimous in its anxiety about these French slaughters," according to Churchill's letter to Roosevelt on the subject—could not derail Eisenhower's decisions about the bombing campaign. On 9 May, Eisenhower lunched with Winston Churchill, who told the general that the Cabinet was still upset about bombings in France, but despite the worries, "I am in this thing with you to the end." Fortunately, intelligence reports from France a week later revealed that the loss of French lives because of the rail-bombing campaign was below even the most conservative estimates. Eisenhower was as relieved by the news as the prime minister was. General Pierre Koenig, the Free French commander of all Forces of the Interior (FFI), also asked Eisenhower to reconsider his decision to bomb targets embedded in the French population, proposing instead that sensitive targets be submitted to an Allied committee that included the French. Eisenhower rejected the suggestion, telling Koenig that he was not ignorant of the ill effects of the bombing, but the goal was so important that he was willing to alienate the French population to achieve it. Koenig, who had indeed received reports from agents in France about French anger over the raids, replied he would approve the bombings if they were done at a low altitude and with pre-warnings to the targeted population. He accepted Eisenhower's assurances that every precaution was being taken to minimize the loss of civilian lives, saying, "*c'est la guerre*," which Eisenhower qualified as "worthy of a soldier."[18]

The air operations against rail centers in northern France began in March with attacks on marshalling yards and repair facilities from the Belgian border to Le Mans. It did not initially achieve great success. Marauders, Mitchells, and Thunderbolts, acting as dive-bombers, peppered the rail centers with bombs. In April, P-51 Mustangs were added to the mix, but the small bomb payloads that the fighters—including the P-47 Thunderbolts—could drop limited the amount of damage they could do. Moreover, the Germans had gotten quite practiced at repairing such damage and it proved to be little more than an inconvenience for them, despite the 33,000 tons of bombs dropped by the Ninth Air Force in March and April. In addition, as the German military lost more rolling stock, they diverted more from French civilian use. The smaller single- or two-engine planes may have achieved greater accuracy than the four-engine bombers of the Eighth Air Force, but they still inflicted damage, death, and suffering on French civilians. In early 1944, 36 Marauders attacked the rail yards at Tergnier, which linked Paris with Brussels and Lille with Dijon. The rails and supporting buildings were completely destroyed along with much of the town. Twenty inhabitants were killed and 60 houses completely leveled. Within 30 hours, the Germans repaired the yards sufficiently to allow trains to pass through; in three days all of the most important services had been restored. French pilots of Pierre Mendès-France's Lorraine Squadron flying light bombing missions against targets in France typically launched their bombs at 1,150 to 1,500 feet—much lower than American or British pilots—in a strenuous effort to achieve accuracy and avoid civilian casualties. Despite their precautions, French aviators faced the same difficulties as Americans: Mendès-France piloting an American-made Boston light bomber against an electrical generating plant used by the railroad hit a nearby chapel instead. It was on a Sunday and a baptism was underway in the church at the time. Sixteen people died.[19]

The British air chief, Trafford Leigh-Mallory, had argued for leaving the bridges in France to the heavy bombers; the American general in charge of all U.S. strategic bombers, Carl A. Spaatz, responded that experience in Italy had proven that tactical bombers and fighter-bombers showed a better record of destroying bridges. Spaatz set out to prove it, and on 7 May he ordered P-47 Thunderbolts to attack four bridges across the Seine at Oissel, Orival, Vernon, and Mantes-Gassicourt. The Ninth Air Force dropped 500 bombs on Oissel in an effort to destroy a railroad viaduct, which killed 14 French and injured 13 without damaging the viaduct. The Americans undertook the same operation at nearby Orival 45 minutes later with similar results: the viaduct was not hit and four civilians died. At Elbeuf they targeted the road bridge across the Seine; a small bridge—not the target—collapsed, leaving eight dead. The Oissel viaduct was finally destroyed in a third raid on 9 May that also destroyed 100 houses. Ten viaducts and 14 road bridges across the Seine were targeted before D-Day, almost all by Marauders or fighter-bombers, and yet most required multiple raids before succumbing. German engineers replaced the road bridge at Oissel with a wooden bridge in a few days. While only the bridge at Vernon was completely destroyed, the others were sufficiently damaged to render them at least temporarily useless. Afterward, Leigh-Mallory ordered a sustained campaign against the bridges across the Seine, Loire, and Meuse Rivers. During the last week of May the Seine bridges were targeted repeatedly; it took until early June to hit them all, and some were only damaged. Strafing attacks hindered German crews sent to repair the bridges, which were bombed repeatedly, and ferries were strafed, bombed, and attacked with rockets. Even though the Germans proved skilled and determined to maintain their lines of communication, the Allies were just as determined to disrupt them, and the constant raids indeed hampered German movement of troops and supplies in northern France.[20]

As Churchill had feared, many French civilians suffered death and injury in order for those bridges to be eliminated. On 27 May, four waves of fighter-bombers hit the rail lines leading out of Rouen and caught the 2 P.M. train bound for Paris. A car caught fire and incinerated 48 passengers; another 34 were injured. The losses were for naught even if the roadway of the bridge fell into the Seine River, because German engineers repaired the damage in a few hours. Tiny Orival had the misfortune to lie in a canyon that contained train tracks leading from the tunnel that cut through the hills south of Rouen. In an effort to destroy the tracks as they exited the tunnel, bombs razed 80 percent of the houses of Orival over four days in May. In one of those raids, 22 civilians were killed in neighboring Elbeuf when a bomb hit directly on a slit trench dug as protection during such air raids. At the same time, American bombers began a series of raids to cut the bridges across the Seine at Rouen. One raid succeeded in cutting the iron bridge across the Seine in two but at great cost to the town and its inhabitants. When the sirens went off, people at first believed the target was again Oissel, but the bombs fell along the Seine in the heart of Rouen along the Rue Jeanne d'Arc, the financial center of the town. A school was leveled with 60 students inside. When the Customs Building collapsed under bombs, 140 people sheltering in its basement perished as the basement flooded with water rushing in from the Seine River. An ancient church, Saint Vincent, and the city's synagogue were both demolished. Although the two raids were carried out by the U.S. Ninth Air Force, the inhabitants of Rouen were convinced English bombers did the deed because of their traditional Anglophobia—the English had Joan of Arc tried and burned in Rouen in 1431. A raid on 1 June set the city's famous and beautiful cathedral on fire. As residents stood in mute horror watching the church burn and its roof collapse in a shower of cinders, the fire jumped the courtyard to the bishop's palace and razed the ancient library there. By the morning of 2 June, the fire had burned itself out and the walls of the cathedral still stood, but the central belfry was gone. Another famous and beautiful church, Saint Maclou, was also hit and its interior severely damaged. The raids continued for the whole week until the bridges disappeared; 200 *rouennais* were dead and 60 were missing. By D-Day, 18 of 24 bridges between Paris and Le Havre were collapsed; the rest were damaged, several beyond use. The bombing campaign against the Seine River bridges could reasonably be judged a success; however, they were temporarily knocked out of use at a high price in historic buildings and French blood. These raids were conducted by Marauders and Thunderbolts, supposedly more accurate than four engine "heavies," but with no better result. The crews were not trained for precision bombing and were learning on the job.[21]

On 20 May 1944, British commander Leigh-Mallory ordered that tactical aircraft go after moving trains in northern France, in the hope that few French civilians would be passengers. On 21 May, 763 American fighters and light bombers were let loose in Operation Chattanooga Choo-Choo. The two-week-long campaign, which stopped only when the planes were needed to directly support the Normandy landings, destroyed 475 locomotives and countless train cars. It also convinced French rail personnel that it was much too dangerous to operate trains under attack by dive-bombers; thus, the Germans had to take over running trains in northern France. Warnings were broadcast over the BBC and hundreds of thousands of leaflets were dropped from Allied planes, warning the French to avoid using trains, especially at night. On the second day, 30 trains were attacked and damaged to some extent, all at the cost of no fighters lost. The Allies claimed to have destroyed 46 locomotives, 11 more probably destroyed, and 21 damaged in the invasion zone north of the Loire River. In eastern France, 500 fighters hit 225 locomotives and destroyed 91; hundreds of cars were targeted and many destroyed at the cost of 16 dead and 65 injured French. A train near Bayeux, Normandy, was strafed, causing six deaths—four of them German soldiers. One passenger train was caught by accident as it entered the rail yards of Massy (a suburb of Paris) on 1 June. Forty French passengers were killed and another 60 injured; 30 people in nearby houses were also killed. Except for a few tragic incidents, the tactic of attacking moving trains proved successful and less costly in French lives than the bridge-busting campaign.[22]

The English translation of leaflets dropped over France in May 1944 read:

The spokesman of the Supreme Allied Commander addresses you.

The bombing of railway centers in France and Belgium, which has been proceeding for some time and on which we have issued so many warnings, is to be intensified in the coming weeks.

Military necessity compels us to bombard by day and by night key centers of the enemy communications in occupied countries as well as in Germany. The enemy's means of concentrating men and material must be disrupted. To achieve this, the weight of these attacks must necessarily be heavy and sustained.

This grave military decision has been taken reluctantly. It is realized that the increased volume of these attacks is liable to involve even greater risks than hitherto for the civilian populations in the vicinities of these targets. Our pilots realize that the lives and homes of our friends are at stake. They will therefore exercise the greatest possible care, but the scale of these attacks will inevitably add to the sufferings which you, our staunch friends, have so courageously endured in this war.

We know the extreme difficulty of evacuation at the present moment. Nevertheless, we ask you most earnestly to take every step possible to move away immediately from the vicinity of all important railway installations.

With the same earnestness, we ask those who are in safe areas to throw open their homes to those who must move.

All key railway targets throughout France and Belgium will be subject to heavy air attacks in the coming weeks. Get away from the vicinity of these targets.[23]

Free French airmen also played their part in the bombing campaign of northern France. When Allied planners decided that bombers should target a major locomotive roundhouse and repair shops in Tourcoing (near the Belgian border), they concluded it was close up against houses and factories, making it almost impossible to avoid hitting civilians. Bomber Command recommended the attack be undertaken by the French airmen of the Groupe Lorraine. Charles de Gaulle personally approved the raid, but told the commander of the squadron, Lieutenant-Colonel Gourri-Fourquet, he could decline if he did not want the assignment. He passed the option along to each of his 12 teams equipped with Boston bombers; none declined. At 11 A.M. they bombed from 1,640 feet and caught 23 locomotives along with tenders and many cars, two of which contained V-1s and another that held U-boat torpedoes on their way to sub pens. They caused not a single French casualty on the ground. Most damage and injury to eight civilians was caused by AA fire falling back to earth. The French resistance was also busy on the ground: on the night of 6–7 June, FFI working with French railroad workers sabotaged 52 locomotives at Neuville-sur-Ain (northeast of Lyon) without any loss of French lives.[24]

The French press in occupied France continued to try to wring the maximum anti-Allied propaganda out of the air campaign. When 52 B-17s hit Troyes for the first time on 1 May, the press in occupied France exaggerated the number of victims, claiming 103 lives had been lost when in fact the toll was four dead and 13 injured. Nonetheless, most French could not fail to notice the high price being paid by French civilians for the stepped-up air campaign: 56 dead, including 17 small girls and six young boys, in a raid on Sarreguemines by 64 B-17s; 42 dead in Mantes; 100 in Metz; 35 at Valenciennes; 80 at Mézières; 74 dead on 10 May in Creil, a small rail junction north of Paris. The next day, 48 Flying Fortresses hit Forbach, Haut Rhin, leaving 56 dead. With the number of dead mounting and the destruction wrought upon French towns intensifying, French cardinals and the bishops of Lille, Paris, and Lyon wrote a public appeal to the bishops of the United Kingdom and United States to condemn the bombings and save innocent populations from death, misery, and homelessness. The appeal was printed throughout France on 24 May after a dispute with German ambassador Otto Abetz over the wording (the bishops refused to change). Belgian cardinal Jozef-Ernest van Roye added his own call to stop the bombing. The Allies responded by dropping hundreds of thousands of leaflets from bombers over France, saying the pilots were aware of the sacrifices made by "our friends" and did all in their power to minimize suffering. Despite all the suffering and anguish, when an American bomber was shot down on 27 May over Amiens during a particularly violent raid (146 dead and several hundred injured), a crew member parachuting to the ground was met by a French woman who immediately gave him a kiss.[25]

Cities in eastern France, such as Metz, Strasbourg, and Epinal, were beyond the range of Thunderbolts and Marauders, and thus were targeted by four-engine B-17s and B-24s, with unfortunate consequences for the towns and their inhabitants. The Air Force targeted train stations, which were usually located in the busy centers of the towns. On the afternoon of 11 May, 68 B-24 bombers struck the center of Epinal, razing much of the town's commercial district, destroying 30 buildings, badly damaging 50 more, razing numerous shops, and killing 204 French civilians. Most of the damage to the rail system was repaired after a few days. Sometimes Allied bombers hit their targets and hurt no one, such as on 27 April, when bombers destroyed three gasoline storage tanks (empty at the time) in Longwy without injuring anyone. The same day bombers cut a rail line and telephone communication between Belfort and Chaumont, without any French casualties, when bombs fell in the countryside outside of the village of Jussey. People living near the German airbase in Essey-lès-Nancy were less lucky the same day when American B-17s struck it and a nearby German munition dump: 12 houses were destroyed and 23 damaged; six French were killed and 19 injured—perhaps a small number considering the massive damage inflicted. The town and airbase had been targeted by B-17s the previous fall, damaging only a few buildings and killing nine people, including the mayor's wife. One resident, who later wrote about the attack, remembered, "people said it was a miracle that Essey was mostly spared, being only a few blocks from the airfield. Thousands of people could have been killed. We were in awe of the Americans—that they could bomb with such accuracy." This comment was not often repeated. On 26 and 27 May, Allied bombers struck a German airfield and barracks near Toul, inflicting heavy damage to both without injuring any French. This, of course, was the preferred outcome for all involved; however, the losses in Essey-lès-Nancy in the fall and spring would probably have been considered an acceptable price to pay by not only the Allies but by the French as well. General Koenig agreed that the bombing campaign was needed and that it would necessarily incur French losses, which should be kept to a minimum through warning leaflets. By May, Allied fighters were added to the mix. The sky on 12 May was crowded with Allied and German fighters dueling to control the air over the many miles stretching south of Toul and Nancy. The Allies bested the Germans that day, with 10 German fighters shot out of the sky and six pilots killed, to two American fighters downed and both pilots surviving. While several houses were damaged, and one cow and a horse were injured, no civilians were hurt.[26]

It was often difficult for either the Allies in England or the French to really know the damage inflicted by a raid. Both formed diametrically different
assumptions, for example, about an RAF raid on a large German complex in
Mailly, north of Troyes, on the night of 3–4 May 1944. Prime Minister Churchill was under the mistaken impression that no French civilian lives were lost
in the raid. He wrote to General Tedder, ". . . we . . . [should] continue to
give a high priority to operations of this sort, which contribute directly to the
disorganization of the German armies and involve no French casualties. Have
you exceeded the ten-thousand limit [on French civilian casualties] yet?" In
fact, it cost lives because the camp used North African POWs as workers and
many locals had jobs inside the sprawling installation: 37 of the POWs were
killed along with 62 French civilians. Some workers sought shelter in a quarry
that took a direct hit; others were caught in the village of Poivre, next to the
camp and hosting 20 German antiaircraft cannons that attracted the attention
of the bombers. Thirty-nine French lost their lives in Poivre, and the lists of
victims drawn up by gendarmes reveal that a number of families lost multiple members: four Pierrons, four Villemins, five Garniers, four Goudards, and
three Goberts. The total count of civilians killed in the raid on Mailly was later
raised to 111 after more bodies were uncovered in charred buildings and some
of the hospitalized died of their injuries. Stories that circulated around Troyes
at the time put the number of deaths at around 1,000, with 50 bombers shot
down. Gendarmes counted three bombers crashed in the region. Officials later
counted nine crashed planes, including German fighters downed in the fight.
People also believed a German troop train crammed with 2,400 veterans of the
Eastern Front was smashed in the camp rail yard. Such a train may very well
have been destroyed, but the Germans never informed the French of German
casualties from any raid. A death toll could only have been the subject of spec-
ulation. In fact, the damage wrought upon the Germans was great, but not as
great as believed by the French, nor was the cost as low as believed by the British, nor as high as assumed by some French. Stephen Bourque points out that
the official British estimate of 33 dead caused by a raid on Boulogne in May
1944 has become indelibly embedded in the literature even though French officials counted 212 dead.[27]

Southern France was beyond the reach of light and medium bombers. Con-
sequently, when planners decided to expand the air campaign to the south, they
elected to use heavy bombers that dropped bigger bombs from higher altitudes

with less accuracy. Using heavy bombers did little good and bred resentment among the French who suffered their attacks. Lyon, Saint-Etienne, Grenoble, Avignon, Marseille, and Nice were all targets of heavy bombers of the U.S. Fifteenth Air Force based in Italy. In two days in May, 600 B-24s and B-17s ranged over southern France, targeting French rail yards. Despite what Bomber Command called "excellent results" and "light civilian casualties," French civilians and rail workers nevertheless paid a dear price. Aerial attacks in the south in support of Operation Dragoon, the Allied invasion of southern France, began on 29 April with a raid on Toulon, when 573 bombers hit the port. Over 200 *toulonais* were killed, mostly when people exited their shelters after the first wave, mistakenly believing the raid was over. Toulon was the target of three more raids before Dragoon finally landed Allied soldiers on southern beaches in late August 1944. B-24s caught an unlucky train during an attack against a bridge across the River Var, west of Nice, in Saint-Laurent in May. Its cars were sprayed with bomb fragments, and when it arrived at the station in Cannes blood dripped from the cars. When the doors were opened, dead bodies tumbled out: 52 passengers had been killed. Train service across the River Var was broken, and for several weeks passenger had to disembark at the river and walk across a footbridge to waiting trains to finish their journey. After a raid on Marseille on 27 May left 752 dead, 2,761 injured, and 18,000 homeless, the clandestine resistance newspaper of Marseille, *La Marseillaise,* indignant at useless deaths, proclaimed, "The massacre of innocents by the American Army must stop!" The bishop called the bombings "a crime against our city." French resistance agents in touch with de Gaulle protested vigorously against the atrocities in Saint-Etienne and Marseille; Massigli lodged another protest in London, decrying the cost in French lives.[28]

Despite French protests, the Allied bombing campaign continued to wreak havoc in France. Lyon was hit in a deadly raid on 25 May and again the next day, with bombs spread inaccurately over a wide area. Among the trains caught in Lyon's sprawling rail yards was one specialized train used to aid victims of air raids. Schools, churches, hospitals, homes, and shops were all hit, leaving behind 717 dead and 20,000 homeless. At least the Gestapo headquarters was leveled, killing several high-ranking Gestapo officials. The head of the regional FFI, Alban Vistel, sent this message to London: "the effects of the bombing on Lyon are more disastrous for morale than in material damage. Population is sadly indignant, enormous sacrifices for insignificant results." That same Friday,

26 May, B-17s raided Saint-Etienne with even more tragic results: 1,084 dead and around 2,000 injured. The city was unprotected by antiaircraft artillery, which convinced locals to think the bombers could have struck from a lower altitude than 10,000 to 13,000 feet. The B-17s razed whole neighborhoods of workers' housing, leaving 15,000 homeless without doing much damage to the rail yards. In the wake of the useless destruction, the Anglophobe mayor ranted against the Allies. Many locals who were neither anti-Allied nor pro-Vichy were very angry about the raid because it was so ineffective and killed so many for no good reason. That was frequently the French response: deaths, injuries, and destruction could be accepted if they advanced the defeat of Germany, but too many raids were obviously ineffective against the enemy and devastating for the civilian population. Those raids were generally viewed as the work of incompetents and were greatly resented. Free French agent Rémy was horrified to learn of the terrible destruction wrought upon Bordeaux in 1940 by RAF bombings that resulted from his alert about German U-boats in the harbor. But, he noted, the choice was between such destruction or slavery. The damage to Bordeaux was worth the harm done to the German war effort. The payoff was obvious, and efforts by Vichy and collaborationists to exploit the raids to whip up Anglophobia or to rally French to the cause of collaboration proved in vain. A French officer, Philippe Ragueneau, parachuted into France to lead an FFI team, asked that only the RAF bomb a rail site in the Loire-Inférieure because he had little faith in the accuracy of the Americans. This, too, was a commonly held opinion among the French: they would rather suffer bombing by RAF Lancasters and Sterlings than American B-17s and B-24s. A French resistance agent in Paris reported in May 1944 that he no longer wanted to help identify targets for Allied bombers as the price in French blood was too high.[29]

A little discussed yet tragic campaign launched by order of General Eisenhower was Operation Quicksilver IV, the diversionary bombing of German military sites in northern France to keep the Germans believing that the main invasion would come in the Pas de Calais. Paradoxically, accuracy was not necessary to achieve the raids' goal of distracting the Germans' attention from Normandy. Three French departments, the Pas-de-Calais, the Nord, and the Somme, contained the most elaborate coastal defenses erected anywhere by the Germans and large concentrations of military units expected to fend off an Allied invasion. British bombers repeatedly targeted the port city of Boulogne in May 1944 until little remained standing. Although four-fifths of the civilian population had been evacuated by the Germans, 10,000 remained in the town, and they suffered grievously from the bombing. In one raid in late May, 200 civilians sought refuge in a shelter that suffered a direct hit by a British bomb and collapsed, killing everyone inside. On 2 June, the Eighth Air Force sent 540 B-17 bombers to attack German bunkers on the beaches around Boulogne. Releasing their bombs from 20,000 to 25,000 feet ensured minimal accuracy, and indeed most bombs landed miles from their targets. The small beach resort of Equihen-plage was "completely destroyed," leaving 33 dead and another 30 injured. Later the same day, 862 heavy bombers from the Eighth Air Force ranged along the coast, dropped their loads, and destroyed a single German artillery battery. As Generals Harris, Spaatz, Tedder, and Doolittle had argued to Eisenhower, heavy bombers were entirely unsuitable to use as flying artillery. But accuracy mattered little in this decoy bombing campaign, as the purpose was not to destroy military targets, but to convince the Germans that the Allies intended to invade northern France rather than Normandy. In two days in June, the charade destroyed or damaged 41 French towns and villages from Dunkirk to Berck (50 dead), killed 253 French civilians and an unknown number of impressed foreign laborers, and left over 2,000 French homeless.[30]

The Allied bombing campaign against the French rail network achieved most of its aims. Eisenhower had ranked the sustained assault against rail targets as the most important objective of the Eighth and Ninth Air Forces under his command that spring. By mid-May, the German military reported that Allied raids on rail yards, bridges, and repair facilities had made it almost impossible to move troops or supplies around France by rail. Damage to rolling stock and locomotives had severely undermined their ability to get the system back up and running anytime soon. Reports reaching England from France asserted that the raids on the rail systems of Belgium and northern France during April had a terrible impact on the functioning of the trains and had caused rail traffic to slow decidedly. By May, a routine train trip from Le Havre to Paris that should have taken slightly over two and a half hours could not be made in a single day! And a routine hour and a half (express) trip from Rouen to Paris took eleven and a half hours! The Council of Ministers in Vichy heard a report on 31 May that since the beginning of April, 29 major rail yards had been rendered unusable, leaving only 24 still operational; 70 of 167 major depots were destroyed; only three of nine repair works remained available. Perhaps more alarming, 470 rail workers had been killed since the first of the year and 1,100 more injured. Until the beginning of 1944, the toll had been 464 dead and 244 injured. Scheduled train trips had been reduced by 80 percent from the 1938 schedule. In 1943, SNCF—the French state rail company—had loaded 232,000 wagons per week; by January 1944 that number had fallen to 188,000; by the end of May 1944 loadings had declined to 93,000. Even German military trains, which continued at the expense of French civilian train service, were down by 50 percent in western France and 80 percent in the north. Vichy authorities counted 793 locales bombed in 1,284 raids. Bomber Command noted 13,345 sorties against French rail lines alone in 1944. A railroad worker in Marseille, packed like a sardine into a shelter by the train station during a violent American raid, grumbled, "we no longer die for France, but for the railroad!"[31]

LITERATURE FROM THE SKY

Not everything that fell from the bellies of American bombers was to be feared. Allied bombers dropped billions of single-sheet leaflets intended to inform civilians and enemy soldiers alike of Allied actions or intentions. Much of it was informational, such as warnings to avoid trains and similar potential targets. Many drops contained propaganda intended for the French to keep them informed about the war from the point of view of the western Allies. They also dropped enormous amounts of literature intended to keep the French informed about news in the rest of the world, free from Axis and Vichy propaganda, with an emphasis on developments in the United Kingdom and the United States. Most of the pamphlets appear to have been prepared by British writers and sought to convince the French of British power, tenacity, and devotion to liberty. One pamphlet explained in impressive detail about the Beveridge Report, which proposed to set up a national health plan for the United Kingdom after the war. Another pamphlet was entirely devoted to how the BBC was organized and operated. Much of the literature celebrated the successes of the Allied armies and discussed munitions, training, and equipment. Several pamphlets were devoted to the Royal Air Force and revealed information about the Wellington bomber and the Typhoon fighter-bomber, stressing their superiority over their German rivals. Allied psychological warfare specialists guessed—no doubt rightly—that Allied aircraft would be of special interest to the French. Not surprisingly, most pamphlets gave upbeat pictures of events in Britain and the United States, with optimistic projections about ultimate military success.

L'Amérique en Guerre presented news of the U.S. war effort. (NARA RG 331, 93A SHAEF Psychological Warfare Department, box 102)

Le Courrier de l'Air gave news of the world war. (NARA RG 331, 93A SHAEF Psychological Warfare Department, box 102)

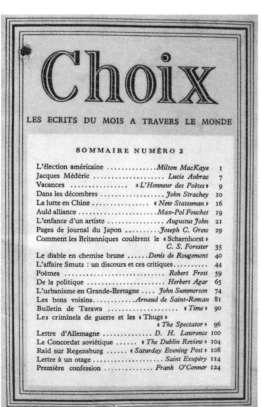

ABOVE: Pamphlet by "Mariette." (NARA RG 331, 93A SHAEF Psychological Warfare Department, box 102)

LEFT: *Choix*. (NARA RG 331, 93A SHAEF Psychological Warfare Department, box 102)

Nevertheless, the information presented in the various pamphlets was free of heavy-handed propaganda and appears to have related nothing that was obviously untrue. *Les Commandos au Combat*, a 152-page booklet with few photographs, related the exploits of British and Canadian commandos who raided the French coasts. The booklet went into some detail about the 1942 Saint-Nazaire and Dieppe raids and, needless to say, did not portray the Dieppe raid as the fiasco it was. Some pamphlets were aimed expressly at children. One purported to be written and illustrated by a young girl, Mariette, explaining the Allied cause and its leaders to French children. Like many of the works dropped by Allied planes, Mariette's work carried a heavy dose of information about France and the Free French. Allied planes also distributed a lot of material in German, intended for German soldiers.

The Allies dropped a literary magazine, *Choix* (Choice), which offered essays, poems, and articles on literary or political subjects by well-known authors of their day: Alexander Werth, Herbert Read, George Bernard Shaw, Jacques Maritain, Harold Nicholson, Ernest Hemingway, Virginia Woolfe, Edmund Wilson, Carl Sandberg, and Georges Bernanos, to name just a few of the better-known authors. *Choix* brought to the French discussions of ideas that would not have been welcomed in Vichy or occupied France, and it kept alive the idea of free speech in a civilized and humane society. *Accord*, a monthly illustrated news magazine that provided news about the war in France, delivered articles about the capture of Caen and Cherbourg with plenty of photos, especially of surrendering German soldiers. It revealed that towns had suffered damage in the fighting but gave only hints at the real extent of the destruction and emphasized the role played by the FFI in the fighting. *Accord* also ran more light-hearted fare, such as "Entente Cordiale" about a blossoming love affair between "Dorothy," a British WREN (female naval volunteer), and "Bébert" (Albert), a Free French sailor, who met in a fish-and-chips shop, began dating, learning each other's languages, and eventually married. This, the author asserts, is the real meaning of "Entente Cordiale." The magazine pushed a distinctly British point of view—and offered a biographical profile of General Bernard Montgomery— but emphasized French participation in the overall war effort.[32]

Five B-17s could drop 3,360,000 leaflets over France in a single night in the spring of 1944. Allied pilots were instructed to drop their loads of pamphlets from 12,000 feet. From there it would take an hour for individual sheets to reach the ground. Sixty-page pamphlets would reach the ground sooner but could still float for up to 15 miles, so precision "bombing" was not expected. Pilots were warned not to drop their loads into clouds, as the material would get wet and material with glossy pages would be damaged. French workers interviewed by Allied psychological warfare officers related that they had access to many Vichy-approved French newspapers and publications, but they did not believe them. They placed more faith in materials dropped from Allied planes, though they rarely saw them. When they did get their hands on them, they appreciated the information provided. While the Germans made an effort to collect all Allied propaganda, only three of 33 workers could recall any French being punished for possessing such materials. Only one ever saw a leaflet advising French to avoid train stations. The interviewed workers also had little access to Allied radio broadcasts, especially after the Nazis confiscated all radios on the Normandy coast. When they did hear broadcasts emanating from Britain, they found them more trustworthy than anything broadcast from German-occupied France. Norman teenager Armand Idrac related that he saw Allied bombers fly overhead and drop leaflets that he was instructed to turn over to the Germans unread. Like many people, he read them before surrendering them to authorities. Norman farmer Xavier de Guerpel saw numerous Allied newspapers dropped from planes and reported that information from them was reprinted in underground newspapers, spreading the word further afield.[33]

French reactions to their first encounter with Americans during the war—those in the air—were mixed and complicated. Frenchmen conscripted to work on the *Westmaur* and later interviewed by Allied psychological warfare officers related that they believed that Allied bombing of German fortifications was very effective, though they voiced complaints heard elsewhere: low-flying medium bombers were more accurate than high-flying heavies, and British bombers were greeted by the French below with relief, while American heavy bombers were dreaded for their inaccuracy. Nevertheless, it took even the accurate Marauders an average of 91 sorties to knock out a single bridge over the Seine River; 57 Thunderbolts dispatched on 3 June to finish the job in Rouen failed to hit the remaining bridges. Of 161 bombs dropped by Marauders on a bridge across the Seine at Mantes, six or seven found their target. Despite frustrations, the bridge demolition campaign on the Seine and the Loire Rivers indeed proved effective in keeping German reinforcements from arriving in Normandy during the first crucial week after D-Day. And even if light and medium bombers proved no better than heavy bombers at hitting bridges, they at least caused fewer casualties and less unintended damage. Reports of the bombings and their negative impact on French opinion reached the CFLN in Algiers, which became greatly agitated by the distressing number of French deaths brought about by the Allied bombings and told the British and Americans so. Most of the population well understood the purpose of the bombing raids and grudgingly accepted them so long as they contributed to an end to the hated German occupation. Those raids that caused too many deaths and injuries, and too much destruction without obvious purpose, were greatly resented. The decision to conduct attacks on French cities with high-flying American strategic bombers came at great cost to the French without inflicting the intended damages that might have justified the death and destruction that contributed little to ultimate Allied victory. Despite French misgivings, their reaction to meeting downed American flyers face-to-face was often, perhaps usually, to offer aid if possible. Many French put their lives at risk to help the downed Allied fliers, whether British, American, or Canadian. They faced stiff fines and imprisonment in order to put a simple bouquet of flowers on the graves of dead Allied fliers. These actions offer powerful testimony about the French response to their American friends and tormenters in the sky.[34]

An unknown number of French perished because of the air war conducted by the Allies over France. Estimates range from 50,000 to 70,000; French historian Eddy Florentin gives us two different numbers calculated by the French government: 47,771 and 67,078. Two historians who have looked closely at the air war over France, Claudia Baldoli and Andrew Knapp, assert that the number of civilian deaths and casualties is not knowable, but that around 60,000 is probably close. Of that number, 25,266 French are known to have lost their lives from air raids from March through June 1944. Allied air forces, of course, also suffered casualties in the war over France: American losses incurred over Europe before June 1944, which would have included France as well as the Low Countries, Germany, and elsewhere, totaled 23,931, with 7,504 dead and another 800 missing. The battle for Normandy (6 June to 24 July 1944) cost the Eighth and Ninth Air Forces 2,506 killed and 2,690 shot down and captured. An additional 5,559 Air Force casualties (2,261 killed) were incurred over northern France from 24 July to 14 September. Combined losses over France for the American Eighth, Ninth, and Fifteenth Air Forces operating from 6 June 1944 to 25 January 1945 came to a total of 22,558 casualties, of which 10,605 were killed and 7,249 captured. These sad numbers give us some idea of "acceptable losses" to Allied leaders and commanders. We also know that at 10:30 in the morning of 14 May 1944, a particularly intense dogfight occurred between Allied and German fighters over Blénod-lès-Toul, Meurthe-et-Moselle, when a machine gun bullet dropped from the sky to strike four-year-old Gilles Mouilleron in the head, killing him instantly.[35]

3

NORMANDY

When massive numbers of Allied troops arrived on French soil in June 1944, they overthrew the authority of both the occupying Germans and their Vichy vassals in a small but expanding zone of Normandy. The invading American troops introduced into this liberated zone the Civil Affairs officers who President Roosevelt imagined would govern France. Following the practice of the British, the U.S. Army established a Civil Affairs division under General Eisenhower's command to handle all matters concerning civilians in formerly occupied territories. Hundreds of officers attended training courses in politics, history, sociology, law, and other helpful fields at a school set up at the University of Virginia in Charlottesville. The officers attached to the Allied armies had no more interest in running French affairs than de Gaulle's officials had in allowing them to. However, it turned out Civil Affairs (CA) officers were obliged to intrude on French sovereignty more than they had expected to, and there was little de Gaulle's men could do about it but protest. CA officers established themselves in French towns and quickly proved their worth to both the French and the Allied armies. The first sizeable town liberated by the Americans, Carentan, offers an example of what American CA officers faced and could accomplish. Major John J. Maginnis struggled to get heavily damaged Carentan back into working order.[1]

When the Allied armies landed in Normandy on D-Day, 6 June 1944, citizens of metropolitan France had their first encounter since 1919 with American soldiers. Like their encounter with American bombs dropped from planes, it was a meeting in the violence of war and, hence, often an unhappy encounter. Living in a war zone proved a trying experience for any civilian, and such an environment did not provide the best conditions in which to meet Americans. The first paratroopers to encounter French civilians on the night of 5–6 June reacted with extreme caution. Not knowing where German soldiers might be, paratroopers searched farmhouses, treating the inhabitants as hostile until satisfied they were not. Paratroopers from the 101st Airborne banged on the door of a farmhouse near Brucheville and demanded everyone leave the house. They complied, and all, including small children, were lined up against a wall outside with rifles trained on them while soldiers searched the house. When no Germans were found, the soldiers relaxed, patted the householder, called him a "*bon français*," and allowed the family back inside. This first encounter, with fear and suspicion on both sides, was common in Normandy that night and much repeated. Paratroopers of the 101st shot at the window of a house in Sainte-Marie-du-Mont, scaring the French civilians inside. When a young boy inside, Michel de Vallavielle, went outside to alert the Americans that only civilians were in the house, he was ordered to advance with hands up. As he did, an over-excited paratrooper put five bullets in his back. At the sight of their son shot down by soldiers, his parents ran out of the house to their son but were not harmed. Michel was patched up by an American medic and later dispatched to England to recuperate. Soldiers of the 4th Infantry Division, who landed at Utah Beach, treated the first French civilians they encountered in Sainte-Marie-du-Mont as hostile. The Frenchmen were marched to the beach with their hands on their heads and held there in temporary pens as POWs. They were then taken back to England as POWs and interrogated. Although they later said they were treated well in England, they were not returned to their families until mid-July.[2]

Despite such initial unpleasant encounters, most French were overjoyed to meet their American liberators. The paratroopers of the 82nd Airborne who landed in and around Sainte-Mère-Eglise impressed the mayor with their quiet determination. After two days of close-quarter combat—American reinforcements had not yet arrived from Utah Beach—a paratrooper promised a frightened French woman, "We will never abandon you. We will die right here." The battalion medic, Lieutenant Lyle Putnam, cared for wounded French civilians with the same dedication he gave to wounded paratroopers. Many French civilians who found wounded paratroopers often gave them what aid that they could. The mayor characterized the soldiers of the 82nd as the "brave among the brave." A French schoolteacher who greeted American paratroopers on the night of 5–6 June and let them use her house in Graignes as their temporary headquarters recalled that all of them were "impeccably correct." This embrace of American soldiers by the French was not evident to all. Captain Harry C. Butcher recalled that the French civilians he saw in public on 12 June seemed listless and apathetic; some waved at Eisenhower as he drove by, a few gave the

"V" sign, but for the most part "they seemed numbed and disinterested." He assumed that the French most affected by the fighting had seen too much in the last few days and just wanted to be left alone. This proved an astute guess. Most French were thrilled to be liberated from the Germans, but the violence of that liberation dampened the enthusiasm of those most directly affected. War zones are terrible and frightening places for people to have to live, and soldiers trying to stay alive, fed, and dry rarely give much thought to the interests of civilians caught in similar straits. Sometimes the liberators liberated a widow's only chickens for their dinner. For the most part, the response of the liberated French was heavily influenced by the bombardment they had to endure on D-Day. Many had suffered mightily under the intense naval bombardment that continued until all resisting Germans were cleared away from areas within reach of big naval guns. Most had gone through the hellish experience of the Allied aerial bombardment that accompanied the invasion, an experience many French resented for long afterward.[3]

THE AIR WAR IN NORMANDY

The bombing and strafing attacks that sorely tested the resolve of the French in the months preceding the Normandy invasion intensely targeted the invasion zone in the days leading up to and then following the D-Day landings. Both General Eisenhower and German commander Erwin Rommel assumed that if the invaders could be stopped on the beaches in the first day or two of the invasion, the Allied offensive would be crushed. The side that could rush the most military might to the beaches as quickly as possible would win. In order to prevent the Germans from doing just that, the Allies set into motion an air campaign of interdiction and isolation to destroy all communication centers at choke points within the invasion zone. General Bernard Montgomery identified 26 towns in Normandy that should be bombed on D-Day after the landings—to avoid alerting the enemy that the invasion was imminent—in order to block the roads. His recommendation to bomb the *carrefours*, or main crossroads, which always lay in the center of towns, doomed the 26 towns that would be subjected to Allied bombs. General James Doolittle, placed in charge of the Eighth Air Force, reduced the list to 13 and moved the bombing date to the day before D-Day rather than the same day as the landings. There was lively debate about the wisdom of the entire plan among those involved, not least the aviators charged with carrying it out, who doubted the attacks would do much good and protested the expected loss of French civilian lives. Generals Spaatz, Harris, Tedder, and Doolittle all argued that heavy bombers were entirely inappropriate for the job assigned to them and the damage would be too great. With only 48 hours to go, Air Chief Marshal Trafford Leigh-Mallory, pushed by Montgomery and Eisenhower, insisted on the plan and refused to budge. Caen, the administrative center of the department of the Calvados and lower Normandy's largest city, was saved by clouds at first, but when they cleared later in the day Caen was struck by a wave of British bombers. Damage to the beautiful medieval city was enormous while all four bridges over the Orne River remained standing.[4]

On the evening and night of 6 June—D-Day—the Eighth and Ninth Air Forces, along with the RAF, began systematic bombing of the other selected towns and villages on the list. B-17s of the Eighth Air Force struck Saint-Lô, the administrative center for the department of the Manche. Just after 8 P.M. a small force of 14 bombers dropped their loads on the center of the small city, killing hundreds of people who never suspected such a thing could happen. Even those who tried to take shelter in their basements were not safe: the entire Fabre family burned to death in theirs when the city center caught fire. The city's firemen were completely overwhelmed, and much of the town burned uncontrollably, in part because the Germans had requisitioned the fire department's pumps for work on the West Wall. Just after midnight the heavies came again. The fires that still burned made the target easy to find. This time hundreds of people sought refuge in a large tunnel being excavated in the chalk hills on the edge of the town by the Germans to serve as a military hospital. When bombs hit the prison full of French patriots arrested by the Germans, 76 of around 200 died. One World War I veteran had the instinctive reaction when he heard the news of the landings earlier in the day to dig a slit trench in his back yard. He, his wife, and young daughter huddled in the trench during the first wave, but no bombs hit close by. When the bombers returned after midnight they again sought the sanctuary of the trench, and this time a bomb landed directly on their house, reducing it to a pile of splinters and rubble. When the bombers left, the family decided it would be best to get out of town, so that when the B-17s returned for a third raid before dawn they were a safe distance south of town. Other town residents had the same reaction and started to walk out of the town after the second raid. The Germans allowed over 1,000 people to stay in the tunnel in the chalk hill for the next few days as they feared further bombardments. Other people were never seen again or accounted for, presumably buried in the rubble or reduced to ashes in the fires. The tunnel served as the town's emergency center and hospital for several days as supplies, food, water, and medical equipment were gathered, stored, and distributed there. When the generators that provided air failed, the mayor ordered the tunnel evacuated.[5]

Saint-Lô had the misfortune to be a minor rail and highway hub only a few miles from Omaha Beach and to host several bridges over the small Vire River. Allied planners saw it as a principal choke point of the invasion region. Saint-Lô also served as the German headquarters for the military administrative area. Prior to 6 June several thousand German soldiers had been quartered there (U.S. Army intelligence put the number at possibly 40,000, which seems unlikely). By one report, on the night of the bombing raid there were no more than seven Germans in the town as the others had all rushed toward the beaches as soon as word of the landings arrived. On the night of 6–7 June, 900 French died in Saint-Lô; another 400 perished in further raids over the next week. The town was left a vast heap of rubble. The official history of the USAAF in World War II claims that leaflets were dropped warning the French population of impending aerial bombardment, but no one in Saint-Lô reported seeing any leaflets. Sometimes such warning leaflets were picked off the ground many miles from their intended destination. A Norman witness, Xavier de Guerpel, deplored that the people of Auney-sur-Odon were forewarned of imminent carpet bombing by leaflets dropped by Allied planes that drifted in the wind many miles away and were seen by no one in the town. Other times the leaflets arrived only moments before the bombs did—too late for inhabitants to clear out of harm's way. Inhabitants in Vire reacted with excitement and awe at the sight of American bombers overhead. Children clapped and people rushed to their windows to see. Then the bomb bay doors opened and bombs began to rain on the shocked town's inhabitants. Caen, Coutances, Falaise, and other Norman towns received similar treatment on 6–7 June and the days that followed for the same reason: "interdiction." Carentan was targeted by Marauders and Bostons of the Ninth Air Force on 6 June. Six French civilians died during night raids and 18 more by noon; 39 more were killed and 50 injured in Volognes. The hospital in Argentan was hit on 6 June and 12 patients in the tuberculosis ward died; 48 other people died in the town, provoking most of the inhabitants—and all of the hospital staff and patients—to flee to the countryside. Lisieux was targeted on 6 June and again on 8, 9, and 10 June. At 8:20 P.M. on 6 June, 72 B-24s hit Lisieux from 23,000 feet; they returned at 1:20 A.M. and again after daybreak, dropping 180 tons of bombs from 20,000 feet that finished off the town, killing 781 plus an unknown number of refugees from elsewhere who had sought sanctuary in Lisieux. German engineers quickly repaired the bridge over the tiny La Touques River and made a path around ruins of the town. Lisieux was bombed another 24 times by 3 July. Volunteers and laborers conscripted by the Germans kept streets clear after each attack. They also pulled 500 bodies out of the rubble and buried them in mass graves. Two-thirds of Coutances was destroyed by a bombing raid on 6 June, killing 312 French civilians. One young girl remembered, "we thought that our house was the only one that had been hit, but there was absolutely nothing left around it. The whole neighborhood was in ruins. Panic and terror set in when we saw the train station and realized the magnitude of the disaster." Seminarians used pitchforks to retrieve mutilated corpses from the ruins. When B-26s targeted the bridges over the Orne River in Caen on 6 June, the after-action report claimed to have hit a German armored car on a bridge. In fact, it was a Croix-Rouge ambulance driven by 27-year-old Teresa Hérilier, who was thrown into the river, where her body was discovered weeks later. Bernard Goupil, a supervisor of an aid station during the raids on Caen, wrote in his journal, "I feel a sense of outrage at the massacres of which I do not understand the military purpose."[6]

By the morning of 7 June, 2,200 Normans had died in Allied air raids. The Normans reacted badly to the devastation of their towns. An American captain who escaped from a column of Allied POWs being marched to the rear by Germans had difficulty finding Norman civilians willing to help him get back to American lines. "They were really pissed off." One family he barged in on fetched a local boy who knew a little English and wrote, "Why did you bomb our magnificent city [Vire]?" American bombers had targeted the bridges over the Vire River and razed most of the town. Jean-Marie Houet, a 20-year-old parish curé in Vire, described trying to save people after the bombing. He was badly shocked by how people could be so mangled, torn up, torn in half, and have limbs ripped off. A young boy with badly burned legs begged the curé to kill him. He "could not but help retain his resentment before such barbarity by the Anglo-Saxons." Norman farmer Xavier de Guerpel noted in his diary for 8

June: "Truly, one cannot conceive of such destruction, the annihilation of our old cities, loaded with history and a memorable past. In full night, the hurricanes of iron and fire came to sow devastation and death." He received with horror reports of the destruction of Caen from neighbors who had witnessed it and heard people say many times, "They're going to liberate only cemeteries!" De Guerpel could plainly see that constant attacks by Allied fighter-bombers kept the Germans off the roads during the day and severely hindered their ability to bring reinforcements to the fight, but he and everyone he knew questioned the effectiveness and thus the rationale for "carpet bombing" that brought death and utter destruction to towns and villages. It became difficult for Normans to venture outside during the day, as anything or anyone that moved attracted the attention of Allied fighters hunting targets. De Guerpel was warned not to dig his air-raid trench during the day because to a fighter pilot he would look like a German preparing a position. He dug at night. He could not venture into his fields during the day for similar reasons: movement attracted unwanted attention. He warned his workers that if they heard a plane, stand perfectly still if they could not hide. Ultimately, 11 percent of Normans in the Cotentin Peninsula reported that a family member had been "a victim of Allied bombing."[7]

After the Normandy invasion the air war against rails, roads, and bridges continued far behind the lines of Normandy in the enduring effort to keep German troops and supplies from reaching the battlefront. Allied fighters and bombers ranged far and wide over northern France seeking targets. Blainville, home to a major rail-switching yard in eastern France, south of Nancy, was targeted in a major raid on 29 June when hundreds of bombs rained down on the yards. The attack came suddenly without warning; the bombing was very inaccurate and hit many houses and buildings in surrounding communes, destroying over 50 houses; 27 French civilians lost their lives and around 100 were injured. At least the rail bridge over the Meurthe River was collapsed and the rail yards were effectively destroyed. A German troop train was coincidentally parked on the tracks and caught in the raid, which killed around 30 soldiers, so more Germans than French lost their lives in the attack. On 20 July, 150 bombers struck the rail yards at Revigny-sur-Ornain, just west of Bar-le-Duc, where they caught a German train packed with munitions heading for Normandy. Nine cars exploded and 12 more burned fiercely in the center of the small town. Three factories alongside the tracks were badly damaged, a retirement home for workers was largely wrecked, and 150 houses were destroyed. Almost miraculously, only three French were killed and six injured. Five more were seriously wounded when they tried to clear away unexploded bombs. Two hundred people were left homeless by the raid and a military cemetery was badly churned up. Despite relatively few casualties, cases like this provided a good argument for the British practice of catching trains between towns rather than in rail yards.[8]

As Allied planes plastered France with bombs and bullets in the wake of the invasion of Normandy, French guerrillas of the French Forces of the Interior (FFI) were at work hitting the same kinds of targets. They sabotaged rails, bridges, power lines, and phone lines throughout France, and were especially active in the north. At the time, many French argued that the Allies should have used their planes to drop weapons and munitions to FFI behind the lines who could have more effectively destroyed targets, thus avoiding the injuring or killing of many hundreds of innocent French civilians with inaccurate Allied bombs. After D-day the Allies vastly increased their program of parachuting arms and explosives to FFI, especially in northern France but mostly outside of Normandy. FFI launched 2,182 sabotage attacks against rail installations all over France in June 1944 alone. They were convinced such operations were more effective than Allied air attacks, however they failed to convince Allied commanders and planners. FFI blew up a locomotive in the rail yard of Bar-sur-Seine on 6 July without any casualties and destroyed a rail bridge about a mile south of town. FFI sabotage was seemingly almost as effective as bombing and certainly less costly in French lives. Civilians in Normandy complained to the photographer Robert Capa, "if we had dropped as many arms to the French underground as bombs on the innocent French towns, we would have killed more Germans and fewer Frenchmen, and succeeded better in our objective." A French guerrilla in Brittany wanted to know from an American OSS agent behind the lines how USAAF bombers could miss a bridge by a mile. They instead had hit a farmhouse and killed a whole family. The CFLN urged Allied commanders to allow FFI sabotage of French rail networks rather than bombing, without result. In the spring of 1944, the CFLN criticized high-altitude bombing by American bombers and asked that it be stopped, to no avail. They requested to be included in decision making about targets, but were rebuffed by military leaders even though the idea was endorsed by Foreign Minister Anthony Eden. In fact, FFI proved effective at destroying locomotives, blowing rail lines, cutting telephone and telegraph communications, and the like; however, they did not do so without cost to their fellow French. FFI sabotage almost always provoked bloody German reprisals that invariably found innocent victims. Eight men were dragged from their houses not far from Troyes and shot dead in reprisal for FFI sabotage. Five men were machine-gunned in Bar-sur-Seine in early August in reprisal for FFI attacks in the region. French police reports of the era are full of such accounts. Although FFI sabotage and attacks could be carried out without killing any French, innocent French still ended up paying the price with their lives even if the circumstances of their deaths were admittedly different from those killed by Allied fighters strafing trains.[9]

THE BATTLE FOR NORMANDY

Not all misery delivered to the French in the battle for Normandy issued from the Allies. The Germans had expected the Normandy landings in the spring of 1944, and as they feverishly prepared for them, tension mounted and discipline degraded. Norman farm owner Marie-Louise Osmont noticed German soldiers getting drunk, which she had never seen before. After the landings, "correct behavior" by German soldiers quickly degenerated into widespread thievery and abuse of civilians. They stole and shot cows; they also shot people. At 7:15 in the morning of 6 June, a German soldier shot dead a French widow in Sainte-Mère-Eglise who had refused to sell him butter. Other soldiers reportedly shot people in Carentan without any provocation in deliberate acts of murder. SS troops stationed in Saint-Manvieu turned their submachine guns on French residents in their houses when British artillery started shelling the town. Among others, they shot a 24-year-old farm worker who was holding her five-month-old baby in her arms. When bullets failed to kill the mother, a soldier stabbed her with a bayonet. Her husband witnessed the slaughter, and their baby daughter survived. When French civilians in Trevières sought shelter from British bombardment in trenches they had dug, a German officer lobbed a grenade into one. When that failed to kill everyone in the trench, he used his pistol on those who remained alive. Not all died, however, and one lived to testify to the event. Similar incidents were reported in other sectors of the Norman battlefields as German soldiers turned murderous against French civilians who had done nothing to merit attacks. The entire Duhoux family, including five children, the youngest of whom was four months old, was massacred in their basement in July as the Germans were being pushed out of Caen by the British and Canadians. One refugee woman staying in Louvigny, whose husband was a POW in Germany, was beaten, choked, and raped by a young SS soldier as British troops advanced on 4 July. When he was through, he invited other German soldiers to rape her as well, but as she lay on the ground sobbing, they evidently took pity on her as no one else touched her. Her neighbor, Mme. G., was less lucky: when she (presumably) fought back against another SS trooper, he shot her twice and pushed her lifeless body down the steps into her basement.[10]

The comportment of SS troopers was not always murderous; when the 10th SS Panzer Division arrived in Normandy, its men were ordered to adhere closely to regulations on requisitions: looting or robbery would be severely punished. And when the staff of an SS division appeared at the doorway of Xavier de Guerpel's farmhouse near Carville, demanding accommodations for the night, they were polite and even friendly. Not having much choice, de Guerpel turned his home over to the officers while men in the ranks set up tents in his yard and garden, and he hoped for the best. The soldiers of course helped themselves to whatever food they found in his kitchen and larder, but when they left the next morning the only item missing was a taurine that had been freshly filled with *paté du porc*. Not all Normans were so fortunate as de Guerpel. When SS troops from the 17th SS Panzer Division retook Graignes from American paratroopers, they shot all the Americans taken prisoner, including all the wounded found in a makeshift hospital in the church and the parish priest. They looted the homes of the locals, taking anything that might be useful as well as a lot of things that could not possibly have been of use to soldiers, such as children's toys and dolls. What they did not take, they often smashed.[11]

Much of Normandy received pretty rough treatment during the fighting. The tactic adopted by General Eisenhower and used throughout the war relied on massive firepower to break the enemy's will to resist before committing infantry to capture ground. This was intended to save American soldiers' lives and no doubt did exactly that; he expended high explosives rather than American blood. This tactic guaranteed massive physical destruction of the countryside and towns caught in the way of the advancing American forces. Captain John K. Slingluff, an infantryman from Baltimore, entered Isigny on 7 or 8 June, the day after it had been bombed by Marauders, and thought that "it looked as though somebody had picked it up and dropped it. It was just piled up and the rubble was burning. You have never seen such a mess in all your life." French Republican Commissioner François Coulet, who had arrived in Normandy on

13 June to represent General de Gaulle, wrote to his superior in London, General Pierre Koenig, that Isigny had been destroyed by the Allies "preventively." American commanders wrongly believed that Isigny was heavily defended by Germans, when, in fact, there were few Germans there. The strategically located town was subjected to a hail of shells from 15-inch (380-mm) naval guns on the morning of 8 June, leaving the center of the town completely flattened and 20 residents dead. Even though most inhabitants fled that afternoon, when bombers struck that evening another 12 civilians died, including a husband and wife buried alive in their trench shelter. On 10 June, General Omar Bradley drove into the sad remains of Isigny and saw its inhabitants trying to salvage what they could from the debris. "For more than four years the people of Isigny had awaited this moment of liberation. Now they stared accusingly on us from the ruins that covered their dead." Determined to link up Utah Beach with Omaha Beach, General Bradley instructed Lieutenant General Joseph Collins, "If it becomes necessary to save time, put 500 or even 1,000 tons of air on Carentan and take that city apart. Then rush in and you'll get it." This well sums up American determination and thinking about capturing towns from the enemy. It reveals the scant consideration for the people caught in between, who in the Normandy campaign happened to be French. The single-mindedness of the Allies might have been necessary to defeat a determined and ruthless enemy like the Germans under Adolf Hitler; however, the application of that Allied resolve provoked resentment among many French civilians who had to suffer the consequences. The tactic used by General Collins in his fight across and then up the Cotentin Peninsula was to bomb an area from the air first, then drench it in artillery, and then send in infantry patrols to see what was left. Often no German troops had been in an area thus devastated by U.S. firepower. Some brave Frenchmen crept out of their shelter during the American bombardment of Colombières to seek out American troops to tell them there were no Germans in the village and they should stop shelling it. The French were amazed to discover that the Americans shelled anything that looked like it *might* harbor Germans without bothering to send in patrols beforehand to find out if there were actually any enemy there. The Americans shelled first and then sent in patrols to verify any German presence. This greatly agitated the surviving French who had to endure the tactic. Norman peasants soon hesitated to tell GIs about Germans hiding in a barn or farmhouse because they knew the Americans would lob artillery shells at it rather than go in and root the enemy out. When told

that Germans had been seen in a barn the night before, GIs set fire to the barn even though the Germans had left hours earlier.[12]

How much violence French people had to live through in order to meet their American liberators frequently determined the greetings given to arriving American soldiers: those who had suffered through bombardment were less than thrilled to meet GIs; those that had escaped being targets were ecstatic. *New York Times* correspondent Hansen Baldwin described Normans as late as 20 June as "cautiously friendly" and showing "shy fear." Overall, he judged the Norman reception of the Allies to be "cool." The inhabitants of devastated Valognes, not far from Cherbourg, gave the Americans a muted greeting when they finally arrived; 39 inhabitants had been killed in Allied bombing raids and 50 injured on the night of 6 June alone. Before the Americans liberated the town, another 175 perished in Allied air raids. Normans who lived in the bocage between the demolished towns of Vire and Caen and who had suffered routine bombing and strafing by Allied fighter-bombers evinced little enthusiasm for their liberators and were commonly described as "indifferent" and "apathetic." They took no comfort in rumors that bombing raids that razed towns were the result of "regrettable mistakes." Many people Xavier de Guerpel talked to could see no reason for the destruction of their "beautiful and peaceful towns" that housed not a single enemy soldier. By the time American troops finally arrived at Avranches, one-third of its houses had been completely demolished and another third damaged; most of the population had been evacuated by the Germans, so there were few casualties, but those who remained received their liberators with a muted response. Some of the British and Canadian soldiers who liberated Caen were greeted by the French with hurled rocks. Chester Hansen thought the popular response to the Allies who had demolished so many of their towns and villages was remarkably accepting, but French resistance fighters he met worried that people would hold the destruction against the Allies. OSS officer Crane Brinton disagreed: "There is no open bitterness about the destruction the fighting in the Manche has brought about, and I think most people do not blame us."[13]

After breaking through the shattered German lines, GIs encountered French civilians who had so far escaped living on the front lines, who lived in peaceful houses untouched by the war, and whose livestock had not been slaughtered by artillery fire and fighter-bombers. These Normans were delighted to see the Americans at last, though an old lady farmer perhaps expressed a common sentiment: she was happy to meet U.S. paratroopers until she learned there might be fighting simply because they were there. She then seemed less pleased to see them. Generally, towns that had been relatively undamaged by the war rendered an enthusiastic welcome to their liberators; when Allied troops entered towns devastated by fighting, their reception was somber and "apathetic." The people of the newly liberated region accorded Gaullist authorities, who arrived in the wake of the U.S. Army, an enthusiastic reception. A rally to celebrate the liberation of Granville, which had hardly been touched by the fighting, attracted 10,000 people who repeatedly shouted "vive de Gaulle!" and "vive la République!" When Colonel David Bruce of the Office of Strategic Services (OSS) entered Granville, he found the French very friendly, "smiling, waving, and giving the V sign." A few days later just south of Granville he encountered people still waving, throwing flowers (one woman threw a bunch of carrots) at Bruce and his crew in a jeep. That day he record in his diary, "for the moment, the Americans are enjoying a honeymoon of popularity." French Army colonel Claude Hettier de Boislambert, who led a French liaison team with the Americans, reported that the people he came across in the villages were very happy to see them and eagerly embraced General de Gaulle as their new leader. General Leclerc's French 2nd Armored Division was almost always accorded a full-throated welcome. When crowds—many of them refugees—in the Orne rushed his tanks rolling through town, one old man's legs were crushed under the treads.[14]

Indeed, as battle moved into the region—even if mercifully only briefly— civilians inevitably suffered the consequences. In the fast-moving battle, soldiers on both sides resorted to foraging at the expense of French civilians in order to feed themselves. Germans, Americans, and French alike ate the dead pigs and cows caught in the cross fire of battle. Farm animals abandoned by fleeing farmers were seen as fair game by soldiers on both sides. During the intense fighting around Mortain, surrounded GIs holding out against a determined German onslaught once again were forced to sustain themselves by digging for potatoes and radishes in farmers' backyards. As the Americans pushed through the area south of Saint-Lô, some GIs found time to stop and milk Norman cows for a fresh treat. Fresh vegetables, meat, milk, and eggs were greatly prized by the soldiers, and GIs bartered, paid cash, or swiped (if no one was looking) to obtain them. GIs longed for fresh bread, which could often be obtained through barter from French farmers or villagers. Hand grenades proved useful when searching for fish in streams and ponds. Orchards lay exposed to hungry soldiers, even if the fruit was not yet ripe. Many apples in Normandy were bred to make cider or calvados, and not for eating, but that did not stop GIs from sampling them anyway. Soldiers still had to improvise to stay fed, and the cost fell on French peasants, even if the price was a rather small one to pay for liberation.[15]

A tally of the damage inflicted on just the department of the Manche is sobering: 187,000 inhabitants out of 438,000 reported property damage; 617 out of 648 communes suffered damage; 313 out of 648 churches were partially or completely destroyed. (Church towers were favorite perches for artillery spotters, making them favored targets for artillery on both sides. An old priest picking through the rubble of his church in Maisy, near Omaha Beach, told Chester Hansen its edifice had 37 holes in it from U.S. artillery trying to knock out a single German holed up in the tower). It took two days for Army bulldozers to clear a primitive path through the rubble of Saint-Lô for U.S. tanks to move through the town as the front moved south. It took 5,000 German POWs three years to clear away all the wreckage. Normandy, which was (and remains) famous for its cheese and apples, lost 105,000 cows and 300,000 apple trees. The human toll was sobering, even if not so high as some such as Winston Churchill had feared it might be: 16,630 French civilians were killed in Normandy from 6 June to 31 August 1944. Half of those died in the two weeks after D-Day. Evrecy, southwest of Caen, lost the most: 130 of 400 residents died in the battle, a 32 percent death rate. In the first three weeks of the battle for Normandy, the United States lost 8,975 soldiers and sailors, slightly more than the number of French civilians killed. Despite the sad toll, most Normans in the Manche told French pollsters hired by the American Psychological Warfare Division that the destruction, disruption, and dead cows were an inevitable part of the war. OSS colonel David K. Bruce observed in late June, "The natives seem to accept stoically the destruction of their homes. We have seen many refugees sheltered by their neighbors, and all of them have expressed their relief, in spite of their own losses, at being rid of the Germans." Today, Caen hosts a Rue du Général Harris, in honor of "Bomber Harris," who oversaw much of the city's ruin.[16]

CARENTAN

The small town of Carentan in the department of the Manche, which Omar Bradley was so keen to capture for the Allies, lay at a key juncture between the left and right wings of the American sector of the front. The Germans realized this and were determined to take it away from the Americans in order to split them into two isolated forces. The Germans, expelled by U.S. paratroopers on 12 June, counterattacked the next day and were beaten back. Thereafter Carentan remained in American hands; however, it sat on the front line for weeks to come. It was the first town liberated by Americans in France and placed under the authority of the U.S. Army Civil Affairs Department (known as G-5 within headquarters). Major John Maginnis commanded the small squad of G-5 men tasked with restoring civil life and smoothing the way for the U.S. military in the badly damaged town. His record of how that task unfolded provides us with an exceptional window into how American CA officers accomplished their duties and how they interacted with the French—civilians, officials, and military. Maginnis had been given the assignment of overseeing civil affairs of Carentan while it was still firmly under German rule and he was still billeted in England. He had served in the U.S. infantry in France during the First World War, attended the Sorbonne for a year between the wars, and taught economics at Massachusetts State College before taking over as president of a coal distribution company in Worcester. He was one of only two G-5 staffers assigned to Carentan who spoke passable French.[17]

Major Maginnis, his small crew of Civil Affairs officers, and his staff came ashore in an LST (Landing Ship, Tank) on 8 June while Utah Beach was still under enemy fire. His LST ran aground about 50 yards from the shoreline, forcing Maginnis and his jeep to plunge into deep water. The jeep sank, forcing his rescue. Major Maginnis and his team first entered the shattered and burning town of Carentan on 12 June 1944, the same day that German paratroopers were forced out and six days after the first American soldiers waded ashore on the Normandy beaches. They set up a temporary headquarters in the Hôtel de Ville (city hall) and met with the mayor and the heads of the police and fire departments. Only two days before, Mayor Joret had been assistant mayor, but on 10 June a bomb from an American plane killed the mayor, Dr. Caillard, and 19 other residents. The elderly M. Joret emerged from six days in his cellar to assume the post and promised Major Maginnis his complete cooperation and support in anything the U.S. military might require. Maginnis and his team immediately set to putting out fires that still smoldered. Their efforts were hindered by a disruption to the town's water service but aided by intermittent rain. The town had neither electricity nor phone service. As Maginnis arranged for debris to be cleared from the streets the next morning, soldiers of the 17th

SS Panzer Division counterattacked and briefly retook the town before being driven out again by American paratroopers from the 101st Airborne Division and newly arrived tanks of General Maurice Rose's 2nd Armored Division. Maginnis and his team reentered the almost deserted town at 4 P.M. before deciding it was too dangerous to stay. As the town was still the target of German artillery, there was little point in again putting out the fires and clearing the streets. The CA team left again that evening.[18]

Maginnis and his staff returned to stay on 14 June and set up headquarters on the second floor of the Hôtel de Ville. They decided that two problems required immediate attention: clearing the roads of debris and burying the dead cows that littered the entire area and emitted a noxious stench. Maginnis asked Dr. Simon, head of the local hospital, to gather French crews to bury the animals and promised Army assistance in clearing mines from nearby pastures that hindered the operation. Twenty American soldiers were detailed to bury dead soldiers who still littered the area. Security for remaining civilians worried both Maginnis and the French. Maginnis's team made a census of available gendarmes and saw right away that there were not enough. The head of the local Gendarmerie would need to recruit 15 auxiliaries and give them rudimentary training. A local woman was pointed out as "a Gestapo agent" and handed over to the gendarmes. This probably ended badly for the woman, as the Allies made a practice of hiring FFI as auxiliary police, who "behaved like hoodlums" according to one CA officer. They answered to no one and scared civilians more than they added to their security. Maginnis declared a curfew from 10 P.M. to 6 A.M., but otherwise people were free to move around as fighting permitted. Subsequent days were taken up mostly with arranging billeting for various American units that would be stationed in the area for the foreseeable future. The team received a stream of anxious local civilians with problems and questions about making the town livable again. Captain Hugh Walker—assigned from the British Army—talked to the local representative of the Crédit Lyonnais bank about the condition of the local banks and finances available to municipal governments.[19]

The team's job was not made any easier by German artillery shells that continued to rain on the town throughout 16 June. The front lines remained stubbornly close to Carentan throughout June, complicating all efforts to restore the town to a peaceful existence. Additionally, GIs saw the town and its environs as resources to help them stay alive and fed. GIs helped themselves to whatever lay at hand: wood was taken for fuel or shelter; chickens, eggs, cows, and ripening vegetables in gardens provided food; piles of bricks, stacks of lumber, and seemingly abandoned property all served as useful materials for building shelters. Unfortunately, all these things belonged to the French inhabitants who were frequently still around and saw this resourcefulness on the part of American soldiers as theft. Major Maginnis also saw it as theft, and when he received reports of pilfering, which occurred daily, he did what he could to stop it, or at least to see that the abused locals were fairly compensated. CA requested that complainants fill out requisition compensation forms. Pilfering came to be known as "irregular requisitions," and an agreement was eventually worked out with de Gaulle's authorities about how to handle the problem. Both the Americans and the French recognized that procurement by soldiers on the move would not always conform to regulations and there was little that could be done to stop it. Because both wanted victory over Germany, they agreed that irregular requisitions would be necessary to keep men in the field provisioned and fighting. But not all irregular requisitions were necessary. The school principle reported the theft of some cutlery, two clarinets, a violin, and a bow. MPs showed up with the musical instruments shortly afterward. When Mayor Joret asked Maginnis's help to prevent looting of a train car of condensed milk on the east end of town, MPs were detailed to guard the car. However, such looting was just as likely to be by French as by Americans—perhaps more so—and MPs had no power to arrest French citizens. French civilians complained to Commissioner Coulet about pillaging committed by French in the liberated zones and wanted to know why French police would not stop it. Such looting should not have been too surprising, as many French found themselves lacking not only necessities of life but any means of acquiring them. They had to scrounge just like the GIs.[20]

As Carentan lay on the front lines, it was a dangerous place to live. Civil Affairs arranged to use Army trucks to evacuate the population that lived south of town and close to the front lines. When farmers protested that they did not want to leave their animals, some volunteers were chosen to stay behind to look after them. Shortly after the town was liberated, Generals Maxwell Taylor, commander of the 101st Airborne Division, and Anthony McAuliffe, his second in command, attended a ceremony in Carentan's main square to award decorations to paratroopers for distinguished service during the Normandy landings. Mayor Joret, most municipal officials, and a large number of the town's population crowded the square for the ceremony. After General Taylor addressed the crowd in French, an eight-year-old girl, Danielle Laisney, presented the general with a bouquet of flowers in gratitude for the town's liberation. As she did, the first of many German 88 mm shells rained down on the crowded square and surrounding buildings, killing 44 French civilians—including Danielle Laisney—and injuring another 30, many of them quite badly. None of the U.S. soldiers who filled the square was killed and only a few received minor wounds. The next day, General Taylor and Major Maginnis visited the injured French in the hospital and promised that Dr. Simon would have all the medical supplies he needed to care for them. Besides the danger of German shelling, land mines and unexploded ordnance from both sides littered the town. The Germans had used a local school as an ammunition dump, which had to be cleared out. For weeks munitions continued to turn up and land mines continued to be unearthed along roads. In the second week of July, unlucky cows continued to tread upon land mines; at the end of July, farmers were still afraid to harvest their crops. Even when the Germans had been pushed back from the town so it was no longer subject to shelling, hidden mines and unexploded shells made it too dangerous for residents to return to their farms and villages south of town. Requests for engineers to clear mines and unexploded ordnance came in to Maginnis until the day he left on 29 August, when he declared the French government was now in charge.[21]

The economy of the town had almost completely come to a halt on D-Day. The Germans burned down one creamery, the phosphate factory was badly damaged, and the brickworks was missing its roof. Maginnis and his band did what they could to get local works functioning again. Captain Walker was pleased to report that the Crédit Lyonnais was reopened by 20 June and that deposits outpaced withdrawals five to one. Then again, four days before, Commissioner Coulet in Bayeux had issued an order that no one could withdraw more than $100 (5,000 francs) from any bank. All local adult men aged 16 to 55 were required to register with the mayor for work; over the next several weeks he proved accommodating in finding men to carry out various tasks requested by Major Maginnis. Roads needed urgent repair, pipes needed replacing, railroad beds required rebuilding, buildings had to be pulled down and usable scrap salvaged from the wreckage. Smashed stone houses turned out to be excellent quarries when Army engineers came looking for stone. The stones also proved a good source for gravel to repair roads, so that some people returned to their villages to find not a single trace of what once had been their homes. They had been transformed into gravel for roads. All of this work was performed by local men with the assistance and supervision of U.S. Army personnel. Dead cows that required disposal kept turning up, as did bodies of dead Germans and American paratroopers who had to be buried.[22]

Normandy was normally a food-exporting province, excepting grains, so finding food for the local population did not present an overwhelming challenge. Maginnis arranged for 1,000 bags of flour and 2,000 bags of buckwheat to be released by the quartermaster for civilian use. Much else had to be brought in by scarce Allied shipping and deposited in overburdened landing zones. Many people stranded in the battle zone had lost everything except the clothes on their backs and were heavily dependent on the Allies. One man asked if the Army would replace his blankets. He had used one to cover the body of a dead paratrooper and another to wrap his wounded buddy, who had been taken away to a hospital along with the blanket. Maginnis was obliged to check out the man's story, and when it was confirmed he ordered Army blankets released to replace those the man had lost and a receipt to prove he had come by them legitimately. According to one war correspondent, nearly 1 million blankets abandoned by GIs in Normandy were ultimately picked up by civilians and put to use. One thing the Army could not provide was baby food, because no one had thought to stock it. Diapers were also in short supply.[23]

As head of Civil Affairs in Carentan, Major Maginnis had to look after the welfare of GIs and civilians alike. He had to find quarters and some supplies for the Army that could only be had from the French. When the Army newspaper, *Stars and Stripes*, needed facilities to work out of and a place to print its newspapers, Maginnis located a print shop in Carentan. Bombed out houses were ransacked for serviceable desks and chairs and whatever else might prove useful. The Red Cross had the responsibility of providing entertainment for American troops, so a club was set up, staffed, and furnished. After electricity was restored to the local cinema, it was requisitioned to show films to the troops. Cafés and enterprising French civilians were asked to stop selling liquor to American troops, most of whom were not used to the powerful local *eau de vie*, calvados, made from fermented and distilled apples. Maginnis blamed the calvados for a minor riot between paratroopers of the 101st Division and First Army MPs, who tried—unsuccessfully—to stop drunken paratroopers from shooting up the town. On the night of 21 June, a drunken GI shot a farmer—a father of five—who resisted efforts of the GI to teach him English. The farmer was treated at an Army hospital and survived the ordeal; Maginnis made sure his family was supplied with whatever they needed from Army stores. The day before saw the first of several accusations of rape or attempted rape by GIs. This was not the last time that U.S. paratroopers would cause major problems for both the French civilian population and American authorities responsible for the comportment of their soldiers. A mayor of a nearby village asked that cafés be ruled off-limits to troops, as they were getting drunk and threatening locals with their weapons. Café owners were informed that Army regulations precluded selling alcohol to GIs. M. Duval-Lemonnier, who owned a grocery wholesale business in Carentan, complained that the remaining stocks of wine and liquor in his damaged warehouse were being looted by soldiers and asked if MPs could be assigned to guard it. Another local proprietor later asked for barbed wire to encircle his place to discourage GIs from sneaking in at night. A farmer complained that GIs had slaughtered and eaten several of his cows; another reported that his buggy and horse were stolen; others accused soldiers of stealing wood.[24]

Such complaints were not limited to American soldiers. French farm owner Marie-Louise Osmont, who lived in the British sector near Caen, made similar accusations against British soldiers. She had previously suffered German troops quartered in her house and observed that British soldiers looted more than Germans did. Even worse, French civilians joined British troops in ransacking the personal possessions that Germans had left behind at her farm. The British did not bother to differentiate German belongings from hers, taking whatever appealed to them. They shot locks off and broke down doors to get into locked rooms of her house that the Germans had respected as off-limits. She had previously complained that the Germans wrecked her house and outbuildings, but the British proved themselves to be virtually professional wreckers. As the Germans had done before and as the Americans did around Carentan, British soldiers dug foxholes all around Mme. Osmont's house, including in her vegetable garden after eating all her vegetables. When she complained to a British officer about two missing outhouse doors taken by soldiers for their foxholes, the resourceful and helpful sergeant interpreter said she was demanding to see a requisition form for the items (she had not asked for and had never seen a requisition form). This got her doors restored. After the front moved a few miles to the south and the infantry were replaced by a Scottish artillery unit, they were no better: they broke into her linen closet and stole her linens. Xavier de Guerpel had few such complaints about either the Germans who had quartered on his farm or the English who followed them. For the most part he found soldiers in both armies honest and trustworthy. However, soldiers occupying farmland and buildings inflicted damage beyond the usual destruction of war, such as exploding shells. After English troops left, de Guerpel reported to a Canadian Civil Affairs officer, who asked for an estimate of damages to his farm caused by Allied troops quartered there, that after he had reached 600 he had stopped counting foxholes.[25]

Repairing and maintaining the town's infrastructure kept Maginnis and Army engineers busy for weeks. The town needed its water supply and sewer system restored most urgently. The town's main water storage tank had been pierced by shrapnel and needed repair. U.S. Army medical corps staff tested the water in the reservoir and pronounced it fit to drink, but the lack of electricity made it impossible for pumps to move the water to users. Smashed pipes made the pumps irrelevant in any case. The local fire department used hand pumps to fill a tanker truck at the reservoir to provision the town for a few days, but this could not meet the town's needs for long and did nothing to address the utility disruptions below the streets. Army engineers, assisted by French civilians hired to help, used rubble from buildings to fill shell holes in the streets without first fixing utilities under the streets that inevitably suffered damage. Water and sewer pipes seeped their contents into the rubble-filled gaps, creating a stinking mess for the town. Additionally, the firetrucks were entirely dependent on gasoline supplied by the Americans to get to the reservoir and back. The septic tanks of Carentan were normally emptied by a *vidangeur* (an "emptier" truck) every two weeks, but the truck had gone missing at the beginning of the invasion. Moreover, the sewer system of the town relied on the tides in the Douve River estuary to carry sewage away from the town and out to sea. Locks on the canal that connected Carentan to the river and thence the English Channel had been damaged in the fighting and were stuck open. This allowed sea water to enter the canal at high tide, both spoiling the fresh water of the river and bringing the town's sewage back into town at high tide. Fixing the locks to restore the water and sewage system would allow the Allies access to the minor port with craft small enough to use the canal. The canal was intended only for small tenders and fishing boats; the Allies were already using tenders to bring supplies to the beaches from larger craft in the Channel, and with the canal operating they could bring supplies directly to Carentan.[26]

American soldiers had dug numerous latrines for their use, so at least they were not overly contributing to the town's sewage problem. However, when MPs gave up their billets at the Institute de Notre Dame, a local Catholic school, the refugees who moved in complained about the awful odor of the place: the sewer lines in the school were clogged and the toilets full and unusable. Some people had taken to using one side of the building as a latrine and left heaps of untended excreta. G-5 arranged to have it buried. The task of repairing the sewer lines was turned over to the municipal administration, but as late as 11 July the problem still had not been fixed. The heavy traffic of Army trucks caused pipes underneath the main street of the town to rupture and drainage ditches on the sides of roads outside of town to collapse. Heavy Army water tankers backing up to the town's reservoir to fill up caused the rim of the reservoir to collapse. Even worse, the mayor complained that the heavy demands upon the reservoir were actually draining it. Then in late July—after pumps had been restored and the water tank fixed—heavy Army trucks crushed the main pipe carrying water from the reservoir to the town. Maginnis promised the mayor that all of these problems would be addressed. Engineers who repaired the pipes under the roads warned Maginnis they would just break again unless truck traffic were rerouted.[27]

The local gas works was unavailable as well. It was repaired and ready to return to production by 23 June, but the supply of coal on hand to convert into gas would last only three weeks. Carenten needed 30 tons of coal a month for the gas works alone and had on hand only 20 tons left behind by the Germans. Commissioner Coulet judged that getting the tile works in Carentan back up and operating would go far in helping the population repair their many damaged roofs. As there was no way to get coal to Carentan for the time being, there could be no coal to fire the ovens necessary to make tiles. Coal would have to be shipped from England to keep the town provisioned with gas. However, it seemed unlikely that space could be found for it on ships or at the crammed and busy beaches serving as a temporary port until port facilities in Cherbourg could be restored. Coal for Carentan would have to wait. The first train from Cherbourg, which arrived at the station in Carentan on the morning of 11 July, consisted of two cars serviced by a railway operating battalion made up of American trainmen. They promised that service would be twice a day and soon four times per day. The short distances available to the railroads made them impractical for use by the Army, so they were available for civilian use, which was a good thing because the roads were not open to much civilian traffic.[28]

The first six weeks of liberation for Carentan showed that the front line of battle was not a place anyone would want to live. Life for the French civilians who remained in Carentan was difficult. However, the Civil Affairs operation led by Major Maginnis showed that goodwill on the part of admittedly amateur military administrators, still learning on the job, could produce swift and positive improvements in living conditions for the civilians stuck on the front lines. The CA officers easily gained the cooperation of local officials, who were glad for any help they could get in their dire circumstances. Many local small business owners eagerly volunteered to help out and accept help once it became clear the Americans intended to treat them fairly. Over time, they proved valuable allies and resources for Maginnis in his struggle to revive Carentan. Friction caused by young GIs living on the front, stealing chickens, tools, and building materials, was smoothed over by Maginnis's compensating the victims of pilfering or "irregular requisitions." MPs did what they could to dampen the ill effects of good Norman calvados on GIs seeking relief from the tensions of war. However, there was only so much that any American officer could do to improve peoples' lives so long as they lived on the front lines in Normandy. Major Maginnis, working with the close cooperation of Mayor Joret, had assumed the position of the local administrator, making quick decisions about what was to be done and by whom. This was well within his mandate as prescribed by the U.S. Army; it was what he was expected to do. However, he had no authority to do any of that according to François Coulet, de Gaulle's appointed commissioner of the republic for Normandy, who arrived in Normandy on 13 June to establish the Free French government.

4

THE FREE FRENCH GOVERNMENT
IN NORMANDY

I n June 1944 Charles de Gaulle remained unable to pry loose from President Roosevelt even *de facto* recognition of the Free French movement and feared an Allied deal with the Vichy leadership similar to the one made by Eisenhower with Admiral Darlan in North Africa and with Marshal Badoglio in Italy that would preserve the authority of a thoroughly discredited and unworthy regime. The Comité français de Libération nationale (CFLN) in Algiers had voted on 26 May to transform itself into the Provisional Government of the French Republic (Gouvernement provisoire de la République française, GPRF) in anticipation of an Allied invasion. De Gaulle was anxious to plant his French flag upon French soil as soon as possible to firmly assert the authority of this Provisional Government within France. He and many in his administration believed they were in a race against the Allies and the Communists to create a new government. In fact, all of the alternatives to de Gaulle were dreaded with horror not only by de Gaulle but by most Free French and even most Allied leaders. As it turned out, there was little likelihood of any of the alternatives becoming reality, but that was true only because de Gaulle ensured they did not happen. The Allies, and especially the British, had a strong dislike of the Vichy regime and would not have tolerated its continuation while Allied troops remained in France. Nor did the Communists pose a real threat to the Gaullists because the PCF had orders from Moscow to make no trouble for the Allies or de Gaulle: winning the war had priority and the time was not yet ripe for revolution. That left only AMGOT, the Allied Military Government of Occupied Territories, as a potential rival to the GPRF. While AMGOT was indeed the preferred instrument of President Roosevelt, he was almost entirely alone in hoping for it. The opposition of his top military staff, who would have been responsible for overseeing it, condemned the idea to irrelevance almost from the start. Even the State Department wanted a formal agreement with CFLN, but Roosevelt refused to consider it. Churchill kept Roosevelt's formal proposal of March 1944 for AMGOT languishing somewhere in his desk without reply-ing to it or passing it along for action within his cabinet. The head of the Allied Expeditionary Force, General Dwight D. Eisenhower, had no more interest in being pro-consul in France than he had in running North Africa; his experience with the snake pit of French politics in Algiers convinced him to avoid any repetition in France. Eisenhower was happy to turn over civil responsibilities to French officials who were willing to cooperate. So long as the Americans ac-knowledged French authority over France, the officials appointed and put into place by de Gaulle were equally happy to cooperate with the Allied militaries.[1]

Regardless of the strong forces working against Vichy, the PCF, and AMGOT, the GPRF took charge in France only because de Gaulle and his as-sociates in the Free French movement made it a reality; it did not come to life spontaneously. As the liberated zone of France expanded, so did the confidence and ability of the Provisional Government's officials to impose their will on both the liberated French and the Allied armies—even if their capacity to contest the Allies remained limited. The ensuing competition for authority between the Allies and General de Gaulle's Provisional Government pitted some very de-termined French against Americans who really wanted no contest. Eisen-hower recognized well in advance of the invasion of Normandy that his armies would need the cooperation of local governments in order to utilize available resources for the Allied cause. De Gaulle had proposed to Roosevelt and Chur-chill in September 1943 a draft accord on cooperation in France once the Al-lies (including the French) arrived. Roosevelt never responded. Churchill, who would have liked to have accepted the agreement, deferred to Roosevelt and put the suggestion aside. Eisenhower also approved of it but had to defer to Roo-sevelt and so said nothing. In December 1943, Eisenhower told de Gaulle that he wanted no responsibility for AMGOT in France. By May 1944, even Secre-tary of State Cordell Hull—no partisan of de Gaulle—favored U.S. recognition of the CFLN. In Roosevelt's conception, Allied military officers would simply present their demands to whomever they met on the spot in France. In fact, that is more or less what happened. With the experience of North Africa and Italy under his belt, Eisenhower was well aware that dealing with one central authority on issues was easier than cutting a thousand local deals with a thou-sand officials. At Eisenhower's direction Allied officers negotiated an agreement with de Gaulle's CFLN in Algiers in March 1944 on acquiring and paying for services in France after D-Day. To ensure greater cooperation from the French in France, the Allies benefitted from the services of Colonel Claude Hettier de Boislambert, an energetic and talented officer who had rallied to de Gaulle from the first hour. He headed a corps of 220 English-speaking French officers (50 of whom were women) of the Mission militaire de Liaison administrative (MMLA) to liaise with British and American Civil Affairs officers (G-5). To the French, including de Boislambert, the mission of the MMLA was to insert themselves between the Allied military and French civilians, and assume control of civil affairs in France. The head of training for the MMLA, Pierre Laroque, who previously had been a high-level functionary in the French government, was shocked to hear from a British brigadier in Civil Affairs that the Allies expected to find no functioning administration in France and they would be forced to establish one. As late as June 1944, Churchill believed the MMLA consisted of a corps of translators for the Allied forces! By October, Laroque and others had convinced their British counterparts that it would not be necessary for the Allied military to provide governors for the French, who would be able to fend for themselves with a little help. Eisenhower's designated head of Civil Affairs, General John Hilldring, also assured Laroque that the Americans had no interest or desire to take over civil administration in France.[2]

When the Allies landed, they found Normans expected de Gaulle to be in charge of French affairs. A British CA officer, Lieutenant Colonel D. R. Ellias, noted, "We received enthusiastic welcome, taking Norman reserve into account. First troops into Bayeux were greeted with cheers and flowers. Celebration held on D+3 with flowers thrown at troops. . . . Everywhere the reception has been friendly." Yet Normans that he met soon after D-Day accepted that de Gaulle would be in charge, saying, "We expect him; there is no one else." They wanted to know when de Gaulle's government would be installed. "Whether he will be provisional or temporary doesn't seem to concern them. They want a French government and he seems to be it. If he landed in France there is no doubt the people would rally to him. Mayor and police commissioners in Bayeux say they want to know in whose name they are to act. They cannot bring anyone to trial until they know who is the constituted authority." Colonel David Bruce of the OSS was convinced that at the time of the landings the vast majority of French accepted de Gaulle as the leader of Free France. Bruce also judged that de Gaulle's followers in the resistance were not sheep or gullible worshipers and there was little danger of him being foisted upon the French as a dictator.[3]

De Gaulle, for his part, was intent on establishing the Provisional Government within liberated France, with or without the cooperation of the Allies. He was furious about being kept in the dark on the details of D-Day until 4 June and ordered that none of the liaison officers accompany Allied troops. He initially refused to make a radio broadcast over the BBC requesting French cooperation with the Allies. Not having any real options, he soon relented, yet remained determined to set foot upon French soil and reestablish the French Republic there at the first opportunity. De Gaulle's order that no MMLA officers accompany Allied troops on D-Day came too late to recall 30 who came ashore on the beaches on 6 June. He set off on the French destroyer *La Combattante* from Portsmouth at dawn on 14 June with Commissioner François Coulet, Colonel Pierre de Chevigné, and other aides on board. Churchill had hoped to control de Gaulle's visit to Normandy and limit his contact with the Normans: arrive on a British destroyer at 11, lunch with Montgomery, back onto the destroyer by 4, and back to London. De Gaulle did not cooperate. De Gaulle was insulted that he was met on a beach crowded with Canadians by a Scottish captain rather than General Montgomery himself. Regardless, when he set out in a small procession to see the liberated land his first stop was the trailer used by General Bernard Montgomery as his command post. There the British general gave de Gaulle a briefing on the progress of the invasion so far. De Gaulle did not think to bring Republican Commissioner Coulet with him to introduce the new GPRF in Normandy to the British commander. Few French people who met de Gaulle recognized him and, to his chagrin, he had to announce to them who he was. This would not do. To ensure that he would receive a more appropriate reception, when he encountered two gendarmes on bicycles, who also had no idea who he was, he asked them to turn around, go back to Bayeux, and alert the people that General de Gaulle was coming. De Gaulle dispatched Coulet to establish himself—and the French Republic—in the office of regional commissioner in Bayeux in advance of de Gaulle's arrival. Despite Coulet's presence and the call by the local liberation committee for his immediate dismissal, Sub-Prefect Pierre Rochat officially welcomed de Gaulle and his party to Bayeux and gave a report on the situation. Before de Gaulle's arrival at the Hôtel de Ville, Rochat removed the photo of Pétain that still hung in a prominent place. When Rochat bothered to acknowledge Coulet, he addressed him as an underling. General de Gaulle then spoke to an enthusiastic crowd that had gathered in front of the Hôtel de Ville, promising victory and liberation for France. Bayeux had been relatively lightly touched by the war, but that was not so of his next stop, Isigny, in the American zone. That unfortunate town had been nearly flattened by American bombers and the dead were still being dug out of heaps of rubble when de Gaulle viewed the pathetic scene with astonishment. After witnessing the progress of the invasion, de Gaulle returned to the destroyer and sailed back to Portsmouth, leaving Coulet, Chevigné, and Laroque behind in Bayeux to administer the GPRF in the liberated region of France.[4]

Republican Commissioner Coulet set about reestablishing the French government in Normandy and asserting French sovereignty with a minimum of resources. The 38-year-old former diplomat issued a stream of *arrêtés*, or executive orders, declaring his authority as the delegated power of General de Gaulle and laying down the law for French citizens in the liberated zone. Coulet was an English-speaking anglophile who disliked politics and politicians. He was unimpressed by de Gaulle's less admirable qualities, finding him irritable, intolerant, and supremely judgmental. Even if Coulet shared most of de Gaulle's principled beliefs about French sovereignty, he clearly saw that de Gaulle's prickliness and obstinacy did not always serve the cause well. Nevertheless, in his new position as regional commissioner of the republic (*commissaire de la République*), Coulet would have ample opportunities to stand up for French sovereignty against Allied encroachments and be every bit as prickly and petty as the general. Coulet and de Gaulle argued against Allied encroachments on what the Frenchmen claimed were exclusive prerogatives of the Provisional Government. In preparation for the invasion, the Allies had printed several million "supplemental francs" and handed them out to soldiers, thinking they might come in handy once ashore. They did: the Allied armies used them to buy local goods and pay workers, which planners thought would infuse cash into a moribund economy that they assumed—incorrectly as it turned out—would be starved of currency. De Gaulle characteristically blew up when he heard about the Allied armies' printing "counterfeit francs" and posters in French with Eisenhower's signature announcing that the French population should accept "*francs complimentaires*" as legal tender. The outraged GPRF denounced the currency as counterfeit and demanded it be recalled. It was not and de Gaulle fumed about the matter as he crossed the Channel in *La Combattante*. Allied soldiers spent their francs in Normandy, and CA officers reported that local farmers and shopkeepers were happy to accept them. Normans proudly wore them pinned to their lapels with the tricolor flag showing. An Allied finance officer claimed the populace accepted supplemental francs more readily than French bank notes. Cafés in Cherbourg gladly took them, but preferred being paid with dollars or pounds, which, of course, was entirely illegal. For his part, Coulet protested to his superior in London, General Pierre Koenig, that Normans did not receive Allied francs with enthusiasm, but accepted them reluctantly and with suspicion, and tried to dispose of them as quickly as possible. The truth, while somewhere in between, was probably closer to the G-5 version than Coulet's. De Gaulle initially would not budge from his position that the "fake currency" was entirely illegal and an infringement on French sovereignty. His appointees in France followed his policy but were in no position to do anything about the "counterfeit francs." When French Army officers assigned as liaisons to Allied units protested about the francs to their Allied colleagues, Civil Affairs officers suggested to SHAEF that they be recalled from Normandy and replaced.[5]

Refusing to accept Allied supplemental francs put Coulet's government in Normandy in a difficult position. Coulet had crossed the Channel with a steel box containing 25 million francs in Bank of France notes, but such a sum would not last long. Coulet promised to pay each family 1,500 francs ($30) per month for those without habitation and 1,000 francs ($20) for those with damaged homes, but he did not have enough francs to pay the bills that were quickly mounting and could not make good on his promises. Still, de Gaulle refused to accept supplemental francs as legal currency. When Coulet took control of hiring and paying French working for the Allies to repair roads, load trucks, and the like, he would not accept the Allies' francs to satisfy the invoices he submitted in order to pay the workers. After Coulet ordered that the Allied francs not be accepted for taxes due, administrative cooperation with G-5 began to look like it might break down. The Allies paid French workers to perform various tasks in Normandy in supplemental francs (at a rate set by CA on the spot and not according to pay rates set up by the GPRF). CA hired FFI to serve as auxiliary police and paid them in supplemental francs as well. When Army officials felt obliged to pay the widow of a local FFI commander killed in the fighting, they did so with supplemental francs. Nevertheless, the issue failed to arise when de Gaulle visited Roosevelt in Washington in early July. In any event, the horse was already out of the barn: the notes were circulating and French shopkeepers accepted them. When local tax collectors looked to Coulet for guidance on how to handle the supplemental francs when civilians tried to pay their taxes with them, he advised them to keep the Allied francs in separate accounts until the question was settled. The issue put Coulet and the Provisional Government in a delicate spot: because the locals readily accepted the money as legal tender, to refuse the money was to jeopardize Norman acceptance of the fragile new government. In July, Coulet informed Koenig in London that the government's accounts in Normandy were now empty, so either London had to come up with several million Bank of France notes or start accepting Allied francs. In a showdown meeting with CA officers in Normandy, Coulet agreed to accept the Allied francs as a temporary expedient, with the understanding that they would be retired as soon as possible and replaced with Bank of France notes. The next day, he reassured French holders of bonds issued by Vichy that their investments would be honored by the new regime and that any French franc, regardless of where or when it was printed, was legal tender. Money printed by Vichy and bearing the imprint "*Etat Français*" was still legal; their money was secure. His announcement also conveniently circumvented the problem of "supplemental Francs."[6]

While the population gladly accepted the supplemental francs and Coulet grudgingly agreed they could circulate in Normandy, French bankers doubted their legality. When G-5 asked the regional manager of the Bank of France in Cherbourg, M. Duni, if he would open an account for Civil Affairs, he hesitantly agreed that G-5 could store their francs in his strong box, a compromise that was accepted by the Allies. M. Duni had good reason to be accommodating, because a British major of the G-5 financial section was driving him around the region collecting bank records and money that had gone astray in the previous few weeks in an ultimately successful attempt to restore banking to the department. With American assistance, he retrieved 100 million in Bank of France notes from a vault in Valognes to restock the banks of Cherbourg. The banker at Credit Lyonnais in Bayeux did the same on July 3: he accepted 60 boxes of supplemental francs and held them in his vault rather than use them to open an account for G-5. With the temporary agreement, Allied financial officers set about trying to find the ship off-shore that held 650 more boxes of the supplemental francs, worth 1.5 billion francs, which by 12 July remained undiscovered. When M. Duni of the Bank of France in Cherbourg was instructed by Coulet to accept supplemental francs as legal currency equal to Bank of France notes, he informed Coulet that no one, not even de Gaulle, had the authority to tell the Bank of France what currencies to accept or reject. The bank was an autonomous institution that did not answer to politicians or generals. The director agreed to abide for now by whatever agreement Coulet had signed with the Allies, but not before he had received a copy and had the opportunity to review it. The question of the Allied francs arose at a meeting in Paris as late as January 1945, when AFA (Aide des Forces Alliées) chief Jacques Lévy assured all that supplemental francs were legal and accepted at par with Bank of France notes. In October 1945, Allied francs continued to circulate in France despite efforts of French officials to replace them with Bank of France notes. The matter still stuck in Coulet's craw when he wrote his memoirs in 1967.[7]

While the issue of the supplemental francs may have been settled for the time being, questions of sovereignty attached to them continued to roil relations. CA had approved the printing of a poster in French, signed by Paul Renault, the Vichy mayor of Cherbourg, reassuring the populace that Allied francs were legal and warning the people not to accept foreign currency in payment for anything. Coulet steamed when he saw the poster and blamed the Allies rather than "that old guy" mayor. When Coulet discovered that the Allies were contracting with printers in France to print their broadsheets instructing the French about what they could or could not do—without consulting either him or Koenig—he issued a decree forbidding French printers from printing *anything* without prior approval from his office. Paradoxically, the Head of Civil Affairs at SHAEF, British general Edward A. Grassett, was under the impression that Coulet had to clear all public announcements with SHAEF before releasing them. After dining with Coulet in Bayeux, Brigadier General Thomas Robbins pronounced Coulet "quite correct," but "determined to take charge," prompting Grassett to blurt out, "all is going well in France. It's just this damn fellow de Gaulle." Actually, it was not just that damn fellow.[8]

Coulet was handicapped in asserting the authority of the new regime by both energetic Allies who acted in their own interests in order to get things done despite infringements on French sovereignty and a lack of staff to implement policies. Coulet had brought with him two Frenchmen to serve as his lieutenants, Raymond Haas-Picard and Colonel Pierre de Chevigné, but they were quickly overwhelmed with tasks and set about finding candidates in Normandy to assume official functions. He lamented the dearth of talent among municipal councilors he encountered in Normandy and found it difficult to appoint mayors for liberated towns who were untainted by association with Vichy. The GPRF had decreed that the only legitimate municipal councils were those elected before the war, though this posed a problem: many councilors had fled, been arrested, died, or left office for diverse reasons. Vacancies had been filled by appointment by Vichy-approved mayors or prefects, and Coulet discovered that frequently the Vichy-appointed council members were the most energetic and cooperative. He appealed to London to allow him to keep those councilors in office or allow him to reappoint them to their posts so their useful services could be employed by the new regime. Even though Assistant Mayor Joret had stepped into the mayor's position in Carentan, and, according to CA officer Maginnis, performed quite admirably, Coulet found him lacking and wanted to replace him. The 82-year-old mayor of Arromanche had the assistance of his daughter, but according to G-5 he was "over his head . . . [and beset by] problems beyond his ability to solve." The head of CA in Cherbourg, Colonel Hawley, gave the GPRF a free hand to appoint anyone to administrative posts who they saw fit. When Coulet appointed Lebas as prefect in the Manche, the U.S. Army immediately recognized his authority. Although Coulet was nominally in charge and cooperative, G-5 recognized that, lacking both mail and phones, he had no means to coordinate or supervise administrators in the Manche from his office in Bayeux even if local officials in the American zone accepted his authority. Coulet was unable to enforce French wage scales in the American zone (the Americans paid more) because in late June he had not a single labor inspector to oversee pay or work conditions. He urgently required more translators with good command of English. This need only increased over time; Coulet further demanded that they must work for France and not the Allies. They could be fed and housed by the Allies but they must be paid by the French government. Isolated in Bayeux without phone links to London or within Normandy, Coulet had little idea of what was going on in Normandy, or Algiers, or anywhere else. He pled with Koenig in London to regularly send newspapers and some PTT (phone company) specialists to get the phone system in Normandy connected.[9]

Everywhere he went Coulet found the populace enthusiastic about the new Gaullist regime emerging in Normandy and claimed to have met no one who challenged its legitimacy. When he put together a ceremony to raise the national flag over the main square of Coutainville, several thousand people attended on short notice and responded with great passion. "Their fervor was greater than any I have encountered yet in Normandy including in Cherbourg. I made a short speech using an American sound truck that happened to be there and was interrupted many times with cries of '*vive la République*' and '*vive de Gaulle.*'" An American CA officer reported in late June that he had encountered less enthusiasm on the part of Normans in the Manche. In his view, General de Gaulle was almost universally accepted in Calvados (the British sector), while about half the population in the Manche was at least *attentiste*—waiting to see what happened. There, he continued, many people thought that de Gaulle was being foisted upon the French by the Americans! Perhaps most French looked sympathetically upon de Gaulle and the GPRF because they feared a return to prewar *parlementisme,* with its gaggle of squabbling parties and no one in control. Even worse would have been a seizure of power by French Communists. As observed in Calvados soon after D-Day, people in the Manche also said, "there is no one else," reflecting resignation more than enthusiasm. Still, the people who mattered the most—the FFI—squarely favored de Gaulle. In early July the resistance group Combat got in touch with Coulet to inform him that the resistance was delighted that the French government had been reestablished and its leader was de Gaulle.[10]

Even if the people in Normandy embraced the new Provisional Government, the Gaullist regime ran into repeated difficulties convincing their allies to take them seriously. Shortly after implanting themselves in Bayeux, Colonel Chevigné called on British general Bernard Montgomery and told him Coulet, too, would be calling on him soon, to which the general replied "gladly." Coulet was anything but glad when Chevigné told him of his visit, telling Chevigné that it was not for members of the Provisional Government to call on foreign military on French soil, but for Montgomery to pay a call on Coulet. Coulet was just playing the hand dealt to him by de Gaulle, who had told Coulet days after the invasion that the Allies recognized the GPRF "*de facto*" and now it was time for them to recognize it "*de jure.*" When no one called on Coulet, he called a press conference, utilizing the overabundance of Allied newspapermen in Normandy, to proselytize for recognition by announcing on 16 June that the GPRF was now in charge of civilians in Normandy. The journalists pushed back and asked by what authority? Would the Allies allow it? Much to Coulet's delight, they pressed the issue, handing Coulet the opportunity to assert that there was no AMGOT in France and that the Allies had no say in the matter. Moreover, he contended, the Allies had used AMGOT in Italy to empower the mafia in Sicily and they would not be allowed to do the same in France. Not only might Roosevelt and Eisenhower reach an accord with Laval and Pétain to remain in control of France, as they had done with Darlan in North Africa and the Fascist Marshal Pietro Badoglio in Italy, they actually wanted to. This was not just posturing on Coulet's part. Gaullist paranoia about American intentions remained strong until FDR recognized the GPRF in October. American journalists took the bait: The *New York Herald Tribune* reported on 16 June that de Gaulle had announced that he was in charge of civil authority in liberated Normandy, Coulet was his representative in France, and that SHAEF had no say in the matter. According to de Gaulle, he had passed a suggested accord on administration in liberated areas to the Allies in July 1943 and never received a reply, thus, there was no agreement. While this was not quite true, the *Tribune* nevertheless wondered by what authority de Gaulle assumed civil control in Normandy and effectively answered its own question by noting that the population of Normandy left no one in doubt that de Gaulle was their leader. Edgar Mowrer of the *Boston Globe* ran an article on 18 June chiding the United States for not recognizing de Gaulle, who refused to allow French liaison officers to go to France except as recognized representatives of the Provisional Government and not just the French Army. The American position invited nothing but trouble. Cordell Hull, who had altered his views on the matter, referred all questions on the matter to the White House.[11]

Because Coulet had no access to newspapers, he had no idea of the impact of his news conference. And there was impact: three days afterward, a group of British Civil Affairs officers presented themselves at Coulet's offices in Bayeux, according to Coulet's memoirs, uninvited and without an appointment. SHAEF's designated link to the French, Britain's Brigadier General R.M.H. Lewis, who had yet to meet Coulet, spoke for the group when he barged into Coulet's office and addressed Coulet, Laroque, and de Courcel in English. Boiling mad, he told Coulet that the Twenty-First Army accepted him as the administrator of civilians because the Allies had a war to fight and no time to trouble themselves with civilians. Coulet replied they were all in perfect accord and the GPRF would assist the Allies in any way possible. Coulet then slammed his fist on the table, spilled his ink well, and said forcefully that he was in Bayeux on orders and by authority of the GPRF and he did not need the Allies' permission to carry out his orders. The CA officers made no reply. When Coulet stood, all others stood (Laroque and de Courcel had been standing the whole time as there were not enough chairs for all to sit) and Laroque opened the door for the Allied officers to leave. General Lewis shook Coulet's hand and all left without a word. Historian Charles Robertson found Coulet's report on the incident to General Koenig, which related little of the confrontation described in Coulet's memoirs. He reported to Koenig that the two parted with mutual understanding of their respective roles in Normandy. Lewis's version of the meeting was rendered in an interview in November 1944 and also failed to mention any shouting or unpleasantness: "the meeting passed off very amicably and satisfactory personnel [sic] relationships were established."[12]

Indeed, the next day, 20 June, Coulet wrote to Koenig that he had received visits from both Lewis and the head of British Civil Affairs, Brigadier General Robbins, and the latter had shown himself to be "most favorable to 'fighting France.'" Despite disagreements between de Gaulle and Allied leaders, in fact relations between Coulet and Allied Civil Affairs officers were very good. Coulet had known Brigadier General Robbins when he was in charge of CA training in Wimbledon, and the two were very friendly when they met again in Bayeux. Coulet invited Robbins and his American counterpart, Lieutenant Colonel Damon Gunn, for a lunch of beef from a cow freshly killed in the fighting—a rare treat for anyone used to London under ration laws. Robbins told Coulet that the British were glad to see him in charge and they were "in no way interested in assuming responsibility for Normandy. And that Civil Affairs has no responsibility in France other than to help us to resolve our problems." When Coulet met with Colonel Gunn, the colonel assured Coulet he was eager to assist in any way and Coulet was entirely pleased with his attitude toward the French Provisional Government. However, lack of liaison officers made it difficult to implant French authority in the American zone, where CA was pretty much on its own to do what it thought best.[13]

General Montgomery eventually did call on Commissioner Coulet to vent his anger over the Liberation Franc controversy. He stormed into Coulet's office and, without exchanging any greeting, launched into a tirade about the supplemental franc, calling Coulet "a politician," which was taken by Coulet as an insult, as Montgomery had intended. After making his usual assertion that Norman peasants refused to accept them, Coulet rebuked Montgomery: Coulet would not order French officials to submit themselves to a new foreign occupation having just got rid of the Germans. Pierre Koenig, who was present, tried to make light of the exchange by telling Montgomery (all of this was in English) that Coulet was "a hard man; a Protestant." With that, Montgomery, the son of an Anglican bishop, immediately changed his attitude toward Coulet and became very friendly. When he left he called him "Mr. High Commissioner" and said he would like to help the new French administration in any way possible. When Coulet later informed Minister of War André Diethelm that the bishop of Lisieux-Bayeux had objected to the appointment of a Protestant as commissioner in Normandy, Diethelm (also a Protestant) replied that Coulet should have arrested the bishop.[14]

Coulet struggled to assert French sovereignty and impel Allied officers to recognize the legitimacy of French law. Koenig was eager to see that French justice was operating in the liberated zone and dispatched five military judges to Normandy to preside over trials of collaborators being rounded up by FFI and French police. When he heard that both the British and Americans were delivering food and supplies directly to French grocers and charging the deliveries to the French government, he insisted they stop; all deliveries were to go to Ravitaillement Générale (General Supply), a government body created to buy and distribute civilian goods. The Allies agreed to work through General Supply and keep accounts with AFA when such offices were fully functioning, but in the meantime they would deliver supplies to whoever was best situated to receive them. By July, French food inspectors were overseeing dairy products sold to the Allied armies and, in the opinion of American Quartermaster Corps officers in charge of buying the goods, were disqualifying for sale food acceptable to the U.S. Army. CA asked Coulet to allow the inspectors to set lower standards for sales to the Allied armies. This demonstrated that the Allies at least recognized that the French set the standards and that any deviation had to be authorized by them.[15]

Coulet lamented to Koenig that getting the Allies to take his government seriously was only half the problem: French officials from London behaved as if the Allies were in charge and not Coulet. After Coulet had been in Bayeux for a month he remained frustrated that French officials visiting from London met with their Allied counterparts before they met with Coulet. French financial expert Jacques Lévy, for example, dropped in briefly before returning to London to inform Coulet of his discussions with his Allied counterparts only after the meeting had taken place. Coulet's biggest complaint was provoked by Winston Churchill's visit to Normandy in late July, when the prime minister failed to pay a courtesy call, which Coulet viewed not as a personal affront but as a snub of the French government in the liberated zone. Churchill was repeating a pattern he had set when he visited Algiers in January 1944 on his return from the

Tehran Conference and did not bother to call on General de Gaulle, who was incensed by the slight. Coulet's response was not only to protest to Brigadier General Robbins, but also to Captain Charles Grey, a Liberal Member of Parliament. Coulet's hopes that Grey would raise questions in Parliament about such misconduct by the prime minister were dashed when Grey was killed on the battlefield in France only days later. Shortly afterward, on 3 August, Coulet received a note from Britain's General Robert F. Naylor that Vice Prime Minister Clement Atlee would be visiting Normandy and would be happy to dine with the commissioner at the British officers' mess on 4 August. Coulet declined, telling Naylor that he was otherwise engaged. Surprised, Naylor paid a call on Coulet and renewed his invitation, which Coulet again rejected with the explanation that it was not Naylor's place to invite Coulet to meet with Atlee; Atlee or his secretary should have approached Coulet directly. Secondly, it was not the British vice prime minister's place to invite Coulet to dine in Normandy, but Coulet's to extend the invitation to Atlee. When Coulet further bristled about the insults occasioned by Churchill's visits to Normandy and Algiers, Naylor inquired if the commissioner would be free to receive a visit from Atlee the next morning at 9 A.M. When Atlee arrived at 10 A.M., Coulet invited him and General Naylor to dine with him at noon. The meal went splendidly, with a very friendly Atlee assuring Coulet that relations among the Allies would be much smoother now that de Gaulle had visited the White House and Roosevelt had agreed to recognize the Provisional Government as the legitimate government of France. Atlee also thanked the French government for its crucial cooperation during the Battle of Normandy. Coulet expressed his satisfaction to Koenig that the visit from Atlee had proven entirely successful. However, Coulet continued to register slights to the GPRF and felt compelled to redeliver a formal protest with SHAEF when Rear Admiral John Wilkes refused an invitation to a reception in Cherbourg hosted by the French Navy. Wilkes proffered the explanation that the United States did not recognize the Gaullist regime, and, thus, he was unable to recognize Commander Jacquinot as the commander of the French Navy. This was an extraordinary position for the admiral in charge of the U.S. Navy in Normandy to take and was received by Coulet as an insult by a "rude American admiral." In this case, Coulet was backed up by the heads of both British and American Civil Affairs, who agreed to take the matter up with SHAEF. Wilkes's refusal was all the more amazing because only days later, on 8 August, the Americans officially turned control of Cherbourg back to the French—meaning the Gaullist GPRF.[16]

So long as French civilians required substantial material assistance from the Allied armies, the French Provisional Government was not fully in charge. By mid-July, the Allies were transferring as much responsibility as possible to the French. Allied engineers had made emergency repairs of water, phone, and electrical works, and were glad to turn such matters over to the French even to a limited extent. French medical personnel had arrived from Britain in sufficient numbers to assume responsibility for injured and sick civilians even if the French still relied on the Allies for medical supplies and items like shoes and smocks for doctors and nurses. As French services were reviving, CA staff were relieved of numerous burdens they were happy to relinquish. On the other hand, CA officers then had to fill out more paperwork to satisfy both Allied authorities and the French, provoking protests from the officers, who clamored that they already had their hands full enough. Regardless, CA agreed to take charge of printing tens of thousands of ration cards for French civilians because the task was still beyond the abilities of French authorities in Normandy. At the end of July, SHAEF reached an agreement with officials of the GPRF that the Allies would deliver on a regular schedule essential goods to French warehouses in Normandy operated by General Supply. The goods would be subject to rationing established by the French, who would pay for the deliveries within eight days of receiving and inspecting them. The French were especially interested in shoes, work clothing, and fuels, all of which were in short supply and great demand in Normandy. Deliveries were to be made in both British and American zones on an equal basis. The French agreed to conduct a census of civilians in the liberated zone to determine how much was needed and how the supplies were to be distributed. Throughout June, many of the supplies delivered to the French—especially gasoline—were not charged against the French Lend-Lease account, but some were, which created confusion among all parties. The agreement of 31 July ended the conflicting ad hoc agreements that had been worked out by officers doing what they had thought best, and codified deliveries as commercial transactions between friendly governments. Still, the Allies occasionally reverted to their old ways: a dairy operator in Isigny who proved to be a reliable source of cheese, butter, and milk for the U.S. Army sold his products directly to the Army rather than going through General Supply because he had been accused of collaboration and could not get contracts approved by the French. As late as 22 August, he was still selling his products for cash to the Americans in violation of agreements between the Americans and the French.[17]

The Provisional Government moved quickly to gain control of the working lives of civilians in the liberated zone. French society traditionally had been highly "associative," with working and professional people organized into professional associations, either voluntarily or compelled by law, with formal contracts with French governments. The Vichy regime continued this practice in the National Revolution, encouraging or demanding that people belong to various professional or social organizations, and the Gaullist regime did as well. The Gaullists were eager to see that labor unions, professional societies, and employer associations got back up and running as quickly as possible so that the French—and not the Allies—were in charge of affairs. The populace was just as keen to see their organizations functioning, and when Gaullist officials called for members to reanimate their associations—such as dairy farmer co-ops— they sprang into action. This placed the French in charge of resurrecting commercial activity and took initiative away from Allied Civil Affairs officers, much to the satisfaction of the latter, who wanted as little responsibility for French affairs as possible. Members of the builders' association of Cherbourg similarly volunteered their assistance to CA to get streets clear and rubble cleaned up. CA was happy to accept their offer, and Coulet's office took note approvingly. The head of the builders' association in Caen, also a vice president of the Chamber of Commerce, jumped into action offering his association's assistance to the British in clearing the debris that filled Caen.[18]

French labor leaders in Normandy proved very useful in seeing that the Allies paid workers according to French government pay scales and made the appropriate contributions into government social welfare accounts. M. Bocher, a socialist (SFIO) labor leader with the CGT, a French labor organization at the Arsenal in Cherbourg, took the initiative of calling on his members to help the Allies in any way possible. Workers responded with enthusiasm, winning Bocher the praise of CA and Coulet's labor office alike. When the Americans told the French labor inspector, Garnier-Thenon, that they were unable to pay French-mandated social charges—family assistance, sick leave, retirement, vacation, health insurance, and such—he looked to his own people for help persuading the Americans they could find a way to do so. Getting the Americans to agree to pay the social charges and adhere to the proper pay scales proved difficult, especially because Coulet had only Garnier-Thenon as the sole labor inspector for the entire liberated zone. Two labor inspectors for Calvados, based in Caen, "disappeared" during the bombardments, presumably under the rubble of the city. Union leaders keeping an eye on workers' benefits helped the Provisional Government immensely in pushing the Allies to abide by French laws. The head of the rival Catholic labor organization (CFTC), M. Huet, and the Communist head of the CGT in Calvados, M. Boisjoli, all volunteered to enlist their members to support French labor laws. The Americans also made a practice of hiring whichever civilian workers happened to be on hand to perform a large variety of tasks—as seen in Carentan. The GPRF did not want any foreign army on its soil hiring French civilians without the explicit consent and cooperation of the government. French workers and their political representatives had struggled for decades to rid France of exploitative private hiring halls and replace them with government-run labor exchanges. Having won the battle, both workers and the government jealously guarded their prerogatives and were not willing to surrender them to Allied armies, who would have to hire French workers through government-run labor exchanges, as French employers did. Coulet, his aides, and Garnier-Thenon scrambled to get these exchanges up and running as quickly as possible, opening them in refugee camps when they could. This not only served the cause of the GPRF, but that of the Allies as well, who were glad to have any assistance they could get from the French in finding workers to perform the many tasks that needed doing.[19]

Commissioner Coulet informed Brigadier General Robbins that the French were setting up labor offices to hire workers for the Allies and henceforth the Allies should submit their labor requirements to Coulet's office. He would see they were met. He also informed Robbins that workers hired through government labor exchanges would require pay according to French-set payment scales and social charges paid into accounts. While the social charges added 50 percent to the cost of workers, following government pay scales saved the Allies money, as the Americans in particular were paying higher than normal wages. On 9 August, British and American representatives formally accepted all French demands on labor, including paying 10 percent income tax and applying the agreements retroactively to 1 August. The British had already been following French law for some time, so the agreement really applied to the Americans. When Garnier-Thenon made an inspection tour of the recently liberated American zone in early August, he reported that the Americans were being most cooperative and following French labor law even before the signing of the 9 August agreement. Coulet's concern to keep wages low was not to save the American Army money, but to prevent French workers from gravitating toward the U.S. Army for work rather than the French government. He did not want the French embroiled in a wage-bidding war in a zone with a labor shortage. Moreover, higher wages would have encouraged prices to rise in a zone with a drastic shortage of goods—mostly subject to rationing. More disposable income—presumably in "supplemental francs," though they were not mentioned by Coulet—would thus encourage higher prices and a general movement of goods to the black market. Coulet noticed, as well, a trend: employers who had served the Germans too well and profited too much eagerly offered their services to the Allies rather than work through French government offices, such as General Supply. Coulet looked to the employers' associations to rein in such undesirable mavericks.[20]

When Omar Bradley's armies finally punched through German defenses on the west of the Cotentin Peninsula at the end of July, the liberated zone quickly expanded and de Gaulle's Provisional Government just as quickly rushed to reestablish French sovereignty. As the liberated zone grew in size, so did the responsibilities of the GPRF. Coulet was keen not only to replace suspect Vichy administrators, but to prevent either Americans or Communists from filling the void. Coulet need not have worried overly about the Americans, as AMGOT was all but dead everywhere outside the Oval Office. Colonel de Boislambert followed in the van of the American armies and made contact with the underground resistance and extant liberation committees to ensure their loyalties were to General de Gaulle. He met with French politicians and appointed officials on the spot and, assisted by the liberation committees, made snap judgments about who would serve the new order well and who should be replaced. When the U.S. Army recognized an inn keeper as mayor in a village in Cotentin because he greeted them at its entrance with an improvised American flag, de Boislambert quickly disappointed him and replaced him with the candidate of the local FFI. Coulet and his growing corps of assistants visited the newly liberated zones as soon as possible to confirm officials in their posts. In Coutances he met a sub-prefect, M. Endelin, recently appointed by Vichy, who had courageously remained at his post during the worst of the fighting and helped the anti-Nazi resistance. He favorably impressed Lieutenant Colonel Gunn of CA when he greeted the Americans as liberators and proved himself cooperative and helpful. Even though Endelin was a Vichy appointee, he also impressed Coulet, who pronounced Endelin "a courageous true patriot" and confirmed him in his post.[21]

The new administration installed in Rennes shortly after it was liberated by the Americans on 4 August was readily accepted by the populace. The republican commissioner at Rennes, Victor Le Gorgeu, immediately proved himself accommodating to the U.S. Army and agreed to allow French technical experts to work directly with their American counterparts to make quick decisions about what needed to be done with roads, electricity, water, and the like. Pierre Laroque, on inspection tour, feared this would allow the Americans to do whatever they wanted without clearance from the new commissioner. Laroque was further distressed to learn that the French military commander for the newly liberated area, Colonel de Chevigné, had issued public orders (*arrêtés*) on military powers of arrest that did not conform to government policy. This was surprising because de Chevigné was no neophyte. He was trusted and had more experience than most in dealing with the Allied military. To ensure that French sovereignty was unquestionably in place, Laroque called a meeting in Rennes of CA officers, heads of French technical services, and the republican commissioner to explain that CA and the section heads were just liaisons between SHAEF and the Provisional Government, and everyone had to respect the agreements between SHAEF and the GPRF already in force. Assuring compliance by French officials eager to help the Allies defeat the Germans was going to be a trial for de Gaulle's new administrators.[22]

On the whole, the Americans proved very cooperative with the new French government and recognized their authority over civil matters. CA officers had a clear incentive to defer to the Gaullists: it meant fewer responsibilities and headaches for the U.S. Army. The eagerness of the U.S. Army to hand over civilian matters helped Coulet and other newly arrived commissioners and prefects to establish the rule of the GPRF in the liberated zone. The willingness of the French populace to embrace the new regime made the transition easier. The Allies generally stayed out of internal French affairs, turning a blind eye to summary executions of collaborators and mostly ignoring kangaroo courts run by liberation committees and FFI. The looming menace of the French resistance in the form of FFI and liberation committees also helped convince the liberated French to embrace the Gaullist officials as they arrived in the wake of the Allied armies.

5

LIBERATED CHERBOURG

As Carentan was the first town of any size to be liberated and placed under American control, Cherbourg was the first French city taken over by the American armies and used as their main supply base until larger Channel ports were liberated in September. Once liberated from the Germans, Cherbourg lay far behind the front lines and so escaped the trials of exposure on the battle front as experienced by Carentan and its people. Because Cherbourg was larger, the problems faced by the Allies there were also larger. The importance of the city as a supply base made overcoming those difficulties all the more urgent. The Americans almost completely dominated the city and kept thousands of its residents from returning in order to make space for the Allied military. Yet the Americans tried to accommodate the French to the extent possible and the French cooperated in many ways to make the city an important element in the liberation of France. Thus, Cherbourg gives us an example of how the French and Americans each managed their forced interaction during wartime. The American military had to accommodate both the French populace and the new Gaullist administration anxious to assert its authority in the liberated zone.

General Eisenhower and the planners of the Allied liberation of Europe had counted on liberating a major port early in the operation to serve as the principal supply depot for Allied armies fighting in France. Cherbourg was not by any means the biggest port in Normandy, but it was the closest to Britain and the only one likely to be torn from German control soon after the landings. Cherbourg was the largest city in lower Normandy and the busiest French port between Le Havre and Brest. The American landing on Utah Beach and the airborne operations by the 82nd and 101st Airborne Divisions on the Cotentin Peninsula were planned to facilitate its capture. Thus, the American divisions headed as quickly as possible to isolate and wrest Cherbourg from the Germans. Ultimately, Marseille, in the south of France, became the largest Allied port of supply in France, but until then Cherbourg played a crucial part in the war and liberation. Even after larger ports became available to the Allies, Cherbourg continued to provide important services to the war effort until Germany's surrender and beyond.[1]

Starting in April 1944, the area of Cherbourg had been targeted by medium and heavy bombers of the Eighth and Ninth Air Forces in preparation for seizing the Cotentin Peninsula from the Germans. Allied bombings of Cherbourg throughout the war until the city's liberation left 1,800 buildings badly damaged and hundreds of French dead or seriously injured. The assault on the city was preceded by a massive air bombardment by thousands of planes of the Ninth Air Force that tore up the already battered city. The AAF used tactical bombers (B-26s) and fighter-bombers to assault the city because they judged that strategic bombers (B-17s and B-24s) would create too much devastation in a port they planned to rely on after its capture. Nevertheless, determined German antiaircraft fire kept the attackers too high for accurate bombing. To defend the city from assault by Eisenhower's army, the Germans gathered around 40,000 men—anyone who could fight—to defend it: port personnel, sailors, mechanics, antiaircraft gunners, clerks, laundry workers, and stragglers from a dozen units that vainly tried to stem the U.S. advance up the Cotentin Peninsula. This included about 2,000 Todt Organization workers: Romanians, Poles, Spaniards, Belgians, Dutch, Russians, and some French. This rag-tag German force had too few men to defend the approaches to the town, yet it still put up a stiff resistance before retreating into a series of forts built by the French to defend the port from an attack by land. American soldiers began assaulting these forts one by one on 22 June and surrounded the German commander, General Karl von Schlieben, in an underground complex with 800 defenders. He decided that further resistance was futile on 26 June and surrendered his fort with its men. However, he did so without ordering the surrender of all German defenders in the city. The next day the Americans stormed the principal bastion defending the port, Fort Roule, whose big naval guns kept Allied warships—even battleships—far away from Cherbourg. When the fort surrendered the next day, organized German resistance in the city collapsed. Most of the remaining defenders surrendered on 28 June. A few die-hards continued to resist within the old French naval base until the next day. However, even then the battle continued because some 4,000 Germans still held on to another fort at Cap de la Hague, to the west of the city, with long-range naval guns that could pound the port Until these guns were silenced, the port remained unusable.²

The Germans holding out at Cap de la Hague turned their naval guns to face inland and reduced the town of Beaumont-Hague into a heap of rubble. But big guns are poor defense against infantry closing in, and on 1 July the last Germans manning the guns surrendered. The next day, when the Americans herded the German soldiers through the streets of Cherbourg, "French residents of Cherbourg came out to stand on the sidelines, spitting at the Germans and throwing rocks. [Private First Class] McDonnell and his buddies got a great kick out of this until they met a GI who had been captured early in the invasion and brought to Cherbourg by the Germans. When the Germans marched him and his fellow captives through the streets, the French had stood on the sidelines, spitting at the Americans, calling them names, and throwing rocks." By 1 July, the Americans had taken 39,000 German prisoners. Over the next few days French civilians accused some men in civilian clothes of being Germans trying to escape and turned them over to U.S. Army MPs.³

Even before the Germans surrendered, GIs discovered vast stocks of French brandy, wine, and liquor stowed by the Germans for what they had anticipated would be a long siege. Word quickly spread among the troops, who exploited the find to celebrate the capture of the city. The commander of the 9th Infantry Division, General Manton Eddy, tried to stop the massive GI party, but he decided the effort would be hopeless and that his men needed to blow off some steam after a hard fight to seize the Cotentin Peninsula. He gave them 24 hours to get drunk.⁴

Cherbourg had a prewar population of around 39,000. By the time American troops approached the city in June 1944, the French civilian population had shrunk to around 5,000. The Germans had ordered a mandatory evacuation of all French civilians on 13 June, but as the evacuation was supervised by the municipal police, it was less than thorough and about 2,000 still remained by the time the first U.S. troops arrived on 20 June. Among those still in the city were the firemen, police, and civil defense volunteers—all services thoroughly penetrated by the French resistance; the chief of the civil defense was one of the heads of the resistance in Cherbourg. A separate naval police force of 45 responsible for the Arsenal and Navy base also remained in town, as did French and foreigners who worked directly for the Germans. While the fighting raged within the town, the remaining civil defense workers, firemen, and police carried on their duties, rescuing many people trapped in buildings shattered in the bombardment. The city was divided into 20 civil defense districts, each one headed by a chief who assumed responsibility for his zone. Along with digging people out of rubble, they arranged for bread to be baked and distributed to the remaining civilian population. Nurses, stretcher bearers, and auxiliary medical workers stayed on the job during the fighting and saved many lives. They scurried about in active combat zones and crossed front lines to move wounded out of harm's way. More than 200 injured civilians were treated during the fighting; nurses often dressed wounds on the front lines as fighting raged. During the height of the battle, 25-year-old Annie Le Tallec drove an ambulance through the thick of the fight, picking up wounded for three days without respite. The head of the Croix-Rouge (Red Cross) ambulance service in Cherbourg, 31-year-old Cecile Armagnac, drove her ambulance through war zones despite being caught in cross fires numerous times and her ambulance being strafed by American planes in the days leading up to the battle. On 26 June, she carried on even after her helmet was blown off her head. One nurse and a female ambulance driver were killed and seven others were injured while persevering in their duties during the fighting. Other French inhabitants helped the Americans liberate their city: a gendarme and a fireman, both active in the resistance, ventured out of the besieged town and contacted American soldiers to point out German positions within the town. Another French civilian, M. Guermeur from suburban Octeville, was badly wounded while guiding soldiers into Cherbourg. A French naval officer, Lieutenant Guidicelli, was killed directing the attack on the last German defenders holding the Arsenal.[5]

Thirty-five city police had remained on the job throughout the fighting and enforced the law as they deemed appropriate under the circumstances. They were soon joined by other police who had fled the town and added new members by early August. Gendarmes (national uniformed police) also mostly stayed at their posts during the battle, and upon liberation the Americans were eager for them to resume their responsibilities—mostly patrolling the roads and under-policed villages in the region. U.S. officers thought there were too few gendarmes to keep order effectively and suggested more than doubling their numbers to 46. The U.S. military was also eager to see the Renseignements Généraux—national plain-clothes detectives responsible for internal intelligence and public investigations—most of whom remained in the city during the fighting, resume their duties. The intelligence agents quickly switched allegiance from Vichy to de Gaulle, added to their numbers, and worked in close cooperation with the Allied CIC (counter intelligence) as well as with the newly installed French CIC agents, who reported to General Pierre Koenig. Despite the shortage of French police throughout the Cotentin Peninsula, law and order did not break down. Only Sainte-Mère-Eglise was mentioned as a site of problems, and trouble there was attributed to unsupervised foreign Todt workers. Civil Affairs was generally satisfied with the behavior of GIs, even if the French had their own complaints. The Americans had expected to find a thriving black market but were pleasantly surprised by its absence. Of course, there was indeed a busy underground economy even if the Americans failed to see it.[6]

Before giving up the port, the Germans had done a thorough job of rendering it useless. All cranes were wrecked and dumped into the harbor to join sunken tugs, boats, ships of all kinds, and port railroad equipment. The quays were likewise blown up, as were the dikes and breakwaters protecting the *rade* (anchorage). The Germans sank boats on top of boats in the harbor, so that when the Americans clearing the harbor raised one they found another underneath. The harbor was strewn with mines that initially prevented all but the smallest wooden boats, which did not trigger magnetic mines, from entering. All this damage had to be cleared and equipment replaced before the port could be used by the Allies to support the Normandy invasion. The first ship unloaded in the harbor on 24 July. The approaches were not declared mine free until mid-September, only after many tugs, barges, and small ships had been sunk by lurking mines.[7]

Soldiers of the U.S. 26th Infantry Division arrived off Cherbourg days after its liberation and had to be ferried from their ships to a beach adjacent to the port in landing craft because mines and sunken craft still clogged the harbor. One soldier observed, "what we could see of the docks and cranes was a mass of steel junk caused by the explosive charges set by the Germans to destroy them before they left." Riding through Cherbourg in open trucks, "we looked up at the remainder of homes and apartments that had been bombed and shelled. It looked like pictures we had seen only two weeks before in *Life* magazine, only this time, it was real. We all pointed out the third-floor bathtub sticking out in the air all by itself, supported only by a drainpipe since the two floors under it were all rubble in the cellar. As we moved through the outskirts of Cherbourg, French people came out to the trucks and gave us apples. One man had several bottles of wine, and I hastily got out my canteen cup which he filled with white wine."[8]

The Allies could not afford to wait for the harbor to be completely cleared and rebuilt in order to rely on it as a landing place for supplies. Mountains of debris, some of it hauled out of the harbor, were bulldozed into the waters off the beaches and made into ramps for landing craft to unload trucks, tanks, and other vehicles. Armies of stevedores—foreign Todt workers, German POWs, GIs (usually black), and Frenchmen hired locally—unloaded tenders, landing craft, and dukws (amphibious 2½ ton trucks) at makeshift docks and ramps starting on 17 July. Fleets of dukws and small tenders off-loaded supplies from larger ships outside the port; by August the port was handling 20,000 tons a day. By late July, U.S. Army engineers had constructed a pipeline to off-load gasoline directly from tankers and pump it into a new pipeline laid across the Cotentin Peninsula that fed the fuel close to the front lines. All this frenetic activity contrasted dramatically with the quiet town that people had come to know since 1940. Cherbourg had been only a minor port before the war and had seen almost no shipping since the Germans occupied the town. The small fishing fleet had carried on to some extent, and small German naval vessels used the port for patrols. Otherwise not much had happened in Cherbourg for four years.[9]

The Civil Affairs unit arrived in Cherbourg on 27 June, set up headquarters in the Chamber of Commerce building, and began meeting with all city officials right away about bringing the town back to life. When the fighting stopped, the town had few operating services. There was no water, sewers, electricity, gas, phones, or trams. Rubble and garbage clogged the streets. Water mains had ruptured all over town; storm drains were clogged and pools of stagnant water filled the streets. All of this needed to be addressed immediately, as the town had to work not only for the returning population, but for the Americans who would use the port. Repairs to the main water and sewer lines were effected fairly quickly through close cooperation between French water workers and Army engineers so that drinkable water was widely available by 10 July. Many buildings in Cherbourg were not connected to the sewer system but had cesspools that required frequent emptying. Engineers contracted with local workers to empty the overflowing cesspools that made many otherwise usable houses uninhabitable. A Navy ship was brought into the harbor to act as a temporary generating station, and power lines ran from it to the town to provide electricity. Teams from the local electric company worked with Army engineers to testing lines to restore as much power as possible as quickly as possible. A shortage of coal to fuel the generators, which were returned to working order fairly quickly, posed the biggest challenge to restoring power. The U.S. public health officer argued forcefully that coal was desperately need to heat water for the public baths, as they were the only facility available to civilians to wash themselves. The bathhouses could also be used by U.S. paratroopers, most of whom had not bathed in weeks.[10]

The Germans also had sabotaged the phone system by lobbing grenades into the main switchboard room and taking an ax to its main cables. This was a hurried last-minute job and stopped phone service for only a few days. The U.S. Army Signal Corps proved much more effective in keeping phones dead when they commandeered the PTT (Postes, Télégraphes et Téléphones, the government service in charge of the post office and telephones) center for their own use. Not only did the Signal Corps expropriate the PTT offices, they refused to allow PTT employees access so they could effect repairs. The mayor appealed to Civilian Affairs to intercede with the Signal Corps on their behalf, but this was one instance where G-5 proved powerless to intercede. After three weeks the Signal Corps agreed to allot wire to the PTT so its workers could rehang lines damaged in the combat. It did not help matters or relations when some Corpsmen cut a PTT cable by mistake while installing their own system and neither repaired it nor allowed PTT workers to repair it for several weeks. On 16 July the Signal Corps announced it would allot 100 lines in the main exchange for French civilian use. This allowed the PTT to reconnect the fire, police, civil defense, mayor's office, and other important agencies. Service for everyone else had to wait.[11]

The civilian population began to return from the countryside even before the last Germans were chased down and captured in the city. There had been a good deal of looting of shops and some houses by both GIs and the French who had remained in the city during the fighting. Most such pilfering was probably the result of people helping themselves to whatever they needed to survive under difficult conditions rather than wanton thievery—although there was perhaps some of that as well. The police who remained in the town made no effort to intervene in the looting. Many people rummaged through buildings and houses that had been occupied by the Germans, taking whatever appealed to them. Unfortunately, the furniture in such places usually belonged to the previous occupants, who then had to undergo great exertions to get it back from both GIs and locals making themselves comfortable. In the days after the liberation, as the civilian population tried to settle in, many could be heard muttering about the looting and thievery by the Americans, but according to MPs much of the looting was in fact by their compatriots and not the invaders. In an effort to maintain order, the U.S. Army put into place a 10 P.M. to 5 A.M. curfew. Under the Germans the curfew had started at 11 P.M., a point underscored by the French to the new American authorities, who controlled this aspect of life in the town.[12]

The fight to take the city had inflicted an enormous toll on its physical condition. An estimated 25 percent of the city's buildings had been damaged to some extent, many of them completely demolished. Thus, the troops had their pick of those that remained habitable and took up informal quarters where they pleased. As the town's people returned, they wanted their homes back from the GI squatters. By 1 July, 17,000 had returned; 5,400 of them were children under five. G-5 was not supposed to be responsible for billeting GIs, but they were tasked with seeing that civilians had somewhere to live, so they found themselves trying to find alternative housing for GIs as often as for *cherbourgeois*. In principle, G-5 wanted to see all French civilians restored to their rightful homes, but this was not possible. In some cases, they negotiated a room or two for the unfortunate residents forced to share their houses with American soldiers. One woman whose husband was a POW in Germany had been staying in a house in the countryside that was destroyed in the fighting. With nowhere else to go, she returned to Cherbourg to find her house full of American soldiers. She begged for just a room or two in her own home, which she was willing to share with U.S. naval officers. Her appeals to G-5 failed to get her house back. Dealing with pleas from French civilians seeking to live in their own homes once again proved to be just one of the challenges Civil Affairs had to meet. Scores of people were living in squalid air-raid shelters and filthy barracks, which the Civil Affairs public health officer wanted condemned as uninhabitable. The Americans pleaded with French officials to keep all nonessential people out of the town. But where were they to go? Back to the barns and sheds they had been living in since the invasion? Civil Affairs turned to the prefect's office to see if some program could be established to house nonessential residents outside of the crowded town. Thus, Civil Affairs took an active part in finding locations outside of town to erect temporary housing for the displaced.

The U.S. Navy requisitioned a primary school to house personnel only to find the school already occupied by 33 injured and displaced civilians put there by French hospital staff trying to make room for more severely injured within the hospital. The Navy insisted on having its way and most of the injured civilians were sent to a makeshift refugee camp outside of town. Over time, as the Provisional Government gained confidence and personnel, it was able to impose its will more effectively, but for a town like Cherbourg, so dominated by the Allied military, the Allies generally got their way.[13]

The housing shortage was further complicated by 2,000 undocumented stranded foreigners, who exasperated both French and American officials faced with the responsibility of caring for them. It was hard enough coming up with enough housing for the Allied military in town, and the Army was reluctant to find housing for the Todt Organization workers stranded in Cherbourg. The Germans had imported 240,000 foreign workers to labor beside 360,000 French workers in the Todt Organization to build the string of defensive works along the French coast intended to keep the Allies from successfully invading. Many of the French workers were in fact from Normandy but were still housed in barracks built for them or any accommodations the Germans could find. By and large, housing for Todt workers provided by the Germans was reasonable; liberated workers complained more about German food than their housing. After the liberation, Todt workers from Normandy were free to go home if they could get there. French authorities were clearly responsible for French workers, but who was to take charge of the others? From the first week, G-5 did not want to be responsible for them, and VII Corps commanders could think of nothing more creative than to round them up as POWs. Civil Affairs officers rejected that solution for workers from Allied countries: Czech and Polish workers would be treated as displaced persons (DPs). French authorities already hard pressed to provide services and essential goods—food, clothing, soap—to their own population balked at having to provide for hordes of foreign workers stranded in Normandy. No one knew what to do with the numerous Russians, who included women, because of their suspect allegiances. Once the French retook possession of the main hospital in Cherbourg, which had been requisitioned by the German military in 1940, they wanted to reserve it for French civilians who needed it and refused to treat foreigners who came there for help. One pathetic injured Russian who had been turned away from the hospital was turned over to MPs as a POW because he needed immediate help and no one knew what to do with him. As a POW he would see a doctor, get fed, and be given a place to sleep. In the end, only a small number of foreigners were turned over to MPs as POWs. The CIC had decided their sympathies were either overtly pro-German or were insufficiently pro-Allied. When it became clear that the displaced foreigners marooned in Cherbourg were the Army's responsibility, it decided to make the best of the situation and put them to work under the guidance of the Corps of Engineers clearing the port of wreckage. One of their first tasks was to clear all the ammunition out of an ordnance factory near the port so 300 foreign workers would have a place to live.[14]

Civil Affairs estimated there was enough food in the city to feed 5,000 civilians for a month, but that would not last long if all the town's residents returned. Enormous stocks of food captured from the Germans in the Arsenal, some of it perishable, was handed over to the 4th Division and the rest given to Ravitaillement Général (General Supply), the French government office responsible for feeding the population. Civil Affairs officers teamed up with French volunteer relief workers to set up locations to receive returning civilians and see that they got something to eat. They were registered and given ration cards while the supply lasted. The Army had printed 6,000 ration cards to distribute to the civilians in town, but they were quickly exhausted as nearly 30,000 residents attempted to return before the end of July. The outlook for feeding the population in the longer run looked good: Normandy produced a surplus of milk, meat, and vegetables that normally fed the population of Paris. However, it lacked and would continue to want whatever was not produced regionally, especially wheat and sugar. Stocks of flour captured with the Arsenal were turned over to General Supply, but as that would soon be exhausted, CA saw to it that Army biscuits and flour were set aside for civilian consumption. Fort Roule was found to contain an enormous bounty of tobacco stockpiled by the Germans, which was divided between the French and the Americans. Ten tons of potatoes found there were judged unfit for human consumption and were used to feed pigs. During the course of the fighting, livestock held by the Germans had gotten loose, and some of them survived the battle. U.S. soldiers were detailed to corral the errant animals, and on a single day, 2 July, they rounded up 98 cattle, 49 cows, 43 pigs, and six horses, which were turned over to French authorities to feed the town's inhabitants. Dozens of horses left behind by the Germans and offered to the French by the U.S. Army found no takers. Farmers complained that cavalry horses trained for riders would not pull plows or work in teams, and in any event they were too small for hard work. Just keeping an eye on them proved difficult for the Army, as GIs kept taking them out for recreational rides.[15]

The returning population needed more than housing and food. They needed soap, shoes, and clean clothes. Most had not washed or changed their clothing for weeks, and many had spent considerable time outside exposed to the elements and suffered poor health. Children and babies suffered the most, so French relief workers appealed to the Allied military most urgently for sheets that could be made into diapers and women's undergarments. The U.S. Army Quartermaster Corps proved reluctant to take on the responsibility of supplying Cherbourg with soap, but ultimately cajoling by Civil Affairs convinced them to release 3.5 tons to General Supply for civilian use. General Supply, in turn, handed it to commercial outlets that offered it for sale to the population.[16]

The local French proved well organized to pitch in and help in the effort. Major Henderson, who oversaw civilian relief for CA in Cherbourg, found during his time there that people working for volunteer organizations were more energetic and helpful than government employees. Minor officials in the French relief agency "contented themselves with the routine (and sometimes apparently unsympathetic) implementation of their regulations. Often enough where there were no regulations to meet the unusual situations which arose there was a tendency to fold the hands and await instructions. Great tact was required but sometimes pressure had to be applied through the sub-prefect by means of a liaison officer." Private and semi-private agencies were much different, "the personnel active and ingenious." Numerous organizations already existed that could put their expertise to work in these dire circumstances. The Croix-Rouge immediately jumped into action and worked closely with G-5 trying to find food and shelter for returning and displaced *cherbourgeois*. They started a registry to reconnect families dispersed in the chaos of war. By 6 July a representative of the American Red Cross arrived to work out a way to forward mail from the liberated zone to French POWs still held in Germany. A semigovernmental organization established to help the families of soldiers, Secours National (National Emergency Assistance), had been operating under Vichy patronage in Cherbourg during the occupation and now turned to the same task under the GPRF. Right away its head came to G-5 with a list of items needed to help displaced families. Secours National collected clothing and shoes for refugees and found people to convert Army bed sheets into layettes and women's undergarments. Catholic agencies such as the Centre d'Action Sociale teamed up with G-5 to deliver aid to those in need. Communal kitchens had been operating before D-Day and picked up again as soon as the Americans arrived. A kitchen destroyed in the aerial bombardment had to be replaced, and the relief section of G-5 set about trying to find a place to put it.[17]

Although finding workers for vital tasks posed challenges, the Allies persevered. The head of the Civil Affairs Economic Section, responsible for recruiting local labor, found that M. Bocher, the head of the local CGT (the national syndicalist labor union) and the town's Socialist party, "stands out" as helpful; he was "pro-Ally, a member of the resistance, a good mob-orator [and] a let's-get-it-done guy . . . [even if he was] . . . rather heavy handed." M. Garnier-Thenon, the French official charged with getting workers in the liberated zone back to work and paid properly, also expressed his high opinion of M. Bocher, who encouraged union members to take up any task asked of them. Positive reports about the helpful M. Bocher even reached the U.S. First Army commander, General Omar Bradley. On the other hand, when the first civilian manager of a printing plant hired by the U.S. Army wanted to see things done by the book, his American supervisor had him drafted into the French Army and replaced. His replacement was a resistance hero who in the opinion of the same supervisor spent too much time on "resistance matters" (probably meaning politics), so he, too, soon found himself wearing a French Army uniform. His replacement was found in a refugee camp 20 miles outside of Cherbourg, and a certain amount of arm twisting had to occur to get him permits to travel to and live in Cherbourg. CA wanted to be rid of the problem of the Todt workers and foisted them onto the French, who decided to draft them into labor battalions and put them to work clearing up the city under the supervision of French Army NCOs. The French herded them into a filthy barrack in the Arsenal and, to the thinking of CA relief officers, treated them badly. Civil Affairs called this to the attention of SHAEF, who objected to involuntary conscripted labor even though it was permitted by the rules of war followed by the Allies. Russians and others of dubious allegiances were then offered a choice: work as paid labor or be sent to a POW camp. This met with SHAEF's approval. However, when foreign Todt workers mixed with French laborers hired by the Allies to clean up the town, the French workers often reacted with hostility to the foreigners.[18]

Taking charge of the streets and roads in and around Cherbourg proved a challenge for the U.S. military. The Army most eagerly wanted to keep all civilians off the clogged roads. Over 7,000 refugees from Cherbourg scattered over the Cotentin Peninsula wanted to return to their homes; the Army wanted to keep them out. U.S. Army drivers often took pity on French civilians trudging along country roads with their meager belongings trying to get back home to Cherbourg and gave them lifts, so that large numbers of returning *cherbourgeois* arrived in Army vehicles only to be told to leave again. MPs tried to persuade drivers not to pick up civilians without travel permits, but the overworked MPs had no real way to enforce such orders and most Normans had no way to get around other than catching rides from sympathetic GIs. Fortunately for the French and unhappily for the MPs, there were many such GIs. Without them, French teenager Armand Idrac would never have been able to move around the liberated zone. Before long, he was catching rides in jeeps, trucks, and amphibious vehicles while hitchhiking around the zone. Eventually French police were forced to take responsibility for evicting French from the city—again—who could not gain approval to stay.[19]

Both the French and American authorities wanted to bring back means of transport for civilians to get around the area, which presented numerous obstacles to overcome. Army transportation officers worked with the Office of Ponts et Chaussées (Bridges and Roads) to revive civilian circulation in the town and region. The tram system that served not just the town but the surrounding areas was not running. Only two busses remained in town and one did not work; the other had no gasoline. Civil Affairs arranged with the Quartermaster Corps to deliver gasoline to Ponts et Chaussées (PC), which took responsibility for doling it out for civilian use. PC commenced a census of all vehicles in town and set out to determine which were operable and which might be good only for spare parts. No civilian automobiles or spare parts had been manufactured in France for five years, so most cars were old and run down. Those that still ran had been converted to run on charcoal rather than gasoline, as no gasoline had been made available by the Germans for private cars. By 4 July, PC had counted 50 cars—half of them in private hands—not one of which had either tires or batteries. The Germans had seized all batteries and tires not hidden by their owners. But those items turned out to be numerous, as the accessories soon emerged from their hiding places. No sooner had PC established a motor pool of cars to be used for official purposes than the French military announced they were requisitioning all vehicles. Then, G-5 had to mediate not only between the American military and French civil authorities, but between civilian officials and the French military. If CA were in France to "help out in any way," then negotiating differences among the French became part of their brief. Because all gasoline derived from the U.S. military, the French military had good reason to listen to suggestions by G-5 about how it should be distributed: precious autos were allotted to PC's motor pool to be used by emergency and social services. Twelve captured German vehicles were also handed over to PC by the United States, but only four worked.[20]

While the American military lent a minimal hand to revive civilian traffic, its principal objective had to be winning the Battle of Normandy. Thus, the Allies took any and all measures they believed necessary to aid the fight. U.S. Army transportation officers preferred to keep civilian traffic off the streets and designated certain main thoroughfares off-limits to civilian traffic. It also put up one-way signs that directly contradicted one-way signs already posted by the French—and without consulting PC. Some of those thoroughfares also contained or crossed tram lines, which complicated efforts to get the lines up and running again. Some city streets were too narrow to accommodate big American trucks, so engineers demolished buildings that hindered long trucks from making tight turns. Often this, too, was done without consulting PC. All Army traffic signs were in English and often of little information value for the locals. G-5 officers realized quickly that restoring civilian trucking was crucial to reviving civilian life and would lift the burden of moving small items around town from the Transportation Corps. As was often the case, businessmen proved easier to work with than did the sometimes prickly or sluggish French bureaucrats. The manager of "a well known oil company," M. Coupard, proved not only cooperative but imaginative and energetic. He organized a company, Service de Répartition de Fret (Freight Distribution Service), SRF, to deliver people and goods within the region. M. Coupard also set up a permit system that allowed only drivers with permit stickers in their windows to have access to gasoline from PC. This was acceptable to PC, but the prefect's office and U.S. authorities wanted a say about who got permits.[21]

In order to move supplies landed at Cherbourg to troops at the front, the Allies had to restore to operation the railroad system thoroughly blasted by the Ninth Air Force. Army engineers set to work repairing rail beds and relaying rails where necessary; in some cases engineers laid new beds and new lines. When the Americans arrived, there were 25 locomotives in Cherbourg; three of them worked. The Transportation Corps estimated that most could be repaired fairly quickly, and they immediately set to it with the help of French railroad workers. It took two weeks for French and American workers to effect sufficient repairs to allow trains to run between Cherbourg and Carentan. The first American locomotive was unloaded at the port on 27 July. Once the system was running again, the U.S. military assumed complete control over its use with crews from the New Haven Railroad brought over to operate the foreign equipment. These trains were initially reserved exclusively for military use, and it took some cajoling by French officials to allow civilians to ride them. Any civilian wanting a ticket needed a permit issued by both French and American officials. The French also wanted to haul freight, and M. Coupard's SRF was prepared to arrange freight shipments, but the U.S. military was not eager to give up precious space on the limited number of freight cars—about 1,000 were rounded up from around the liberated zone—for civilian use. The Transportation Corps agreed to attach full cars of civilian goods to the trains; however the SRF never assembled a complete car of goods to ship by 4 August, when G-5 stopped concerning itself with such matters.[22]

Military authorities were not much concerned to revive civilian commerce in Cherbourg and revealed themselves more interested in catering to the comfort of their soldiers. The owner of the major local department store, Mme. Ratti, was reluctant to accept that her store, Le Ratti, had been taken over to serve as a Red Cross club for the 15,000 African American engineers working to clear the rubble from the town and restore the harbor to working condition. Mme. Ratti objected that she wanted to get the store back into operation. When negotiating the requisition with Mayor Renault, G-5 deputy commander Rupert L. H. Nunn, a British officer, pointed out that the store was stripped of any merchandise, with little likelihood of obtaining anything to sell anytime soon. Moreover, the building had sustained some damage, and while the building served as a rest and relaxation center for American soldiers, materials for reconstruction could be obtained and the U.S. Army would undertake the repairs. If the building were to revert to Mme. Ratti, no building materials would be available as it would not be supporting the war effort and thus would not qualify for hard-to-get supplies. Besides, the U.S. Army would rent the building from Mme. Ratti for much more than she could get from whatever meager sales she could ring up in the same period of time.[23]

While the Allies worked cooperatively with local authorities, the Provisional Government incrementally inserted itself into the administration of Cherbourg and its region. Even while the fighting still raged for the harbor, Commissioner for the Republic François Coulet arrived in Cherbourg for an inspection tour and to plant the flag of French authority. On 28 June, he met with the head of the departmental liberation committee, various newly appointed officials, as well as American Civil Affairs officers. Americans who met with Coulet assured him they had no intention of interfering in the administration of the newly liberated areas and would fully cooperate with the new French administration. An official handover of power and reestablishment of the Republic was declared at a grand rally the next day at the Place de la République in front of the Hôtel de Ville. Both the French and the Americans who witnessed the event judged the crowd of several thousand to be very enthusiastic, cheering and applauding de Gaulle's name every time it was spoken. The Americans presented Mayor Renault (temporarily accepted by Coulet as mayor) with a French tricolor flag patched together from American parachutes. Coulet praised local resistance leaders M. Gresselin and Captain Schuman, helping to bind the new regime with the resistance, who had already been in close contact with de Gaulle's organization via General Koenig. The attitude and policy of Coulet toward the resistance echoed that of the Americans: he welcomed leaders of local resistance into the new administration so long as they were cooperative. Both the Allies and the Gaullists integrated themselves with the locals by accepting as partners almost anyone willing to cooperate. The new administrators of the Provisional Government (GPRF) often had to negotiate with local resistance committees about who stayed in office, who was ousted (or arrested), and who was appointed to vacant posts. The Americans stayed out of such decisions and worked with any French who would work with them.[24]

Because of the overwhelming American presence and the speed with which Commissioner Coulet asserted the authority of the GPRF, local resistance fighters did not gain control of Cherbourg. This dampened the general settling of scores after the changeover soon to be seen elsewhere in French towns and cities. Only two Vichy officials were removed by Coulet, both without consulting the Allies. Coulet dismissed Sub-Prefect Bourdin, who officially greeted the Americans and turned the city over to them. Coulet deemed him too attached to Vichy and replaced him with a member of the local resistance committee. The head of the naval port police, Maurice Mesmacre, was also replaced because he had been too cooperative with the Germans. The jail filled up with the newly arrested: 152 people were picked up for a variety of offenses, many of them accused of collaboration, and crammed into a jail designed to hold 100. The Americans stayed out of these affairs. The French negotiated among themselves to send some of the overflow prisoners from the municipal jail to a secure facility in the Arsenal controlled by the French naval police. Civil courts reopened with a formal ceremony on 6 July, and judges began hearing cases right away. On 8 July, two young men were tried for serving as informers for the Germans during the occupation and sentenced to life imprisonment at hard labor. A Civil Affairs major attended the trial and judged it fair, even if he found the sentences too lenient.[25]

Cherbourg witnessed few head-shavings of women accused of having consorted with Germans, as occurred elsewhere when French control was reestablished, because the police in Cherbourg prevented it. The Germans had maintained brothels in Cherbourg for the exclusive use of their troops and had brought women from all over France and other conquered countries, especially Poland, to service their soldiers. They instituted the practice of rotating prostitutes to different garrisons around France and, thus, most of the women serving the Germans were not Normans yet were stuck in Cherbourg after the German surrender. Other women, some from Normandy and some from Paris, had served as "chambermaids" to German officers and were widely assumed to have also served as mistresses. These women were not always appreciated by the locals and were sometimes isolated from other French. A genteel Norman farmer, Marie-Louise Osmont, who was the proprietress of a stately farm near Caen, disliked and distrusted the French "kitchen women" brought by the Germans to perform menial tasks for them. While the four brothels in Cherbourg were off-limits to GIs, American soldiers frequented them anyway. Locals assumed that the same women who had served the Germans were then sleeping with the Americans and labeled them *"femmes internationales"*—international women. Many Normans—widely characterized as phlegmatic—shrugged off the situation as "to be expected." When Allied authorities got serious about enforcing the ban on GI visits to houses of prostitution, what was to be expected also occurred: the prostitutes left the established brothels and established unofficial houses of leisure that were sought out by GIs. This caused much consternation and ultimately anger as misdirected drunken GIs in search of prostitutes banged at night on doors of unsuspecting *cherbourgeois* roused from their sleep. Both military and local police were stretched too thin to hunt down and close the illegal brothels that sprang up. As feared by the French doctor in charge of public health, venereal disease rates that had been kept low under the Germans climbed alarmingly after the Americans arrived and placed registered brothels off-limits to GIs. Local women began to complain of being accosted in the streets and their homes by GIs looking for prostitutes. On 28 July, Civil Affairs received its first report of three rapes in Hameau Gallis, a village outside of Cherbourg. More rapes followed. In mid-December, five soldiers were tried for rape; by the end of January another 17 trials were held. Rape accusations by French women against GIs became a major discordant note in relations between the U.S. Army and the *cherbourgeois*.[26]

Allied authorities wanted to restore newspapers to Cherbourg to inform civilians about rules and requirements put into place by the military authorities. To that end, the Americans published a French-language information sheet in late June that provoked the wrath of Commissioner Coulet, who admitted his inability to prevent it from appearing. Upset that a foreign military was printing unauthorized propaganda in France, regardless of its good intent, Coulet appealed to General Koenig to see it stopped. According to the Provisional Government, all newspapers appearing in the liberated zone had to have the approval of the departmental liberation committee and permission of Commissioner Coulet. Newspapers began to reappear on 3 July, when *La Presse Cherbourgeoise* became the first French newspaper to appear in the American liberated zone. Making newsreels accessible to the civilian populace would make it easier to inform them about the course of the war and other news. All movie theaters in Cherbourg had been off-limits for civilians and reserved exclusively for the German occupiers since 1940. That changed on 5 July, when the Omnia Cinema was reopened to the French with great fanfare organized by the Psychological Warfare Division. The Omnia offered British and American fare for the first time in four years. The first radio station started up as well in early July when Radio Cherbourg began relaying BBC broadcasts, U.S. Armed Forces radio, and French-language programming. It was reportedly hugely popular with the civilian population.[27]

The generally good relations and close cooperation between the U.S. military and the newly established French authorities were complicated by the constantly changing commands within the Cherbourg region. Cherbourg initially fell under the responsibility of the 4th Infantry Division, which handed it over to the 101st Airborne, which then gave way to the First Army, which in turn handed responsibility to ADSEC/COMZ (Advanced Section, Communications Zone), which ultimately assumed responsibility for all of Normandy. Each one of these units had different generals with their own staffs that had to reestablish relations with French civilians and officials all over again. Fortunately, many G-5 officers remained on duty until early August 1944, when the French government under Commissioner Coulet took over relations directly with the heads of COMZ. With that, Civil Affairs no longer ran interference between civil authorities and the U.S. military. Toward the end of their tenure in Cherbourg, G-5 increasingly relied on the restored French naval command to act as French ambassadors to the revolving door of U.S. commanders. The heads of Civil Affairs in Cherbourg were mightily impressed by the diplomacy with which the French naval officers dealt with the newly arrived American chiefs. They helped things go more smoothly and served as an exemplary model of how good relations at command levels provided critical lubrication between the two principal actors—the U.S. military and the renewed French authorities. Both French naval officers and civilian authorities—Mayors Renault and Schmitt, Prefect Lebas, and Commissioner Coulet—worked cooperatively with the Americans to the benefit of both the Americans and the French civilian population. The helpful part played by the French Navy in assuring cooperation with the Americans makes U.S. Rear Admiral John Wilkes's refusal to recognize the authority of French commander Jacquinot as head of the French military in Cherbourg all the more regrettable.[28]

By mid-August the necessary cooperation forced on both the Americans and the French began to erode as both sides centralized decision making and took away much of the ad hoc agreements that had been so useful to all involved. SHAEF concluded that the port could not have been restored to service without the help and cooperation of the French population and officialdom that had been secured locally through handshake agreements. Throughout most of July, G-5 had acted as a mediator between French officials and various levels of Allied command. That role was greatly reduced at the insistence of French officialdom, which centralized most decision making within the offices of the prefect or Commissioner Coulet. On 15 August, the Quartermaster Corps stopped making deliveries of oil and gasoline to various French agencies that had directly requested them; instead, allocations were handed over to General Supply. All French requesting supplies or assistance from the Allied military, such as G-5, the engineers, or the Signal Crops, were told to apply at the prefecture, which then passed the request on to the proper Allied authorities. This was greeted with relief at some levels of the military, but not by G-5 officers in Cherbourg responsible for restoring civilian life. They believed it would slow down responses and make life more difficult. Lieutenant Cote of the Quartermaster Corps, assigned to G-5 to settle supply problems and see that things got done, recognized that his job was essentially over. He was reassigned and left Cherbourg.[29]

Bureaucracy made other tasks more difficult. When the Americans liberated Cherbourg, fishermen had stopped their trade entirely. Before the invasion, the Germans had severely limited the amount of fishing allowed. Only boats licensed by the Germans could fish, and only up to three miles into the English Channel. With the invasion, fishing stopped altogether. Mines dumped off shore by the Germans prevented fishing from resuming until the Allies could locate and remove them. All fishermen had to register with the new authorities and be cleared by counter intelligence (CIC). Once the mines were cleared away by mid-July, fishing still did not resume because all registered fishermen then had to be accepted by French naval authorities. Then, it turned out that the liberation committee also wanted a say in who was allowed to fish. Fishermen still had to obtain clearance from the Gendarmerie. The first thirteen boats ventured into the Channel on 26 July and their catch was small. By 3 August, when G-5 stopped filing reports, the fishing situation had changed little. Fishermen were allowed to keep only the first 50 kilos of their catch; the rest had to be sold to General Supply at prices set by the prefecture. Low prices gave fishermen little incentive to catch more than 50 kilos, and few did. With the Allies removed from decision making after 13 August, their aid also disappeared; all fishermen had to obtain fuel from the prefect's office instead of the U.S. Army Quartermaster Corps.[30]

By early August the French administration was sufficiently back on its feet to take charge of running civilian affairs outside of active combat zones. In October, Prefect Lebas ousted Mayor Renault and replaced him with a local socialist resistance leader, René Schmitt, who SHAEF credited for the smooth operation of the Allied port through 1945. The Allied military presence in Cherbourg remained massive until after the war was over in Europe, and many thousands of troops continued to clog the city houses and streets. The Allied military ran the port of Cherbourg even after Germany surrendered, not handing it back to France until October 1945. The port was far from fully functional by mid-August 1944, when the city—excluding the port—was handed back to French control.

Only five ships could berth at the quays at one time until the end of 1944. Despite its limitations and the opening of larger ports, such as Antwerp, Le Havre, and Marseille, before the end of the war the Allies used Cherbourg to unload 20,000 railcars and 1,400 locomotives, and over 1.5 million metric tons of petroleum were fed into the pipeline built by the U.S. Army Corps of Engineers to fuel Allied engines. And by the fall of 1945, 124,000 German POWs and 148,000 wounded American soldiers were loaded onto ships that sailed out of Cherbourg. At its peak of operations, 18,000 American GIs, 9,000 POWs, and 900 French civilians labored seven days a week, sometimes for up to 15 hours a day, loading and unloading ships at the port and seeing that the supply chain functioned as effectively as possible.[31]

Despite the relatively cordial relations between the French administration and the Allied militaries, popular opinion of the Americans began to wane in August as the food situation became dire. As was to become common around France, liberation did not bring abundance—far from it. Food became scarcer rather than easier to obtain. Lack of bread was the number one complaint of the French surveyed by the Psychological Warfare Division in August. Even tobacco, which U.S. soldiers obviously possessed in abundance, became harder to find rather than easier, adding to civilian frustration. As the popular mood soured, rumors that cast the Americans in a disfavorable light circulated freely. Army authorities were forced to clarify that 8,000 *cherbourgeois* did not perish in the battle for Cherbourg, rather around 75 did. G-5 made concerted efforts to turn French opinions around, but propaganda was no substitute for bread and soap.[32]

6

LIFE DURING WARTIME
IN NORMANDY AFTER D-DAY

The liberation of France was an event lived by both GIs and the French populace. Most of France witnessed little fighting and destruction; some regions of the country experienced a brief baptism of fire as the Germans and Allied armies raced through to the east. The Allied invasion of Normandy promised deliverance to the French people, however it first brought devastation. Most displaced French did not live in the liberated zone but in areas still occupied by the Germans. The initial Allied bombardments and artillery duels with the Germans caused much damage in the invasion zone and created refugees despite much of the local population having been forcibly removed from the beach areas by the Germans prior to the invasion.

On 6 and 7 June, thousands of Normans fled their towns and villages because of Allied aerial attacks and artillery bombardments. Norman farmers near the front opened their doors to shelter over 100,000 refugees. All available space was filled, with people sharing barns with cows, horses, and chickens. When cows left for pasture in the morning, farmers hastily mucked out stalls and replaced straw in horse barns so that people could take their places during the day. Some farms harbored dozens of people, some hundreds. Coutances, far from the invasion beaches but heavily bombed by the Americans, emptied out as people fled to nearby farms and empty beach houses. When the invasion began, construction work on the coastal defenses came to a stop and most Todt Organization workers were sent away from the coastal regions. Surprisingly, the Germans left many to shift for themselves and find what shelter they could. In the week after D-Day, wandering workers seeking shelter began to show up at the de Guerpel farm near Vire, Calvados, bringing with them stories of the devastation they had seen since leaving the coast. Xavier de Guerpel helped them with food, rest, and advice about how to reach an area safer than his own; above all, he cautioned that they should travel by night. Two weeks later, Normans fleeing the war zone with only the clothes on their backs arrived at de Guerpel's farm asking for refuge, which he gave willingly. As the Allies slowly advanced, more displaced French trudged down the road in front of de Guerpel's house, risking attack by Allied fighters. When one old lady was hit in the thigh and face by ricocheting debris, de Guerpel took her in and insisted a young German medic billeted in his house take care of her, which he did. On 23 July, the inhabitants of his village, Carville, were ordered to evacuate. De Guerpel himself stayed behind as a civil defense warden to watch helplessly as Germans looted empty farms.[1]

Republican Commissioner François Coulet spent much of his time in July and August circulating around liberated Normandy assessing the situation and was distressed by what he saw. He had been eager to visit liberated Caen because it had been the *chef lieu*—the administrative center—of the department of Calvados, and when he did on 10 July he found it "in a complete shambles and mostly still under German control." Even while the battle for Caen continued to rage for weeks between the Germans and the British and Canadians, government officials appointed by Vichy remained at their post in the prefecture, the main administrative building of the department. Fortunately, the prefecture had been built during the reign of Napoleon III of stout stone, like much of the city, and withstood a great deal of punishment during the fighting, surviving many direct hits from shells from both sides and continuing to serve as the administrative nerve center of the city throughout the siege. After British troops penetrated as far as the center of the city, they implored the civilian staff to evacuate the battered structure. The officials, however, refused to leave because of the negative impact their departure would have on the morale of the 6,000 to 8,000 *caennais* who remained in the city. Coulet was very impressed by the performance of the town's civil defense teams and the medical staff, who had behaved heroically during the fighting, and asked his superior in London, General Pierre Koenig, to dispatch medals he could award to keep up morale.[2]

The majority of the remaining city residents sheltered in the Lycée Malherbe, which was older than the prefecture and built on the foundations of an abbey that dated back to the time of William the Conqueror. Much of the substantial building also was constructed from massive stones, making it the safest place in the city to take shelter, even if it offered no guarantees. To ward off Allied bombers, volunteers stretched an enormous banner with a red cross on the roof and an even bigger one in the center court. Because paint was unobtainable in France during the war, the red cross of the banner was made from sheets that had been used to swab blood from the floor of the emergency operating room. The banners successfully warded off Allied planes, but not artillery, whose spotters sometimes could not see them. From 5,000 to 6,000 *caennais* found refuge in the lycée for weeks amid conditions that deteriorated with each day until British soldiers arrived during the second week of July. After the British and Canadians seized control of the northern sections of the city, 1,500 refugees still remained in the lycée amid horrific sanitary conditions, somewhat relieved by the steady stream of food and water delivered by the Allies from the beaches. The survivors were among the lucky. By 10 July, civil authorities in Caen estimated that around 2,000 to 3,000 civilians had died since 6 June, with about 1,200 of those confirmed.[3]

Throughout Normandy, finding hospital beds for all the injured and sick posed a great challenge. Bon Sauveur—also an ancient abbey built with huge limestone blocks—housed the only working hospital in Caen and cared for thousands of injured with 81 medical doctors, 22 interns, and 114 nurses, who remained at their posts throughout the siege. While the fighting raged they performed 2,300 operations; 253 of their patients died in the hospital. Like the lycée, Bon Sauveur escaped aerial bombing but not artillery shells. After the British and Canadians arrived, most of the 1,347 patients in the main hospital were evacuated to the hospital in Bayeux, but the last 120 were in such serious states that they could not be moved and stayed along with staff who cared for them. The hospital in Coutances was emptied of 400 patients and as much equipment as could be moved quickly after Allied aerial bombardment made it too dangerous to stay. Patients, staff, and equipment were crammed into all available transport, which was not much, and taken to Coutainville—a nearby beach resort—where a new hospital was improvised in vacation villas. The big houses of tiny Boucé hosted the hospital of Argentan, a town in the Orne far from the invasion beaches but subjected to destructive air raids on the night of 6 and 7 June. The French Croix Rouge took charge of thousands of refugees in improvised camps in the Cotentin Peninsula and flew or draped big red cross flags over them to protect them from Allied air attack.[4]

Most Normans who fled their towns and villages left with only minimal provisions, so teams were sent back into towns to scavenge supplies. Some people returned to their towns to see if their houses survived and if anything was salvageable. People daubed walls and doors with messages about where the inhabitants could be found. Pillaging of the emptied buildings was common, especially by German soldiers, who looted abandoned buildings at will. People put up "unexploded bomb" signs hoping to discourage looters from entering; many who found valuables intact buried their goods or hid them as best they could to try to keep them safe from plundering. A team of 500 men circulated though Caen to keep an eye on premises and discourage looting; they arrested around 500 French for looting in Caen between 12 June and 7 July. They could do nothing to stop the Germans—not even German MPs could stop SS troops from rummaging through empty buildings. However, it was difficult to distinguish looting from scavenging, which became essential to survive in the ruins of Caen as food and supplies ran low.[5]

The civilian population caught in the middle of the fighting was understandably frustrated by the lack of progress made by the Allied forces. What was taking so long? The French could easily see not only the vast fleets of vehicles, the mountains of supplies, and the hordes of soldiers available to the Americans, Canadians, and British, but also the paucity of material available to the small number of German troops. Civilians constantly crossed back and forth over the front lines and brought information to Allied troops about German troop strength. When the Imperial forces took half of Caen, civilians who moved between sides urged the British to advance, as there were few Germans to oppose them. They were bewildered by the British "lack of audacity." They were similarly surprised by the failure of the Americans to push the Germans aside and just walk into the rest of France.[6]

Saint-Lô, the *chef lieu* of the Manche, remained behind German lines. Upon its liberation by the Americans on 24 July, only around 90 inhabitants remained in the town that had been home to around 12,000 before the war; the town was almost completely razed. As in Caen, the stranded civilians sought refuge in the basement of the teachers college, and when the Americans arrived the huddled French had food and water for a only few more days. Some elderly residents continued to live in the basements of wrecked buildings. Commissioner Coulet judged that "the town is absolutely and completely destroyed . . . dead, and incapable of resuscitation." Unlike Caen, no officials remained in Saint-Lô, and Coulet wondered where he could find anyone—former teachers, professors, or municipal councilors—to assume responsibility for the town. For their part, American Civil Affairs officers were willing to step in to do whatever needed to be done to set the town on its feet again. For the immediate future, Coulet would not allow any of the former inhabitants, now scattered widely over the surrounding countryside, to return as the town was incapable of supporting more than a tiny population. Moreover, the U.S. Army did not have trucks to spare even to supply the town with basic necessities, and at the end of July the town remained littered with unburied bodies of German and American soldiers.[7]

The refugee problem vexed the Allies and French alike. Initially, the Allies wrested control of only a narrow strip of land along the coast, and the displaced Normans within the liberated zone had few options about where to go. When the front became bogged down, the narrow band was crammed with demolished houses and homeless French refugees, mostly dependent on the good will of the Allies. In late June, Coulet did not have an accurate count of the number of displaced French civilians in liberated Normandy and guessed it might be around 30,000; 12,000 refugees from the fighting around Caen were crammed into the British sector. By 21 July, 5,900 homeless civilians— mostly from Caen—found shelter in and around the small town of Bayeux. Coulet asked General Koenig if some way might be found to transport women, children, and old people to temporary camps in England, but this did not prove practical. Fortunately, the Allies were disposed to treat the French with good will to the extent that the difficult situation allowed. The British created a Franco-English committee that met every morning in Bayeux to review the refugee situation and decide what could be done about it. The British military worked cooperatively with French authorities appointed by Commissioner Coulet, while the Americans resisted efforts to establish parallel committees in the American zone. Once the Americans had cleared the Cotentin Peninsula of German forces, it offered lots of places to host camps for refugees. Nevertheless, most displaced French remained stranded in the narrow British sector with inadequate facilities to care for them because they had no means to travel to the more spacious American sector. The inadequacy of the roads did not allow refugees to leave the crowded British eastern sector for the larger American zone in the Cotentin Peninsula that by late June was also more secure. The Americans refused to allow the French to establish camps for refugees in the central sector (the American left wing) because it was too narrow, continually subject to German artillery fire, and too congested with military transport constantly clogging the roads. Camps were duly set up in the Cotentin Peninsula and had capacity to house more people, but getting people to the camps posed the real problem; 4,500 refugees from Caen soon found shelter in a camp in

Barfleur, just east of Cherbourg. An American-built camp in Fontenay-sur-Mer, near Valognes, was intended to house workers and their families, who would help clear up badly damaged Valognes. It had capacity for 700 but housed only 127 people in early August. French officials were impressed by the facilities of the camp and its efficient operation, and were eager to assume responsibility for it and move more people into it from the overcrowded British sector. A camp at Chateau de Cavigny was jointly run by the U.S. Army and a French aid group, Volontaires Françaises, and had room for 600 people; however, in early August it housed only 240. This camp was poorly situated and hard to reach, so French authorities who expected to assume responsibility for it in August hoped to convert it into an orphanage or temporary home for convalescents. The situation of all the camps in late July was deemed satisfactory by French officials who kept an eye on them. However, the camps needed more of everything: beds, supplies, linens, sanitary supplies, and the like. Coulet was determined to take charge of French refugees in the liberated zone; however, he had neither personnel nor supplies to do it and accepted reluctantly that the Allies must manage the camps until the French were able. By early July, French officials started setting up their own camps for displaced persons in the American zone; one opened in Saint-Marguerite-d'Elle, Calvados, and was run with the assistance of local volunteers. By the time of the big American breakout at the end of July, Normandy was full of refugees, but many did not live in camps run by anyone; they lived with sympathetic neighbors or relatives who could offer some form of shelter widely dispersed around the Norman countryside, mostly on farms.[8]

The Allies were initially surprised that the fierce fighting in Normandy had not killed or wounded more civilians. Almost certainly the German evacuation of most people from the immediate coastal areas saved many lives. Civil Affairs officers remarked how few young men were to be found, as they had all been taken for work by the Germans, sat in POW camps, or had fled to the *maquis*. When they started looking for locals to hire, they found only the elderly. The health of the remaining Normans was better than expected. Allied medical authorities had feared epidemics among local populations but found no such problems in Normandy. French doctors had reported cases of typhus in Cherbourg; captured German doctors denied it. The Americans chose to believe the French but also concluded any cases of typhus that had been present had been cured before the U.S. Army arrived. The hospital at Bayeux was the first to fall into Allied hands and was reserved for civilian use. In just a few days, it became home to 200 injured civilians. However, there were few French doctors or nurses to treat the patients, so Allied military medical personnel had to fill in. As these Army and Navy doctors and nurses had plenty of military cases to keep them busy, Allied authorities sent urgent requests to London to find French doctors and nurses to be brought to Normandy. By the end of June, only 10 French doctors and nurses could be found in England to come to Normandy, by which time the number of French patients in the hospital in Bayeux had swollen to 1,300. By mid-July, enough French doctors and nurses had been located to take care of French patients in both liberated zones, but they still relied on the Allies for all of their supplies; Civil Affairs put out a rush order for 200 uniforms for French nurses to be shipped from England. There was no hospital in the U.S. zone until Cherbourg fell, yet local French doctors somehow took care of the civilian population adequately without a hospital in the early days of June, with the U.S. Army providing them with medical supplies.[9]

The refugee problem was compounded by large numbers of foreigners brought into Normandy by the Germans to work for the military. Most of these people were men from Poland, Czechoslovakia, Hungary, and Russia and had worked for the Todt Organization on the West Wall fortifications. Large numbers of homeless and aimless foreign men created a security problem, especially around Sainte-Mère-Eglise, where French complaints about thefts convinced Civil Affairs to request the curfew be changed from 11 P.M. to 9 P.M. The people of the Cotentin Peninsula were especially afraid of the Russians, who were seen as predatory. OSS Colonel Bruce noted near Saint-Malo, "An ancient in the bar told us there had been many Russians quartered in the village and that their conduct had been very bad. He described them as being ignorant and brutish, unaware at what the fighting was all about." Civil Affairs did not want to take charge of these foreigner workers and wondered who was going to pay the 200 who had been put to work clearing the beaches and working as stevedores to unload ships. Would French labor laws apply to them? Another 800 were rounded up by the U.S. Army and slammed into POW camps. Almost everyone objected to this solution, but suggestions to house them in refugee camps were rejected by French officials, who were trying to assert their authority over the camps in the U.S. zone. Once the French Labor Office, responsible for recruiting workers for the Allied military, was up and running in the Manche, it accepted responsibility for 140 Russian women who had been brought to Normandy by the Todt Organization The French judged that with so many needs, they could easily be put to useful service. However, many French resented the presence of the foreign workers and wanted them closely supervised or shut up in POW camps. Eventually, the U.S. military agreed to take responsibility for Czech and Polish Todt workers and employ them, as there was plenty for them to do.[10]

The cramped conditions for the French populace in the liberated zone were eased when the American Army swarmed out of the Cotentin Peninsula in late July. In order to break German resistance at the base of the peninsula, General Eisenhower decided to smash the German lines west of Saint-Lô by massing 1,500 B-17s and B-24s to kick off Operation Cobra. The operation did not come off quite as foreseen and killed 102 U.S. soldiers and wounded 380. Among the dead was Lieutenant General Leslie J. McNair. Although German casualties from the operation were evidently not great, the massive bombardment accomplished its goal of breaking the German line and U.S. troops rushed through. The number of French civilian casualties resulting from the carpet-bombing operation is unknown. As American troops overran the zone devastated by the bombing, they encountered French civilians caught in the zone as well as dead or disoriented Germans; American medics attended to them all. Photographer Robert Capa drove through a scene of devastation: "The first towns through which we drove had suffered much from our heavy raids. Our tactical air force had bombed them to a shambles in order to cut off the communications of the retreating Germans. In those towns, the French were only half-happy and complained that if we had dropped as many arms to the French underground as bombs on innocent French towns, we would have killed more Germans and fewer Frenchmen, and succeeded better in our objective. The coastal town of Bréhal was the first town we reached that was unscarred by the war. The Germans were on the run, and the good campaign began. Here the French were fully happy. The food was good, and the first glass of wine was free at bars."[11]

The breakout from the Cotentin Peninsula finally allowed the transfer of displaced people from the overcrowded British sector to the American zone with camps already established to receive them. A trickle of people—350— started to move from the British zone to the American zone to relieve the British sector of its enormous burden of refugees. The Americans had recognized the problem and sent Army doctors to camps in the British zone to help out the overburdened British. U.S. Civil Affairs estimated that 10,000 French needed to be moved into the American sector, mostly because better facilities could be found to house them—better than the stables then used in the British to house too many homeless French. Despite the slow pace of French surveys of damaged villages, some refugees were already returning to their homes—wrecked or not. French officials also saw the American push to the south as a big opportunity for them. Facilities until then used by the military, such as Blanche-Lande, a religious institution near La Haye-du-Puits that housed 300 American officers who would soon be moving along, were eyed eagerly to house French civilians.[12]

The hard-pressed Allies and French found help to meet their plights from the Red Cross. Volunteers from both the British and American Red Cross arrived in Normandy to assess the needs of the populations early in July and by early August had arrived in large numbers to help take care of displaced civilians. They had no formal agreement with the Army, but Civil Affairs agreed to work closely with them and was pleased to turn over to them care for civilians. By end of August the Red Cross was deeply embedded in Normandy, helping to look after war-damaged Normans and foreigners alike stranded in France. Commissioner Coulet appealed to the British and American Red Cross to hurry up the small stream of supplies that was trickling through by early August. And the need for supplies was great. French officials gave a wish list to the Red Cross: 3,000 brooms, 3,000 dust brushes, 60,000 rolls of toilet paper, 5 tons of bleach, 20 tons of soap, 20,000 mattress covers that can be filled with straw, 800 woodstoves, 1,000 storm lanterns, 15,000 wash basins, 300 pickaxes, 600 shovels, 200 reams of paper, and much more. Most of the refugees had little more than the clothes on their backs, which had not been changed or washed for weeks. Many of them had not bathed for weeks, and the state of their hygiene was appalling. Civil Affairs was surprised to note that many French farmers wore not their work clothes when they fled their homes, but their "Sunday best," which was not the optimal choice for rough living. Thus, French officials also sought from the Red Cross 5,000 pairs of baby shoes, 7,000 pairs of baby socks, 10,000 women's socks, 20,000 women's blouses, 10,000 dresses, 7,000 dresses for young girls, 10,000 men's suits, 50,000 cans of condensed milk, 50,000 safety pins, 20,000 diapers, and much more. In fact, the Army was doing what it could to deliver such supplies; only one-half ton of soap for civilian use had been brought ashore in July, which increased to 12 tons in August; 52 tons of flour turned over to the French in July became 514 tons in August. Because the Allies wanted to put as many Frenchmen to work as possible—the need for laborers was so great—they called on the Red Cross to supply as many strong boots as could be spared. Relying on the Red Cross rather than the military was a practical consideration, as anything supplied by the Red Cross was free to the French, while anything provided by the Allied military had to be paid for through reciprocal aid. In July, the American Red Cross had gathered 100,000 tons of donated clothing—much of it for children—that was waiting to be transported across the Atlantic to clothe 30,000–40,000 refugees. The British Red Cross pleaded in late July that they had their hands full seeing to the needs of British civilians—especially children—made homeless by the then relentless bombardment of German V-1 flying bombs.[13]

The Red Cross also inspected POW camps filling up with Germans. As the International Red Cross Committee, headquartered in Geneva, had been the conduit for mail for POWs on both sides of the conflict, their services were now requested to move mail from the liberated zones of Normandy to the rest of still-occupied France. Normans with relatives held as POWs in Germany wanted to send and receive mail in the liberated zone and looked to the IRCC for help. This, however, posed a security problem for the Allied military, who insisted on the right to read and censor all outgoing mail.[14]

With the Germans nearly expelled from Normandy (the frantic and bloody German withdrawal at Falaise was over by 22 August), the number of French refugees mounted steadily beyond the capacity of existing camps to house them. Many displaced people were losing patience and beginning to return to their villages and farms, even if French officials had not yet approved them for rehabitation. The tens of thousands of Normans removed from their villages by the Germans during the worst of the fighting now wanted to go home. The population of Cherbourg—still held outside the battered town—was filtering back, and Major W. C. Henderson of Civil Affairs had the unpleasant duty of telling returning refugees they could not move back into their own homes—often because GIs were living there and the Army needed the GIs but did not need the refugees. He suggested building a camp for returning *cherbourgeois* just outside the city, but higher authorities feared (probably rightly) that it would be a mistake to situate them so close to their homes and then forbid them access to the congested and still bombed-out town. Cherbourg remained an important port for the Americans even beyond the end of the war, which kept most *cherbourgeois* out of town into 1945. In principle, only those with work in the port city could gain authorization to live there. Fortunately for Major Henderson, that

determination fell to the French by August 1944 and it was up to French officials to tell people they could not return to their homes. Despite all the difficulties, Major Henderson still worked closely with French officials to find places
for returning French to live. He cooperated with the newly in-charge French
officials and tried to find rooms in returnee's own houses if they were occupied
by Allied military, with GIs making room and sharing facilities with their hosts
and hostesses. Most people seem to have accepted this situation. Henderson
even agreed to find a place to serve as a nursery school (crèche) for returning
toddlers. [15]

The breakout from Normandy complicated the refugee quandary as displaced
Normans sought to return home and there was no way to get there. Major roads
in the Manche were closed to refugees trying to get home and reserved for military use. Major routes were clogged with U.S. Army vehicles of all sorts rushing to the south. Refugees who elected to return had to find their way on back
roads. Commissioner Coulet suggested that empty trucks heading back to the
beaches could pick up refugees and take them to points in Normandy. A varia-
tion of this proposal was eventually implemented, but in the meantime American truckers frequently stopped on their own initiative to give rides to hapless
French—often whole families—walking on the roads. MPs were supposed to
prevent Army vehicles from giving rides to civilians, but the overwhelmed police had more pressing worries to occupy them and Army drivers continued
to pick up refugees hitching rides. The lack of available transport encouraged
French officials to eye hungrily all trucks seized from the departing Germans.
The US Army had different ideas about those vehicles. The Quartermaster
Corps already had to race to collect equipment and vehicles abandoned by the
Germans in their flight before French civilians claimed them.[16]

Food for civilians generally presented little problem in Normandy, as the
region produced lots of it. Allied bombardments killed so many cattle that there
was an abundance of fresh meat for soldiers and civilians alike. Fresh meat, of
course, does not stay fresh for long, so that feast lasted only as long as cattle
continued to be killed in combat, which they did throughout July. Not surprisingly, many animals were unfit for consumption and had to be buried, which
kept many farmers employed for weeks as the Army paid them to perform this
service. Farm animals treading on mines and unexploded ordnance also proved
to be a too-common occurrence, but at least it kept the supply of fresh meat
flowing. The vast supply of slaughtered animals was a good thing as far as Civil

Affairs was concerned, as the Allies had their hands full handling supplies for the military and had little surplus capacity to land and transport food for civilians. As Allied armies poured into the small liberated zone in June, they took over farm fields and pastures for supply dumps, camps, and vehicle parking lots. While the displaced farmers were paid, their animals had nowhere to graze, provoking a crisis for the surviving livestock in Normandy. Because Normandy housed a vast supply of milk, cheese, and butter that far surpassed what could be consumed by the local French, Commissioner Coulet declared all was available for sale to Allied soldiers. After Allied armies broke out of Normandy, cheese and butter became officially unavailable to soldiers but was often acquired by barter. Yet, much dairy product was available only so long as it could be stored. British Civil Affairs proposed to buy the surplus and ship it to England, but Coulet judged that would be too detrimental to French morale and vetoed the suggestion. Due to lack of refrigerated storage, large volumes of dairy products had to be declared unfit for consumption because of spoilage. French veterinarians in charge of inspecting animal products like cheese declared much of it unfit for consumption during a time when the need for the food was great. Cut off from supplies of flour, Normans had to improvise to make bread in revived ancient bread ovens still sometimes found on farms. Ground apple and tomato seeds were added to barley and bran to improvise flour; straw was also milled to add filler. The "Norman sandwich" was made of slabs of butter between two slices of Camembert cheese, which replaced bread.[17]

Both the Allies and the French wanted water and electrical services restored as quickly as possible so that normal life could begin. U.S. and British Army engineers worked with French engineers to get services restored. In most cases the French did the actual work, supervised by Allied officers, who scrounged the materials. Water and electrical services were restored to the extent that limited coal supplies allowed in both Cherbourg and Caen by late July. Demolished Saint-Lô took longer: water and electricity were not restored there until the end of August, but even then the town remained dangerous because of unexploded ordnance. The French worked well with Allied specialists and said they were especially impressed with the American electrical engineers. The shortage of coal would continue to plague the French until well after the war was over and most Allied troops were gone. When the Germans were pushed off the beaches and immediate hinterland, they left behind huge amounts of construction equipment and supplies intended for building the *Westmaur*. The

Allies were able to put much of this material to good use. It also saved them from having to bring similar materials—concrete, cement, lumber, and cement mixers—from England. Civil Affairs saw urgent need to build temporary hospitals, prisons, and shelters for civilians, and both the French and Civil Affairs wanted materials to repair storage facilities for food. With all the strong arms and backs required by the Allies to move supplies and by the French to rebuild—or at least patch—war-damaged buildings, a labor shortage quickly developed. Americans thought that French fishermen—temporarily diverted from fishing—made excellent workers and snatched them up for unloading boats. Even old men were requisitioned for work on the beaches and to repair roads, although Civil Affairs worried that it took them away from their farm fields that needed attention. The Army also figured that most of the refugees were fit and in good health and could perform useful work repairing roads and clearing rubble out of towns and villages. But to do that, the Army would have to come up with not just food but suitable clothing and shoes. Shoes and boots proved to be in short supply.[18]

After the Americans cleared most of the Germans out of northwestern France, they inherited the refugee problem created by the Allied bombing campaign. They found camps established by the Vichy regime all over France. A vast camp in Chateaubriant—south of Rennes—held 30,000 bombed out of Saint-Nazaire and Nantes; over 200,000 homeless French were found scattered throughout the Loire-Inférieure. Gathemo—just south of Vire—held nearly 90,000 people, mostly from Calvados. New refugees were created by fighting in Brittany; Plabannec—just north of Brest—was found filled with 19,000 residents of Brest who had fled the battle raging there. Another 9,000 brestois were found sheltering in Mayenne. Once the Americans arrived, it became unclear who was now responsible for these camps. The American Red Cross agreed to take over the supply and running of several camps, but they could hardly take care of all of them. Civil Affairs did not want responsibility for them and urged French officials to take them over as soon as possible. But how were the French, without trucks, fuel, or supplies, supposed to provision these camps without the close cooperation from the U.S. Army? For that reason SHAEF readily agreed to supply French authorities with all the food and other supplies necessary to keep the refugees in the camps. The Army scrambled to find thousands of blankets for refugees scattered around Brittany. Civil Affairs found accommodations for 3,000, along with blankets and food, at Saint-Malo. Civilians filtering back into smashed Caen were causing headaches for the British Army and French authorities, who could not care for them. At least everyone agreed to the necessity of moving the thousands of wretched *caennais* out of the quarry caves near Fleury, where they had found shelter during the seemingly endless fighting.[19]

Housing the displaced population in Normandy became crucially important as the weather turned cold. French officials also coveted barracks vacated by the fleeing Germans, especially those that had housed Todt workers. However, the Americans thought such accommodations would make good housing for GIs. Civil Affairs officers remained involved and tried to help the French obtain supplies. However, everyone realized that France would not be able to provide enough material to build temporary housing for both refugees and American servicemen, who also required winter shelter. In November 1944, the Army estimated it needed to build shelters for 50,000 GIs and 120,000 displaced French; French factories were then turning out 9,000 units of housing per month—only a fraction of what was required. Normandy and Brittany together needed 20,000 temporary huts. The French estimated that 200,000 homes had been totally destroyed in Calvados and the Manche; another 800,000 homes were damaged. A French survey of the displaced revealed: 100,000 "total war victims" and 250,000 "partial war victims" in the Manche alone; numbers for Calvados were the same. Other departments were less devastated but still accommodations had to be found for 200,000 in Finistère, 100,000 in the Seine-Inféreure (mostly from devastated Le Havre), and another 30,000 each in the Eure, Ille-et-Villaine, and Orne. French authorities believed that most of these people could still be housed in their own homes with repairs (many needed patched roofs and replaced windows), but finding materials for those repairs was going to be difficult.[20]

Norman refugees created by the invasion and the precautionary German evacuations posed great challenges for both the Allied armies and the French officials eager to reassert French sovereignty. French officials appointed by de Gaulle's CNLF indeed wanted to help their suffering countrymen, but they also wanted to be in charge in their own country. Once it became clear that the Allied military was eager to pass the caring for displaced persons on to French civilians and that the Allies would help out to the extent they could, the two forces cooperated smoothly. The additional help from the American and British Red Cross, added to existing French aid agencies—including those established by Vichy—made the difficult burden lighter on Commissioner Coulet and his subordinates. However, the Allies' will to help was greater than their capacity to handle provisions on the beaches and the limited port facilities available. Roads jammed with military vehicles made it difficult not only to move supplies intended for the refugees and civilian population still in place but also to move the homeless to more salubrious accommodations. The breakout from Normandy at the end of July did not alter that quandary much. The roads were still congested, ports and beaches were still operating at full capacity, and the number of displaced in need of care only increased.

7

THE U.S. ARMY MEETS THE FRENCH
FORCES OF THE INTERIOR

After almost two months of grueling combat in Normandy, the American forces on the western end of the front broke the German line and rushed into the interior of France. This was the beginning of the end of the Battle for France in 1944. The collapse of the German Army in Normandy by early August left the rest of northern and western France open to Allied forces fanning out in all directions. After the doomed German counterattack at Mortain failed to cut the American armies in two, the remaining German troops in France either barricaded themselves into coastal enclaves or fled for the safety of the Siegfried Line in Germany. This left the vast expanse of France open to the French Forces of the Interior (FFI), waiting in the wings to play their part as l'Armée Secrète, which General de Gaulle hoped would rise up and seize France for the Provisional Government. In the excitement of the German retreat, hordes of men and women flocked to join the FFI to participate in the final days of fighting and share in the pride of liberation. As the Germans had denuded their defenses in Brittany, practically the only armed men initially encountered by the advancing Americans in Brittany, Maine, and Anjou were French resistance fighters of the FFI. Although greatly weakened, German forces still remained in Brittany, and engaging them in combat often proved deadly for poorly armed French irregulars who tried. Ambushes staged by the FFI often resulted in German attacks on nearby French farms and villages, resulting in burning, looting, and massacres. The French responded by shooting any German soldier who fell into their hands.

THE FRENCH FORCES OF THE INTERIOR

The French Forces of the Interior (FFI) was supposedly the French army within France awaiting the day of liberation to take up arms en masse. General de Gaulle ordered the creation of l'Armée Secrète (AS), uniting the various armed resistance groups in France in January 1943, and tried with only limited success to instill some discipline in the groups. The AS was supposed to lay low and prepare for the "great day" of the Allied invasion and then lead a national uprising to ensure that the liberation of France would be by the French and not by the Allies. To more firmly legitimize the French part in liberating France, in March 1944 de Gaulle established the Comité français de Libération nationale (CFLN) to unite all fighting French and act as a partner in the liberation of France, and to assert his control over the armed groups of the interior, renamed the French Forces of the Interior to emphasize that the resistance within France was another arm of the Gaullist Free French. He greatly worried that the French Communists would try to build up and keep active an army loyal to them alone to challenge de Gaulle's claim to leadership in newly liberated France. De Gaulle appointed General Pierre Koenig to take charge of the FFI and placed him in London in April 1944 to be in direct contact with General Eisenhower and be part of his team. Eisenhower gladly accepted Koenig as a member of his command, under the broad umbrella offered by Roosevelt to accept the assistance of any group willing to fight the Nazis. This gave de Gaulle and his CFLN a formal stake in the Allied invasion. The acceptance of Koenig's authority by the Communist partisan group Francs-Tireurs et Partisans (FTP) avoided a rift among the fighting groups within France and ensured the FTP, too, a recognized role in the Allied invasion. French Communists did not want any schism within guerrilla groups and were eager to have official links to the Allied forces of liberation. They also worked assiduously to dominate the FFI and marginalize its non-Communist leaders. While waiting for the great day, the FFI had many small tasks to perform: gathering intelligence, sabotaging, circulating pro-Allied propaganda, and helping downed flyers to escape, among other chores. Once the invasion was launched, Eisenhower counted on the FFI to disrupt Axis communications and serve as military auxiliaries to Allied soldiers in France.[1]

Much of Koenig's control over guerrilla groups in France was entirely theoretical; most resisters within France were more or less freelance men and women trying to stay out of the clutches of the Vichy paramilitary police, the Milice, and the Germans. Most of the freelance resisters within France who took up arms upon the Allied invasion did not answer to anyone, but were volunteer guerrillas, or *maquis*, operating in small groups under their own commanders. The term *maquis* was applied to those who had fled their homes—

most often to avoid the obligatory labor service—and made a precarious life for themselves in the bush (*maquis* is a kind of brushy vegetation common in the south of France) and outside the law. Most *maquis* were unarmed; a lucky few wielded hunting rifles, shotguns, or weapons left over from past French wars. *Maquis* bands grew in number and size under the imposition of labor conscription introduced by Premier Pierre Laval in late 1942 (STO, Service du Travail Obligatoire) to send French workers to German war plants. The increased destruction rained upon German factories by Allied bombers made the service not only detested but also dangerous in late 1943 and early 1944. The best way for young men to avoid being sent off to Germany was to take to the hills, which thousands did, and 30,000 to 40,000 ultimately joined *maquis* bands. The German High Command (OKW) ordered in March 1944 that *maquis* caught with arms were not to be treated as combatants, but to be summarily dispatched as terrorists.[2]

Most evaders of the STO did not take to far-away hills however, but stayed close to home, hidden and helped by friends and relatives. Those that did not have local support took to forests, hills, and marshes to hide and live by their wits. *Maquis* hiding in the forests and hills of France often resorted to poaching animals—too often farm animals—stealing crops, and other petty crimes in order to survive. Those closer to towns often raided stores for provisions and municipal offices for ration booklets and other handy documents. This and the unwanted attention that such outlaw acts attracted from the Germans and Vichy Milice tended to make the *maquis* far from popular among the farmers who had to suffer their presence. Sometimes, but not often, such small bands of mostly young men were in close contact with formal resistance rings and cooperated with them to the extent that it was mutually beneficial. Because Brittany offered many places to hide—whereas Normandy did not—many STO resisters and evaders flocked there. Most did not join armed resistance groups while the Germans and Milice were still active and feared, but by the end of June 1944 around 19,500 had joined FFI bands in Brittany, of which only about half actually had weapons; by mid-July—before the breakout—the ranks had grown to 31,500, though only 13,800 had arms. By mid-August, as Patton's troops were pushing through Brittany, the FFI that greeted them counted 80,000 men and women in their ranks—20,000 armed with weapons.[3]

The Allies tried to improve the fighting effectiveness of the FFI, even while discouraging them from engaging the Germans in combat, by dropping arms, supplies, and military officers to act as advisors. The British sent officers from the Special Operations Executive (SOE), the Americans dispatched officers attached to the OSS, and the French sent agents in a parallel organization, the Bureau central de renseignements et d'action (BCRA), all of whom worked in teams in the spring of 1944 to prepare the FFI for the Normandy invasion. The campaign, named Operation Jedburgh, grew in size after D-Day as more bombers were freed up to support it. The Allies believed that armed *maquis* might finally play a useful role in the fight against the Germans. The Americans grew alarmed when they learned the scale and scope of the guerrilla war that had erupted in the south of France after D-Day. Fearing disaster, the OSS successfully appealed for 180 bombers to drop 300 tons of supplies to *maquis* in the south on 25 June. Another Air Force mission to drop arms and supplies in southern France on 14 July 1944 employed 359 B-17s. By then the United States had dropped 70 agents and around 1,000 tons of supplies—mostly captured Axis arms. Before the end of September 1944, the Allies had inserted 25 Jedburgh teams into southwestern France in an effort to coordinate scattered FFI units there, many of which suffered bloody encounters with withdrawing German units. That many Allied and Free French officers took charge of FFI units in a region heavily influenced by Communist FTP units made their presence especially welcome to the Gaullists because they undercut the influence and weight of the Communists within the armed resistance. At the end of May and throughout the summer of 1944, Allied planes made 80 drops of arms and supplies to *maquis* in the department of the Yonne alone. Besides submachine guns and ammunition, they dropped shoes, clothes, explosives, and bazookas—the latter much prized by the FFI. Three British Special Air Service (SAS) groups and three Jedburgh teams parachuted into the Yonne to help organize the FFI that summer. Leadership offered by the Jedburghs and SAS helped defuse fears of many in the Yonne that the FFI were simply an underground Communist army waiting for the right moment to seize power. The French Communist Party (PCF) was in fact powerful within the FFI there, and General Koenig was pleased that British agents went in to help undercut the Communist hold over local *maquis* until a reliable French Army officer could be dropped in early August to assume command. If the FFI looked to Allied agents for training, guidance, and supplies, that meant they looked less to the PCF for leadership. Resistance leader Pierre Villon, with deep roots in the PCF, called for a "national insurrection" in June 1944 to forestall the imposition of AMGOT. All Jedburgh officers ultimately answered to General Koenig, so having British or American Jedburghs taking command of FFI units really introduced no confusion into chains of command, even if Koenig believed that the role of Jedburghs was to liaise with and arm FFI, and not to command them.[4]

Jedburgh teams first dropped into Brittany two days after D-Day and radioed London, asking for arms drops to supply 4,000 FFI. To provide supplies to their swelling numbers as American forces pushed into the province, the Allies mobilized 250 bombers in the last week of June to drop provisions, including 10,000 arms and even six jeeps. More OSS, SOE, and French officers in 14 Jedburgh teams jumped into Brittany to lead and advise FFI groups. In late July, Eisenhower authorized 35 drops of arms per night to *maquis* in Brittany. One Jedburgh team in Brittany organized the escape of 200 Russian POWs, who had been pressed into work for the Wehrmacht, and enrolled them into the ranks of the FFI. Operating with Allied commandos, the *maquis* made the lonely roads of Brittany unsafe for German troops, hampering their movement. SHAEF gained new interest in the possibilities of the FFI because the armed French irregulars had proven helpful and effective in the battle for Cherbourg, especially when acting as guides for American troops. General Koenig thought that the FFI, guided by Jedburgh teams, could prove especially important in the liberation of Brittany. General Bradley's aide Chester Hansen was impressed that they were willing to give their lives for the joint cause and said they performed "magnificently." Eisenhower did not believe the FFI could achieve much by themselves, but he wanted them to help the U.S. Army capture the city of Brest. In fact, engaging German troops, supported by Milice, in combat usually proved disastrous for *maquis* in Brittany, even when led by "Jeds."[5]

One of the American commandos parachuted behind the lines to link up with the FFI in Brittany, OSS Captain William B. Dreux, left a lively and informative account of his experiences that illustrated the strengths and weaknesses of the *maquis*. Along with British and French colleagues, Dreux quickly met up with some veteran members of the Communist-aligned Francs-Tireurs et Partisans (FTP), who knew the area well and had experience laying ambushes for isolated German units. OSS and SOE leaders in London were leery of FTP fighters and did not really trust them as loyal allies. Dreux also had moments of hesitation, but ultimately grew to respect and trust them. He was greatly saddened when one of those he had gotten to know well was badly injured by a mine. Many FTP, like *maquis* everywhere, were untrained and undisciplined teenagers of dubious value in battle. Robert Capa noted that they seemed to be mostly "young boys and girls." They were easily distracted, too given to displays of machismo, took foolish chances, and did not know how to hold their fire. They were as likely to shoot a cow or each other as a German. On the other hand, they were eager to help, knew the land and people well, would go to the last degree to accomplish a mission, and were easy to like. Unfortunately, their self-assurance and immature judgment often made their "intelligence" about the whereabouts of German units doubtful and frequently flat wrong. That proved to be a problem since Dreux's main mission was to find the Germans and report their strength. Dreux was initially excited to have Algerians and Senegalese join his FFI band, because as escaped POWs he assumed they were veterans with military training. Indeed, they were veterans, but they were also desperately seeking a way to hide from the Germans and had little enthusiasm for fighting alongside French teenagers. Dreux found the African members of his team to be unreliable in battle. He regretted that he had no legal authority over them and thus could impose no penalty on those who ran away in the face of German fire aside from expulsion from his troop.[6]

The FFI encountered by Dreux were poorly armed. Those that had any arms at all carried a wide assortment of weapons: British Sten guns (notorious for jamming), captured German rifles, shotguns, and a variety of pistols. Some had old French rifles from who-knows-what-war. Dreux guessed the rifles were probably half from the 1940 army and half from the First World War, though some looked like they might have been antiques from the nineteenth century. Sometimes FFI units had the luck to have captured German machine guns or submachine guns, though too few actually knew how to use a machine gun. Many had little idea how to use any firearm. OSS Colonel David Bruce observed that it was common to see FFI discharge their weapons by accident and that simply being around them could be dangerous. They usually made an effort to outfit themselves in some kind of uniform: military jackets or shirts and perhaps an Army cap. They almost always sported armbands with either "FFI" or "FTP" written on it, and many tried to wear helmets—American, British, or French, but never German. Sometimes the FFI took the initiative and forced the hand of Allied commanders, who had little choice but to change plans and lend a hand to out-matched FFI. An American major found himself in charge of an FFI contingent in the Norman town of Granville, on the western edge of the Cotentin Peninsula. The Americans had planned to bypass Granville, but with the FFI locked in fierce combat with the German garrison, the U.S. 4th Armored Division sent a small force into the town to help out. It may not have been needed; when the armored cars arrived, the town's populace was in full celebration over its liberation and capture of 150 Germans. Robert Capa witnessed the scene and his first sight of head-shavings dealt out to women accused of consorting with the enemy.[7]

Most GIs who fought in the Battle for Brest formed positive opinions of French irregulars. First Lieutenant Donald L. Van Roosen, formerly a student at Harvard College, found the French neither warm nor welcoming, but he regarded the lightly armed *maquis* as fairly effective in helping to liberate Brest given their limited arms and training. Chief Warrant Officer William Gideon remembered FFI he encountered as "very effective" and held a high opinion of them. Tech Corporal John J. Somers, in the 29th Division, thought the FFI helpful in the Battle of Normandy but not in the taking of Brest, where they disappeared when faced with danger. He remembered that they reappeared to pick up supplies, rations, guns, and ammunition after the fighting died down. Private Raymond E. Konrad, from Detroit and with the 2nd Infantry Division, was one of many soldiers who found the French volunteers to be "friendly" and very useful to the GIs; they were tough and dedicated, but neither disciplined nor prone to follow orders. Staff Sergeant Robert T. Thompson, from Pennsylvania, similarly found the French to be eager and helpful, but after he had spent two weeks training them, they all disappeared when ordered to depart for the Ardennes. Fighting in Brittany was one thing, but shipping off to "foreign" parts of France was apparently asking too much. Nevertheless, the general consensus among soldiers in the 38th Infantry Regiment that slugged away to root the Germans out of Brest was that French who volunteered to help out were "a great help," "great guys," "very friendly," and "always willing to help." Only one corporal in the regiment said he did not respect them as soldiers. Sergeant John Savard fought alongside a group of French irregulars who attached themselves to his company and stuck out the entire battle. Savard appreciated their help because they knew the city and acted as reliable guides. They also showed determination, courage, and initiative, which could easily be confused with lack of discipline. At one point in the battle, while American officers discussed how best to approach a building full of German soldiers, the French volunteers charged in with submachine guns and quickly reemerged with a batch of German prisoners. Some German officers, under a white flag of truce, complained to General Middleton that FFI in Brest were mistreating captured Germans, to which Middleton responded that he could not guarantee treatment meted out by FFI as they were not under his control.[8]

A 4th Infantry Division antitank company picked up 30 FFI during the breakout of Normandy. They proved so useful and reliable that they were given American uniforms and equipment, and kept on as members of the company all the way through the fighting in Germany. Colonel Narborne Gatling, the regimental commander, had nothing but praise for the performance of the FFI, who were treated as regular GIs. They proved especially helpful in gaining the cooperation of French civilians as the division swept across France. North of Saint-Quentin, Gatling's unit came across an active firefight between local FFI and Milice units. The FFI asked the Americans to stay out of it as it was "their fight." But "their fight" was holding up the American advance, so GIs inter-vened on the side of the FFI. The greatest service provided by the FFI in Dreux's opinion was the valuable knowledge they provided about the land and the peo-ple who lived there. French-speaking West Point graduate Lieutenant Colonel John B. Beach of the 1st Infantry Division agreed; he found French civilians generally helpful in providing advice to American forces. He judged the FFI he encountered "very effective," and, like Dreux, believed their most important contribution was providing field intelligence.[9]

The FFI also earned great gratitude from Americans who had become iso-lated from their units and became their charges. General Patton's aide-de-camp, Major Charles R. Codman, judged during the breakout that the FFI "have given real and valuable assistance, not only in mopping up operations, but in sabotage, bridge-blowing, and ceaseless harassment of the retreating Germans." Codman could speak from personal experience: during the wild rush over France, he became lost around Le Mans while trying to find Gen-eral Leclerc's French armored division's command post. He was sharing his jeep with Crown Prince Félix of Luxembourg when they decided to abandon the vehicle as hopeless in the thick underbrush. When they heard thrashing in the bushes Codman assumed his number was up, and they prepared to de-fend themselves with tommy guns. Instead, they were confronted by several members of the FFI, who served as guides to get them out of the woods and on the right path. James T. Lingg of the 1st Infantry Division was wounded and captured in fighting around Mayenne in early August. He was evacuated to a hospital in Paris, where he remained for less than a week before being put on a train with other injured POWs bound for Germany. French partisans saw to it that the train never reached Germany or even got very far out of Paris. Lingg escaped with the help of the *maquis* and was given over to the care of a French doctor in the suburbs of Paris, where he could hear the fighting that soon led to the city's liberation. When German troops left Paris, they prepared to take all wounded POWs with them, but were dissuaded by the French Red Cross, who took charge of them and the hospitals as the Germans left. Captain William T. Dillon was captured in early July near Caumont and managed to escape from a column of POWs marching to the rear by running away from the column and hiding in a haystack. He emerged from his hiding place that night and surprised a young French woman going to the well. She tried to get him to go away, but he insisted on staying. Her parents were no more enthusiastic about hiding an escaped American prisoner and tried to convince him to leave their house, which he did after they gave him some bread, cheese, and clothes. They pointed him in the direction of Vire, still far behind German lines, and he walked for a while. Hungry, he stopped at another farm inhabited by an old woman and two teenagers, who were no happier about helping an American soldier. Eventually the *maquis* came for him with bicycles. They took him on a bike to an empty farm and left him there. He awoke to a .45-caliber pistol pointed in his face by a *maquis*, who refused to believe Dillon was an American until Dillon showed him his tattoo. A woman who spoke English came and talked to him. Finally, an American Jedburgh man told him to find his way to Blois and hide by a lake until a man came to take charge of him. He eventually was lodged with over 300 downed airmen in a forest outside Blois until liberated by Patton's troops on 13 August.[10]

Some FFI fought in their own units rather than as irregular soldiers attached to U.S. units. One FFI group that operated in the lower Loire Valley, near Angers, grew to nearly 1,000 members after the Allied landings in June 1944. Its leader, Marius Vanneyre, had been a captain in the French Army before linking up with a group of *maquis*. He helped downed flyers by hiding them and contacting London by wireless to arrange their repatriation. Like most others, his group was poorly armed, and after D-Day parachute drops of arms and supplies to his group became less frequent just as regional resistance groups ballooned in size with fresh volunteers. Vanneyre begged London for more arms, but to no avail. When Vanneyre helped two American flyers cross the front lines in August, one of the airmen, Lieutenant Colonel Robert L. Coffey, tried to cajole arms out of the members of the Third Army that rescued them. When that failed to produce results, he sought out General Patton and argued that if given arms, supplies, and only a small American force, the FFI could seize Angers from the Germans and secure Patton's southern flank. Patton saw the attractiveness of such a plan and agreed to release arms for the FFI, and tanks and artillery to accompany Captain Vanneyre back to Angers. Guided by locals, American tanks and infantry were able to cross the Maine River unopposed and outflank the German garrison, making the city untenable.[11]

Many Americans who ran into FFI came away with ambivalent impressions of them. Colonel Gatling learned not see the FFI through rose-tinted glasses. When his regiment entered Etampes, south of Paris, the local resistance had declared the entire administration of the town "collaborationists" and arrested them. Gatling smelled a strong whiff of political machinations in the detention and assumed authority over the "collaborationists" himself and handed them over to American MPs for safekeeping. Gatling was also in Paris during the liberation and was even less impressed by the performance of the resistance there. He saw them riding around town in heavily armed commandeered cars and trucks posing dangers to everyone on the streets. When shooting broke out during de Gaulle's visit to Notre Dame, Gatling believed much of it was wild firing by ill-disciplined resistance fighters who shot at anything that appeared suspicious. Captain Dreux witnessed similar behavior in Brittany after the liberation of Cobourg: new ranks of FFI suddenly sprang up after the Germans surrendered, and the newly minted maquis commandeered cars and trucks, painted "FFI" in white on the doors, and scouted the countryside looking for German stragglers and "collabos," rather than sticking to the mission of locating German units. Dreux wondered what the FTP veterans he had fought alongside must have thought of their new comrades. Private Konrad also believed FFI fighting with him in Brest were more interested in finding collaborators than in liberating the city by digging out well-entrenched Germans. Civil Affairs officer Major John Magginis met the local FFI who had implanted themselves as the new authority in Charleville-Mézières—near the Belgian border—and also had mixed feelings about them. They had faced real danger and acted selflessly for a number of years, and he thought "they were entitled to this moment of power and glory while the flush of liberation lasted—provided they did not get out of hand. Their attitude of being above the law, however, did not sit well with some of the citizens of the community." In the Ardennes, FFI doggedly combed the hills and forests for German stragglers, and "sometimes they brought them in as prisoners of war and sometimes they simply liquidated them."[12]

Some GIs came away from their encounters with FFI with distinctly negative impressions. Major John Henne of the 29th Infantry Division remembered, "the FFI and the *maquis* I met were not impressive, quite opposite." Sergeant Leroy N. Stewart, of the 1st Infantry Division, found French irregulars who tagged along to join the fray simply nuisances and tried to shed them as quickly as possible. In early August, near Mortain, Stewart's unit found itself in the cross fire between some *maquis* in a commandeered fire truck and the occupants of a house who had just served the GIs lunch. The *maquis* claimed the family were collaborators. Stewart's men convinced the family to go quietly with the *maquis* to an unknown and presumably dire fate. A first lieutenant attached to the 29th Division counter intelligence unit, William C. Frodsham Jr., accompanied *maquis* into newly liberated towns and saw them shoot dead accused collaborators on several occasions. For Frodsham, this was a "bad job." Like Private Konrad, many French also thought the newly emergent *maquis* were more interested in finding collaborators—real or imagined—than in fighting Germans. Many French at the time and historians in retrospect concluded that the *maquis* who sprang up in August 1944 were primarily interested in settling accounts with other French, who may or may not have been collaborators. The FFI were responsible for two-thirds of the summary executions and three-quarters of the head-shavings that accompanied the liberation of Brittany. Even though SS prisoners were not always accorded the protection of the Geneva Convention by American soldiers, Americans could still look disapprovingly at ill-treatment of SS prisoners by the French. Three FFI joined up with the 4th Infantry Division's intelligence and reconnaissance unit in Vincennes—an eastern suburb of Paris—just before the city's liberation and stayed with them all the way to Belgium. In Belgium, the unit captured 20 SS who had just massacred the inhabitants of a small village. The FFI were given the task of guarding their prisoners while the Americans scouted the area. When they returned, the FFI were still there but the SS had vanished and the Frenchmen claimed to have no knowledge of their whereabouts. Assuming the FFI had killed them and disposed of the bodies, the Americans decided they no longer needed the assistance of the FFI and sent them home. Of course, few FFI spoke or understood English, just as few Americans understood French, so communication difficulties influenced both the effectiveness of the FFI and the opinions of GIs who could not really understand them. Sometimes, FFI groups would contain Spanish-, Russian-, or Polish-speaking fighters who could communicate with GIs who knew such languages from their families. Some GIs from New England and Louisiana spoke archaic forms of French at home, which could be understood by FFI. Almost all "Jeds" were fluent in French and tended to form high opinions of the FFI, perhaps because they were well aware of the limitations of the FFI.[13]

Sometimes the exploits of the FFI were exaggerated to inflate the participation of the French in their own liberation or by the Allied press for propaganda purposes. William Dreux found that the damage inflicted by FFI forces in Brittany was overestimated in official reports, such as those he later saw in London crediting the FFI in Brittany with destroying over 100 German trucks and capturing 1,400 POWs. Dreux guessed that most of those trucks had been destroyed by Ninth Air Force fighter-bombers or U.S. artillery and then claimed by FFI as their own accomplishment. Most POWs taken by the FFI were German service troops left behind or lost, and not regular Wehrmacht infantry. In the wake of the liberation of the Yonne, local authorities claimed FFI killed or captured 12,000 Germans—a number which is probably inflated. The American Army newspaper Stars and Stripes also liked to play up FFI participation in the fighting. A September issue relayed the story of a 19-year-old woman, dubbed "Marianne," who reportedly served in the maquis for two years and had been tortured by the Gestapo for three days. Stars and Stripes credited her with helping to capture the town of Baume—just east of Besançon—when she reportedly led Lieutenant William Duff across fields to a ferry and then across the Doubs River into Baume, which was still on fire. They found a basement crowded with terrified women and children in need of medical attention, so they went into a nearby hospital to look for supplies. Instead they found 12 German soldiers there. Assuming they would need help taking the Germans, Duff went in search of American soldiers, found a platoon, and returned with 20 infantrymen, only to find "Marianne" waiting for them with her 12 prisoners. That story may have been true, or exaggerated, but its appearance in Stars and Stripes suggests its editors wanted it retold to admirably reflect the help of French civilians in the war of liberation.[14]

In mid-September a collection of nearly 20,000 German Marines, Wehrmacht, and Luftwaffe personnel strung out in a column 30 miles long gave up the trek while still west of the Loire River at Issoudun, near Bourges. The column was under constant attack from American tactical bombers and constant harassment from nearly 3,000 *maquis*, which convinced the German commander, General Botho Elster, that the flight was hopeless. He made contact with the *maquis*, the core of whom were not the typically ad hoc collection of STO evaders and last-minute enthusiasts, but 2,400 members of the Armée Secrète, regular French soldiers of the demobilized "Armistice Army," equipped with artillery. However, the German retreat from the Gironde had been a brutal trek, with prisoners taken by neither the Germans nor the FFI. The Germans had massacred French civilians, and burned and looted farms and villages. Elster thus feared surrendering to the vengeful FFI and asked them to contact any nearby American units. The FFI found a squad of 18 GIs, led by Lieutenant McGill, scouting the areas west of the Loire and brought the American to Elster. When Elster asked McGill if a token battle could be arranged so that he could surrender with dignity, McGill answered that his were the only U.S. troops anywhere nearby, so even a mock battle could not be arranged. Would the threat of aerial bombardment be inducement enough asked the lieutenant? General Elster agreed and McGill arranged a show of bombers overhead, convincing the Germans to lay down their arms to McGill, who still did not have sufficient soldiers to take the 20,000 Germans prisoner. McGill's men led the German column to the Loire River, where it was handed over to the 83rd Infantry Division. At least, that was the colorful version of events as related by the American press. Benjamin Jones describes a more drawn out affair, with Elster negotiating surrender terms with British and American officers, who accepted the surrender of the German soldiers, who were allowed to keep their weapons until they were beyond the range of vengeful FFI. The FFI and the Jedburgh and SAS officers with them were outraged by the lenient treatment accorded Elster and his troops.[15]

ERNEST HEMINGWAY AND THE FFI

One American in particular got along easily with French *maquis*: war correspondent Ernest Hemingway, who found himself leading a band of *maquis* around Rambouillet, southwest of Paris and Versailles, in August 1944 in the days leading up to the liberation of Paris. Hemingway had been traveling with the 4th Infantry Division, attached to Courtney Hodge's First Army, when it made a wide swing south of Paris in an effort to cut off German troops fleeing to

Germany. On 19 August, Hemingway and his driver drove east from Maintenon (near Chartres) in an effort to find the front and encountered a forward U.S. command post and some French civilians. The civilians, who had bicycled out from the town of Rambouillet, reported that the last German soldiers had left the previous night and mined the road as they departed. As Hemingway was the only American present who spoke French, he took this information from the civilians and passed it to the company commander on the spot. Hemingway thought this intelligence would be valuable to the regimental commander back in Maintenon and had his driver turn around to head back, taking one of the civilians with him to give his firsthand account of the situation.[16]

When he returned to the command post, Hemingway encountered two car loads of French resistance fighters armed with pistols and Sten guns. He interrogated them as well about the situation in Rambouillet and they confirmed the previous information given by the civilians: there were no Germans in Rambouillet and the roads were indeed mined. Hemingway again headed back to Maintenon with the guerrillas—Hemingway's term for them—to convey what they knew to the regimental headquarters. Afterward, Hemingway and his new friends headed back to locate the mined sections of road and waited for Army engineers to render the mines harmless. During this foray, Hemingway maintained that the guerrillas placed themselves under his command, "ignorant of the fact that a war correspondent cannot command troops, a situation which I explained to them at the earliest moment." Regardless, Hemingway and his resistance crew posted themselves as guards to make sure no American soldiers blundered onto the dangerous stretches of road. Eventually American sappers arrived and, aided by the French resistance fighters, cleared the road of mines. When the guerrillas again asked Hemingway to act as their commander, he again advised them he could not—but he could offer them "advice," which he was happy to do. He advised them to first establish themselves as the civil authority in Rambouillet, which they did, even though FFI had not shown themselves reluctant to take charge elsewhere and needed no instructions from American "advisors" to do so. Hemingway then suggested they reconnoiter the roads out of town leading to Paris to ensure there were no further German obstacles to the American advance. This they also did until American infantry arrived to take over that job. Finding themselves again without useful employment, they went to Hemingway and asked his advice. He suggested they screen the town in case the Germans tried to come back. At this point the American military presence in Rambouillet was still minimal and would have been unable to repel a determined German counterattack if they launched one.[17]

On 20 August, OSS Colonel David K. E. Bruce arrived in town to discover the strength of German forces south of Paris and got into contact with Hemingway, who, according to Bruce, "was attaining information by running French patrols through the [front]lines." Hemingway then passed all useful information to Bruce, who agreed with Hemingway and his French associates: the town was vulnerable to German counterattack and the Germans had larger forces in the immediate area than the Allies did. Hence, Bruce saw the merits of using French irregulars to guard the area and requested that Maintenon rush 40 FFI veterans to Rambouillet. Bruce found himself serving as the chief of all FFI in the area, the Civil Affairs officer, and the counter intelligence officer for the region even if these were not his responsibilities. Hemingway told an Army investigator, "as senior American officer present in the town, Colonel Bruce had a great many problems to deal with." Hence, when Hemingway offered to help Bruce in any way that he could, Bruce was only too happy to accept. Hemingway was the only person fluent in both French and English who knew the area and the situation, thus he served as Bruce's liaison with the FFI, who scouted the entire area and reported the whereabouts of German troop concentrations, artillery, mines, antiaircraft guns, strong points, and the like.[18]

Hemingway found himself comfortable quarters in the Hotel Vaneur, which he made his headquarters, with French *maquis* coming and going, passing along information and requesting new duties. They also left their weapons there while in town—as did Bruce, who ordered more weapons for the FFI, which were doled out from Hemingway's room. All of this was going on as Rambouillet filled up with American and British war correspondents hoping to get the big scoop when Paris was liberated. Many made jokes or muttered about Hemingway's strange doings in Rambouillet, ultimately leading to an Inspector General's investigation of the writer to determine if his actions with French guerrillas violated the Geneva Convention. The Inspector General concluded Hemingway did not violate any rules even if he did gather intelligence from *maquis* and pass it along to OSS agents. The information about German troop dispositions southwest of Paris gathered by Hemingway's crew was ultimately used by General Leclerc's 2nd Armored Division when they planned their advance from Rambouillet into Paris for the liberation on 25 August.[19]

Hemingway's experience leading a band of French irregulars was itself not exceptional; Jedburgh teams of French guerrillas and Allied officers were performing similar tasks throughout France where the Germans were still threatening. Close cooperation between the "Jeds" and the *maquis,* with Allied officers providing advice and leadership, also typified relations between the allies during the summer breakout. Only Hemingway's fame and position as a war correspondent made his situation unusual. Hemingway's band of volunteer irregulars performed the sort of tasks taken on by FFI everywhere. They played an important part in gathering information about the enemy and applied their deep knowledge about local conditions to help the Americans advance. Passing along Bruce's instructions and perhaps just showing good sense, Hemingway told his men to avoid fighting the Germans, who had advantages over the poorly armed and untrained volunteers. Nevertheless, some of Hemingway's band got into firefights with German soldiers and two were killed. Before the Germans were completely expelled from France in May 1945, 24,000 FFI died. Americans who spoke French—as both Bruce and Hemingway did (and surprisingly few American war correspondents did)—got along better with FFI than those who did not. Not surprisingly, those Americans who knew and understood the French—as many "Jeds" did—got the most benefit from working with them and enjoyed good relations with their extraordinary allies. While their usefulness had diminished with the waning German threat and many perceived the FFI as pests, if not nuisances—and often for good reasons—as of August 1944 the FFI still had a large and important role to play within the Alliance. The FFI took a leading role in the liberation of Paris and in containing German pockets of resistance on the Atlantic coast.[20]

THE FFI ON THE ATLANTIC COAST

As Patton's Third Army swept around Paris, tens of thousands of German troops were cut off in southwestern France. German troops in the southwest did not withdraw until Paris was threatened with immediate capture. They then made a mad dash to the northeast, seeking the safety of Germany. The occupiers in Bordeaux did not leave until 23 August and did not completely quit the city until 27 August—two days after French and U.S. troops flooded into Paris. Other German units were ordered to hunker down in French Atlantic ports to keep their facilities out of Allied hands. Neither the French nor the Americans had the military forces to spare to reduce the German pockets along the French Atlantic coast. After the fall of Brest and the remaining isolated German garrisons in Brittany, the American troops mostly withdrew from western France to take on the larger challenge of defeating Germany. The tenacity with which the Germans defended Brest and the casualties taken by the Americans and FFI convinced Eisenhower and the French alike to lay siege to the remaining pockets of German resistance rather than try to take them by storm. One American witness described liberated Brest as "utterly destroyed. All buildings left standing are completely gutted by fire. We brought up three bulldozers and spent the night opening up a couple of streets through town, bulldozing the fallen walls of the buildings into the basements." Chester Hansen called the battle for Brest "the worst street fighting since Stalingrad." Some in the American Army believed the Germans held out so fiercely in Brest because they feared being handed over to the FFI, who would likely kill them. In any event, Eisenhower did not have the forces available to root out the remaining Germans after the fall of Brest on 19 September and preferred to leave them isolated, holed up in their coastal fortresses. After the surprise capture of Antwerp, left unsabotaged by the Germans, the French Atlantic ports were judged by the Americans as unimportant to the war effort. Not surprisingly, de Gaulle did not share that assessment, but he had no more troops to spare than the Americans. De Gaulle also agreed that defeating Germany had to be the principal concern of the Allies, and because he was determined that France should play a real part in Germany's defeat, de Gaulle directed the flow of American military equipment to French divisions engaged against Germany. De Gaulle chose to utilize the FFI units in the west and appointed General Edgar de Larminat—who rallied to de Gaulle in Lebanon in 1940—to shape them into a real fighting force capable of not only containing the Germans, but of defeating them. Unfortunately, the FFI were starved of equipment and supplies, so building a force capable of ousting the 280,000 Germans from their remaining fortified positions proved impossible, even when supported by American units.[21]

The 50,000 to 75,000 barely trained FFI left behind to contain the Germans were upset and frustrated by what they saw as lack of support by the Americans. In the fall of 1944, the poorly armed FFI expected the U.S. Army to fully supply them with everything they needed to carry out their tasks even though the U.S. Army did not have sufficient supplies to conduct its own operations in France. Liaison officers and supply units were left behind by Patton—nominally in charge of the remaining U.S. operations on the Atlantic coast—to assist the FFI, but they were unable to help them enough to make much difference. This angered many in the FFI, who felt betrayed by their reluctant allies. Although regular French Army officers got along well and cooperated easily with their American counterparts, the average FFI mistrusted and disdained them. This led to numerous incidents, such as FFI looting U.S. supply depots and helping themselves to whatever they wanted. This, in turn, angered the Americans, who became fixed in thinking of the FFI as just a source of trouble rather than help. This American attitude was shared by many local French civilians who also saw FFI as little more than opportunistic brigands. The stance of local Communists in the west added fuel to these fires as they whipped up anti-American sentiments among Communist-dominated partisan units and their civilian admirers. In fact, most members of FTP units were barely acquainted with communism and belonged to their units not because of faith in Marxist-Leninist ideology, but because Communists ran the regional FFI operations and if a Frenchman or woman wanted to fight, he or she joined with the Communists to do so. Nevertheless, Communist agitation confirmed the image of Communist revolutionaries in the eyes of many conservative civilians inclined to distrust the PCF and their armed cohorts. Much of the civilian population was caught between a Communist Scylla and an American Charybdis.[22]

Friction between the Americans and civilians mounted even without the encouragement of the Communists because many—and probably most—French had exaggerated beliefs about what the Americans were capable of delivering. Both the FFI and the civilians expected much more from the Americans than the U.S. Army could deliver. Eisenhower and de Gaulle both had taken the view that the Atlantic coast was a side show not deserving of the military support necessary to eliminate the German hold-outs. Nor could they magically transform the FFI into professional units capable of dealing with the Germans by themselves. Allied failure to adequately supply the FFI led to looting of American supply trains in Morbihan and Côtes-du-Nord in Brittany and numerous "regrettable incidents" between GIs and FFI near the front at Lorient, spurring a further decline in relations between the two. Antagonism mounted when the Americans fired 160 French workers employed on the docks in Morlaix for stealing American supplies, angering much of the local population. The commissioner of the republic in Rennes, Victor Le Gorgeu, convinced the U.S. Army to take the men back and address some of the complaints of the FFI and the population of Brittany. Popular resentment often focused on the seemingly sympathetic treatment accorded German POWs by the Americans at a time when many civilians in the war zone still endured precarious lives in miserable conditions. Many complained that, if the Americans were not going to feed the displaced French, then at least they did not have to feed German POWs so well. FFI and GIs also clashed in the south, where the irregulars were slow to be integrated into the French Army. FFI were still mounting checkpoints on roads around Marseille in December, and U.S. Army vehicles did not feel obliged to stop for them, when by agreement they were supposed to. FFI fired in the air when one U.S. truck refused to stop at a checkpoint near Draguignan. The GIs in the truck then returned fire, leading to an extended fusillade that left two GIs badly wounded. Tensions mounted in the area between GIs and FFI; a fight that started in a bar in Martigues spilled into the street and both sides started firing guns, leaving at least one brawler badly injured. A few days later, MPs stopped a truck filled with FFI and 315,000 packs of American cigarettes, resulting in the arrest of the FFI, including their commander for Avignon. Even de Gaulle found it difficult to domesticate the FFI and the liberation committees in the south. The Gaullist commissioner of the republic in Rennes worried that these tensions served to promote the PCF, which would have regrettable results when local elections were held in the spring of 1945. Despite problems, those French who dealt directly with their U.S. counterparts understood and accepted the limitations on U.S. aid and got along well with the Americans. American officers and Gaullist officials tended to hold similar views of many problems encountered with the newly liberated French.[23]

In many French versions of the history of the liberation, the FFI played a leading role. The most inflated is probably Robert Aron's *Histoire de la Libération de la France,* which gives the FFI a place of honor at the center of the story. The most recent histories by Robert Gildea and Olivier Wieviorka offer a measured assessment of their importance to the overall liberation of France. Both works stress the psychological and political importance of FFI participation in the fight against Germany. The impact of the FFI fighters on French morale was no doubt great; however, many French feared the FFI as much as the Gaullist GPRF did (although the nature of their worries differed). The FFI did play an important role in the liberation. They effectively sabotaged many communication systems in northern France in preparation for D-Day, hindering the German response to the invaders. The intelligence they provided Allied advance forces no doubt saved many lives and much time. They rendered many small services to frontline and rear echelon troops that helped the American Army advance quickly through France. Such assistance was recognized by many

American soldiers, who were grateful for the help. But the overwhelming majority of FFI were military amateurs who sometimes just got in the way. Their enthusiasm could not always compensate for their lack of skill and training. Experienced saboteurs helped delay the German response to D-Day by disrupting trains, trucks, and communications heading to the front. But most FFI were not saboteurs; most were not even armed. Nevertheless, they still had experience and knowledge of the local roads, woods, and villages to help out the Americans once they advanced off the beaches. Once the Allied armies had passed through areas, such as the Yonne and Aube, the FFI left behind did not always reassure the liberated French. The population had little to fear from the FFI who worked well with liberation committees and newly appointed Gaullist officials, yet the interval between the old and new regime could be scary with young undisciplined FFI careening around towns and along country roads in commandeered vehicles looking for enemies to vanquish. Fortunately, even if such adventures were common enough, they were the exception and not the rule. Most FFI had little taste for vengeful escapades; they made their contribution to liberation and quickly returned to their civilian pursuits.[24]

8

SURVIVING THE BREAKOUT

The Allies and the Germans fought ferociously for two months in Normandy over a relatively small portion of France, wreaking havoc on its land and people. Much of the population was forced out of their homes and into temporary shelters of all sorts, as far from the fighting as possible, which was not always very far. After the Americans broke through the German lines in the Manche, the fluid character of battle (with the large exception of the Battle for Brest) lightened the impact of the war on the French people. The war brought liberation without massive devastation. Nevertheless, in much of liberated France, freedom from German rule still came at a price, some inflicted by the Allies, much more wrought by the retreating Germans, and some exacted upon the French by the French themselves. With the breakout from Normandy came liberation for towns, villages, and hamlets across France, and American troops encountered French civilians who had not suffered life on the battlefront. Many of them had, however, lived under bombardment from Allied planes. With liberation both the Germans and the threat of bombardment disappeared. A new set of challenges faced both the French and their American liberators.

THE AIR FORCE ADVANCE GUARD

After the breakout, the Allies launched an intensified campaign by fighters and tactical bombers of the Ninth Air Force against communication networks and German installations in eastern France to prevent German reinforcements from moving west and to hamper the withdrawal of the large German forces still in France. Systematic and widespread bombing raids against rail lines, rail yards, and bridges became almost daily events. Already targeted in previous raids, the extensive rail yards of Laroche-Migennes, in the Yonne, were hit yet again by 200 Allied bombers on 31 July—just weeks before its liberation. Nearby

Saint-Florentin, already targeted 10 times, was bombed again on 11 August, killing 20 more residents. Allied bombers unleashed a storm of bombs on the train station in Champigny-sur-Yonne in an effort to destroy a train transporting tanks spotted parked there. Instead, they caught a passenger train headed for Paris, killing 40 French civilians and injuring 70; the panzers remained untouched. On the afternoon of 2 August, bombers followed the Seine River south of Troyes and struck every town and burgh with a bridge: Bar-sur-Seine, Virey-sous-Bar, and Polisot. They cut rail lines, hit bridges, and destroyed rolling stock and a locomotive, as well as houses and buildings. The attack killed and injured civilians in several towns: two married couples, a married woman, and a young woman in Bar-sur-Seine were killed. The same day, bombers struck a great many sites with bridges and rail yards in a wide swath of territory east of Paris, destroying at least 50 locomotives. A train with fuel cars in Châlons-sur-Marne was hit and burned, damaging buildings in the center of town but injuring no civilians. Rail, telephone, and telegraph services east of Paris were temporarily put out of service.[1]

In a single week in early August, Allied planes struck dozens of sites in an arc from Troyes to Longwy, close to Luxembourg. They bombed and machine-gunned vehicles on roads, trains, rail yards, bridges, canals, German bases, and industrial sites serving the German military. On 7 August, Allied bombers struck Nogent-sur-Seine for the seventh time in a continuing effort to destroy a single bridge across the Seine River. They failed to hit the bridge again, but they destroyed several buildings, wounded four people, and killed 21 cows. One unfortunate woman was caught on the road and "shredded" according to local gendarmes, and a farmworker was inexplicably cut down by machine gun bullets in a field not far away. Eighty heavy bombers returned the next day to attack German bases in the area, especially the large German airbase at Romilly-sur-Seine. This time they destroyed 16 houses and badly damaged 10 more. Luckily, only a single civilian was killed, a woman in her home. Fifty planes struck Essey-lès-Nancy the same day with more deadly results: six people were killed in one canal barge, five in a single house, and a woman "died of fright." When the bombs struck the rail yards and bridges, a German truck was thrown 40 meters and its two occupants killed.[2]

While targeting bridges and rail facilities, significant damage was still inflicted on towns caught in the bombsights. An industrial suburb of Troyes, Saint-Julien-les-Villas, was badly mauled on the afternoon of 3 August by waves of bombers targeting its rail yards. The station, its yards and switching facilities, as well as many train cars were totally destroyed. A fertilizer factory and flour storage bins caught fire and burned to the ground despite the best efforts of fire brigades from Troyes to save them. Fifteen houses were completely destroyed, 13 rendered uninhabitable, and 17 more partially damaged. Five men and three women were killed, including a husband and wife; eight more were badly injured. The raid cut gas, electric, and phone services in the town. The commander of the regional Gendarmerie reported that public morale was not shaken, in part because the attack had been expected for a long time and "no one was surprised."[3]

During the breakout, Allied fighters hunted trains, distinguishing passenger from freight trains, and in all cases targeting the locomotives rather than the cars behind. They caught trains moving between towns as well as trains sitting in stations and yards, but usually only strafed moving trains and saved bombs for those in yards. Targeting locomotives on moving trains usually resulted in fewer civilian casualties, even if French train crews paid a dreadful price. Unfortunately, sometimes passenger cars were indeed strafed by Allied fighters. On 2 August, Allied fighters targeted two trains traveling on tracks, one a troop train near Metz and the other a passenger train between Bar-le-Duc and Nancy, full of French civilians. The troop train was badly mauled and its locomotive demolished, but fighters missed the engine on the passenger train and hit two passenger cars, killing a woman passenger. Ten days later, fighters caught passenger trains going from Dijon to Nancy and Verdun to Lérouville, killing 12 and eight passengers respectively. The same day, fighters hit a train packed with Senegalese POWs being transported to serve as laborers in Toul, killing or wounding seven. The Paris-to-Belfort train was strafed by fighters on 8 August, resulting in only four injuries—none serious—and leaving the locomotive untouched. Attacks against trains sitting in yards and stations proved more destructive, but not necessarily more costly in French lives. When bombers struck the rail yards in Bar-le-Duc on 12 August, 40 locomotives were destroyed at the cost of a single railroad employee's life and one injured. Ten more French were injured and a woman killed when a train was strafed while stopped at the station of Aingeray. The outcomes on the same day at nearby Mussey and Longeville were optimal: a fuel train and a supply train wrecked without any loss of French life. Nevertheless, the toll for raids around Bar-le-Duc on that single day added up: six civilians and two German soldiers were killed on a train caught at

Woimbey. The town of Islettes was severely mauled when a German munition train was hit and exploded, miraculously injuring only three Germans and no French civilians. The tally for civilians in the Meuse for one day: 14 attacks left 11 dead and six severely injured. While an unhappy outcome for the dead and injured, that was the sort of toll acceptable to both Allied planners and French civilians waiting for liberation.[4]

Allied fighters hunted vehicles on roads believing that only people important to the Germans or Vichy could obtain scarce fuel to be driving. Among those with a car and gasoline on 12 August was the commander of French gendarmes in Longwy, Meurthe-et-Moselle. While the commander drove, he had a gendarme assigned the specific task of watching the skies for hostile—meaning Allied—planes. The commander noticed farm workers in fields looking at the sky before his lookout spotted American fighters descending on them. They seemed to come out of nowhere and strafed the car. The commander immediately jumped from the still-rolling vehicle, but his lookout was caught by a 13 mm machine gun bullet that ricocheted off the road, passed through the floor of the car, and struck the officer in the buttocks. With the commander lying in a ditch and the wounded gendarme lying in the road, and the car stopped in the middle of the road, the pair of fighters made a second pass. They evidently identified their targets as French and flew by without firing a second time. The gendarme was hospitalized without serious wounds. On 7 August a commercial truck was targeted on National Route 77 near Bouilly, south of Troyes, where its 41-year-old driver was killed and his passenger gravely wounded. A passing car took the passenger to the hospital in Troyes, where he was received "bathed in blood." The next day another commercial truck was strafed not far away near Rances, destroying the truck while leaving the driver unharmed. Two trucks, a milk delivery truck and a moving van, were caught on the road in the Meuse and destroyed. Only the requisitioned moving van was serving the Germans, yet the two Frenchmen operating the milk truck were both killed.[5]

As American troops approached eastern France, the air campaign that preceded them intensified, and with the Wehrmacht in full retreat across France the planes found a target-rich landscape. Fighter-bombers searched to intercept German columns and strafed any train on any track and any vehicle on any road. On 26 August, the first day that B-26 Marauders started operating out of a base in Lessay, Normandy, Allied planes ranged widely over the department of the Vosges and strafed a French truck, badly wounding the driver. They caught an ambulant basket weaver on the road and killed him; they strafed a German convoy at Harol, setting several trucks and a house on fire. Two German trucks were caught by fighters on the road to Richardménil, strafed, and set on fire; one carried machine guns and the other cases of champagne. Allied planes also struck a German troop train on the tracks at Chames, setting it on fire; two tanker cars were also hit in Harol, and the resulting fire burned down a nearby house—no French were killed or injured. In Bains-les-Bains, Allied planes attacked two locomotives in the rail yard, but they were already disabled so the targets were of little value. No one was injured in that strike either. A German munitions trains sitting at the station at Ludres was bombed and strafed, destroying 60 boxcars and either killing or injuring the stationmaster, his wife, and two children (local witnesses were unsure). Bombs and bullets also found five nearby farmhouses and a barn, killing the cows inside and burning the year's harvest. On that day it seems fair to judge that the aerial attacks accomplished what they set out to do, disrupt German troops on the move, yet inflicted some damage on the civilian population in the process. It was certainly a tragedy for the basket weaver, the truck driver, the stationmaster's family, and the people who lost their homes, yet the price was most likely seen as not too dear to both Allied forces and French civilians alike, all of whom expected some civilian deaths. The wife of a French physician, who had to have both her feet amputated because she was in a café south of Paris as Allied planes attacked a passing German convoy, told a visiting OSS colonel with resignation, "*C'est la guerre.*"[6]

French police reports—still under the Vichy regime and bearing the Vichy "Fransique" stamp—always referred to "Allied planes," "English planes," "American planes," "Anglo-American planes," or "planes of unknown origin," but never to "enemy planes" except one quoting a German officer warning about unexploded bombs. Their tone was uniformly sober and neutral and never anti-Allied. Unsurprisingly, they were never anti-German either. A leaflet dropped by a British plane warning French train personnel of the risks they ran carried the salutation, "Your Friends of the RAF." The planners and pilots of the USAAF and the RAF were painfully aware that French citizens lay in harm's way underneath, and planes ranging over the Meurthe-et-Moselle for targets in August 1944 made efforts to minimize French casualties and maximize damage to the German war effort as General Patton's troops brought the war closer. One of those pilots was American Marc [or Mark] Kennon, whose P-51 Mustang was shot down on 24 August while attacking trains on the line from Paris to Strasbourg. Paul Bodot of Coincourt saw his parachute descending, jumped on his bicycle, and found the pilot. He took Kennon to the local FFI, who hid him, gave him clothes, and fed him until an American patrol showed up on 11 September. Even while suffering from aerial attack by the Allies, many French took enormous risks to shelter and aid pilots who shot up French trains.[7]

The air campaign in one small swath of territory south and east of Lunéville, Meurthe-et-Moselle, illustrates what Germans and French alike endured during the weeks before liberation. On a single day, 28 August 1944, Allied planes attacked trains in Avricourt, Emberménil, Saint-Clement, Blainville, and half a dozen nearby burghs in a small corner of Meurthe-et-Moselle. The munitions train struck in Emberménil caught fire and burned uncontrollably; only one person died and no one was injured. Another munitions train caught fire and exploded in Saint-Clement, destroying the train station, six houses, and seven nearby buildings; five other houses were rendered uninhabitable and 80 percent of the windows in town were shattered by the exploding boxcars. Munitions, fragments, and burning embers rained down on the town, setting numerous roofs on fire and leaving the streets littered with unexploded ordnance. A 33-year-old man was badly injured when one of those shells exploded. A parallel incident in nearby Baccarat killed a 47-year-old railroad employee, a father with three children. Exploding machine gun bullets caused minor scattered fires, quickly extinguished by municipal firefighters. When another munitions train caught on the tracks near Lunéville blew up, it destroyed a farm and killed a 30-year-old woman who worked there. A truck was strafed on the road near Thiacourt and its French driver injured. The attack also cut phone lines and, thus, local phone service. A German convoy was caught on the road near Hudiviller, burning six trucks and damaging four more. French police reports almost never mention German casualties, but they did report a French passenger car caught in the raid by accident, which killed a 16-year-old boy passenger. This rendering does not exhaust the police reports of bombings and strafings on one day but does provide an image of life under Allied air attacks, which proved effective in destroying German targets. The toll imposed on French civilians was small compared to the miserable havoc wrought by four-engine bombers attacking at high altitude. The medium bombers—mostly two-engine B-26 Marauders and DH.98 Mosquitos—and fighters hunting German targets over the Meurthe-et-Moselle were vastly more effective and preferable to the French below. Only

one day later, 29 August, the Gendarmerie in Nancy received reports of bombings and strafings at Chambley, Homécourt, Conflans, Mars-la-Tour, Jarny, and
Vellecey. While damage was inflicted on military targets, no civilian injuries
were reported. Such results were desired by French and Allies alike and were
more likely to result from the use of tactical aircraft than four-engine bombers.[8]

THE GERMAN RETREAT

The deadly price of liberation extracted by the Germans was many times greater
than that extracted by the Allied air campaign after D-Day, even when considering the passengers killed on trains and the innocents caught close to rail yards.
The German soldiers, who had behaved so correctly and with such discipline
during the occupation, reverted to brutes on their way out. Looting that might
have been seen as scavenging by troops in Normandy turned into wholesale
theft as German soldiers robbed and stole from houses and stores on their route
of retreat. They stole carts, bicycles, wagons, and horses from refugees they had
forced from their shelters. They often coerced men to work for them or serve
as drivers without pay. In the Falaise pocket, German soldiers forced a group of
French civilians out of the trench they had dug for their shelter from air raids
and used it themselves. Villages liberated by Leclerc's Free French division had
to be abandoned by order of General Omar Bradley, and were then reoccupied
by German troops and looted. People caught with Allied flags were shot. The
Breton town of Saint-Pol-de-Léon, on the north coast of Brittany, fell victim to
German barbarity after the residents celebrated their liberation prematurely.
When the town was abandoned by most of its German garrison on the night of
3 August, many residents decided to celebrate the following morning by looting the abandoned German barracks, tearing down German placards and signs,
and burning in the main square of town a portrait of Hitler that had been left
behind. French and American flags were hoisted over the town hall, the church,
and numerous houses amid the celebration. Young men seized arms left behind
by the Germans, despite the police posted to guard the former barracks, who at
least prevented young boys from making off with any weapons. Duly armed, the
spontaneous militia set about rounding up notorious collaborators and any German stragglers they could find, which amounted to several dozen—including
many Russians—before the afternoon was over. The armed band then set off
to liberate the nearby port of Roscoff. As the townsfolk and area farmers re-

joiced to music in the square, around 4 o'clock a column of German soldiers rolled into town. They immediately began to shoot anyone they saw, beginning with some armed men at the church, but their violence soon extended to women and unarmed men unlucky enough not to have disappeared when the Germans arrived. The Germans discovered their comrades held prisoner and machine-gunned the police and volunteers acting as their guards. As they ransacked the town, stealing food, drink, and anything that seemed valuable, they threw grenades into all the important buildings and loaded 15 men onto a truck to be taken to a place unknown. In fact, they were taken to nearby Morlaix and shot. Several farmers cultivating their fields and within easy range of German rifles were shot as the German column drove by. In all, 26 were killed and nine wounded, including four women—one a nun. On 4 August, U.S. troops were still far off, but racing for the port of Brest at the tip of the peninsula. They arrived in Morlaix on 8 August, while the main American force was busy bottling up the remaining Germans in Brest. While American troops prepared to take Brest by storm, they left mopping up operations in the burgs of Brittany largely to the French Forces of the Interior.[9]

In the department of the Aube the retreating Germans committed massacres in 52 out of 433 communes. When the Vichy Milice quit Troyes, the main city of the Aube, they turned over to the Germans 49 prisoners, all of whom were shot dead that night before the Germans left town. In all, the Germans killed 74 people in Troyes, 14 of them women, before quitting the town. They pillaged and burned Buchères, just south of Troyes, and massacred 62 people, including 25 women, 17 children, and seven old men, as they departed. They committed similar atrocities in Creney, Jully-sur-Sarce, Saint-Mards-en-Othe, and Mesnil-Saint-Père, where they killed 132 people altogether. Throughout the department of the Aube, German soldiers killed 442 French civilians in a few days in late August, not counting FFI or irregular fighters who died actually fighting German soldiers. Every one of the 442 was unarmed and murdered in cold blood as Germans rampaged their way through the department. Additionally, they burned substantial portions or all of 22 towns and villages, and pillaged and looted 54 others. German soldiers also raped four French women in Bar-sur-Seine. While many French civilians were accidently killed or injured by Allied fighters and bombers in departments across eastern France, that sad toll did not begin to approach this atrocious cost in innocent lives exacted by the Germans, every one of which was taken deliberately.[10]

As American troops raced through Troyes and the area, FFI units and the newly created and maladroitly-named "Milices patriotiques" (patriotic militias) scouted out abandoned German supply dumps and placed guards around them to gain arms and prevent looting. They were too late in one quarter of Troyes, where the locals jumped at the opportunity to plunder warehouses filled with Wehrmacht supplies. This seizure of German supplies by the FFI and gendarmes added fuel to a Franco-American quarrel over war booty. As the supplies were secured by the French while the Americans raced through, the French claimed the booty as theirs—with much justification. Outside of Alençon, Americans encountered French civilians looting a supply wagon abandoned by the Germans in their headlong flight to get away from the advancing American tanks. The looters took cigarettes, black bread, cheese, boots, underwear, and trousers—some of which may have been made in France but was not likely to have been stolen by the Germans. In this case, civilians could not plausibly argue they were simply taking back that which was theirs; it was looting abandoned German property, which, no doubt, struck the French as entirely justifiable. It is difficult to say they were wrong even if U.S. Army policy claimed all such abandoned property belonged to the U.S. Army.[11]

Immediately upon the liberation of Troyes, "popular justice" was rendered by the population with the guidance of the FFI, the FTP, and the Milice patriotique, beginning with women accused of "horizontal collaboration" with the Germans. A jeering crowd shoved 50 women to the police station, where they had their heads shaved. Afterward, the police judged that most people were outraged by the spectacle and that many of the women were either entirely innocent of any wrongdoing or that their transgressions were minor. They received reports that some women were falsely accused by enemies seeking revenge for entirely different matters or, in fact, the accusers were themselves guilty of consorting with the enemy. This was not an isolated negative reaction. American war correspondent Charles Wertenbaker met a young woman resistance fighter in Chartres who thought the head shavings were a disgrace to France. "It is cruel and unnecessary. They were soldiers' women and tomorrow they will be sleeping with the Americans. What difference does it make whether the man is German or American or Japanese? I have worked for the liberation . . . and I do not demand such a thing as this." Pierre Maillaud, who fought with Leclerc's soldiers from Normandy to Paris wrote, "I would rather have dispensed with a practice borrowed from the other side of the Rhine." Jean

Paul Sartre, who witnessed the spectacle of a shaved woman paraded by a jeering crowd down the Boulevard Saint-Michel in Paris, called the ritual "medieval sadism." On the other hand, *New York Herald Tribune* reporter Richard Tobin related a conversation with a female *résistante* in Cherbourg in July 1944 who saw head shaving as a relatively minor punishment for a relatively minor crime. She did not believe it worthwhile to fill the prisons with women who had committed offenses against the country that really hurt no one. "Women who had their heads shaved do not merit prison . . . these women who have betrayed in spirit, we treat them more lightly. We shave their heads. . . . In a few weeks or a few months their hair will grow again and all will be forgotten."[12] Most American and British soldiers were also repulsed by the head shavings they witnessed, yet few intervened in what was usually seen as a matter for the French alone. Despite the disgust it evoked among many Americans who witnessed it, the U.S. military did not interfere. Major Maginnis of Civil Affairs wrote:

> Today I saw one of the less pleasant aftermaths of the liberation—a parade of women accused of having cohabitated with Germans. Their heads were publicly shaved and they were marched through the main street with few clothes on. It was possible that this sort of public expiation was justified, but their appearance evoked more pity than disgust. I told all of our personnel to keep off the street and away from this demonstration, so that there would be no involvement in it. This was a French affair, which was not our business to condone or to criticize, although it seemed to me that there were other methods of punishment more effective and less degrading than this.[13]

The myth of the murderous and vengeful French lovers of German soldiers quickly gained currency among Allied troops. Rumors persistently circulated among American troops that young French women, left behind the lines by their German lovers, served as snipers picking off GIs from hiding places. Efforts by G-5 to prove these rumors true or false ran into only dead ends. Journalists latched on to the rumors and kept them alive because they made good copy. Edwin Hoyt recounted how GIs were held down by machine gun fire from the attic of a farmhouse outside of Saint-Laurent-sur-Mer, on the west end of Omaha Beach. The shooter was silenced with some hand grenades pitched through the window, and when a soldier "entered the house. Up in the attic they found the gun on its side, and the body of a 13-year-old French girl beside it." He also related that in the POW cages of the 2nd Division "there was a woman in a white beret, a French Nazi sympathizer who had been caught firing at American troops." British journalist Alan Moorehead wrote, "one correspondent reported blithely: 'Every French woman here [in Normandy] is a potential sniper. The French are against us.'" An American infantry captain in the 29th Division was certain that his company took sniper fire in utterly smashed Isigny on 7 or 8 June from "German men and French women." American journalist Charley Wertenbaker repeated stories of women snipers to Chester Hansen, claiming some were the German wives of officers and others were French mistresses of German soldiers. He claimed one threw grenades at him. Hansen was skeptical, the "general tendency is to disbelieve such stories—they occur in every war. . . . Stories of French women shooting our troops are largely fiction." Colonel Bruce of the OSS noted in his diary on 29 June, "Probably too there were German agents left behind [in Cherbourg]. In Carentan last night about fifteen men in civilian clothes were picked up who were supposedly sniping or directing artillery fire. They were reported to have been sheltered by women with whom they were living." It is noteworthy that Bruce was relating rumors he picked up in Cherbourg about Carentan but that Major John Maginnis's reports as CA officer in Carentan fail to mention such a momentous event. Had it occurred, surely Maginnis would have recorded it. Antonio J. Ruggiero, a Ranger in the 76th Infantry Division, related that his men met some French women in Brittany outside Brest: "They were friendly. They were mingling among us. They were bumming cigarettes and candy bars." The women came down to the camp one day, chatted amiably as one gave haircuts to the GIs, and then suddenly announced they had to leave. "They left, and it was maybe an hour after, all at once, the shells started to come in." Patrick O'Donnell, who quoted Ruggiero, concluded, "the Rangers realized, to their horror, that their new French 'friends' had tipped off the Germans to their location." Such stories about French women persisted and persist despite efforts to prove them true or false because many French women did indeed take German soldiers for lovers, and not always for money. However, evidence of actual French women firing on American soldiers, such as that above, is pretty thin, whereas evidence of French women taking German lovers is abundant.[14]

Some Franco-German liaisons were indeed affairs of the heart. An elementary school teacher in the tiny Norman village of Saint-Germain-du-Pert, near Isigny, was arrested shortly after D-Day because of her well-known liaison with a German NCO. As an elementary school teacher, she was also secretary to the mayor, who had no complaints about her until D-Day, when, as a French woman with a German lover, she became inconvenient. She had been trapped in an abusive marriage that had fallen apart by 1942, when she and her husband separated, and he left to work in Germany. She claimed that only one man in the village had been hostile to her despite her openly acknowledged affection for the German sergeant. When arrested and interrogated, she denied having any animosity against the British or any political thoughts at all; her attachment to the German soldier was entirely personal and had nothing to do with politics or admiration for Germany. Both the mayor and the police inspector who interviewed her called her "none-too smart." The police inspector warned her that she stood to lose not only her ability to teach in France, but her ability to live there unless she renounced her attachment to her German, which she refused to do; indeed, she insisted they intended to marry when they had the chance. She was taken away and put into police custody at least in part for her own safety, as one local man had threatened to hang her from her apple tree. Such relationships were not uncommon. German troops fathered an unknown number of children in France during the occupation, with estimates running between 50,000 and 200,000. Around 2,000 to 3,000 children were supposedly born to German fathers in the region around Rouen alone.[15]

THE REGIME OF THE FFI FILLS THE VOID

The speed at which Patton's tanks and infantry raced around Paris to the south and then departed to the east mystified and upset the French. German units and stragglers remained scattered throughout the region and were justifiably seen by the lightly armed, poorly trained, and hardly organized FFI as mortal dangers. The French *maquis* were bewildered that the Americans would leave them so exposed to enemy forces still lurking in the region. Nevertheless, many FFI units saw this as their opportunity and leapt into independent action to assume control of regions bypassed by the Americans. FFI units attempting to fight German soldiers by themselves, without Allied assistance, usually met with disastrous results. FFI staged numerous uprisings in the department of the Yonne and took over many small towns on the night of 6–7 June. None of the liberated towns had any German troops, so the risk seemed small; however, German soldiers showed up soon enough and the rebels took to the woods, leaving the inhabitants of the towns to fend for themselves. Events turned out poorly for FFI units that attacked a column of the Das Reich SS Division passing through the Yonne on 24 August. The clash left many FFI dead, and the SS shot up the town of Vézelay as they drove through, randomly throwing hand grenades at shops and houses. When the SS abandoned Troyes, they took up positions in Lusigny, to the east, and were quickly surrounded by FFI bands in the area's woods and marshes. The mayor of Lusigny set out to find American troops and begged them to come and save them from the SS. The American officers contacted by the mayor replied that they did not yet have sufficient forces to take on the Germans and, in any event, they had to press on and bypass the region. The FFI then tried to take on the SS by themselves, with predictable results: the FFI were easily repulsed, and 50 were captured and immediately shot dead in a field. The SS then set upon the town, looted it of anything of interest to the Germans, and massacred 14 civilians who took no part in the *maquis* attacks. American tanks arrived in Lusigny the next day, 28 August, after the SS had departed for their next victims. When the SS passed through Bar-sur-Aube, they stopped to ransack the town, steal anything with wheels, stock up on food and drink, and round up 20 hostages held against the peaceable behavior of the citizenry. No French were killed by the passing Germans. Although the SS troops dug in to defend the town against an expected American attack, they freed the hostages and quit the town before Americans arrived on the evening of 30 August. When American troops finally came to Auxerre to stay, the FFI (unhappily) turned over to them 180 "German soldiers" held as POWs, including 30 Russians captured at Saint-Florentin.[16]

When American tanks failed to appear to take over areas abandoned by the Germans, local FFI took command of the situation. After the Germans evacuated Auxerre, the administrative center of the Yonne, FFI walked into the town and immediately arrested several hundred people, detaining them in the jail, prison, lycée, barracks, and wherever space could be found. One merchant was beaten by a crowd and had an eye knocked out. Twelve civilians were subjected to drumhead justice and immediately executed in Quarré-les-Tombes, a village deep in the woods. By December, 60 accused were killed by local FTP acting outside the court system. "Justice" was also served to local women accused of consorting with Germans by shaving their heads in the central market square on liberation day, 24 August. More suffered the same ritual in the days that followed. In Laroche, women were not shaved, but were forced to serve meals to the FTP and sew their clothes. Some women were stripped of clothes and driven out of Sens. Women were shaved, beaten, or subjected to public humiliation in many towns and villages in the Yonne. The widely disseminated photos of French women having their heads shaved caused revulsion in much of France and the rituals of "popular justice" soon diminished, but they did not disappear. In the view of a police commander who survived the purges of 1944 but did not seemingly share the views of most FFI, "these [head shavings] had the effect of calming the nerves of the population over-excited at having regained their liberty and who cried for vengeance against all the humiliations they had endured during the German occupation and the bitterness that had accumulated." In such cases, sexual relations with the enemy often played little part in the ritual, even if the women (and sometimes men) were still called "prostitutes."[17]

In the wake of General Patton's tanks, some FFI units successfully liberated towns and regions. As the Germans began to disappear from Sens—east of Orléans—on 16 August, the police and gendarmes also left to join the *maquis* in the forests outside of town. The few remaining Germans did nothing to stop them. On the afternoon of 17 August, the police returned with bands of armed men to round up any Germans who remained in town. Fighting lasted until evening, when the surviving 115 Germans surrendered. Only five Germans had been killed, at the cost of 108 FFI killed in the fighting, including two police. The lopsided toll and prisoners illustrates the uneven match between the Wehrmacht and the FFI. When a horse-drawn German column passing through the Yonne from Poitiers on 22 August found French and Allied flags on the monument to the war dead in one town, they burned the local school and several nearby farms. This caught the attention of nearby FFI units, Jedburgh teams, and a small force of American infantry who closed in on the column and soon found themselves in an intense firefight. The Germans, believing themselves under attack by a much larger force, beat a hasty retreat from the area.[18]

The official account of an FFI group in Migennes is probably trustworthy. A small-scale reign of terror was unleashed in Migennes by the FFI under the command of "Camille," who, according to police, was a practicing Catholic known as M. Chanard and had also belonged before the war to the rightist Parti Social français. During the occupation, one of his daughters was engaged to marry a German officer. Despite that misalliance, he sat on the newly reconstituted Municipal Council of Migennes and on the local liberation committee. Camille organized an FFI "tribunal" for two Italian immigrant brothers, Guido and Guerino Gasparini, before a crowd of 200 in front of the city hall of Migennes. The older brother, Guido, was accused of serving as an informer for the Gestapo, while the younger, Guerino, was simply in the wrong place at the wrong time: he was hiding out at his brother's house after having run away from his Todt Organization unit and was guilty of nothing. The "trial" sentenced them to death, and Camille immediately shot them both dead before the crowd. The events occurred on 24 August, the day of liberation before legitimate authority had been reestablished in the region, when the FFI in Migennes arrested 70 other people, including 29 women, and shaved the heads of 16 of them; some were also beaten. Camille soon set about requisitioning cars from local bourgeois, trucks, tires, and much else from local merchants, and butter, livestock, and whatever he wanted from local farmers. Soon after, storekeepers in town started to receive letters saying it was going to cost them 50,000 francs to stay out of jail. It did not take long for his swagger to alienate much of the population, who became up in arms over his misdeeds. In the days that followed, the new authorities—who among the police were usually the same as the old authorities—wanted to classify the killing of the younger Gasparini brother as murder. The "Red Army" of nearby Saint-Florentin was likewise accused of extorting food and supplies from area farmers in order to keep their names off of lists of collaborators. Widespread brigandage was reported in some regions of the Yonne as FFI stole cars, money, and goods from stores. The mayor of Dixmont was smashed in the head with a rifle butt when he tried to stop a young FFI from shooting up a café and threatening its owner. Gendarmes soon arrived and took away the offender. In October, when authority was finally reestablished by the central government, one FFI captain was arrested for selling stolen cars.[19]

The new regimes imposed by the FFI and liberation committees were unwelcome to many French who had to live under their sway. With both German and Vichy officials gone from the region around Rennes, FFI took over administrative offices and began to pay themselves and disbursed payments for goods from government accounts at local banks. A French Army colonel in charge of government funds in liberated territory noted this with alarm and asked the commander of the new French military district to put a stop to it. Farmers who had to endure *maquis* predations during the occupation now had to adjust to having the same "bandits" as their new bosses after liberation. FFI around

Auxerre continued to requisition potatoes, vegetables, and other food directly from farmers in the countryside of Yonne, giving farmers unofficial requisition orders of no value. Ravitaillement Générale (General Supply) had assumed the responsibility of feeding the FFI and claimed to have access to all the food required by local FFI. The farmers stuck with worthless vouchers were unable to claim compensation. They were understandably upset, yet they also were not in any position to refuse food to the armed men who showed up at their doors. Furthermore, General Supply complained to FFI commanders in Auxerre that FFI took more food than they needed from farmers, provoking suspicions they were selling extra rations on the black market. The practice proved difficult to suppress, as the line between FFI and bandits was often difficult to discern. As French farmers famously profited from black market food sales during the war, they were widely believed to be sitting on piles of ill-gotten cash, which some FFI saw as ripe for confiscation. A farmer outside of Joigny complained to police that five armed men forcibly took eggs, cheese, five kilograms of sugar, and other supplies, as well as 25,000 francs in cash. This time, police discovered and arrested the culprits.[20]

THE GAULLIST PROVISIONAL GOVERNMENT
ASSERTS AUTHORITY OVER THE FFI

Triumphal liberations of towns and regions by the FFI, heavily dominated by socialists and communists, prompted concern among both Gaullists and the U.S. Army. Even though Civil Affairs had demonstrated its ability to work with leftist French groups, SHAEF was anxious to see the armed bands disarmed or firmly placed under the authority of the French Army. American authorities were especially eager to see the civilian authority of the police restored and police powers separated from military powers, as the specter of FFI armed control became real with liberation. Although the U.S. Army stayed out of local politics, officers were agitated by what they saw. SHAEF was alarmed about a pattern of actions taken by leftists to dominate all aspects of political activity. They maneuvered to control committees at all levels to take control of purges, political nominations, and appointments. Elected mayors and municipal councils were displaced and supplanted by FFI appointees, usually with loyalties to the PCF or the SFIO. Their political committees submitted lists of nominees loyal to their parties to Gaullists prefects, who mostly deferred to the liberation committees and accepted their nominees for offices. The liberation committees agitated for a single electoral list for upcoming municipal elections and wanted acceptable candidates to be chosen in open meetings by show of hands rather than secret ballot. There was really nothing SHAEF could do to alter this situation other than urge the Provisional Government of de Gaulle to establish control as quickly as possible. The Provisional Government needed no push from SHAEF to undermine the liberation committees.[21]

Certainly not all FFI were crooks or their regimes arbitrary and vengeful. Placed in charge of security, many FFI took their responsibilities seriously and handled them fairly. French police, American soldiers, and FFI usually worked together cooperatively to enforce law and order. Americans were not supposed to arrest French citizens but sometimes did with the cooperation of French authorities, especially in the early days of liberation. French civilians accused of stealing gasoline, tobacco, arms, and food were detained in Auxerre by American soldiers, who then accompanied a French police officer to the town jail to turn them over to French authorities. American soldiers also showed up at the jail in the company of FFI holding civilians for unspecified crimes. One of those detained by the FFI was an American civilian, whose crime was not reported. FFI in the Ardennes continued to hunt German stragglers for weeks after the Americans arrived and turned them over to Major Maginnis in Charleville, who had greater difficulty getting American MPs take them off his hands than he had convincing the FFI to surrender them to the U.S. Army.[22]

In mid-September, French Minister of War André Diethelm announced that all FFI would be absorbed into the French Army and given equal treatment as regular troops. He promised that FFI could serve together in their own units under their own commanders "to the extent possible." They would be provided with Army uniforms, but could wear distinctive patches or markings to showcase their FFI unit. General de Gaulle, of course, would never have tolerated separate Communist units serving under Communist leaders within the Army, so all Milices patriotiques units were ordered to be integrated with departmental FFI. In the Aube, the Communist-dominated FTP was ordered disbanded and absorbed into the FFI as early as 29 August; wearing the FTP armband was forbidden by order of the newly appointed prefect. De Gaulle believed—not without reason—that French Communists intended to grab as much power as possible everywhere possible as quickly as possible and that once established they would be difficult to dislodge. De Gaulle and Diethelm were more interested in demobilizing and thus neutralizing the FFI than in actually enlisting their services. That order, however, was easier to issue than implement. In the Ardennes, all FFI were supposedly enlisted into the French Army, but in the eyes of Major Maginnis and the prefect nothing had changed. While most FFI units in the Ardennes were willing to be absorbed into the French Army, the local FTP resisted and refused to give up the barracks they had occupied. In late October, the district French military commander with the assistance of cooperative FFI convinced the FTP to give up their barracks and enroll in the Army. By the fall of 1944, about 400,000 had flocked to the FFI bands, roughly half of whom actually possessed weapons, and in much of the country they constituted the forces of "order," such as it was. Bands of armed FFI racing around Paris in commandeered trucks and cars convinced de Gaulle that they had to be removed from the scene lest they challenge his hold on power. De Gaulle's newly appointed republican commissioner in Lille, Françis-Louis Closon, was equally alarmed by what he found in the Nord, an industrial region heavily influenced by the Communist Party. Closon found that the PCF was just as interested in stopping FFI brigandage and drumhead justice as the new commissioner. He called a meeting of all FFI and FTP leaders at his office in Lille and demanded that the reign of terror unleashed by ill-disciplined FFI must come to an end, and it did.[23]

De Gaulle wanted the gendarmes to be restored to authority everywhere in France, but especially in Paris, and requested from SHAEF arms and uniforms for 74,000 police and gendarmes to replace the FFI. In October, the French requested from the Americans 320 machine guns, 2,300 light machine guns, 20,500 submachine guns, 14,000 carbines, and 78,000 pistols, as well as 100 million rounds of ammunition for French police and gendarmes. They also asked for police cars, jeeps, trucks, ambulances, radios, bicycles, motorcycles, and two Piper airplanes to keep the police mobile. As for the FFI, the best way to curb them was to draft them into the military, but that, too, required weapons, uniforms, and vehicles—all of which would have to be supplied by the Americans. Eisenhower agreed to Koenig's request that two divisions should be formed of FFI as soon as possible and supplied by the Americans. Units in Brittany were equipped with captured German weapons and put to work mopping up remaining German stragglers and holdouts there.[24]

French civilians experienced the Allied breakout with surprise and uncertainty. In many locales American soldiers arrived unannounced and unexpected, and were greeted with joy. People in other locales awaited their arrival impatiently, especially if German troops were still present, as in Troyes. But also, as in Troyes, initial joy turned to confusion and anxiety as the Americans rushed on to the next town, leaving the civilians in the hands of the local FFI. Often the FFI were well known locals and the new regime proved benign, but not always. For the most part, the chaos and anarchy of the German retreat and the American arrival proved fleeting. In the regions discussed in this work, the interval between the overthrow of the Nazi regime and the establishment of the GPRF was usually brief—a few days, a week at the most. Anxiety about German stragglers and the depredations of undisciplined FFI was real but usually proved without basis. The FFI turned out to be mostly young patriots performing what they believed was their patriotic duty. They did their best when they did not try to be too ambitious and limited their activities to providing intelligence to Allied troops and standing watch in newly liberated towns and villages.

9

LORRAINE AND ALSACE

When George Patton's Third Army reached eastern France, they received the same sort of rapturous welcome meted out to liberating GIs throughout northern France. However, when the front stalled and the war bogged down to artillery duels in the fall of 1944, the French who had to endure the slow slogging American advance became sullen. Impatience at the sluggish American advance that inflicted great physical damage and many civilian casualties spread from eastern France to much of the country. Attitudes of many French evolved in sometimes subtle, and often obtrusive, ways. Enthusiasm for their liberators dimmed throughout France, but it diminished the most perceptively in Lorraine. Unique characteristics of Lorraine that separated it from the rest of France made it a special case for the GIs fighting there. A German dialect spoken by many inhabitants of Lorraine convinced some GIs they were already in enemy territory, and they treated civilians accordingly. Many of the GIs who roughly handled Lorrainers had been fighting continuously since landing on the Normandy beaches and were weary of the war. Having witnessed scenes of horrific brutality for months no doubt hardened and coarsened some GIs, making it easier to behave toward French civilians caught in their advance with nonchalant abusiveness. By the time American soldiers pushed over the border into Germany, many had been fighting in France for seven months and were hardened by the fight. Regardless of coarsened attitudes among many GIs, they could still show great compassion toward French civilians caught in the final German offensive in France, Northwind, and a higher regard for their safety than was shown by those civilians' own Provisional Government in Paris.

By 23 August, even before General Leclerc's tanks and armored cars slipped into Paris, George Patton's tanks had started to run out of gasoline. Some fuel was airlifted in the last week of August to keep his columns rolling east, but when those planes were diverted for a paratroop drop on the Belgian border that never happened, the gas ran low and then out. Patton's forward patrols reached the Moselle River by 1 September, and the next day they ran out of gas. General Eisenhower had made the crucial decision to allocate the meager available supplies to Allied armies pushing into Belgium, allowing General Patton's Third Army to lose its forward momentum just as it reached the ancient capital of Lorraine, Nancy. This permitted the retreating German armies to stop, regroup, and mount a defense in Lorraine, something they had been unable to do in the Orléanais, Champagne, or Burgundy. German resistance stiffened only because the American pause allowed it. That Patton's tanks stalled almost at the gateway to Germany was really just a coincidence. The borders of Germany had been redrawn by Hitler in 1940 to include Alsace and most of Lorraine (Elssas and Lothengrin), forcing a special and unwanted status on the two French provinces. From 1940, three French departments were detached from France and their populations then became citizens of Germany "*malgré nous*" (against our will).

The inhabitants of Alsace-Lorraine had been subjects of the German emperor from 1871 to 1918 and, thus, many of the older residents had long experience with being subject to German rule. Many French in Alsace and Lorraine did indeed speak a German dialect and could readily read and understand German, making the linguistic transition less than onerous. However, several hundred thousand residents in 1940 spoke only French, which in the summer of 1940 was banned in public except by special permission. Eventually a majority of the French-speaking and Jewish populations of the annexed areas were expelled to the unoccupied zone of France. While French Jews in Alsace-Lorraine were initially spared the sort of murderous "special treatment" meted out in Poland, the Germans expelled 3,000 Jews from Alsace as early as July 1940. By the end of the year the number had surpassed 100,000. When Alsace and Lorraine were formally reannexed to Germany in August 1940, German laws became operational, including laws regulating Jews. French teenagers were at first encouraged and eventually forced to enroll in the Hitler Youth for boys and German Maidens for girls. In August 1942 conscription into the German Army was extended to all young men in the annexed departments, herding 130,000 former French citizens into German uniforms. And therein lay an unexpected irritant in Franco-American relations: former Frenchmen wearing German uniforms were seen by many French—especially those in the eastern provinces—as French, while the same soldiers were seen by Americans as German and, thus, the enemy. Because of this, the friendly attitude of many eastern French toward young men in German uniforms angered GIs, who could not understand how French could protect members of the Wehrmacht, hiding them from American patrols searching for German stragglers and rearguard troops left behind to ambush GIs. The French propensity to give Lorrainer deserters civilian clothes and take them into their homes made GIs suspicious of all young men encountered in the eastern departments and, soon after, all residents of Alsace and Lorraine.[1]

Among the 130,000 Alsatians and Lorrainers who served in the German military during the war, the story of Ernest Bartel from Strasbourg illustrates the predicament that these men faced. Before the war he was employed by the municipality in a chemical lab. Called to the colors in 1939, he served in the French Army and was captured in Holland in May 1940. At first he was held in a regular POW camp with other French prisoners, but on 1 September all *Volksgenossen* POWs—those from Alsace and Lorraine—were segregated into separate camps. On 1 October they were released. Bartel returned to Strasbourg—once again *Strassburg*—where he again worked for the city. After Hitler's debacle at Stalingrad, the Nazi government adopted a policy of "total war" and began systematic conscription of *Volksgenossen*. In April 1943, Bartel was drafted into the Wehrmacht, sent to a training camp, and ultimately stationed in Denmark with 120 other Alsatians. In September he and the other Alsatians were reassigned to purely German units fighting in Russia, with no more than three Alsatians per company. Alsatians within the German Army were subjected to considerable propaganda and indoctrination in an effort to convince them they were truly German. Otherwise they were treated just like any other German soldier. That fall, Bartel was struck with appendicitis, which landed him in a hospital in Odessa until spring. He was fortunate, because that winter most of his division was wiped out: only six men from his company returned to Germany. In May 1944 he was assigned to a reserve regiment in upper Normandy (east of the Seine River) and took no part in the fighting after D-Day until early August, when his unit was finally sent into action. Bartel exploited a blown tire on the truck transporting him to the front to separate himself from his unit and disappear in the department of the Eure. There he met a sympathetic Frenchman, M. Lefevre, who gave him civilian clothes and sheltered him in the tiny burg of Les Baux-de-Breteuil until the American Third Army overran the town. Both Bartel and M. Lefevre were probably fortunate that counter intelligence

(CIC) found him in the Eure and not in eastern France, or the reaction of his captors would likely have been different. In Normandy, Bartel would likely still have been considered by Americans as a Frenchman in France; that might also have been the case in Lorraine, but often was not. An Alsatian like Bartel who had deserted the German Army in Normandy and joined an FFI group still had to be interrogated by CIC officers to decide if he should be treated as a POW or a French soldier.[2]

The French government of Charles de Gaulle also harbored doubts about French who had served in the German Army. By late 1944, a significant number of French citizens serving in the German military had been taken prisoner by Allied soldiers in Italy, Russia, or the Balkans. Only a small number were repatriated to France: Stalin shipped 1,500 Frenchmen captured by the Red Army to Algeria in August 1944, but he never repeated that gesture of goodwill. Others managed to escape the German Army and make their way to Switzerland. By the fall of 1944, Switzerland—seeing more clearly which way the winds of war were blowing—allowed them to continue to France. The French government insisted that all French citizens captured as POWs by Allied armies be handed over to France, which the Americans agreed to do. In October 1944, the Americans relinquished around 1,200 Alsatians and Lorrainers taken as POWs. All such men were sent by the French to camps and interrogated about, among other things, their "national point of view." Did they consider themselves French? If they were of military age, they were subject to conscription into the French Army. Even French volunteers for German military service were welcomed into the French Army if they pledged allegiance to France. In 1944, the French Army did not have any spare uniforms for ex-members of the Wehrmacht, who continued to languish in French camps in their German uniforms. Officials of the new government fretted a good deal about what to do with any former German soldiers who refused to fight for France. Only a handful of such men ever came to the authorities' attention—about 50 captured in Italy in 1945, but the source is silent about whether they were from Alsace-Lorraine or were volunteers for the SS from elsewhere in France.[3]

French from the eastern provinces did not react uniformly toward their new status as "Germans." On one extreme there was a high degree of collaboration with the Germans and some even embraced the Nazi cause enthusiastically. Others among the men drafted into the German military may have been hesitant fighters without belief in the Nazi cause, but they also exhibited a high degree of *attentisme*—waiting to see which side won the war. By the time Bartel deserted it was obvious to him that Germany had lost the war, even though as late as September 1944 the majority of his German comrades still believed firmly in ultimate German victory. Numerous French related instances of Alsatian soldiers serving in the Wehrmacht acting with sympathy toward French civilians when the opportunity arose. When the SS Das Reich Division carried out savage reprisals in Dordogne for attacks by FFI, a woman in Mussidan—near Périgueux—reported that she had been set free by a "German soldier with a French accent," while 48 other hostages were shot. According to a French witness, when German troops burned the village of Couvonges, near Bar-le-Duc, on 29 August, a self-identified Alsatian in German uniform "tried to save as many people as he could." That was not always the case. An Italian evader of the Todt Organization in Normandy testified that French guards at a discipline camp for malcontents outside Cherbourg were exceptionally cruel even to French detainees. One officer "with an Alsatian accent" boasted he had formerly been an officer in the French Army, and another guard forced a French inmate to eat his own excrement.[4]

While some Alsatians and Lorrainers shed their French identity and others hedged their bets, many retained their loyalty to France and the Allied cause. Many Lorrainers eagerly helped their American allies, despite the damage done and lives lost to Allied bombers. During the summer of 1944, an American bomber crashed in Germany close to the French border in Lorraine. Two surviving aviators, Daniel Dunbar and Benjamin Rabier, walked for days to find the French border and were discovered in the woods by Mme. Bultez, a widow, and her daughter, who took them home and fed them potatoes, some vegetables, and bread. The two women sheltered them for four days until they could be turned over to local *maquis*, who took them away. Even an American fighter pilot who died when his plane crashed near the Belgian border in early September received good treatment. His body was found by a local carpenter and a teacher, who took his papers and hid them until the Americans arrived. They also claimed his body from the police, the carpenter made him a casket, and the two men paid for his funeral in the local cemetery despite protests from German authorities. The widow Gerardin found a stranded GI in Armaucourt on 17 September and took him into her home until she could turn him over to an American patrol five days later. Paul Druaux, one of the *maquis* who received downed American fliers in Aboncourt, south of Nancy, took in an American pilot from Lake Grove, Oregon, and another from Menosha, Wisconsin, gave them food and civilian clothes, and arranged for them to make their way to Switzerland. He took in other Allied fliers, some of whom were wounded, and cared for them until they, too, could be quietly slipped to safer refuge. The Germans caught up with Druaux in August 1944 and sent him to Dachau, which he survived until liberated in May 1945. These sort of incidents were replicated hundreds of times across eastern France before the liberation, despite the great dangers faced by the Frenchmen and women who helped downed Allied airmen.[5]

When American soldiers finally arrived in September, the French population remained very friendly and glad to see the Americans. Edwin Hoyt recalled approaching the Belgian border after Reims in early September: "we were completely surrounded in the village [Touligny] street by a cheering crowd and I was thoroughly kissed by about 80 women whose ages ranged from 1 to 80. Lots of them were between 16 and 20 though. All the women were on my side of the jeep and all the men were on the driver's side. He got to shake hands. The mayor's wife brought out the calvados and we both had stiff jolts. When I told them in my broken French that there would be *beaucoup de soldats* there tonight, all the girls cheered. Someone is going to have a good time tonight." It would seem the GIs were still happy to meet the French as well. The French helped out if they could, and even if they performed only small favors, the acts were symbolically significant. When an Engineer Corps truck broke down and became stranded on a lonely country road, a local family brought coffee out to the soldiers trying to fix it. One night, Private First Class Richard Courtney was invited to spend the night in a French farmhouse with a family east of Nancy; a young woman of the house served the GIs hot milk. In Zarbeling—just a few miles from Haboudange—Courtney and his buddies were able to heat their rations on the stove of a Frenchman in his warm house.[6]

In Lorraine, American soldiers benefitted from the same help from FFI that they had found elsewhere in France. Americans under General Edmund Sebree liberated the ancient capital of Lorraine, Nancy, from the Germans without crushing it with aerial and artillery bombardments thanks to close coordination with local FFI forces. The Germans had decided that Patton's sweep to the east was unstoppable and prepared to abandon Nancy as early as 1 September. They detonated a large ammunition dump (in a boys' school attached to a girls' school) in the center of suburban Frouard without consideration for the

French population living there, leveling the city hall, inflicting much damage on the town, and injuring six residents. The Germans attempted to sabotage the canal locks in and around Nancy and sank all the barges they found in the canal. FFI pointed out to the Americans where major German military concentrations were in the forests to the west of Nancy, asking that the Americans bomb the forest rather than the town. The Germans sheltered there were thus targeted and forced to withdraw, leaving the wooded heights overlooking the town to American tanks. Nancy would have been difficult to defend from an American attack, but a coup by FFI on the morning of 15 September made the attack mostly unnecessary. Organized French resistance seized strategic locations within the city and handed the town over to General Sebree by 11 A.M., though pockets of German resistance still had to be crushed in street fighting. Before noon, Mayor Schmitt was ousted from his office and a replacement was appointed by Commissioner of the Republic Paul-André Chailley-Bert. General celebrations erupted all over the city before the last German soldier had even pulled out, though some die-hards remained to snipe at the Americans and French for the remainder of the day, until mopping up operations could remove them. Helpful Frenchmen showed the FFI where the retreating Germans had hidden mines and booby-trapped buildings. The FFI passed that information along to General Sebree's men. The U.S. Army's introduction to Lorraine after the long, hard drive from Normandy went very well, and the assistance of the French followed the pattern established elsewhere in France.[7]

The Third Army counted on the coordinated action of Allied commandos and FFI to seize crossings on the Moselle to keep the offensive moving forward. As was so often the case in war, things did not go as planned. The insertion of two Jedburgh teams south of Nancy succeeded in rallying and arming hundreds of FFI but failed to alter the military situation as planned. A group of 10 Canadian SAS troops dropped with arms and three jeeps turned into disaster when the team ran into German troops and was entirely wiped out. An American-led team linked up with a *maquis* group with over 500 men and hoped to secure intact bridges over the Moselle for General Patton's tanks. Their carefully planned raid seized three bridges from the Germans, but Patton's soldiers failed to arrive in time to take the hand-over. Patton's tanks ran out of gas before they reached the river, and the Jedburgh team and their FFI were forced to beat a hasty retreat in the face of a German counterattack on the village of Bayon. FFI were rarely able to hold territory against German counterattacks without assistance from Allied units, and the case south of Nancy was no exception. Another Jedburgh team dropped into the same region of the Meurthe-et-Moselle only a few days later was unable to seize the bridges over the Moselle and accidently skirmished with a Third Army patrol scouting German positions. With the bridges still under German control and the Third Army arriving in force by mid-September, the Jedburghs dropped into Lorraine in September had little role to play. Some of the OSS officers were dispatched to Verdun to take command of FFI being converted into conventional Army units—a task soon enough handed off to the French. While irregular FFI units provided the same valuable intelligence and guidance assistance to the Third Army in Lorraine as *maquis* provided in western France, they failed to achieve their assigned tasks when teamed up with Jedburghs. Planned drops of arms and supplies to FFI faced confusion as fast-moving armies made plans obsolete before they could be implemented.[8]

With Nancy liberated, General Patton's troops crept forward town by town and village by village on the eastern banks of the Moselle beyond Nancy. The behavior of American soldiers changed radically once they crossed into Germany, but the turn started in eastern France. As they advanced toward the 1939 German border, American authorities received a stream of complaints from French citizens about mistreatment at the hands of GIs encountering German-speaking French. As GIs entered villages and towns that looked more German and whose inhabitants spoke a German dialect, GIs began to feel as if they were no longer in France, but in Germany. Americans had already encountered Frenchmen from the eastern provinces who had deserted the German military and been sheltered by French civilians and given civilian clothing, because the French viewed such deserters as "French" and not German. This may have confused some GIs, but the French initially helping the deserters were clearly French in the GIs' eyes, even if the deserters were suspect. When such incidents increased in Lorraine, it convinced many GIs that these French civilians were pro-German, and the American soldiers began to routinely search civilians in this part of France in an effort to find German deserters dressed as civilians and mingling among them. When GIs entered the village of Haboudange, east of Nancy, they encountered four German deserters dressed in civilian clothing sheltered by the villagers. These men, immediately taken as POWs, were almost certainly Alsatians or Lorrainers sheltered by the local population as "French." One Frenchman in Haboudange expressed surprise at being treated as enemies by Americans and told the sergeant, "we are not Germans, we are Frenchmen." As the 4th Infantry Division approached Luxembourg, they encountered a suspiciously large number of civilians on the roads without papers. CIC (Counter Intelligence) kept busy rounding up and screening them all. Many claimed to be Polish—conscripted workers imported to fill jobs in France—but CIC had difficulty determining who was legitimate and who might be a German straggler. According to Private First Class Richard Courtney, the inhabitants of Rodalbe, east of Nancy, proved to be hostile to the Americans: when a German counterattack filled the village with German troops, locals pointed out to the Germans where GIs were hiding in cellars. It is hard to say who "the locals" might have been; possibly this village had been colonized by ethnic Germans when annexed to Germany. And not all Lorrainers were unhappy about annexation to the Reich. Or perhaps the villagers just feared for their lives if they failed to cooperate with the Germans.[9]

As more German soldiers began to doubt Germany's ultimate victory, more decided to surrender to the Allies. That was a hazardous enterprise because if caught by their own officers they faced certain summary execution. When U.S. troops entered Haguenau—north of Strasbourg—in mid-December, they found 300 Germans dressed in civilian clothes so that they could desert the Wehrmacht and surrender. Alsatians in the German Army went to great lengths to desert to the Allies: one soldier supposedly walled himself up in a basement to elude detection and spread black pepper around the floor to throw off the dogs. These deserters, usually Alsatian or Lorrainer draftees, were viewed sympathetically by the local population. It would seem highly unlikely that any of them would have tried to pass themselves off as French civilians in order to carry out guerrilla operations behind the lines; nevertheless, the U.S. Army was obliged to treat them as enemy soldiers and intern them like any other POW. The prefect in Metz tried to convince the Americans that French deserters from the Wehrmacht should not be treated as POWs at all, but seen as the valuable resources that they were: they had valuable intelligence about the German Army to share with the Allies and the Americans should use it. Moreover, he pointed out that the soldiers put themselves in great personal danger by deserting; if recaptured they would be hanged. He did report to his superiors in Paris that he was allowed to visit the French POWs, who were held separately from other POWs, and their conditions appeared to be good; they were allowed to move about freely within villages. Regardless, that the local French population would view these Wehrmacht deserters sympathetically reflected badly on them in the eyes of GIs.[10]

Evidence suggests that the casual vandalism and theft that soldiers inflict on any civilian population unlucky enough to be caught in the path of warring armies, already seen in Normandy, did indeed increase and worsen when American soldiers settled into Lorraine. The people complained that GIs abused houses that they had requisitioned for temporary quarters, using anything that burned as fuel to heat them. They stole vast quantities of wood from public and private forests, which American soldiers used as a good source of fuel to cook, heat water, and stay warm. The French Forest Service protested repeatedly, and the republican commissioner complained, with no evident impact, that this took wood away from villagers who relied on it to stay alive in the winter. GIs continued to harvest wood. They vandalized even properly requisitioned houses, factories, and commercial buildings; they cannibalized machinery, thus ruining industrial equipment that could have been repaired and put to good use. This ill-treatment was attributed by both French and American authorities who investigated it exclusively to individual GIs and not to orders from commanders of troops. It did not reflect Army policy and, thus, represented the nature of Franco-American relations almost from the landings in North Africa: American policy was to treat the French with benevolence, but some GIs contravened the policy and behaved cavalierly toward the French populace and their property. Most Franco-American friction was caused by GIs themselves, the enlisted men who would rather have been elsewhere, spoke no French, and endured weeks of mind-numbing boredom and moments of absolute terror.[11]

The stresses of military life in wartime encouraged soldiers to find relief and solace in bottles, which frequently only added to their problems. Four GIs knocked on the door of a French policeman, M. Rudelli, early in the afternoon in late September and asked to search the house for German soldiers in Heillecourt, a suburb of Nancy. They appeared to be drunk, but having nothing to hide, Rudelli allowed them to search his house. Things took a bad turn when the policeman heard his wife screaming in another room and accused the GIs of sexual assault. Rudelli demanded they leave, which they did—with his revolver and several bottles of wine. They took the wine to the next house and demanded the two women living there drink the wine with them. When pressed to have sex, the women yelled for help and Officer Rudelli came to their assistance. He demanded that the GIs return his pistol, pay for the wine, and then get out, all of which they did. When discussing the incident with neighbors later, a couple said they had had some of the same GIs over for dinner a few nights before and they had been pleasant and polite. The assembled neighbors also concluded that the GIs had started house-to-house searches that morning and each of the residents had insisted the soldiers stay a bit and have a drink of wine or eau-de-vie. After seven such searches the four GIs were stinking drunk by noon and their comportment declined with their sobriety. They were not bad young men, it was drink which had done them in. This incident, while probably not typical, nevertheless stands in for interactions between American GIs and French civilians. The Americans, arriving with good intentions and a bad job—searching people's houses—were met by the French with good will and hospitality. However, the soldiers were bored, undoubtedly spoke no French, and were easily induced to drink too much. When alcohol was added to the awkward circumstances, dealings between civilians and armed men were not likely to go smoothly.[12]

When their principal task was to fight Germans, stay alive, and stay as comfortable as possible under conditions that did not lend themselves to comfort, foreign civilians with problems of their own were often just annoying and unwanted distractions to the Americans. German deserters dressed in civilian clothes and hiding amid French civilians in the small villages of Lorraine added an irritating complication. The gulf of misunderstanding that separated enlisted soldiers from French civilians to some extent also divided GIs from their own superior officers. Republican Commissioner Chailley-Bert in Nancy underscored this point to Raymond Haas-Picard—in charge of relations with the Allies: "we have excellent relations with American *chefs* but less good relations with sub-officers, who lack understanding of our needs and situation. The indiscipline of the troops is shocking and a remarkable contrast to the American soldiers we had known in 1918. There are often drunken attacks upon civilians and much pillaging. The mayor of Contrexéville was attacked and had his arm broken. The authors of these attacks are never identified. . . . Our relations with Civil Affairs are very good and correct, but they have no influence over the troops and can solve no problems. I have to go directly to General Patton to get anything done." Perhaps so, yet dealing with General Patton was more frustrating for the French than with other American generals. Problems between the French and the Third Army were greater than in areas under other commanders. It is possible that units under Patton's command followed the example of their leader and paid less heed to the concerns of civilians in their areas.[13]

As the front stalled just east of Nancy and before the ancient fortress-city of

Metz, French citizens who had been overjoyed to greet the liberators became discouraged. While the French viewed the damage and civilian casualties inflicted by the fierce fighting that had raged briefly in the region as the unfortunate price of freedom, their acceptance began to devolve into bitterness when they saw the advance stop and the fighting transform into long-range artillery duels. People saw American bombers fly overhead and heard their bombs discharge in the distance, but the soldiers remained loitering in their towns and villages with no apparent intention of attacking. The American artillery banged away at the enemy, but the infantry still dawdled behind the front, smoking endless packs of cigarettes and chewing gum nonstop. Depressed by the shelling and cut off from normal services, people despaired and began to leave—if they could. Pont-à-Mousson filled up with refugees from surrounding villages; many of the evacuees had had no time to grab anything from their homes, so they sheltered in the industrial town with nothing of their own. Those who received permission to return home to retrieve some of their possessions were shocked to discover their towns completely pillaged "by the Americans." Food became scarce as civilian supplies stopped arriving from the rear. Army rules forbade civilians to use the roads, even with carts and horses. Late October was potato harvesting season and farmers complained that they could not reach their fields or move their crops even if they could harvest them. The people stranded in villages expected the Americans to share food, especially as it was obvious to all that they had plenty. French children loitered around the Army kitchens hoping for scraps, which they usually received, as GIs often took pity on children. Stories circulated that GIs would trade food for wine or brandy, fostering an unfavorable impression of the liberators. French officials reported that opinion remained pro-American, but predicted that would change if the American troops did not advance and stayed as an oppressive presence much longer.[14]

Soldiers of the 35th Infantry Division continued their slow advance against stiff German opposition in Lorraine east of Nancy in early November. When troops reached the small village of Haboudange, northeast of Nancy, on the morning of 13 November, about 100 German soldiers still occupied the town but quickly thought better of their situation and pulled out. The people of the village, along with a good number of evacuees from other towns and villages, huddled in available basements to shelter from the expected fighting. The local chateau provided the largest cellar and sheltered about 35 people, who spent two days there as American tanks approached the area. Before the Germans evacuated the town, a Wehrmacht captain searched for any remaining German soldiers and somehow managed to miss around 40 who were hiding among the French because they wanted to surrender. When the inhabitants heard American tanks and voices, one man emerged from the cellar with a white flag. GIs searching the village told him to go back into the basement as the town was not yet clear of Germans. About 20 minutes later, when the 35 French civilians were told to come out, about 10 German deserters emerged with them. The American battalion commander sent a message that CIC and Civil Affairs should send officers to Haboudange as there were civilians with German deserters among them (counter intelligence routinely interviewed all POWs). The village also harbored numerous foreigners—including at least one Italian—who had become mixed in with the local people. Because the German deserters wore civilian clothing, all men were segregated from the women of the village and marched with their hands up into a stable to be searched and interrogated, so civilians could be separated from deserters. However, no CIC officer arrived to undertake this task and no GI spoke either French or German, rendering the effort somewhere between difficult and impossible.[15]

The battalion commander was concerned about taking the next village and moved most of his troops out of Haboudange that afternoon. He left his intelligence officer—a sergeant—in charge of the civilians with orders to separate local inhabitants from the rest and find all the Germans. He found an American corporal who spoke some German to act as translator. Although one Frenchman spoke some English, German became the lingua franca of the interaction, setting the tone for the contact. As the residents spoke German, they were treated as Germans by the GIs. The men were forced to remain in the stables for two hours waiting for CIC to show up; in the meantime, GIs held them under guard and forced everyone to empty their pockets. One Frenchman said, "they were very severe and very rough with us." All papers were thrown on the ground by the GIs who were supposed to use them as a means to separate Germans from the locals, but no GI could read them. A Frenchman showed his military discharge papers to a GI, who had no clue what he was looking at. Nevertheless, the Americans found 35 German soldiers and four more the next day. In all probability, the German deserters made little effort to hide themselves from the GIs, as their purpose was to surrender. The civilians were then sent back into different cellars for their protection because German shells still occasionally whistled overhead. Women were allowed to go to their houses for bedding, food, and supplies; men were allowed to leave one at a time the next day to tend to the cows bellowing in the fields. Some complained they had no food for two days. When one asked why they were being treated this way, a GI replied, "you are all Germans." Until a Civil Affairs officer arrived on the afternoon of the 15th, the men were treated as POWs. One of the men, a resident of Chateau Salins evacuated by the Germans to Haboudange, said that when Chateau Salins was first liberated by the Americans in mid-October, the GIs were very friendly. But when the Germans counterattacked and retook the town, the Americans pulled out and left the civilians behind to face the Germans, shocking the abandoned civilians.[16]

Some French later complained they had been robbed by GIs. One French civilian approached an American staff sergeant and complained that he had just been robbed by a medical corpsman. When the sergeant convinced the corpsman to give the man back his watch and some money he had taken, another civilian said the corpsman had stolen his watch, too. The medic gave that man a watch as well. When questioned by the sergeant about why he had taken money and watches from the French, the corpsman said, "I thought they were all Heinies." Some French also claimed their houses had been ransacked by the Americans and the contents of women's purses (left in the cellars when their owners had been ordered out by the Americans) had been stolen. One company commander called the French "uncooperative" because they complained. One thing they complained about was that the guards keeping them sequestered were drinking looted eau-de-vie and were obviously drunk. When one man went to his house from a cellar to get food, he discovered that his house had been plundered and that GIs had used his dining room as a toilet. "They believed they were in Germany," the man related. Although not condoned by the U.S. Army, such behavior was seen as a not unnatural reaction to being in the home of the enemy. One man wrote a letter protesting GI conduct and demanded, "General Eisenhower has stated, 'We will enter Germany as victors, not as oppressors.' How does it happen that his army behaves worse in France than it has promised to do in Germany? Why do we see German prisoners treated with humanity, drinking wine, obtaining milk, while the French, who find themselves in the path of American troops, are despoiled of all they possess, and abandoned without food or clothes on the roads of their country with the sole solace of the address of some information bureau?" In fact, GIs were later accused of widespread theft, looting, and vandalism in Germany.[17]

A nearby village, Achain, experienced much the same sort of treatment at the hands of GIs. The fighting for Achain had lasted for 10 grueling hours before the Germans were driven out, leaving behind scores of dead and 150 soldiers taken as prisoners. The battle cost the Americans 106 casualties. When GIs took the town, they found 35 people sheltering in the local church. As in Haboudange, some were local villagers, some were French dislocated from elsewhere, and some were foreigners—in this case, Poles. The civilians were held in the church without food or proper clothing (it was snowing outside) for 18 hours (some said more than 24 hours) and were not allowed to go to the toilet. Although none claimed to have been hurt by the GIs, they, too, complained about being treated as if they were enemy POWs. According to the villagers, while they were confined in the church, GIs plundered the town, stealing silverware, watches, and all the cash they could find. The French men were searched in the church, as in Haboudange, and one reported that he had 12,000 francs taken from him. People protested that their belongings had been rummaged through and valuables stolen. A woman objected that while they were held in custody her little grocery store had been pillaged and looted. Marcel Bour complained that thousands of marks and francs had vanished from his suitcase and that his house had also been pillaged and valuables stolen.[18]

The American commanding colonel later claimed the people were kept in the church for their own protection as there was still fighting and German shelling, and that when his troops left early the next morning the people were still in the church. He also claimed that the villagers were given K-rations, allowed to fetch bedding and clothes, and no one was searched. In addition, his intelligence officer—Sergeant Andrechak—found a German NCO hiding among the civilians. This repeats on a smaller scale the experience in Haboudange: German deserters were found hiding among French civilians, who probably shielded them. This also most likely explains searching the men in the church and an apparent indifference to their comfort—despite claims to the contrary by the American colonel, who, like the (different) American colonel in Haboudange, had more pressing military matters to worry about. That GIs took the village only after 10 hours of fighting and 106 casualties probably put the soldiers in a less-than-charitable mood, affecting their treatment of the villagers once freed from their shelters. An American captain told a Frenchman who complained about the thievery that "the American Army is not wholly made up of honest men." That was no doubt true, yet their sour moods and the suspicious attitudes of many GIs toward Lorrainers might have made looting easier on some consciences. Achain was also on the front line; houses, stores, barns, and farmers' fields were all seen as ripe and available resources to be exploited by soldiers trying to stay alive under enemy fire. The ransacking of the French lady's store would not have been unusual on the front line, where soldiers looked after themselves as best they could. Since American soldiers left Normandy, there had practically been no front line, so most French between Normandy and Lorraine had been spared such misadventures.[19]

In December, complaints about American soldiers poured into Republican Commissioner Chailley-Bert's office in Nancy. Chailley-Bert in turn alerted Raymond Haas-Picard, appointed by de Gaulle to handle Interior Ministry relations with the Allies, that American soldiers were conducting themselves very badly in the department of the Moselle, in eastern Lorraine and annexed by Hitler to Germany. Chailley-Bert related reports from French police intelligence that American soldiers behaved as if they were in enemy territory and called everyone "boche." They pillaged the vacant homes of French people expelled by the Nazis or forcibly taken to the Reich, and moved in themselves without the benefit of requisition orders. Many such homes had previously been occupied by Germans, and the Americans, according to Chailley-Bert, saw this as an excuse to ransack the places. When systematically searching villages, GIs banged on peoples' doors demanding entry, and when people were afraid to let them in and refused to open, the Americans broke down doors with axes. The Americans requisitioned even government offices without going through proper procedures, pushing out French officials. In Thionville, they ejected a company of French police from their station and threw their furniture out the window before the policemen had a chance to find new quarters. The prefect feared that if these sorts of incidents continued, violent clashes between French and Americans would result.[20]

Two French officers who had accompanied the American troops into Lorraine reported in December 1944 to Renseignements Généraux in Paris their impressions of the American soldiers in Lorraine. Upon arrival in Boulay-Moselle (east of Metz) the Americans set about pillaging the local shops and demanding alcohol from local merchants; any who refused were threatened with arms. When women and girls came to greet their liberators, several of them were raped. The French officers even witnessed a firefight involving machine guns between two groups of (drunken?) Americans settling a dispute. The local population was astounded by this behavior. The officers suggested that the French and Americans did not understand or like each other; in their view the Americans seemed to have a greater affinity for the Germans because the two peoples were more alike. They estimated that the French got along better with the British, who were more like the French, just as the Americans were more like the Germans. Chester Hansen was inclined to agree: "The French are still incapable of understanding the Americans, whom they view as an amenable but completely insane people but are not reluctant to pursue them with their notorious but traditional cupidity[,] for liberation like occupation means soldiers with money to spend."[21]

The people of Lorraine had to put up with the same sort of inconveniences, minor destruction, and petty theft that civilians caught in the war zone endured in Normandy. All across northern France, GIs dug foxholes to protect themselves from German mortar bombs and artillery shells. Private First Class Richard Courtney fought his way across France from Normandy and knew that he might stay in any foxhole for an extended time—he spent two weeks in one foxhole in cold and rainy Luxembourg—so, like many other soldiers, he made himself as comfortable as possible by piling it with plenty of straw pulled out of nearby barns. With tens of thousands of GIs doing the same thing, French barns gave up many thousands of tons of straw to line foxholes all across Lorraine. While holding out in one town's cellars for several days against determined German efforts to retake it, Courtney and his comrades drank several cases of cognac and champagne abandoned by the Germans. And to make their cellars more comfortable, they "went through all the apartments upstairs and brought down all the thick, silk covered comforters from the beds and lined them across our cellar about four deep. It was quite a sight. We had pink, yellow, lavender, blue, we walked on them, muddy shoes and all. We wondered how the civilians would feel when they found all their bedding at one neighbor's house." When the GIs got hungry and tired of their rations, they visited a local corner store and ran into other GIs from a different company with the same idea to help themselves to whatever they could find to eat there. This sort of pilfering did not appear in government reports complaining about the misbehavior of GIs. While no doubt very unwelcomed by those civilians who had to suffer the mistreatment of their homes and possessions by GIs hunkering down for a fight, it was to be expected and on the whole endured stoically by the French. Indeed, three American soldiers who worked cooperatively with civilians and FFI in Maxéville to separate and arrest suspicious men in the town after the Germans pulled out were nominated for Croixs de Guerre by a French delegation from there.[22]

The French however objected to and resented thievery and vandalism that clearly contributed nothing to victory and that they ascribed to simple criminality. The theft of silver, jewels, money, and valuables could not in any way have been justified by wartime circumstances, and wanton vandalism did not advance the Allied cause. Such transgressions were not limited to battlefront villages. The same sort of both casual destruction and making-do with other people's possessions afflicted French government property behind the lines as well. After Nancy was taken from the Germans, the III Corps of Patton's army set up its headquarters in the Ecole des Beaux Art (School of Fine Arts). Although Nancy is a small provincial city, it has a long history as an artistic center, and its art school was world famous by the opening of the twentieth century. The headquarters unit used the building for about three weeks from mid-September to early October before it moved on with the front. When the school's director retook possession of the building, he was shocked and dismayed to see that much of it had been ransacked and looted. The building was a shambles. He complained to the French commissioner that valuable, irreplaceable Asian engravings had disappeared along with most of the tools from the engraving classroom and the woodworking shop. Many valuable vases and figurines held in the school's collection as examples for students to study had been either damaged or stolen. The director estimated the value of damage done at 375,000 francs ($7,500). An investigation by the Third Army concluded that Army personnel probably took the tools, but that the building was already damaged when the unit showed up and the looting had probably been done by civilians before the Army took possession of it. The evidence suggests otherwise. One private admitted to having taken some copper engraving plates and mailed them home as souvenirs. An officer confessed that the unit had used handmade paper—some of it quite old Japanese paper—for Army business. This fit the practice of soldiers making do with whatever was at hand to get the job done in a war zone. Bored soldiers seeking distraction were the likely culprits in the case of the missing or damaged artworks. This was unfortunate, but probably just war in the eyes of both soldiers and the officers supervising them. Discipline was sometimes lax, and officers usually saved real discipline for when it really mattered: in fighting the enemy. To some extent the mistreatment and petty looting of the school—some of which in fact may have been the work of departing Germans—fits in with the wear and tear of wartime: soldiers finding the ancient paper and assuming it would do just fine for letters or memos, finding that the shop tools performed admirably for the purpose of fixing Army equipment, or whatever. But the destruction of objects of art, like vases and figurines, is harder to justify. In fact, it cannot be justified, but it can be explained: bored young men in wartime do annoying things.[23]

The museum in Lunéville suffered much the same fate. It, too, was requisitioned and used as a barracks by first the Germans and then the Americans. When the war erupted in 1939, much of the contents of the museum was packed into crates and stored in the basement. During the occupation, the museum experienced some thefts, but the crates in the basement went unmolested. In October 1944, the Americans replaced the Germans and some of the crates were pried open and ransacked. The mayor wanted to move the crates but was unable to find workers to move them or a secure place to store them; only two cases were taken away. Throughout November and December thefts continued. In January, the building was converted into a recreation center and problems got worse. Not only did all of the cases disappear, the building was generally vandalized, with all the interior windows smashed. When the provost marshal investigated, they discovered the building was guarded by MPs during the day, but not at night. American aviators stationed next door routinely broke in and wrecked the place, taking whatever appealed to them. MPs were able to return a few statues and vases, but most of the contents of the museum had vanished. This could have also been a case of bored and drunken young soldiers letting off steam and amusing themselves at someone else's expense, but it seems more like how soldiers would treat the enemy than friends. The infantry's and subsequent aviators' maltreatment of the building and its contents fit the pattern of American behavior in enemy territory, which, as seen, was where many believed they were.[24]

News of problems created by the men serving under General Patton reached Paris early on and became an irritant in Franco-American relations as early as October 1944. Although a November letter to SHAEF listed complaints against "the Allies," an earlier report on a meeting of French officials dealing with the Allies stated specifically that the problem of indiscipline "does not apply to the British Zone" and that General Courtney Hodge's First Army did not generate the flood of complaints that Patton's did. Almost all mounting French complaints about "the Allies" could be reduced to "Patton's Army." French complaints about lenient treatment of POWs, excessive requisitions of buildings and land, and expansive claims of what constituted "war booty" applied to all American armies under General Eisenhower, but protests about indiscipline, cavalier attitudes, arbitrariness, and failure to live up to agreements signed higher up all applied especially to General Patton's soldiers in Lorraine. The mistreatment of French civilians in Lorraine by GIs was protested to SHAEF by Commissioner Coulet in October 1944, and in December the prefect in Nancy protested to Paris, "I have to say that the population has the impression that the Americans believe themselves to already be in German territory. While one can explain the true situation to the officers and convince them, but this explanation does not go beyond the person present at the moment." As late as February 1945, the chair of an interministerial committee that discussed relations with the Allies protested to delegates from SHAEF that American soldiers still behaved in eastern France as if they were on enemy soil. Chairman Marcel Grégoire noted that Alsace-Lorraine seemed to be treated differently than the rest of France by the Americans. Some American units were applying orders against fraternization with the enemy to the people of Alsace-Lorraine. By mid-December 1944, even before the German Ardennes Offensive, the French population in Lorraine had grown weary and wary of American soldiers. Many fewer civilians invited them into their homes, and they no longer greeted passing convoys with smiles and waves. Mothers warned their daughters to avoid the American soldiers. The cheering had stopped.[25]

When Patton's Third Army turned north into Belgium and Luxembourg, the Allied front of American and French forces was suddenly stretched thin. In an effort to force Patton to pull back into Lorraine and—in Hitler's mind— retake German Elsass-Lothringen, the Germans launched an offensive under Heinrich Himmler's command south into Alsace and Lorraine in early January 1945. Eisenhower was greatly worried that his forces in the region were too weak to withstand the onslaught and gave orders to Generals Jean de Lattre de Tassigny and Sixth Army Group commander Jacob Devers to prepare to pull out of the Alsatian plain. The big prize for the Germans was Strasbourg, liberated only in late November, which de Gaulle was determined not to relinquish. When de Gaulle got wind of Eisenhower's plan to abandon Alsace, he ordered de Lattre to stay put and fight for the city, which for de Gaulle carried enormous symbolic importance. De Gaulle's order to de Lattre went over the head of the French First Army's commander, General Devers, as well as that of the overall chief, Eisenhower, greatly agitating and angering Eisenhower. De Gaulle argued to Eisenhower that the loss of Strasbourg would be a crushing blow to French morale and possibly provoke massive popular unrest against the Americans, who ordered it abandoned without a fight. When Winston Churchill, by chance at the meeting between de Gaulle and Eisenhower in Versailles to debate the matter, intervened on de Gaulle's side, Eisenhower relented and countermanded his order to retreat. De Lattre was allowed to fight for Strasbourg, but the hierarchy of command remained in place: de Lattre followed orders from Devers and not de Gaulle.[26]

De Lattre did not retreat from Strasbourg, yet word of the Allied pull-back had already spread and provoked panic among the recently liberated French population, who feared Himmler's revenge should his troops retake the city and decided it would probably be best if they pulled back too. As German troops surged forward, frightened French civilians fled. Civilians left the region by any means available—crammed into unheated boxcars, in wagons, on horse, or on foot. People left in droves, and Nancy and other towns in Lorraine quickly filled up with refugees from Strasbourg. Almost all hotels had been requisitioned by the U.S. Army, leaving few places to shelter the arrivals. The sight of public officials from Strasbourg, who especially feared being seized by the Germans and deported to concentration camps, aroused much public alarm in Nancy and neighboring areas. Determined to hold the city but presented with a fait accompli of evacuation, ministers in Paris ordered the removal from Strasbourg of children and men of military age; civil servants native to Alsace were ordered out, but other French officials newly appointed by the Gaullist regime were ordered to remain at their posts. Anyone publicly linked to the resistance or FFI was to be evacuated, but otherwise the people of Strasbourg were to stay put. French authorities in Paris were especially concerned to dampen the panic and reassure the civilian population that the renewed French Army would never allow Strasbourg to fall back into Nazi hands. U.S. Army offers to coordinate the evacuation of 150,000 *strasbourgeoise* with French officials in Paris were spurned, leaving any coordinating to be carried out at the local level. French police teamed up with MPs to control the flood of refugees and keep them off the roads needed by the U.S. and French armies, so the U.S. Army accepted that they would have to play a large role in transporting French civilians from Strasbourg and threatened areas of Alsace. Trucks were released from military duty by the Army to be used to evacuate civilians. The U.S. Army stepped in to organize a more orderly evacuation, picking up people at designated points with empty ammunition trucks heading back from the front filled with refugees. One transportation unit helped 2,000 Alsatians per day leave the department for the other side of the Vosges Mountains, away from the fighting. The French refused an offer to have the trucks pick up evacuees in Strasbourg, so they instead resorted to picking up people walking along the roads, who had left of their own accord and ended up riding in open trucks or under canvas tarps in freezing weather; others traveled in unheated boxcars in trains organized to move them out of endangered regions. The U.S. Army organized reception centers to provide hot meals to the evacuees once they arrived. A school in Saverne was turned into a temporary shelter with the French government providing food and the U.S. Army providing medicine and doctors. The Americans also took charge of removing 3,650 German civilians from Strasbourg. Ultimately, the U.S. Army evacuated 6,000 civilians from the town of Haguenau alone, which indeed fell to the German counteroffensive and remained on the front lines until its ultimate liberation on 20 March 1945 after fierce house-to-house fighting. A Civil Affairs officer involved in the evacuation from Alsace complained that French authorities in Paris contributed "nil" to the operation, while local officials had proved to be "remarkable."[27]

The Strasbourg affair ultimately proved symptomatic of how Franco-American relations had developed since the Americans recognized that they would have to deal with General de Gaulle and his committee. As pointed out to Eisenhower by Churchill, Eisenhower should have discussed abandoning Strasbourg with de Gaulle or his Army Chief of Staff Alphonse Juin—with whom Eisenhower had good close relations—before issuing any orders. It may have proven a lapse in Eisenhower's judgment, but fundamentally de Gaulle demanded to have final say over the fate of Strasbourg as a question of French sovereignty and superior authority over SHAEF. Yet French local officials faced with the chaos of fleeing civilians cared little about such matters and eagerly worked with the Americans to move French civilians out of harm's way. American commanders on the scene saw a potential disaster unfolding and moved quickly to avert it, regardless of decisions by French ministers in Paris. At the street level, American officers worked easily and efficiently with local French officials to solve the problems that needed solving, while in Paris, Interior Minister Adrien Tixier and Provisional President de Gaulle wanted to know who is in charge here: the U.S. Army or the French government? The answer was obvious to Tixier and de Gaulle. The French had cooperated with the Allies to a large degree out of necessity, in order to liberate their country. Once liberated, the need to submit the fate of French citizens to Allied strategic purposes greatly diminished. De Gaulle had gotten from the Allies, especially the Americans, most of what he wanted. The French still relied on the Americans for tanks, airplanes, fuel, and the basic necessities of warfare, but it was in the Americans' interest to deliver them, so the French government felt less need to make sacrifices in order to accommodate the Allies. The vast imbalance in the relations between the liberators and the liberated remained in early 1945, but the urgency to tolerate American dominance had much abated.

10

ENDURING WARTIME IN LORRAINE

ife for the French was difficult and unpleasant in Normandy while the battle raged from early June to mid-August—two and a half months. The fighting surged into Lorraine in early September and continued until January, the Germans not being completely driven out of eastern France until March 1945, when they were finally expelled from Alsace. Thus, combat raged in eastern France for a full five months, twice as long as in Normandy, and most of the fighting in the east occurred during often frigid weather. Life for the refugees in crude shelters in Normandy during the summer was relatively easy compared to the conditions faced by many homeless French in Alsace and Lorraine. The east was more thickly populated than Normandy and hosted about one-third more people.[1] The fighting in the east of France was just as intense, and American casualties give some idea of the ferocity of the combat there. Casualties mounted as 1944 dragged on. Between 6 June and 24 July 1944 the Americans amassed 63,360 casualties (13,959 killed in action) in Normandy. The US Army added another 72,014 casualties (15,239 KIA) in the sweep across northern France from 24 July to 14 September 1944, when the front stalled in Lorraine. The months of small gains, October and November 1944, were nevertheless treacherous for American soldiers, adding 94,054 casualties (17,294 KIA).[2]

German soldiers behaved abominably as they withdrew from Lorraine, just as they did elsewhere in France in the summer of 1944. As they passed through the village of Pexonne, they rounded up all 110 adults, men and women, so they could freely pillage the town. They took all of the bread from the bakery and stole 14,000 francs from its cash box. A number of villages around Pont-à-Mousson suffered grievously: the people were expelled by the Germans, who then looted the towns. The inhabitants could take with them into exile only what they could carry. They left all their animals, most of which were dead or missing upon their return. This was a common tale summed up in official reports in early 1945: in Fréménil the Germans stole 59 of 81 cows, 3 of 13 horses, 12 of 18 bulls, and 3 more animals were killed and 2 injured by mines after the return of the villagers; in Hablainville the Germans stole 58 of 119 cows, 19 of 54 horses, and 17 of 38 bulls; in Merviller 70 of 160 cows, 15 of 27 horses, and 2 of 11 bulls were missing; and on and on. Whether this was wanton plundering by the retreating Germans is hard to say. No doubt some French villages were subjected to out-and-out pillaging, but that some farm animals survived in many towns suggests the Germans ate what they needed and left the rest. When the people of Veho returned in 1945 they complained that all of the farm animals and farming equipment was gone, all clothes, linens, and blankets had disappeared from the homes, and all of the firewood had vanished. This sounds like a list of items that soldiers would have helped themselves to in an effort to survive the war on the front in a smashed and empty foreign village. Perhaps the Germans took everything, perhaps it was the Americans, or maybe both, which seems the most likely. It made little difference even if the French indeed blamed the Germans for their losses. Soldiers in wartime take what they need with little consideration for the people who suffer the loss, not out of malice but from necessity and thoughtlessness. Some damage was just accidental. A farm in Champeneux burned down with all the barns and the year's harvest when GIs spilled fuel while trying to light a lamp in the barn. The spilled fuel caught the barn on fire and it quickly burned beyond control. French firefighters arrived to find the GIs attempting to put the fire out, but it was hopeless and all was lost. Yet, the German Army indeed engaged in systematic looting: they stole most motor vehicles, including 80 percent of all heavy trucks in the Haut-Rhin, leaving the entire department with only 300 working trucks in the spring of 1945.[3]

When the 60 inhabitants of Morville returned to their devastated village, they found the place a shambles. Many houses had been destroyed or damaged by artillery; others had been occupied by GIs during the heavy fighting. Soldiers left the houses in states of complete disarray: armoires had been emptied and their contents scattered around the floors; all drawers had been pulled out and their contents ransacked; and what remained of canned food was strewn about in the kitchens. The GIs used furniture for firewood, even burning a bed in one house. The villagers complained that before the Germans left, they systematically searched for any valuables, gold, jewelry, silver, etc., but they did not destroy the places. The mayor complained that "the pillaging by the American troops since they entered the village far exceeds anything done by the Germans. It seems as though the American soldiers lodged in the houses were animated by a spirit of destruction or at least a carelessness or indifference that must be called to attention. In any case, in consequence, the population is furious and very disappointed in their liberators." It is easy to imagine the disheartening response of the villagers of Morville to the condition of their hamlet after the front passed through it, but it is unlikely that the GIs were "animated by a spirit of destruction" quite in the way imagined by the mayor.[4]

The Germans forcibly evacuated most villages and towns near the front in Lorraine, but in one, Faulquemont, 27 people, including 13 refugees from Pont-à-Mousson, hid from the Germans and rode out the battle until the Americans arrived. They paid a high price for their boldness: 10 of them were killed before the town was liberated. Indeed, much of the misery inflicted on the civilian population came from the unpredictable shelling that accompanied the liberation of the province. As General Patton's soldiers approached Nancy, American artillery targeted German positions within the city, but sometimes shells went astray. Nineteen people were killed by seemingly random shelling from U.S. forces to the north of the city on the afternoon of 9 September, and 23 more were seriously injured, including five women. Three people were killed and 11 wounded when a shell hit a trolley stop in the southern section of Nancy; nine more were killed when a shell struck just a block away. Nancy's fire brigade was kept busy putting out fires that broke out around the city because of the American bombardment. A single shell that hit one house took the life of a 65-year-old grandfather, who was caring for his 11 grandchildren. The same night a judge was killed in his bed; his wife and daughter had sought safety in the basement and were spared, although his daughter was still injured. Artillery rounds continued to drizzle onto the city and the surrounding towns for the next few days, killing a man here, a woman there, severely injuring children, and demolishing houses. The remaining inhabitants of an apartment building in Villers-lès-Nancy—women, children, and elderly men—spent nights in the basement listening to the shells whistling overhead and exploding nearby. Only one hit the building the night before liberation and caused minor damage. The fighting to capture Nancy was not intense, but civilians still got caught in the cross fire and some were killed or injured. Some civilians took up arms at the last minute to join the fight against the Germans and paid for it with their lives. Fortunately, most FFI casualties survived. Only 24 died, despite a tough fight against Germans holding out in a French Army barracks in the center of the town.[5]

Unfortunately for Nancy, Patton's tanks ran out of gas just after the city was liberated and it remained within range of German artillery, which rained shells on the town for weeks. On the day that the Luftwaffe's General Krum left Nancy, as Patton's troops neared the city, he told a Frenchman, "I will return in three weeks." In fact, the city was almost empty of German troops and administrative staff as of the morning of 2 September and local FFI begged the Allies to drop arms to them so they could seize the city. While sympathetic, the Allies could not arrange a parachute drop that quickly, and by the time Patton's tanks were rolling again, German troops had returned in strength. After the brief fight for the town, the Germans dragged 280 mm (circa 11-inch) guns into place to lob shells onto Nancy and surrounding towns. Children playing outside in Maxéville were caught by a shell soon after Nancy's liberation: a 14-year-old boy was killed and a 10-year-old girl was badly injured. Shells fell on Lunéville every night in early October, taking the lives of two men and three women, and injuring many others. It was a good day when the sub-prefect could report "light shelling and not much damage last night." The suburb of Malzéville suffered the death of an elderly woman and two infants—a four-month-old and a one-year-old—on a single night. Both parents of one of the babies were badly injured, and their house was destroyed in the shelling. Other houses were wrecked, and many lost roofs as cold weather encroached. On one night in October, a 56-year-old man and his 20-year-old son were lucky when a blast ripped away the front of their house in Nancy but left them only lightly injured as large-caliber rounds fell on the hapless city. An elderly woman suffered a severe head injury when an explosion tore away the third floor of her house. The Germans also tried to hit the city with V-1 flying bombs; several landed in forests to the west of the city, inflicting major damage to trees, but none to humans or buildings. There was even a report of a V-2 rocket attack. Even though the American bombardment of Nancy was relatively brief, and the city was quickly seized by FFI without inflicting much damage on the town, the stalled American advance forced Nancy to sit forlornly on the front lines for most of the next two months. The punishment that the people of Nancy and surrounding towns were spared by the Americans was instead inflicted on them by the Germans.[6]

The inhabitants of Pont-à-Mousson were initially thrilled when American soldiers liberated their town, despite the rough treatment they had endured during the fighting that lasted from 4 September until 17 September. After a tough contest with the Wehrmacht to wrest the town and area from its control, the front then stalled on the Moselle River, leaving Pont-à-Mousson on the front lines and well within range of German artillery. The people became discouraged when the Americans failed to attack. What was holding them up? General Patton's soldiers fired lots of artillery shells at the Germans, and people could see the bombers and fighters overhead flying toward the enemy, but why did the infantry and tanks not drive the enemy back into Germany? People's spirits dipped when the temperature dropped and there was little fuel for heat and food became scarce. The Americans did not provision the civilians even though they appeared to have plenty for themselves. And General Patton kept tight controls on the roads, preventing French farmers from reaching their fields or delivering their harvests—if they had any. French on the wrong side of the front lines suffered under the American barrage: on 6 September, 30 American shells hit Nomény, injuring two people and damaging many homes and buildings. A woman was killed in her farmhouse and others were wounded on farms and in villages nearby on the same night.[7]

When German soldiers retreated, they left behind many mines and booby-traps intended for the advancing Americans; however, many of them were discovered or triggered by French civilians instead. Germans hid explosives in peoples' gardens, in stacks of cabbage, in piles of firewood, and attached to doors—all just as likely to find civilians as GIs. The OSS's Colonel David Bruce heard of an incident near Saint-Dié: "an American soldier yesterday [16 November] went into a house just abandoned by the enemy. Hearing a cat miaowing from the locked closet of a bedroom, he opened the door. The cat sprang out. There was a cord around her neck. The charge exploded. The soldier was killed." A lock keeper in Flavigny-sur-Moselle was killed when he went to the assistance of two American soldiers injured while attempting to extract a mine from a canal lock. One of the soldiers died and the other was badly injured when the mine exploded. When the lock keeper tried to reach the injured American soldier, he stepped on a mine himself and was killed; his wife and another man were injured by the explosion. Abandoned ordnance was widespread and too often was found by curious children before it could be disposed of by Army sappers. Two teenage boys found a mine and tried without success to disarm it; both were seriously hurt and one had to have an arm amputated. A six-year-old boy found a hand grenade in an outbuilding while his parents were visiting friends and picked it up. It exploded, killing the boy instantly. A group of seven children in Nancy found a bomb under a pile of rubbish and were all injured to some extent when they disturbed it. Some of the children suffered fatal injuries despite having been immediately whisked to a U.S. Army hospital by Army ambulances. Two brothers tried to empty the powder from an artillery shell that also went off, leaving them both badly injured in the courtyard of their farm. Their mother ran to her brother's home next door to summon a doctor, but by the time the doctor arrived one of her sons had died of massive blood loss. Two days later, six boys were attempting to empty the gunpowder out of some antitank shells they found when one of the rounds went off. All of them, too, were injured to some extent; a nine-year-old lost an eye, another lost his right hand and forearm.[8]

FROM MISERY TO ANXIETY

After liberation the populace of many places dreaded that the Germans would return. Such anxiety was not widespread before the mid-December German counteroffensive in the Ardennes, but worries become acute in areas of northern France as news of American reverses spread. People in the Meurthe-et-Moselle could see long columns of General Patton's tanks heading north into Belgium but received no news about what was going on and otherwise saw little activity among U.S. troops in eastern France. Rumors circulated about hideous German reprisals inflicted on Belgian towns and villages that fell back under Nazi control. On New Year's Eve, German troops surged over the 1939 border with France and struck southward toward Haguenau, pushing American forces out of regions of Alsace that had been considered safely back in friendly hands, inducing panic among French civilians. These events raised alarms in much of eastern France, stretching all the way to Paris, as fear of a Nazi return deepened. Alarm turned to paranoia as rumors and alerts spread of German agents lurking behind the lines. This fear of Nazi agents was not completely the product of fantasy. French police received and investigated credible reports of suspicious men, lights, airplanes, and parachutes turning up over numerous departments in eastern France, starting as early as 22 November, when police found Panzerfausts and parachutes by the side of the road near Briey. Such reports trickled in through January. However, anxiety grew and spread as the military situation in Belgium deteriorated for the Americans, rather than as more reports of Nazi agents were verified.[9]

As early as August, FFI volunteers were put on patrols in the Yonne looking for suspect men hiding in forests and fields. This made perfect sense, as

large swathes of France in August were teeming with German stragglers left
behind by the retreating armies. But FFI guards were told to watch for not only
small groups of German soldiers trying to elude Allied patrols in order to reach
Germany, but also parachutists and German soldiers acting as saboteurs and
snipers behind the lines. As late as November, gendarmes in Tonnerre, Yonne,
reported that forests nearby were home to armed German soldiers helped by
local sympathizers. They claimed that farmers in the region gave them food
and clothing, and some sectors were too dangerous for the gendarmes to enter
to search for them. Also in December, in southern Yonne, a farmer told police that two suspicious men in U.S. Army uniforms stopped at his home and
demanded something to eat. Only one got out of the truck and spoke, and the
other wore a Wehrmacht forage cap. When the suspicious farmer asked to see
some identification, the soldier quickly flashed a card and put it back in his
pocket before the farmer could see what it was. A similar incident was reported
in the next commune (Escamps) as late as 8 January 1945, when two men in
khaki uniforms came to the farmhouse of Mme. Robert, took her to her basement, and shot her dead. Her 12-year-old son said they stole 12,000 francs and
left. This episode sounds more like typical brigandage of criminals acting under the cover of the FFI in the wake of liberation than German guerrillas. Yet,
the timing of the event persuaded police to suspect German agents rather than
French bandits. Even the earlier incident may have actually been AWOL GIs
extorting food from a farmer (not a common problem that far behind the lines
in November), who preferred to see them as the German enemy rather than as
American friends. Regardless of the facts, that gendarmes accepted these incidents as evidence of "German agents" testifies to the level of nervousness that
pervaded eastern France after the liberation.[10]

Such incidents and anxiety were widespread. Reports of parachutists in the
region of Marseille spooked the officers in charge of security for the pipeline
that carried gasoline up the Rhone Valley to Allied forces. They feared enemy
sabotage and ordered increased patrols of the pipeline from the oil storage
tanks at Port-de-Bouc—on the Mediterranean—all the way to Lyon. The U.S.
Army asked that already overstretched French police mount guards as well and
issued orders that soldiers shoot anyone suspected of sabotage. When the U.S.
Army instituted tight traffic controls on roads in northern France and frequent
identity checks by MPs, some French were annoyed by the inconvenience, but
most welcomed the measures as necessary to locate and capture German par-

achutists sent to sabotage the pipeline. Even General Eisenhower's armored Packard was stopped several times at MP checkpoints. His aid, Harry Butcher, was asked to name the river that formed the eastern boundary of Iowa—he did. Patton's aide-de-camp, Colonel Charles Codman, was shot at in his jeep on the road near Nancy by nervous tankers alerted that German infiltrators were posing as Americans and driving jeeps. In the wake of widespread purges of French collaborators, the populace and officialdom alike suspected that French Nazi sympathizers had been left behind in France to undertake foul deeds. There were also reports of French collaborators who had fled France in the summer of 1944 being parachuted back behind the lines to sow chaos. In fact, over 100 members of the PPF and other assorted collaborators stranded in Germany in late 1944 volunteered to attend a sabotage and espionage school near Wiesbaden set up with the cooperation of the SD. There, both men and women learned how to act as subversives in the new—presumably Communist—France that was to come. Only a handful ever infiltrated back into France; 11 jumped from captured American planes piloted by Luftwaffe flyers into the Corrèze in mid-December 1944 only to be arrested immediately by French forces. Another group parachuted into Burgundy with some SS soldiers in the spring of 1945 to harass the Allies behind the lines. The French saboteurs were immediately captured and the SS disappeared. Others were infiltrated back into France with false papers as displaced persons and were never heard from again. Gendarmes were stumped by the mysterious men who threatened the prosecutor in Troyes charged with investigating German atrocities in the Aube and wondered if they were not part of some "fifth column" of collaborationists working behind the lines. People in Nancy also were worried about "fifth columnists" hiding in Lorraine waiting for the signal to emerge when German troops poured out of Belgium and back into Lorraine. While they waited to attack, they were blamed for the wild rumors circulating around Nancy intended to sow panic among the populace. The large population of foreigners imported by the Nazis and left behind when the Wehrmacht pulled out aroused fears in the populace because their loyalties remained suspect. And what of the German colonists planted in Lorraine and then abandoned; had they all been rounded up and accounted for? People thought the Americans were remarkably relaxed about the danger posed by the German offensive and wondered why they did not rush from Lorraine and into the storm in Belgium. In fact, Patton began gathering troops to move north the day after the Germans launched their offensive, as soon as it became clear to him that it really was a major attack. They were on the move the following day and ready to attack the Germans in Luxembourg by 22 December, or day six of the offensive. This may have seemed slow to nervous French civilians, but it was too fast and perhaps imprudent as far as Eisenhower was concerned.[11]

Much French nervousness was indeed the product of fantastic rumors, but many of the rumors were based on fact: German infiltrators really did dress in U.S. uniforms and carry faked or captured ID papers. How far they operated behind the lines is not really known, but U.S. counter intelligence considered reports of German parachutists dressed like GIs credible, as did French police. In December, the huge Allied installations growing in the Marne attracted the attention of German aircraft and (according to the prefect) fifth columnists, instilling anxiety in the population about their fates. He appealed to Paris for more CRS (militia) to protect French officials from assassination by German agents. Curfews were put into place in the Aube, many miles behind the front lines, yet reportedly the target for parachutists. Seriously concerned about German agents dressed as GIs or civilians trying to slip into Paris to sabotage important installations, U.S. counter intelligence asked French police for their help in checking everyone trying to get into the city. An 8 P.M. curfew was put into place in Paris for Christmas and all evening shows and festivities were cancelled. As late as mid-January, gendarmes discovered parachutes, radios, documents, and a code book near Fontainebleau. Inquiries revealed that three suspicious men had taken the train from Fontainebleau to Paris. When German bombers were able to attack targets in the Marne and Aube, people began to question the abilities and competence of the American military. Refugees from Belgium and French fleeing areas bordering on Luxembourg trickling into Troyes added to popular disquiet, and people who had until then scoffed at the thought of the Americans being defeated started to have second thoughts. As faith in the American military waned, fear of the Germans waxed; rumors spread about secret new rockets armed with poison gas destined to rain on France.[12]

Even though the Ardennes offensive was decisively beaten back by the Allies by the end of January and German losses in men, material, aircraft, and fuel could not readily be replaced; French faith in the U.S. Army, once shaken, proved hard to restore. There may very well have been German agents prowling the roads and railways of France, and German aircraft probably did fly over areas deep inside France until the end of the war, but anxiety over the final outcome likely provoked most of the unexplained and mysterious sightings reported to French police into April 1945. Searches by French police and American MPs following reports of strange lights, flares, low-flying planes, and rumors of parachutists almost invariably turned up nothing suspicious. Police and U.S. counter intelligence focused on three Dutch brothers suspected of signaling German observation planes near the giant American airbase at Brienne, in the Aube. The three immigrant farmers had been arrested as collaborators in 1944 and released in December, only to be arrested again in April 1945 on suspicion of being enemy agents. However, Gendarmerie searches for reported "parachutists" around Brévonnes (close to the airbase) turned up nothing. In one case west of Auxerre, police found three teenagers who had discovered some flares in the woods and set them off "to amuse themselves." They admitted having done such things before and were warned not to do it again. Nevertheless, reports of strange men and unexplained lights continued to come in from the farms and forests west of Auxerre. In the Marne, the Americans' General Thrasher became paranoid about strange lights and flares reported in the woods close to large U.S. Army supply dumps and threatened to have the U.S. Army assume all security responsibility for the department, greatly alarming the prefect. With so many armed Frenchmen of dubious character having emerged from the Milice and FFI with reasons to stay hidden, it proved difficult to distinguish brigands in the woods from German agents. Who were those armed men who robbed a farm at night in Melisey? Police in the Lot-et-Garonne launched a big operation to suppress "bandes armées irregulaire," which might have been composed of brigands of various colorations, "but the leaders got away." They also launched operations aimed at supposed bands of Milice operating in the woods, but found no one, perhaps—according to the republican commissioner—because the reports were erroneous or the products of imagination. From January to the end of the war, police in Meurthe-et-Moselle arrested 15 people suspected of "intelligence with the enemy." How many were guilty is another question.[13]

Even if the Germans were mostly expelled and all of France bordering on Belgium was indeed liberated, peoples' minds remained uneasy. This was especially so after the German counteroffensive in the Ardennes in late December aroused fears of a return of the Wehrmacht. In a corner of Alsace the Wehrmacht really did return and wrest territory from the Americans, ground that had already been liberated. Eisenhower revealed that he was willing to abandon even major cities such as Strasbourg if holding them placed Allied forces in jeopardy. We know he contemplated pulling back Allied lines to the Vosges Mountains and completely abandoning Alsace, but that was not common knowledge among the French in 1944. Thus, liberated civilians in the east really did have legitimate fears. The people of the Yonne and Aube experienced relatively little fighting as Patton's tanks roared through chasing retreating Germans. Nevertheless, they paid a toll when FFI took up arms against the fleeing Germans, who still had time to massacre civilians and destroy towns. The barbarous treatment of civilians meted out by the retreating Germans induced enormous fear among the inhabitants of northeastern France. When it appeared that German soldiers might return with the Ardennes offensive of December, French anxieties turned into fear and paranoia. With the aura of American invincibility greatly dulled by setbacks in Belgium and Luxembourg, French confidence in the future ebbed. The optimism and jubilation of the summer of 1944 turned into a dour skepticism of the winter of 1945.

11

AMERICANS IN LIBERATED PARIS

N
ot all encounters between the French and U.S. servicemen and women occurred amid violence and devastated cities. The junction of the American military and the French in Paris took place in a city renowned for its beauty and charm, which had hardly been touched by the ferocity of the war. The city and its people had been bruised by the 10 days of fighting during the liberation, but compared to Cherbourg, Carentan, or Nancy, the city was unscathed. The story of the liberation of Paris has been told many times, is well known, and this not the place to retell it. Yet, the Paris that American military personnel got to know in 1944 and 1945 was undoubtedly a capital at war, suffering all of the shortages and discomforts experienced by the rest of France. And the men and women who left memories of their time in Paris also reveal that they were well aware there was a war on, even if the fighting was far away. They were foreigners living in a foreign land, trying to do their jobs and get along as best they could under trying circumstances.

After its liberation in August 1944, Paris filled up with Allied soldiers, many stationed there and many others on leave from the brutality of combat, trying to find distraction. Eisenhower did not establish his headquarters in liberated Paris. He wanted to avoid the city. Eisenhower said at a dinner with staff on 12 August 1944 that he disliked Parisians, calling them "unpleasant and filthy people." He had a puritanical streak in him that found Paris repulsive: during a brief visit in 1929 he saw men making advances toward women on the Metro and in the "Dome"; Paris offered "filthy peep shows" and nudity as entertainment. He chose instead to make his headquarters in Versailles and quickly filled the palace and town with 16,000 staff members, who eventually occupied 1,800 requisitioned properties. Despite Eisenhower's disdain, after August 1944 Paris became the headquarters for numerous Allied services, principally the Transportation and Quartermaster Corps, because it was strategically located and offered huge amounts of office and living space. Because of its many hotel rooms, it served as the main rest and relaxation center for Allied soldiers from many armies. The enormous influx of Allied personnel into Paris put pressure on an already burdened populace and infrastructure with scant provisions. Allied sol diers stationed in wartime Paris shared many of the privations imposed upon Parisians, but not all. GIs may not have had heat or hot water, but they had coffee, cigarettes, and plenty of food. Allied soldiers not only had an impact on the city; it had an impact on Allied soldiers stationed there as well. Opinions about Paris by Allied servicemen and women evolved with time, just as French attitudes about their allies also changed as the war dragged on and finally ended.[1]

Before the liberation, military planners continued to worry about what kind of horrors would greet the liberators and how the capital would be provisioned. They knew that France generally and Paris especially lacked soap, and they thus assumed the city would suffer louse infestation and the various diseases they carry: typhoid, diphtheria, and scarlet fever. They assumed the city would need enough food to feed 4 million for 45 days. All of it and the transport necessary to get it to Paris would have to be diverted from stocks needed by the Allied armies. Civil Affairs set aside 3 million C-rations for the city's population and requested 3 million more from the Quartermaster General. He rejected the request out of hand. They also expected to find a city without law or order, yet quickly concluded that would have to be a French responsibility. De Gaulle shared Civil Affair's concerns about chaos in the capital caused by food shortages and worried it would descend into anarchy if Allied troops—hopefully French—did not quickly assume control of the capital.[2]

Army engineer Lieutenant Joseph Miller was among the first American troops to arrive in Paris. They received a raucous welcome. "The broad avenues were lined from curb to curb with laughing, crying, waving Parisians, and the moment we stopped our vehicles, we were practically mobbed. They wanted to touch us, shake hands with us, thank us." Immediately after General Leclerc's troops entered Paris, Civil Affairs officers followed, arriving at Tuileries Gardens at 6:30 A.M. on 26 August while gunfire still echoed across the city. They brought 21 trucks of food, which they turned over to their French liaisons. Civil Affairs officers also received a hearty welcome: "All detachments received a magnificent welcome by the inhabitants of the city and were embraced on every side amid joyous tears and questions." Looking around for quarters within the city, the prefect of police found a building for CA on the fashionable Place Vendôme and hotel accommodations at the nearby Hôtels Lotti and

Normandie. Both hotels had recently quartered German troops, who had made it a practice to requisition the best hotels in town. As the Americans practiced a policy first seen in Cherbourg of occupying buildings previously used by the Germans, Americans ended up in the best hotels in town. However, the Germans made it a practice to ransack places—if they had time—before leaving. When Civil Affairs moved into their new quarters on the Place Vendôme they found it without furniture. Fortunately, the French headquarters of the Texas Oil Company was next door, was friendly, and had furniture to spare. CA found the city with running water but no functioning Metro and no buses because the retreating Germans stole the city buses to get out of town. Before departing, the Germans burned the four mills in the 18th arrondissement, yet did not destroy the warehouses of food, which is why they launched air raids that night targeting them. They mostly failed, but the massive Halle aux Vins was badly damaged, destroying thousands of bottles of wine and causing over 1,000 civilian casualties in the effort.[3]

Lieutenant Miller's engineers arrived in Paris on 27 August with the assignment to check the Seine River bridges for demolition charges and then to guard them. They were soon relieved of the guard duty and happy to have the opportunity to tour the scenic river, inspecting the riverside bookstalls, the Louvre (the museum was empty and closed), the Palais Bourbon, and the Montparnasse neighborhood before taking up other assignments. When he was told to find water for the Americans, Miller used it as an excuse to visit the Eiffel Tower, the Place de la Concorde, and various shops. He wanted a camera to record his visit but could find no store with one to sell, as the Germans had banned camera sales in occupied France. Chester Hansen noted that by 28 August "the French people seem to have quieted down quite a bit from a few days ago, although every time the jeep stops they practically mob it. There's something about this Paris that gets in one's blood. In spite of the war and its privations there's a gala air about the city. Perhaps the abundance of bicycles and beautiful women has something to do with it. . . . All the Parisian women are beautifully attired and coiffed. . . . Not everyone is Paris is beautiful but an uncommon percentage of them are. . . . Anyway I can understand why people go AWOL in a place like this." He was enthralled by the women on bicycles who bummed cigarettes from American soldiers, who gladly gave them away. A week later he added, probably with more credulity than the stories warranted, that "girls[,] soldiers tell me[,] are doing business for several packs of Camels.

One told me the standard rate was also a pack of chewing gum." He talked to an American woman who was living in Paris and "simply had to say hello to every Yank I see." She said the proportied classes of Paris were convinced that de Gaulle was a Communist, the FFI were all Communists, and that FDR was a tool of Stalin; he laid her opinions to "Nazi propaganda." Hansen added that there were few hints that there was a war on, except the occasional damaged building and the many antiaircraft cannons abandoned by the Germans that attracted crowds of curious Parisians who inspected them. They poked around inside the once-forbidden cement bunkers the Germans put up to protect the Hôtel Crillon. German signs were still being removed. American fighter pilots made a sport of flying obstacle courses around Paris; some tried to fly under the Eiffel Tower and pulled up at the last second. A Thunderbolt fighter tried to fly through the Arc de Triomphe, but as he flew closer the pilot saw the arch was filled by an enormous French flag and likewise pulled up at the last second. Crowds gathered to watch, and those around the Arc ducked or ran as the plane nearly collided with the monument.[4]

Paris quickly began to return to something resembling normalcy. Stores started to reopen on Monday, 28 August, when mail and banking service also revived, though few restaurants opened. Water was available, though pressure was low because the retreating Germans blew up a bridge across the Seine, severing large water and sewer conduits underneath. Another major water line had been damaged in a German air raid and urgently needed repair. Garbage had not been picked up for five days, and workers were back on the streets Monday morning hauling away the accumulation. The paving stones torn up to make barricades during the revolt were being restored to their rightful places in the streets. The first train—from Chartres—arrived in Montparnasse Station in Paris on Monday. Phones had been turned back on and electrical workers were busy locating breaks in the transmission lines that carried electricity from hydroelectric plants to the south. Restored Metro service awaited the electrical repairs. Most of this was accomplished by the French on their own initiative and unaided by the Allies. Reflecting his dim view of Paris, Eisenhower noted that upon liberation "the black market is flourishing." Nevertheless, the needs of the city were great and French officials were glad to cooperate with Allied military officials to help get Paris back on her feet. De Gaulle's staff principally worried about getting food and coal into Paris.[5]

The Allies did what they could to help funnel supplies into the capital after its liberation. High on their list of worries was the coal supply needed to provide the city with electricity, heat, and fuel to keep the bakeries' ovens hot for bread. Because of widespread destruction of French railroads and an acute shortage of railcars, coal shipments to Paris had dwindled to almost nil by July 1944. When Paris fell, SHAEF estimated that the coal supply could last from 10 to 17 days, if closely husbanded. CA agreed that coal to operate sewage pumps had first claim on available supplies. When General Patton's troops discovered a stockpile of 10,000 tons of coal about 40 miles east of Paris, General Bradley authorized U.S. Army trucks to move about 800 tons per day to Paris. However, there was still not enough coal to operate the gas works. Due to lack of coal, Paris would remain without gas for some time. Fortunately, French coal mines in the country's center and the industrial northeast fell into Allied hands soon after the capital's liberation. The mines fell to the advancing armies so quickly that retreating Germans had little time to set them alight or flood them, and engineers figured their output could be increased without much difficulty. Thus, coal was available to keep France electrified, supplied with bread, and somewhat heated as winter approached. Eisenhower wanted to facilitate French repair of railroads principally so that coal and food could enter Paris without requiring Allied Army trucks. Even though rail lines connecting Paris with the coal producing regions of the Nord and Nivernais had been restored to service by 1 October, the French still lacked locomotives and railcars to haul coal to Paris. By December the coal situation had improved, but not enough to heat the city; deliveries from French mines to Paris reached only around 5,000 tons in both November and December, which was below requirements.[6]

Chester Hansen noted on 23 September that all the bistros on the Champs Elysées were open and crowded, there were more fruits and vegetables for sale in Parisian markets, and women carried big baguettes in wicker baskets. The "bread looks better than before." That may have been true, but food became scarcer in Paris over time rather than more plentiful. There were many reasons for this: for example, the warehouses of food left behind by the Germans were eventually emptied, and the amount of space on Allied ships devoted to food for civilians remained tight, as did wharf space available to unload it. Increasing tonnage on ships would have done little good so long as the ability to handle it in ports remained limited. Eisenhower knew the limited capacity of the available ports was insufficient to supply his troops; adding the population of Paris to the burden would break the system. The principal port for Paris,

Le Havre, remained in German hands until Canadian forces wrested it from German control in mid-September after a devastating fight that cost the lives of many thousands of the city's inhabitants and destroyed tens of thousands of buildings. It took until the mid-1960s to rebuild the port city. Brest and the smaller Breton ports remained in German hands until only a few days after the seizure of Le Havre and had been rendered useless by German demolitions and the fierce fighting to capture the towns. Beautiful, historic Saint-Malo was almost completely razed by the American fight to wrest it from German control. The French informed SHAEF that Paris required 5,800 tons of food per day; in September SHAEF was receiving contradictory reports on the amount of food actually reaching Paris from all sources, ranging from 1,800 to 6,000 tons. However, as it turned out, Eisenhower's concerns about feeding Paris were alarmist; Paris could be sustained at a minimal level with food available in northern France and with imported supplements—some of it airlifted from England.[7]

In late November only slightly more than half of the supplies required by Paris were arriving by rail. All the rest came by truck. The American Army Transportation Service was eager to keep roads around Paris unobstructed so that the Red Ball Express could deliver supplies to the front without competing with French civilian traffic. Accordingly, French trucks had to apply for permits in order to use back roads to Paris, leaving the main highways to U.S. Army trucks. The French relied on the Allies to supply them with trucks, fuel, and tires, which SHAEF did reluctantly and minimally. It made nearly 1,000 trucks available to supply Paris, but that was woefully short of the city's needs. Civil Affairs estimated that the city needed as many as 200 trucks per day just to deliver milk, which was not only in short supply but becoming harder to find within the capital as the war dragged on. In fact, all supplies for the city became less abundant rather than more with each passing month. Scarce shipping, meager dock space, and shortage of transport allowed only minimal amounts of needed commodities to reach the city. Civil Affairs had counted on bringing in imported goods that had been scarce under the occupation, especially coffee and chocolate, as a means to boost civilian morale and showcase the material dividends of liberation. The French had been drinking coffee mixed with various fillers since October 1940. Until summer 1944 the best mixtures contained 12 percent real coffee; after D-Day even that was unavailable. Most in SHAEF agreed that it was simply good public relations to import scarce luxuries from tropical climes such as chocolate, coffee, and sugar, but the shortage of ships and port facilities to handle the cargo bedeviled the Allies even after Brest was captured in September and Antwerp's wharves became available in late November.[8]

In any case, it was difficult to worry too much about luxuries when not enough meat, potatoes, and milk was reaching the city to feed its populace. General Robert McClure, head of SHAEF's Psychological Warfare Division, worried that there were practically no cigarettes in Paris and Parisians were sweeping through the gutters picking up butts dropped by GIs. He proposed that cigarettes destined for Army PXs be diverted to the civilian population. Transport problems did not improve over time, and less food arrived in Paris during the fall than had been available during the Nazi occupation. The French harvest of 1944 was poor due to lack of fuel, tractors, horses, and trucks, all feeling the enormous pressures of the war. While French rail lines were being steadily restored to operation, locomotives, boxcars, and fuel all remained hard to find. Thus, it remained difficult to move food from the areas that produced it to the regions that needed it, such as Paris. Shipments of flour destined for French civilians indeed fell every month after September, when imports from North America peaked at around 700 tons; by December shipments fell to 526 tons. The vast majority of food for Paris had to come from France itself. Only in October did the amount of food reaching Parisian markets surpass the minimum needed, and afterward deliveries fell short. *New Yorker* magazine correspondent Janet Flanner returned to Paris in November 1944 as an accredited war correspondent and reported the Parisian obsession with food. She wrote in December about the shortage of paper, coal, gas, electricity, jobs, and all kinds of food. Flanner, who evidently did all of her investigating at cafés and dinner tables so that she was well informed by the Parisian rumor mill, ascribed the want of food to the closing down of the black markets. When the Germans had tolerated them, food was available even if prices were high. After the Allies and de Gaulle arrived and effectively quashed the black markets, sulking peasants deprived of their rich rewards withheld their produce from markets. Yet even Flanner recounted that on average Parisians lost 40 pounds during the German occupation. War correspondent A. J. Liebling noticed there were no pigeons in Paris; an old French acquaintance acknowledged that some of those old pigeons made pretty tough chewing. When Gertrude Stein returned to Paris in December 1944, she feasted on K-rations, which she found delightful even if few GIs did.[9]

HQ PARIS

Spared the brutal sort of fighting experienced by some of the unfortunate towns of Normandy, Paris became situated in what the Allies called "COMZ," or Communications Zone, and was the headquarters for numerous support operations—as it had been for the Germans. Paris had quartered up to 40,000 German support troops and soon had a similar number of Allied soldiers stationed there. While hundreds of thousands of U.S. troops passed through the city at some point in the remaining months of the war, 35,000 supply, communication, and transportation troops stayed to work in the various offices and depots established in Paris. The largest establishment answered to Lieutenant General John C. Lee, chief of the Quartermaster Corps for the European Theater, who took over both the former general headquarters for the Germans at the Hôtel Majestic on the Champs Elysées and the plushest hotel in Paris, the King George V, plus 127 other hotels just for his headquarter staff. Eisenhower, who had not been informed of General Lee's move to Paris, became irate when he found out and ordered the move stopped. He was quickly convinced that changing the orders would introduce chaos into the system when the armies moving forward could least afford it. He countermanded his own order but demanded that Lee quarter as few troops in Paris as possible. On 22 September, Hansen noted there were 36,000 Allied soldiers stationed in Paris. Even Paris has a limit to how many guests it can accommodate, so Versailles soon found itself hosting tens of thousands of Allied support troops as well as General Eisenhower's headquarters. SHAEF established itself at Versailles, taking over the palace and many outbuildings, hotels, barracks, schools, and private residences, until 24,000 troops occupied 1,800 properties. According to Colonel Bruce, the palace had escaped the war without any apparent damage.[10]

Initially, the U.S. Army assumed buildings requisitioned by the Germans, but the Allied footprint in Paris and its environs quickly surpassed that of the Germans and required additional space. By October the Americans had requisitioned 1,100 buildings, including 300 hotels, along with movie theaters, warehouses, hospitals, garages, parking lots, and more. Dormitory buildings for the University of Paris, built in the 1920s on the Boulevard Périphérique around the city by John D. Rockefeller, were requisitioned as barracks for GIs. War correspondents had their own quarters in Paris at the Hôtel Scribe, directly across the street from the Grand Hôtel, with its own mess where a dinner could be had for 20 francs (about 40 cents). When correspondents, who ate meals in Army messes provided by the quartermaster, started bringing too many of their French friends to eat as guests, the quartermaster complained. Paris was so overwhelmed by the thousands of service personnel that it could not offer accommodation to all the soldiers on rest and relaxation (R&R) leave who wanted to visit. In early September, only Air Corps members were receiving R&R anyway, so the lack of space posed no immediate problem. Nevertheless, Eisenhower demanded that rooms be found for the thousands who would want to visit on leave and ordered a census of all Allied personnel in Paris so that any deemed nonessential could be banished to the outskirts. By spring, there were 60,000 U.S. service troops stationed within a 15-mile radius of the capital; an additional 15,000 French soldiers were posted to Paris.[11]

By 1945, Paris had become the R&R center of France. The U.S. Army found and set aside 11,000 hotel rooms for soldiers on leave, and by February 8,400 American soldiers arrived in Paris on leave each day. They were joined by around 4,000 British soldiers per day, so that on any day around 13,000 Allied soldiers on leave lingered in Paris. A high proportion of these soldiers were officers: 2,000 on any day, 1,600 of whom were American. The rest were French, British, and Canadian. Captain Aileen M. Witting, a WAC in Special Services responsible for seeing that soldiers on leave in Paris knew about facilities available to them, said most GIs were more interested in "wine, women, and song" than in touring the City of Light. Many enlisted men would have been content with a bed with clean sheets, a shower, movies, music, and meals other than K-rations that could be had elsewhere. A first lieutenant arriving with his company on leave at the Gare de l'Est said his men had no advance warning that they would be granted leave to go to Paris and thus arrived directly from the front "covered with combat grime." To help entertain men on leave in Paris, the American Red Cross operated 10 service clubs for enlisted men and four for officers—almost 30 percent of Red Cross facilities were set aside for officers. They served millions of their famous donuts and cups of coffee at their most famous club at the Grand Hôtel, open to all, and added Coca Cola to their offerings in 1945. The "Pershing Club" operated by the American Legion offered hotdogs and hamburgers to GIs accompanied by dates—no stags were allowed. WAC Frances DeBra reported that WACs called themselves "hamburger tickets" because GIs needed a date to get to those American Legion burgers. At least one "club" set up for "MPs" turned out to be a front for a black market operation set up by a "Russian baroness." The French police had shut down Les Mille et Une

Nuits (The Thousand and One Nights) as a shady operation that had previously served as a German officers' club, however the club suddenly reopened as an MP club (Special Services of the U.S. Army never authorized any such specialty club). The club sold all manner of pilfered PX goods to French customers, who had free entrance to the club, but it specialized in stolen cigarettes. Evidently about 80 MPs had "joined" the club, some of them thinking it really was a special club for MPs, but the rest knowing exactly what it was.[12]

The 180 registered bordellos in Paris may have been an attraction, but all were off-limits to U.S. personnel. Tests by Inspector General investigators showed that American service members who tried to gain entrance were all refused by management, even though the French insisted that barring GIs encouraged unregistered streetwalkers and spread venereal diseases (VD). Both U.S. Army medical teams and the provost marshal agreed with the French, but SHAEF refused to change the policy. French medical authorities estimated that 75 percent of unregistered prostitutes had VD, while the rate in brothels was very low. Demand by GIs created a market for around 68,000 unregistered and illegal streetwalkers, who accounted for an estimated 90 percent of all VD among GIs. The Inspector General reported that rates of VD among black soldiers was considerably higher than among white GIs, suggesting that white GIs more commonly used condoms issued by the Army.[13]

As was usually the practice, the U.S. Army filled many positions in its staff with non-Americans with useful skills. When searching for English-speaking civilians to perform a wide variety of tasks, the U.S. Army easily found foreigners eager for the work. The foreigners were most often French, but the large number of people from other countries resident in France in 1944 for various reasons—some related to the war and others not—gave the U.S. Army a large pool from which to draw. Some with dubious backgrounds sought jobs with the U.S. Army because the Army offered an excellent place to hide for many in France wishing not to be found. The U.S. Army hired first and vetted second, passing lists of names to the French police and the U.S. Army CIC (counter intelligence), which forced the Army to fire people with pasts that disqualified them from work. The reasons for firing varied: Eva Stern, Ernst Hirschmann, Jean Cahn, Aron Blaustein, Ludwig Schwartz, Kurt Levy, Julius Neuberger, and Felix Zedermann were all employed by the Army—many as interpreters—and listed as "German Jew" or "Austrian Jew," and discharged in February 1945 as "enemy national." The paradox of this action needs no elaboration, but one is forced to wonder why it did not occur to the Office of Adjutant General responsible for hiring. The Army hired and then fired many Russians and Poles because they had previously worked for the Germans in France; some were fired because they had worked for a German company. Adele (normally a woman's name) Berthelot, was an American fired for having been an LVF volunteer! Frederick Blair, an Irishman, was fired for having served as a German propagandist. Some French were fired for cause: of scores whose names turned up on lists of terminated workers, only three were let go for being "collaborators," one of whom was listed as "PPF" (the pro-Nazi Parti populaire français); four were let go for belonging to the family of a collaborator; 10 women were fired for having "associated with Germans," one of whom was the American niece of Brigadier General Leonard Townsend Gerow. An unusually large number of Dutch were fired for loafing, strike activity, or refusal to obey orders. Twenty-one workers were fired for stealing, and 46 others for having criminal records with the French police. Lists reveal between 10 and 15 percent of hires were discharged after vetting or for cause, which was probably higher than random hiring would have produced but perhaps not excessively high. French staff who worked for the U.S. Army were recruited by the French government, yet French civilian recruiters encountered the same problems in finding suitable, untainted candidates as the Americans did. While attempting to put together a pool of French who spoke English to serve as translators, the prefect in Auxerre discovered that the translator for the mayor of the city had previously worked for the Wehrmacht.[14]

MAKING PARIS HOME

In early September 1944, Major General Frank S. Ross, head of the Transportation Service in the European Theater of Operations, set up his office on the Champs Elysées in the former Paris home of *Time Magazine*—lately occupied by Joseph Goebbels's propaganda operation in France. Among the staff General Ross brought to Paris was Betty Magnuson, a member of the Women's Army Corps, a WAC, which made her rare enough within the Army. There were about 8,000 other American women stationed in France by early 1945. But as a secretary assigned to the staff of General Ross, Magnuson was fairly typical of many U.S. personnel stationed in Paris in 1944–1945. She left Duluth, Minnesota, in March 1943, landed first in England in late 1943, and crossed over the

Channel to land at Utah Beach at the end of August, when it was still littered with the detritus of battle and German POWs worked slowly to dig up mines that still made the area dangerous. She was impressed by the Norman country-side, thinking it looked a lot like Wisconsin with its forests of apple trees. She arrived in Paris in early September 1944 only two weeks after its liberation. Another WAC stationed in Paris, Frances DeBra, from Danville, Indiana, joined the Army in April 1943 and became a draftsman, learning how to do the letter-ing for Army maps. After spending time living in a tent in Valognes, Manche, she was packed off to the Hôtel Windsor in Paris—the same as Magnuson—on 10 September 1944 and had her first hot bath in several weeks. It turned out to be her last for many weeks, as hot water was unavailable at her or any other hotel in Paris until 19 November, when the hotel offered "a little hot water and heat," which disappeared just as quickly. Magnuson complained that the Wind-sor remained without heat after Christmas and she could see her breath in her room. The hotel had "some heat and hot water" on 10 January 1945, but DeBra lamented the "cement beds" had only blankets and no sheets. She was set to work in an unheated room in the Hôtel Majestic making maps for frontline troops. In the cold fall and winter, the single lightbulb suspended above her desk provided the only heat; she would cup her hands around the bulb to warm her fingers enough to resume work.[15]

Working in Ross's headquarters offered certain perks not enjoyed by most GIs, even WACs: Magnuson ate most days in the restaurant of the requisitioned Hôtel Splendide, waited on by white-gloved waiters. DeBra, who also ate there, was amazed at what confections French cooks could make from C-rations, though she was disappointed at the lack of fresh fruits and vegetables; she did not care if she never ate another beet in her life. The French staff cooked a big Thanksgiving dinner, complete with turkey and stuffing, for the general's entire American staff as a gesture of appreciation for what the Americans were doing for the French. The restaurant staff also got to keep leftovers from the meal. The Army hired French civilians as chambermaids and cleaning staff for Gen-eral Ross's employees; DeBra was impressed by how friendly the French staff was and was very sad when one of their maids suddenly died. Washerwomen took care of the WACs' laundry, except for lingerie, which WACs washed by hand in their rooms. The practice of hanging khaki underwear out to dry on the balconies above the Champs Elysées provoked complaints, however, so other measures had to be contrived. Magnuson was impressed by how chic

Parisian women looked, using their resourcefulness to adapt prewar clothes to new times. New clothing had almost disappeared from shops during the occupation and was slow to reappear after the liberation. Initially WACs wore baggy field dress uniforms, which raised many eyebrows among fashion-conscious *parisiennes*. Eventually they were issued uniforms more appropriate to their functions as clerical staff in Paris. DeBra was chagrined that in the summer of 1945, when Paris temperatures reached into the 90s, WACs still had only their woolen winter uniforms to wear. Magnuson eventually got used to seeing elegant women riding bicycles on Parisian streets, but adjusting to the bad odor of people on the Metro because of the shortage of soap proved more difficult. DeBra was terrified to cross the Champs Elysées—which she had to do twice a day—because of the packs of bicycles that came roaring downhill at high speed from the Arc de Triomphe. And she never liked the crowds of people on the Metro who seemed to lose their manners as soon as they became packed into train cars. DeBra observed, "Parisians individually are quite polite, but in a crowd!" She was once enveloped by two GIs who created a space to save her from being crushed against a door.[16]

GIs stationed in Paris had access to many luxuries still out of reach of the French. Every taxi in Paris had been requisitioned by the U.S. Army and was reserved for use by soldiers with valid chits issued by authorized officers. The Metro was free for U.S. military personnel; the French still had to pay for tickets. While Parisians drank coffee that was 90 percent chicory, Magnuson and other WACs had access to real coffee, though limited to two cups per day. She and other service personnel could also get coffee and doughnuts at the "Do-nut dug-out" maintained by the American Red Cross, though in September DeBra complained that the doughnuts were made without sugar. When GIs ventured out to see Fontainebleau Palace, as Magnuson and other WACs did, they were greeted by more Red Cross coffee and doughnuts reserved for sightseeing soldiers. In order not to divert French food, the Army did not buy French dairy products for its staff in Paris. Butter and cheese were imported from the United States. When Magnuson told her parents of this, a friend sent some Kraft cheese from Wisconsin, which she received as a luxury. DeBra filled letters to her parents in Indiana with pleas for food, cough drops, and Kleenex. By late October, women's clothes did appear in shop windows on the Champs Elysées, but at prices that shocked Magnuson: $16 for a skirt and $90 for a dress. She enjoyed browsing at the big department stores, such as Printemps and Galeries

Lafayette; she could not afford to buy anything but exploited the occasions to practice her French on the saleswomen, who in January were bundled up in the unheated stores. Like other GIs, Magnuson believed the exchange rate agreed to by the Americans was outrageous and all things French were too expensive to buy. Thus, Magnuson and GIs—not just WACs—did most of their shopping in the PXs (the first opened in late September), which accepted dollars. The exchange rate was not just a byproduct of thoughtless policy, it was by intent. The exchange rate and scarcity of consumer goods in France remained a subject of controversy within the U.S. military throughout its time in France. Eisenhower did not like the artificially high exchange rate and believed it was up to the French to ration scarce items. GIs did not like the rate either and many got around it by resorting to the black markets in currencies and goods. Some within SHAEF decided that black markets were not all bad and served as a valuable way to relieve pressure. Nevertheless, some items, like gift wrapping, were unavailable at any price, as Magnuson complained. Chanel No. 5 perfume seemed to be one item not only much in demand by all Americans, but in plentiful supply. Chester Hansen made a trip to Paris especially to buy a bottle for his wife and found the store on the Champs Elysées thronged with "Red Cross women" looking to buy. Frances DeBra and her WAC friends all bought some, and DeBra sent perfume for Christmas to her family back in the Midwest. Hansen noted that the fashionable street was packed with GIs hunting for souvenirs to send back home. In August 1944, there was yet no limit—besides food—on what Americans could buy. Champagne was available if a GI cared to part with $10 to $16 to have a bottle. DeBra found a French camera for 1,500 francs, which she considered a reasonable price. Unlike many others stationed in Paris during the war, she was able to record many sights and friends when she could find film. Getting it developed was another problem.[17]

Men at the front considered posting in Paris a cushy job. Lieutenant Robert S. Gerdy, formerly a student at Columbia University, was one of them—assigned to Paris as a press relations officer for the Ninth Air Force. When the Ninth Air Force moved from England to France in September 1944, Gerdy moved with it and had the good fortune to be posted to Paris for eight months. Like most US officers, he was allotted a requisitioned Parisian hotel room, which he shared with another officer—first a captain and then a sergeant. Initially he slept in an unheated room with no hot water, like everyone else in Paris; in November he slept under three Army blankets and three hotel blankets. Eventually he was assigned a room with a tiny amount of heat in his bathroom and hot water once a week. Gerdy, who spoke a crude version of French, was thrilled to be in one of the cultural capitals of the world and took full advantage of his time there. Like other Americans in France, he was not permitted to eat in French restaurants, but he could drink his fill in cafés and bars, which he did. He too took in shows at the Folies Bergère and other nightclubs in Montmartre, some dingy and sinister, others less so. He toured Paris often and took in the sights during his time off, ruing his misfortune that the Louvre remained closed while he was there. He fully exploited the scarcity of French men in Paris and struck up relationships with numerous women who helped him improve his French. He was entirely aware that the women benefitted from his free cigarettes, cognac, champagne, and other favors often dispensed by friendly American soldiers to cooperative women—not all of whom were French in a cosmopolitan city like Paris. Gerdy met and dated Russian, English, and Dutch women while in Paris. He appreciated French wine and spirits, and sought out interesting conversations with French men and women alike. Gerdy enjoyed the simple pleasures of Paris. "We sat on a stone bench [in the Tuileries Gardens] talking, while the kid took a ride in a wagon pulled by a goat for three francs, then went to see a puppet-show or *guignol* for three more francs." One day he happened to meet Gertrude Stein, who invited him and another officer to her apartment, where he met Alice B. Toklas and viewed Picasso paintings for an hour. His driver, an enlisted man from Chicago, was disappointed when it turned out they were going to see Picasso paintings and not to visit a clandestine bordello. Stein even offered to introduce Lieutenant Gerdy to Picasso, an opportunity he evidently did not exploit. Frances DeBra also met Stein by chance on a bridge over the Seine; Stein talked to her and her friend affably but did not invite them back to her home.[18]

Infantryman John Savard took advantage of what Paris had to offer during his three-month posting in Vincennes as a guard for the railroad. While in Vincennes he received seven months of back pay and visited the city often. He toured the Tomb of the Unknown Soldier under the Arc de Triomphe, the church of La Madeleine, the Opera, the Trocadéro Museum, and the top of the Eiffel Tower, where he joined many others in scratching his initials in the paint on the railing. Savard attended mass in Notre Dame, strolled the Place de la Concorde, watched girls from cafés on the Champs Elysées, took in a show at the Folies Bergère, and tried his luck at a casino. Like most GIs in Paris he

Readers of American wartime memoirs, such as the diary of David Bruce, would be surprised to discover that French restaurants were off-limits to American military personnel. Soldiers often wrote about memorable meals they had in French restaurants. (ADA SC 24642 B poster forbidding American soldiers from eating in French restaurants, 23 October 1944)

DETACHMENT C 1 C 2, COMPANY H, 1st E. C. A. REGIMENT

23 October 1944.

NOTICE to U S. MILITARY PERSONNEL

All restaurants in Troyes are Off Limits to all U. S. Military Personnel. Order of Commanding General, Advance Section Communications Zone, 28 September 1944, provides :

" **Purchase of food in restaurants is strictly prohibited. This prohibition will be strictly enforced by all Commanders and appropriate disciplinary action taken in the case of violations.** "

There is a shortage of food in this area, available food is for civilian population only.

U. S. Military Personnel coming to Troyes must bring their own rations.

The Military Police are authorized to pick up any U. S. military personnel in restaurants.

By order of Major McGUGIN :

ARLO F. BENZMANN,
1st Lieut., Q M C,
Executive Officer.

"Stop off at Paris, Sept. 1944," drawing by John B. Savard. (MHI, Veterans Surveys, 2nd Inf. Div., box 1, John Savard, "My Life Until Now: The Story of a Boy Growing Up in the Thirties")

frequented the American Red Cross hospitality center in the famous Café de la Paix, which served millions of donuts and cups of coffee to GIs passing through Paris. Savard might have had more interest in art than most GIs; he too regretted that the Louvre was closed and, with most of its art still packed away for safe keeping from the war, he would never see all those famous works. However, he did have a street artist draw his caricature "for a few cigarettes." He took advantage of the free Metro and like many others had to rely on friendly natives when he became lost. And like many other U.S. servicemen, he used some of his Army pay to buy perfume and jewelry on the Rue de la Paix, near the Opera, which he mailed home as Christmas gifts for his family. However, Savard did not get to spend Christmas in Paris; he went to Belgium in time to fight in the Battle of the Bulge. His war ended when he developed trench foot in the Ardennes Forest. Savard may have had somewhat more curiosity about Paris than the average GI, but there were many others like him.[19]

Like Magnuson, Frances DeBra became an avid tourist and on her first free day hiked up to the first landing of the Eiffel Tower as thousands of other Americans did. Both DeBra and Magnuson, neither of whom who spoke French, were initially impressed by how friendly Parisians were. Along with other WACs, Magnuson set off to see Paris, taking in Les Invalides, the Eiffel Tower, the Arc de Triomphe, and the Tuileries Gardens. DeBra added the Rodin Museum as one of her favorites and was fortunate enough to wander around the magical Sainte-Chapelle on the Isle de la Cité along with another WAC and no one else. She insisted that another friend had to see the Cathedral of Notre Dame. Magnuson and DeBra were fortunate enough to still be in Paris in May 1945 when the Louvre reopened with around 80 of its masterpieces restored to their proper place, where GIs flocked to see them. DeBra was thrilled to see the *Mona Lisa*, Vermeer's *Lace Maker*, *Venus de Milo*, the *Winged Victory*, Delacroix's *Liberty Leading the People*, and many other famous works. She had hoped in the fall of 1944 to take art courses at the Ecole des Beaux Art in Paris, but there was none offered in the evenings. In March 1945 she was able to attend life drawing classes with French students on Saturdays at the Ecole even though she spoke no French; she reported the French students were very kind and helped her out.[20]

DeBra also set out to see as much of Paris as she could on her days off, although the nearly constant fall and winter rain persuaded her to spend a lot of free time reading in her unheated hotel room. She took full advantage of enter-

tainment offered by Paris, attending many operas and musical performances at
the Paris Opera, the requisitioned Marigny Theater, and other Parisian locales.
She saw *Romeo and Juliet, Faust,* and *Madame Butterfly* in the unheated Opera
House In November; a cold breeze rushed into the audience when the curtain
first rose. Both Magnuson and DeBra kept their coats on while seated in the
Opera to keep warm. DeBra attended *Boris Godunov* in January 1945 when the
theater was freezing, prompting her to resolve to bring a blanket next time.
The Sadler's Wells Ballet came from London to stage many shows, which DeBra
saw four times; she saw Glen Miller twice at the requisitioned Marigny Theater
and other less famous jazz acts. Magnuson took advantage of services offered to
British soldiers stationed in Paris and went to the British theater to see Shake-
speare performed by the leading British actors of the day. Unescorted French
civilians were barred from dance halls reserved for GIs. If the French wanted to
do any dancing, they had to wrangle an invitation to an American service club
because dancing was banned at French establishments so long as resources for
civilian life were so hard to come by. This was not a practical matter but a policy imposed by the French government in view of the harshness of life, seeing
public dancing as inappropriate.[21]

Magnuson noticed something that worried French officials also noted: lines
for American movies were longer than for French movies. After being cut off
from the products of Hollywood for four years, the French eagerly soaked up
whatever they could see, even if it were old releases like Chaplin's 1925 *Gold
Rush,* which played to packed and enthusiastic houses. Walt Disney's 1937 an-
imation *Blanche Neige et les Sept Nains (Snow White and the Seven Dwarfs)* attracted large crowds on the Champs Elysées soon after. Americans generally
went to different movie houses that showed the latest Hollywood movies without subtitles. Most Parisians were unable to appreciate the new films because
few could understand English. Yet enormous crowds tried to gain entrance
to reopened cinemas showing films previously not screened, causing fights to
break out over admission; someone fired shots when 1,600 people tried to get
into the Gobelins Cinema on the Avenue d'Italie in October. By November 1944
American movies began to appear in French cinemas with French subtitles.
Magnuson and other WACs found it amusing to watch American cartoons with
French subtitles and hear the audiences roar with laughter after a delay. Lieutenant Gerdy frequently took his French dates to the movies and improved his
French by watching American films with French subtitles. Numerous French

theaters had been requisitioned by the Army and offered American films without subtitles, but Gerdy preferred the French theaters. Frances DeBra also attended American movies dubbed into French and sometimes with French subtitles in French theaters, which she found amusing. Magnuson was less amused about having to pay "old lady" ushers 2 francs to be escorted to her seat; the ushers refused to let anyone sit until they had been paid. None of the theaters, French or American, had heat.[22]

The winter of 1944–1945 was cold and dumped an unusually large amount of snow on Paris, making it even more difficult for supplies to reach the city than shortly after the liberation. The amount of wheat, potatoes, and milk reaching the markets diminished rather than increased. It had been barely adequate in October, and by December shortages were causing real hunger among Parisians. Transport remained the principal cause for shortages. Six hundred trucks were allotted to bring food to the city every day, but only 350 of them had tires. The amount of French food reaching Paris dwindled from 6,250 tons in October to around 5,000 tons per month in the winter. People were living on about 1,500 calories per day, which was not enough for an active man to maintain weight. At Christmas, most restaurants in Paris were closed for want of food. CA judged there was a deficiency particularly in the meat and potatoes that normally provided the main source of calories. Parisians suffered more than GIs from the dearth of warmth, electricity, and food. Even chewing gum was rationed at the PX: one pack per week. Still, French children begged for gum and chocolate outside WAC quarters, knowing they would get some. Coal was still not reaching the capital, and Parisian authorities announced that no public buildings would be heated until the new year. The department stores were freezing inside, and food was becoming harder to find for the French, who waited in long lines outside of bakeries to get their ration of bread. In January, Paris suffered an acute shortage of food, gas, and electricity. Bakeries were forced to close for want of flour and the means to turn it into bread. Fresh milk stopped arriving and only carrots and small quantities of meat and potatoes were available in the markets. There were limits to what innovative and resourceful French cooks could do. The population was becoming sick, and freezing-cold hospitals were jammed to full. The French begged the Allies for another 200 trucks right away just to deliver milk. Allied soldiers appeared to be living in privileged comfort compared to the deprived Parisians. At first this did not seem to provoke much resentment on the part of the French. During the first heavy snowfall in January GIs and civilians threw snowballs at each other in good humor. Still, when Magnuson groused to a GI on the Metro that she had been in the Army for two years and he replied he had been in for four, a Frenchwoman interjected that she had been in a concentration camp for four years and now had no heat in her freezing apartment. When Colonel William Triplet arrived in Paris as a replacement officer in December, he found Paris "a frigid hell hole," and his room in his assigned hotel "stone cold, like going to bed in a walk-in refrigerator." Only on 10 January, when Paris received three inches of snow, did Magnuson's room receive heat and hot water. Most French still had neither in their apartments, and both French and Americans were aware of the disparity.[23]

Robert Gerdy was very aware that he had a cushy existence far from the war and that many GIs did not. He wrote in mid-February, "Just arrived in the office after a nice afternoon sitting in between two dames on a stone bench in the Jardins des Tuileries watching kids on the swings, the merry-go-round and the puppet show . . . I felt funny walking down the Rue de la Paix with a girl on each arm. . . . It's warm today, and the sun's been out, and all in all, it would be a fine day except for the always horrifying sight of combat men in the streets, reminding you that guys are getting killed in this war, that guys are not sitting in gardens with girls or in hotel rooms with big fancy typewriters. It's horrible that. Produces some guilt sense and an almost constant discomfort, not at what they will think of you but at the difference between your war and theirs." While Gerdy enjoyed Paris and the Parisians, not all Americans posted to Paris did. "Last night, Polly, Blake and I [Gerdy] got into a furious argument about Paris and the people who live here. They said they thought they were all terrible, mercenary, degenerate. I said they were OK and not to make generalizations like that because it leads to fascism. . . . I can't get enough of Paris, can't see enough different places, can't see enough different people—mostly dames, I admit."[24]

THE BEGINNING OF THE END

Friction produced by the enormous number of American service troops stationed in Paris and its environs should have been dampened by a change in policy in March 1945. With the final big push in Germany to crush the Nazi regime, the Allies experienced a dearth of riflemen on the front and looked to make up the shortage from among service troops stationed in the COMZ. After black infantrymen rushed into Belgium during the Battle of the Bulge and showed themselves every bit as tough and effective as white soldiers, SHAEF opened up more combat positions to black GIs, until then mostly restricted to service positions. SHAEF also sought to get white service troops out of desks and from behind typewriters in Paris and into Germany with rifles. Thus, 65,000 service troops of all races were transferred from COMZ to fighting units in Germany in March 1945, and their places were filled with 7,500 WACs and tens of thousands of French civilians. The Army also searched among thousands of displaced persons stranded in France from Allied nations (primarily from the Low Countries) to take over service jobs.[25]

As spring approached, tensions between Americans and the French became more apparent. Magnuson got into an argument with some French soldiers about democracy, what it meant, and how it worked in the United States. Still, when President Roosevelt died, French people stopped American strangers on the streets to tell them how sorry they were. Many had tears in their eyes. Despite his hostility to de Gaulle, Roosevelt remained enormously popular among the French, and when polled in November 1944 almost three-quarters had wanted to see him reelected to the presidency. Robert Gerdy heard stories of commiserating French from his comrades, but no one ever approached him about it. A public mass was said for the late president in Notre Dame, another at the Trocadero, and all entertainments were closed. U.S. service clubs likewise shut their doors in mourning. However, FDR's death proved an exception to the general trend: the French were growing tired of the Americans, who now seemed more like intruders than liberators. And American attitudes toward the French similarly dimmed as the novelty of discovering a new people and new ways wore off. The French resented apparent privileges enjoyed by their allies: American buildings and cinemas had heat when civilian buildings did not. Americans had plentiful food while the French did not. American service personnel rode the Metro for free; the French had to pay. The small annoyances of life mounted for both peoples. Magnuson became exasperated by all the pushing and shoving on the Metro, and she and other WACs stopped being polite and saying "*excusez-moi.*" As the weather warmed, Magnuson's attitude toward the French turned cooler.[26]

Even as late as the spring of 1945, Americans and Parisians had little real human contact with each other. The language barrier probably explains most

of this. When Lieutenant Hans Schmitt arrived in Paris as an intelligence officer in the spring as the war was reaching its conclusion, he was invited to the
Montparnasse home of a French captain, who had met the French-speaking
German-American in line at the Paris Opera. When word spread in Captain
Mayer's apartment house that a francophone American officer was in the building, inhabitants gravitated to the captain's apartment to meet and interrogate
the young lieutenant about America. He spent hours satisfying the Parisians' in-
exhaustible curiosity about his homeland as if they had never met an American
before in a city teeming with tens of thousands of Americans. These Parisians
were far from hostile and in fact very friendly and interested to hear about the
United States, given the opportunity that they never had from chance encounters with a Betty Magnuson or a Frances DeBra, who spoke only English.[27]

As the days grew warmer and the end for Germany appeared closer, even
Gerdy's views of Paris and its people grew less generous. He noticed more beg-
gars and was appalled by the rude treatment they provoked from Parisians. He
started to evince greater irritation with the French. When he saw GIs being
charged 15 francs for a 10-franc beer, he mused that he could understand the
French practicing that sort of subterfuge on the German occupiers, but why do
it to their friends, the Americans? The incident made him remember another
time in September 1944, when he was in a bar where an American lieutenant
complained about being charged twice for the same drink. The captain with
Gerdy responded that they would not pay for their drinks. They drank their
beers and when they began to leave without paying, the barman objected and
told them they had not yet paid. The captain put his hand on his holstered .45
and retorted, we already paid; the barman replied, "oh, yes. I remember, now."
Gerdy had not mentioned this incident in earlier letters, when he was first
enchanted by Paris and eager to get to know its people. Only in the spring of
1945 when the bloom had worn off did he tell the story, which related an event
that probably occurred often. By April, now-Captain Gerdy was ready to leave.
He had grown bored with his French girlfriends and broken off his relationships; he was tired of the French generally and by early April was socializing
exclusively with other Americans and a few British—who he generally liked
and respected more than the French. His admiration for the British waxed as
his regard for the French waned. In late April, Gerdy got into a shouting match
with some French in a Montmartre nightclub when a French woman called all
Americans "cheap." By springtime Frances DeBra was homesick, tired of being

in France, and bored with the Army. She complained about the "tasteless food" and the crowds on the streets of Paris. In March she mused how she preferred Chicago to Paris, and after spending a few days on leave in Brussels she mentioned that she found Belgians friendlier than either the British or French. She never formed any real friendships with any French because of the language barrier. Both French and Americans were growing irritable and losing patience with each other. By May, the Americans wanted to leave and the French wanted them to go.[28]

It was probably inevitable that Parisians and the Americans stationed in Paris would get on each other's nerves over time. SHAEF, the administration in Washington, and the French government were aware of the diminishing sympathies on the part of both the French populace and GIs, and viewed the coolness with alarm. It was not limited to Paris but becoming general around France. GIs returning from Germany became convinced that the French hated them, and GIs began to reciprocate the feelings. In Paris, Americans occupied thousands of hotel rooms and apartments badly needed by returning French POWs, deportees, and others returning to liberated Paris. The French press started to grouse about the thousands of apartments requisitioned in Paris for American officers who frequently spent long periods away from the city, leaving the apartments empty when they were desperately needed by French. This conflict of interests probably had no happy resolution other than an American withdrawal from Paris, which would come eventually after victory. The shortage of food had no solution so long as the French transportation network, from docks to rail depots, remained unreconstructed. Repairing it would take time and resources. Most Americans in Paris would have preferred to have been someplace else—home. That is something the French and the Americans agreed upon, but there was little they could do about it for months after VE Day. Inconveniences imposed on the French by the vast American military presence were tolerated so long as Germany remained undefeated, but with the collapse of the Nazi regime in May 1945 the reason to put up with the Americans had disappeared.[29]

CONCLUSIONS

The Liberators and the Liberated

I
t took the German Army just 46 days in 1940 to rout the French, Belgian, and Dutch armies and the British Expeditionary Force. The Wehrmacht overran about two-thirds of France before an armistice came into force just after midnight on 25 June. The Germans accomplished this feat with great savagery, not hesitating to bomb, machine-gun, and beat French civilians who got in their way. They killed and injured many others who were not in their way. They massacred townspeople in villages that put up too much resistance to the German onslaught and behaved with brutality toward officials who failed to jump to do their bidding. Once the armistice was signed and German forces withdrew to the Occupied Zone in the north and along the Atlantic coast, Berlin ordered its soldiers to behave "correctly" toward the French, and by and large they did. The strict discipline of the German military proved effective in curbing within the Army the sort of viciousness meted out by the Gestapo, the SS, and the French Milice (the militia of the Vichy regime tasked with crushing dissent). After the Allies invaded France in June 1944, the German Army reverted to its brutal comportment of June 1940 and committed wanton acts of murder, rape, and pillage during their ferocious campaign against the FFI and their retreat from France. Not until March 1945 did the Allies completely expel the Germans from their last footholds in Alsace, and it took until May to oust them from their remaining redoubts on the Atlantic coast. The American advance into and through France contrasted starkly with the German onslaught of 1940. Despite the horrific violence of the liberation, American soldiers and French civilians met as friends. The Allied struggle to liberate France from the Nazi yoke necessitated widespread spilling of blood, and much of it flowed from French civilians. The price paid in civilian blood and devastation in 1944 was several times greater than in 1940: many thousands—even tens of thousands—of French civilians lost their lives to American bombs and artillery shells. However, while the Allies and Germans both shed much French blood

in 1944, the Allies attempted to keep French casualties to a minimum while the Germans deliberately and wantonly massacred many thousands of innocent French civilians. Most French civilians who lost their lives during the war died under Allied air raids, mostly in 1943 and 1944. Even after the successful invasion of Normandy in June 1944, Allied bombers continued to hit targets in yet-to-be-liberated France, and French continued to die. But as one French agent in touch with British intelligence noted, the French choice was between death and destruction, and slavery. Almost all French preferred to suffer the casualties and enormous damage of liberation rather than to live under the Nazi heel. And there was an enormous difference between living with the German occupiers and the Americans who followed, even if the vast majority of German soldiers comported themselves "correctly" amid the French populace, while not all GIs behaved so well.

Of course, policy makes a difference. Nazi policy, set by Adolf Hitler in Berlin, dictated that Germany should expend a minimum of resources to keep France docile and under control, while extracting the maximum wealth, without provoking massive resistance. German generals tasked with implementing this policy used the minimum of brute force to gain as much cooperation as possible from the occupied subjects. Because most German soldiers after 1941 viewed occupation duty in France as the best possible assignment, much preferable to subduing Russia or chasing guerrillas in Yugoslavia, they tended to adopt a friendly stance toward France and its people. Nevertheless, the humbled French returned the friendliness only to the extent they had to. Most French hated the humiliating occupation even if the average German soldier was not such a bad fellow. Generally, German soldiers, subject to harsh discipline, "behaved correctly," according to most French. Proper behavior was the American policy, too, but it was not implemented or enforced with the same rigor as the Germans had. Discipline was often lax among the American soldiers who replaced the Germans, and too many GIs behaved boorishly. At times this slackness benefitted the French: MPs tasked with keeping civilians from using roads reserved for U.S. Army supply trucks actually helped civilians find rides; U.S. drivers frequently gave lifts to illegally hitchhiking French and had to be reminded repeatedly that it was against Army regulations to carry civilian passengers. That did not stop GIs and even officers from doing so. While some French civilians were indeed beaten by American GIs and others were even murdered, American authorities made efforts to find the culprits and see them punished.[1]

The responses of French civilians toward their liberators varied depending on the circumstances and setting; they also evolved over time. At first the most common reaction of the French was shock and horror at being targeted by Allied bombs and artillery. Even some who experienced or witnessed the Allied bombardments understood the purpose and accepted the price of liberation. Initial responses by both paratroopers and civilians who met them was mutual suspicion, soon replaced by relief. Normans, who suffered disproportionally from the raging battle, eventually received Americans as friends, but only if they had not been badly mauled by American high explosives for too long. Residents of unscathed Granville put on a joyous welcome for the liberating GIs; those of badly battered Avranches received the Americans with less warmth. Paris, which had been through some tense and bloody days before the Allies arrived in August, gave its liberators, who were initially French soldiers, a raucous welcome. Their recent trials had been inflicted exclusively by the Germans and not by the Allies. The people of the Yonne and Aube were ecstatic about the arrival of General Patton's tanks, yet alarmed when they failed to stay and left the civilians in the care of the FFI. Valuable aid rendered to American forces by FFI in Lorraine left an initial good impression on the arriving Americans. Attitudes of GIs turned skeptical and then hostile only when the advance stalled and German resistance stiffened in the fall of 1944. It is possible that some GIs turned their frustrations against French civilians in Lorraine, but that had not occurred in similar circumstances in Normandy. The differing characteristics of the two French populations probably explains at least some of the different reactions of GIs in the two regions. The attitudes of GIs and WACs waned even in peaceful Paris as time went on. Initial mutual happiness was replaced by boredom and resentment as the war bogged down on the German frontier. The strains of war beat down the morale of GIs and civilians alike as the war dragged on into 1945. Despite such challenges, GIs still reacted with sincere concern and charity to the plight of French civilians caught in the chaos of the German offensive into Alsace in 1945.

The joy of liberation in a wide swath of France turned into uncertainty and worry when inhabitants were left more or less to their own devices while American forces rushed to the east before Gaullists authorities arrived to establish order. The temporary void left behind by the Americans was mostly filled by the French Forces of the Interior (FFI), the bands of civilians who took up arms to help free their country from Nazi rule. Certainly, the reign of the FFI was often (and probably usually) benign and gladly received by the liberated French; however, too often it came with capricious, arbitrary, and unjust retribution against those who had shown too much enthusiasm or cooperation with the Vichy regime. In areas recently vacated by American troops, this often reflected poorly on the Americans who failed to protect French civilians caught in the chaos, even if that was not their responsibility. Both American and French attitudes toward the FFI varied with circumstances: often the FFI were seen as helpful, other times they were perceived as a nuisance, and occasionally FFI were viewed as dangerous. The GI responses echoed those of the French—including the Provisional Government of Charles de Gaulle: many saw them as heroes, others (and not just collaborators) saw them as devils. The French reaction to the FFI depended not only on the individual French fighters, but on whether American soldiers were close by to serve as a counter to the unpredictable FFI. After the war, Gaullists made sure that the FFI were seen exclusively as heroes.[2]

The Battle for France in 1944–1945 was costly in the lives and health of Allied soldiers and French civilians alike. The French response to American and Allied bombings was frequently shaped by the anticipation of liberation: it was an unfortunate necessity leading to freedom from Nazi rule. However, without the prospect of liberation looming in the near future, it was just murder and mayhem. That was true throughout the regions of France that suffered through the chaos and carnage of battle. Only faith in ultimate liberation could justify the death and destruction visited upon France by the Allies. Once the German occupiers had been expelled from most of France, by the winter of 1944, the purpose of French acceptance of the Americans had been achieved. The price had been paid, and yet the Americans were still in France, monopolizing roads, using scarce resources, and making decisions that greatly affected French lives. The necessity for the French to tolerate American dominance over many spheres of their lives had greatly diminished and the French would soon demand greater control over affairs in France.

This work seeks to demonstrate something that should be obvious: living in war zones was a precarious and often miserable experience. Sometimes it proved deadly, even if the vast majority of French subjected to the misfortune survived relatively unscathed. The Americans never sought to turn the French into victims, even if they made decisions that inevitably led to dire consequences for the French. Targeting the crossroads of Normandy on 5 June and subsequent days was perhaps the decision taken by Eisenhower that proved the most lethal for the French. Thousands perished and many more were injured in a gamble to keep German reinforcements away from the landing beaches during the critical early hours of the Allied invasion. Both Rommel and Eisenhower assumed that the first day or two of the invasion would decide its success or failure; hence, Eisenhower was willing to sacrifice French civilians for final victory over Germany. We know now what Eisenhower could not have known at the time: Hitler forbade moving reinforcements from east of the Seine River to support the forces opposing the landings because he believed the Normandy landings to be only a diversion and not the main attack, which would come to the east of the Seine. The bridge bombings and destruction of much of the center of Rouen was for naught. German troops adapted to the destroyed crossroads the same way the Allies did when they eventually encountered them: they went around. The decimation of towns and villages at the *carréfours* slowed the movement of German troops insufficiently to affect the outcome. Yet, Eisenhower sought to tweak the odds for success at every opportunity. He approved any action that he believed would improve the likelihood of a successful invasion, including razing towns and villages and annihilating their inhabitants.[3]

The same dilemma faced Eisenhower and his planners when deciding on tactics to use in the air campaign against French railroads. Here, we have clear evidence that the decision to employ four-engine strategic bombers to disrupt rail lines cost more French lives and destroyed more French property than two-engine medium bombers and single-engine fighter-bombers, which proved more accurate even if they, too, rarely hit their targets. At least when they missed they caused less damage and fewer deaths. The decision to use inaccurate heavy bombers against precise targets in northern France in advance of D-Day and as support afterward seemed reasonable only because Eisenhower wanted to use all available weapons to win. The bombers were there, so they should be used even if they were not ideal for the job. In fact, as Operation Cobra at the end of July 1944 made clear, using strategic bombers in support of ground troops was still an acceptable option, even if they already had been proven to put both friendly soldiers and civilians below them in harm's way. Similarly, the differing tactics of the British and Americans in attacking trains showed that the British approach of targeting locomotives of moving trains was just as effective as the American practice of hitting trains standing at sidings, and at far lower cost. The British attacks in the open country avoided the casualties inherent in attacking trains in towns. Targeting locomotives reduced the number of civilian casualties among passengers on the trains. Hitting standing trains packed with German soldiers certainly increased the number of dead Germans, but it was equally lethal when packed with French civilians. The British tactic recommended itself, and fewer French would have paid the ultimate price had the Americans adopted it.[4]

I have employed "acceptable price" many times in this work because that was the term employed by many French and Anglo-Saxons at the time. Heartrending death, destruction, displacement, and injury in France were unavoidable consequences of the brutal and bloody liberation. Allied planners knew that innocent French would sacrifice their lives in the struggle, but how many deaths were "acceptable" to achieve victory? Winston Churchill had stated that he wanted to keep the number of French casualties from British air raids on France "under 10,000." In fact, the number of victims was many times that figure, counting the dead alone. No French authority has been able to calculate a reliable number of French civilian losses caused by aerial bombardment; estimates range between 48,000 and 70,000 dead, and another 70,000 injured. Claudia Baldoli and Andrew Knapp posit around 60,000 dead. The land war to liberate France also proved costly. The French, who pay close attention to statistics, nonetheless have been unable to arrive at a reliable number of French civilians killed during the war; the best most recent guess puts the figure at around 250,000. This number includes French workers killed in Germany (maximum of 40,000), deportees who never returned from German concentration camps (about 36,000), "collaborators" killed during the violent passions of the Liberation (about 9,000), hostages shot by the Germans (7,000–12,000), FFI killed in combat or summarily shot dead (about 13,700), and civilians lost to Allied bombers. Indeed, the Allied aerial bombardment may have been the largest single cause of French civilian deaths, and yet RAF personnel recorded very little resentment against them by the French, once liberated. In total, around 80,000 French civilians died violent deaths in 1944 from causes linked to the war. There is no way to affirm that these deaths were "acceptable," but they were the price paid by France for liberation, and French documents of the era contain few references bemoaning that toll. During the war, Charles de Gaulle said hardly a recorded word about the toll of bombing campaigns. A poll commissioned by the GPRF in the fall of 1944 revealed that 70 percent of French believed "deliverance" was worth the horror of the destructive war for liberation. Some believed it was the harvest reaped by the French for their "errors of the past."[5]

Government inspectors counted 452,000 houses totally destroyed by the war and 1.4 million damaged (including destruction wrought in 1940). Somewhere around 64,000 houses were completely destroyed, 37,000 rendered uninhabitable, and 90,000 severely damaged in the Allied air campaign alone. In 1945, French civil defense officials counted 60,000 buildings destroyed by Allied bombing and 130,000 damaged. Many more homes were destroyed or damaged in the fighting in France than in the Allied air campaign; most of that damage was wrought in Normandy and Alsace-Lorraine, where fighting was the most intense. While the numbers are subject to debate, the war undoubtedly brought much destruction to France; however, the French seem to have expended little energy blaming the Allies at the time or in subsequent decades.[6]

Allied soldiers also paid a price for French liberation. The number of dead airmen from both the American and British forces should give some idea of "acceptable losses" among the Allied air fleets. We have no estimate of casualties among airmen from bombing raids over France alone, but we do have reliable numbers for Allied losses in the European air war. The American Army (excluding the Air Force) suffered 552,117 casualties in the European Theater from 6 June 1944 to 9 May 1945, of whom 122,754 died on the battlefield, in hospitals, or in POW camps. Again, that was the toll, whether an "acceptable price" or not. Between 250,000 and 270,000 of those casualties were incurred in France; 55,590 American soldiers (including flyers) were killed in action in the European Theater (excluding Italy) between 6 June and 1 December 1944. We know that General Eisenhower approved tactics that minimized casualties among American soldiers, so that he could keep "the price" low. He was appalled to learn from Marshal Georgy Zhukov that the Red Army cleared German minefields during battle by having Soviet infantry advance through them as if the mines were not there. As seen in the bombing campaign against crossroads in Normandy, Eisenhower approved tactics intended to lower casualties *in the long run*, even if the plan to keep German reinforcements from reaching the invasion beaches was expected to be costly in French civilian lives in the short run. It *was* costly in French lives and made almost no difference to the battle, but was a calculated risk taken by Eisenhower amid conflicting advice over its wisdom.[7]

French historian Eddy Florentin points out that despite frequent and devastating bombardment by Allied heavy bombers in Brittany, Bretons flocked to the FFI to join the Allies in their mutual cause. The same applied to Normans, even more devastated than Bretons by Allied planes. Some reports from Caen relayed that when the city was finally liberated, the inhabitants, emerging from their cellars, danced for joy and applauded the British and Canadian soldiers who first appeared. The deputy mayor noted, however, that the population greeted the ranks of French-Canadian soldiers who later marched into town with restrained emotion: "We had suffered too much . . . to greet them with unrestrained emotion, those who the necessity of war had obliged to do us so much harm." This at least recognized that though the harm was real and great, the war had demanded it. Similar sentiments were encountered by liberating Americans in devastated Valognes: they were greeted by subdued residents who had survived the horrendous pounding the town had taken from American forces. The American liberators of Brest received a comparable welcome from the remaining residents who had lived through the horrific battle. The pattern seems to have been that those French who had personally experienced the wrath of war generally showed less enthusiasm for their liberators than those who had only secondhand experience of the violence, or whose exposure to the horrors of war had been brief. As French agent Rémy noted after the RAF inflicted great damage to Bordeaux in 1940, the choice was between such destruction and slavery. Around 12,000 Frenchmen and women risked execution or deportation to help downed Allied flyers get back to England to return once again to bombing.[8]

Although many French expressed gratitude to their liberators, they nonetheless were determined to oppose any effort by their Anglo-Saxon allies to impose a government of occupation in 1944. In the French imagination, the Allies, especially the Americans, were determined to prevent Charles de Gaulle from heading a provisional government in France and planned to establish their own occupation authority similar to the one in Italy. The myth of the Allied Military Government of Occupied Territories (AMGOT) was a large foundation upon which rested one of the pillars supporting de Gaulle's authority. In the Gaullist view, not only had de Gaulle been crucial to ousting the Nazis from France, he saved France from the bitter fate of occupation by the perfidious British and their crude, rude, materialistic, and uncivilized cousins, the Americans. That the Allies planned to impose a military government or puppet regime on France was more or less received wisdom during the war and persists to this day in France. The French, including many scholars who should know better, continue to wave the bloody shirt of AMGOT as an example of what awaited France if de Gaulle's perseverance and toughness had not prevented the Allies from having their way. This is mostly nonsense, even if President Roosevelt had favored AMGOT until he abandoned the idea in October 1944. Roosevelt was never in a position to impose AMGOT, not least because he could not impose it on his own commander, General Eisenhower, who would have been responsible for implementing this bad idea. Winston Churchill never gave the proposal any serious consideration. Perhaps Roosevelt would have dropped his attachment to AMGOT if some other more charming and flexible Frenchman, Jean Monnet, René Pleven, or Pierre Mendès-France for example, had come to the fore instead of de Gaulle. De Gaulle was undoubtedly a problem in U.S.-French relations, but he was not *the* problem; Roosevelt contributed as much to discord as de Gaulle. Régine Torrent argues convincingly that the specter of AMGOT was kept alive in the years since the war because of Gaullist resentment of the United States as the new power in the world that displaced France.[9]

Regardless of President Roosevelt's very late recognition of de Gaulle as the head of state of France, both the French and the Americans saw each other as valuable allies in their common struggle. The Civil Affairs Corps proved to be an inspired invention, whether its original purpose was to govern the French or to assist them; it more than proved its worth. American officers specifically tasked to liaison with French civilian officials earned almost universal praise from their French colleagues and French civilians who dealt with them. Civil Affairs officers usually spoke French and had some experience of France and its people before arriving. They appear to have been well chosen and performed their assignments with enthusiasm and integrity. I saw few complaints against CA officers by French officials who dealt with them, although there were some. Cooperation between French and American officials at that level made the alliance successful. Officials who had to get along and work together to win the war were more important to the alliance than administrators in Washington and Paris, who did not always work together so smoothly. Republican Commissioner François Coulet was undoubtedly a talented and dedicated public servant who accomplished much against the odds; however, if French officials of lower rank reacted to every complication and problem as peevishly as he often did, compromises and agreements to settle minor conflicts would have occurred less often or taken more time. Friction between the two partners would have been greater, with consequential impact on overall effectiveness.

French admiration for their American liberators noticeably declined over time. Anger and dismay over the devastating bombings mounted in the fall of

1943, peaking in June 1944. The Normandy invasion muted much of that, but bitterness among some remained. French regard for their allies slipped markedly in December 1944. Many wondered why it was taking the Allies so long to break out of Normandy during the summer, although the impressive sweep through northern France in August and September 1944 wiped away most doubts. Once the German military collapse began in August, the rout was even more complete than that of the French Army in 1940. However, the Germans had somewhere to retreat to, which in 1940 the French did not. The inability—or in the view of some French, unwillingness—of the U.S. Army to push the offensive against the Germans in Lorraine in the fall of 1944 to completely rid France of Nazis diminished the awe with which many French regarded the Americans. Many believed the war would be over by Christmas 1944, and when it ground on the mood of the populace darkened and the high regard for their American liberators dimmed. Popular morale never really returned to the high point of late summer 1944, when complete liberation seemed imminent and the damage inflicted on France seemed worth the cost. Exaggerated expectations of deliverance from both Nazis and want contributed to French popular disappointments in the winter of 1944–1945. Even the victory of May 1945 failed to revive the optimism and grand accord of 1944; however, the brevity of the joy of victory had numerous explanations: the shock of the return, or failure to return, of concentration camp inmates and POWs; the suspicion and quarreling between French Communists and Gaullists; the failure of the government to deliver food and rapid material relief. The Americans had little to do with much of these plaints, but resentment against the Americans grew nevertheless. French officials had a more realistic idea than many civilians did of how much material relief the Allies could be expected to deliver to the French populace. Officials knew they could expect little and, thus, set to doing what they could to take care of their own. The shortage of shipping, port facilities, and trucks for civilian use ensured that the civilian economy would lag and that consumption would remain minimal, and the Americans could do little about it. However, many French noted that even if rationed, bread was available in the shops during the German occupation; after September 1944 it became scarce and at times disappeared entirely. Many French blamed this on the Americans.[10]

The liberation era was chaotic, full of violence and uncertainty about the future. The Provisional Government of General de Gaulle acted quickly to guide

France with a firm hand, but it faced many challenges. The Americans could help the French with some of those challenges and not with others. Reining in the FFI and reestablishing an orderly police and justice system was largely up to the French; however, rearming the police and the revived French Army could only be done by the Allies in the short run before the French arms industry could be restored. That the U.S. Army, instead of installing an AMGOT, actually helped de Gaulle reestablish orderly government in France could be viewed with amazement, though it only made sense. Eisenhower had no interest in embroiling himself and his staff in French political disputes and wanted a stable country in the Communications Zone, free of hunger, epidemics, fighting, and mobs. Helping the Provisional Government was the only reasonable option. And there is no doubt that even if German soldiers behaved "correctly" during the Nazi occupation, and GIs sometimes comported themselves boorishly, the American military presence was much preferred by the French to the German occupation. While Americans rounded up and detained some hundreds of French in the heat of battle, U.S. policy never sanctioned killing any of them, unlike Nazi policy that authorized mass murder of French civilians. As fraught as the rapport between Roosevelt and de Gaulle was, relations between Vichy and Berlin were much less equal than between Washington and Paris under the GPRF, and there was no doubt that Berlin could and was capable of doing its worst. In contrast, despite Roosevelt's dream of imposing a temporary military government on liberated France, there was never any American plan or desire to conquer France and turn it into a vassal state. The occupation of France ended when the German armies were expelled. The administration of France was turned over to the GPRF almost in its entirety by the end of 1944 even if the Allies retained many privileges in order to defeat Nazi Germany. When the war was over, the French wanted the Americans to leave. And by January 1946 they did.

NOTES

ADA	Archives départementales de l'Aube (Troyes)
ADBdR	Archives départementales des Bouches-du-Rhône (Marseille)
ADMM	Archives départementales de Meurthe-et-Moselle (Nancy)
ADY	Archives départementales de l'Yonne (Auxerre)
ANF	Archives nationales de France (Pierrefitte-sur-Seine)
comm. rép.	commissaire de la République (commissioner of the Republic)
comm. police	commissaire de police (police commissioner)
COS	chief of staff
CWO	chief warrant officer
Dir.	director
ETO	European Theater of Operations
FRUS	Foreign Relations of the United States (documents published by the U.S. State Department)
MHI	Military History Institute (at the U.S. Army War College, Carlisle, Pennsylvania)
Min. Int.	Ministère de la Intérieure
NARA	National Archives and Records Administration (College Park, Maryland)
PFC	private first class
Préf.	préfet (prefect)
PWD	Psychological Warfare Division
QMC	Quartermaster Corps
RG	record group
Ren. Gén.	Renseignements Généraux (government domestic intelligence agency)
Sous-Préf.	assistant prefect in charge of a suboffice

INTRODUCTION

1. Rick Atkinson, *The Guns at Last Light: The War in Western Europe, 1944–1945* (New York: Holt, 2013); Max Hastings, *Overlord: D-Day and the Battle for Normandy* (New York: Simon and Schuster, 1984); John Keegan, *Six Armies in Normandy, from D-Day to the Liberation of Paris* (New

York: Penguin, 1983); Charles B. MacDonald, *The Mighty Endeavor: American Armed Forces in the European Theater in World War II* (New York: Oxford Univ. Press, 1969).

2. On the episode of AMGOT, see Charles Robertson, *When Roosevelt Planned to Govern France* (Amherst: Univ. of Massachusetts Press, 2011), and Régine Torrent, *La France américaine: Controverses de la Libération* (Brussels: Editions Racine, 2004).

3. In fact, I undertook research in the archives in Marseille to investigate the Franco-American experience in the south of France, but the events there largely duplicate what I found in northern France, so I decided to cut out discussion of the south of France to produce a shorter, more manageable work. Hilary Footitt examines the Franco-American interaction in Marseille in *War and Liberation in France: Living with the Liberators* (New York: Palgrave Macmillan, 2004). I discuss the Allied requisition of the port of Marseille in *The Struggle for Cooperation: Liberated France and the American Military, 1944–1946* (Lexington: Univ. Press of Kentucky, 2019).

4. Footitt, *War and Liberation in France*; William Hitchcock, *The Bitter Road to Freedom: A New History of the Liberation of Europe* (New York: Free Press, 2008); David Reynolds, *Rich Relations: The American Occupation of Britain, 1942–1945* (New York: Random House, 1995); Mary Louise Roberts, *D-Day Through French Eyes, Normandy 1944* (Chicago: Univ. of Chicago Press, 2014); see for example: Françoise Passera and Jean Quellien, *Les Civils dans la Bataille de Normandie* (Bayeux: OREP Editions, 2014); Peter Schrijvers, *Liberators: The Allies and Belgian Society, 1944–1945* (Cambridge: Cambridge Univ. Press, 2009).

5. Torrent, *France américaine*; Claudia Baldoli and Andrew Knapp, *Forgotten Blitzes: France and Italy under Allied Air Attack, 1940–1945* (London: Continuum, 2012); Claudia Baldoli, Andrew Knapp, and Richard Overy, eds., *Bombing, States and Peoples in Western Europe, 1940–1945* (London: Continuum, 2011); Stephen Bourque, *Beyond the Beach: The Allied War Against France* (Annapolis, Md.: Naval Institute Press, 2018); Eddy Florentin, *Quand les Alliés bombardaient la France* (Paris: Perrin, 1997); Robert Gildea, *Fighters in the Shadows: A New History of the French Resistance* (Cambridge, Mass.: Belknap Press, 2015); Benjamin Jones, *Eisenhower's Guerrillas: The Jedburghs, the Maquis, and the Liberation of France* (New York: Oxford Univ. Press, 2016); Richard Overy, *The Bombing War: Europe, 1939–1945* (London: Allen Lane, 2013); Olivier Wieviorka, *The French Resistance,* trans. Jane Marie Todd (Cambridge Mass.: Harvard Univ. Press, 2016).

1. THE AMERICANS, THE FRENCH, AND CHARLES DE GAULLE BEFORE D-DAY

1. I use Arthur Funk's translation from *Charles de Gaulle: The Crucial Years, 1943–1944* (Norman: Univ. of Oklahoma Press, 1959), 214; the complete transcript of the conversation between Generals Eisenhower and de Gaulle is found in: Charles de Gaulle, *Mémoires de Guerre, L'Unité, 1942–1944* (Paris: Plon, n.d.), 320–22.

2. Yves-Marie Péréon, *L'image de la France dans la Presse américaine, 1936–1947* (Brussels: Peter Lang, 2011), 154–57. One of the most influential and ultimately important Frenchmen working to guide American policy during the war, Jean Monnet, actually had been a traveling salesman in the United States between the wars for his family's cognac firm.

3. Charles de Gaulle, *The Complete War Memoirs of Charles de Gaulle*, trans. Jonathan Griffin and Richard Howard, 3 vols. (New York: Da Capo, 1984), 1:6–7, 16, 26; Jean Lacouture, *De Gaulle*, vol. 1, trans. Patrick O'Brian (New York: Norton, 1990), 21–22, 56–60, 71–73, 75–88, 99–102; Milton Viorst, *Hostile Allies: Roosevelt and Charles de Gaulle* (New York: Macmillan, 1965), 2, 5–6; Julian Jackson, *A Certain Idea of France: The Life of Charles de Gaulle* (N.p.: Allen Lane, 2018), 217–23, offers a good discussion of the problems caused by de Gaulle's difficult personality; Duff Cooper, *Old Men Forget: The Autobiography of Duff Cooper* (New York: Dutton, 1954), 314.

4. Pierre Mendès-France, *The Pursuit of Freedom* (London: Longmans, Green, 1956), 53–54, 60–61; Raoul Aglion, *Roosevelt and de Gaulle: Allies in Conflict: A Personal Memoir* (New York: Free Press, 1988), 51; Charles de Gaulle, *The Speeches of General de Gaulle*, trans. Sheila Mathieu and W. G. Corp, 2 vols. (London: Oxford Univ. Press, 1942), 1:1–4; Viorst, *Hostile Allies*, 31, 41.

5. Aglion, *Roosevelt and de Gaulle*, 52–54; Lacouture, *De Gaulle*, 1:220. On de Gaulle's politics, see Jackson, *A Certain Idea of France*, 12–16. See, for example, Henri de Kérillis, *I Accuse de Gaulle* (New York: Harcourt, Brace, 1946), an ex-deputy for Paris who took refuge in New York and became vociferously anti-de Gaulle.

6. De Gaulle, *Complete War Memoirs*, 93–96; Viorst, *Hostile Allies*, 35–36, 41–42. Joan of Arc usually served as a symbol of anti-English French patriotism, closely linked to the Catholic Church.

7. De Gaulle, *Complete War Memoirs*, 107–8; G. E. Maguire, *Anglo-American Policy Towards the Free French* (New York: St. Martin's Press, 1995), 8, 10; Henri Michel, *Histoire de la France Libre* (Paris: Presses Universitaires de France, 1972), 17–18.

8. De Gaulle, *Complete War Memoirs*, 111–13, 127–30, 133; Winston Churchill, *The Second World War*, vol. 2 (Boston: Houghton Mifflin, 1949), 488–93; Péréon, *L'image de la France dans la Presse américaine*, 272–73; Robert Murphy, *Diplomat Among Warriors* (New York: Doubleday, 1964), 69–70. On French naval officers as the most reactionary of all in the French officer corps, see Ronald Chalmers Hood, *Royal Republicans: The French Naval Dynasties between the World Wars* (Baton Rouge: Louisiana State Univ. Press, 1985).

9. Péréon, *L'image de la France dans la Presse américaine*, 211–20, 222–23; Charles Robertson, *When Roosevelt Planned to Govern France* (Amherst: Univ. of Massachusetts Press, 2011), 15; William L. Langer, *Our Vichy Gamble* (New York: Norton, 1966), 85–86.

10. Maxime Weygand, *Recalled to Service: The Memoirs of General Maxime Weygand*, trans. E. W. Dickes (London: Heinemann, 1952), 347–52; Langer, *Our Vichy Gamble*, 233–37; William D. Leahy, *I Was There: The Personal Story of the Chief of Staff to Presidents Roosevelt and Truman* (New York: Whittlesey House, 1950), 24–25. On the importance of supply in North Africa, see Martin Van Creveld, *Supplying War: Logistics from Wallenstein to Patton* (Cambridge: Cambridge Univ. Press, 1977), 181–201.

11. Richard Griffiths, *Pétain: A Biography of Marshal Philippe Pétain of Vichy* (Garden City, New York: Doubleday, 1972), 169; Harold Macmillan, *The Blast of War, 1939–1945* (London: Macmillan, 1967), 207; Langer, *Our Vichy Gamble*, 117, 123; Viorst, *Hostile Allies*, 57; Julian G. Hurstfield, *America and the French Nation, 1939–1945* (Chapel Hill: Univ. of North Carolina Press, 1986), 17.

12. Murphy, *Diplomat Among Warriors*, 85, 89–90, 94–95, 109–10; Langer, *Our Vichy Gamble*, 135, 228–32.

13. Hurstfield, *America and the French Nation*, 26, 33, 48, 50–53, 59, 85–87; Murphy, *Diplomat*

Among Warriors, 235; Aglion, *Roosevelt and de Gaulle,* 124; Péréon, *L'image de la France dans la Presse américaine,* 224–34, 269. One result of Chautemps's staying in the United States was to feed Gaullist paranoia that America was keeping him in reserve to head a U.S.-imposed regime after the liberation. See George McJimsey, ed., *Documentary History of the Franklin D. Roosevelt Presidency,* vol. 47, *Establishing Civil Government in Occupied Europe* ([Bethesda, Md.]: University Publications of America, 2001), 182–83, Memorandum [to FDR], 4 July 1944.

14. Hurstfield, *America and the French Nation,* 22, 36; Viorst, *Hostile Allies,* 68–70, 76; Aglion, *Roosevelt and de Gaulle,* 33–34.

15. Aglion, *Roosevelt and de Gaulle,* 35, 37–40, 73, 72–73; Robertson, *When Roosevelt Planned,* 35; Viorst, *Hostile Allies,* 75.

16. Langer, *Our Vichy Gamble,* 176–77, 183–84, 193, 199, 175, 210–11; Aglion, *Roosevelt and de Gaulle,* 30–31, 110; Viorst, *Hostile Allies,* 76–77; Macmillan, *Blast of War,* 204–5; Cordell Hull, *The Memoirs of Cordell Hull,* vol. 2 (New York: Macmillan, 1948), 1042; Weygand, *Recalled to Service,* 383–86, 390–93. Historians disagree about the reason for Weygand's recall, see Robert O. Paxton, *Vichy France: Old Guard and New Order, 1940–1944* (New York: Columbia Univ. Press, 1972), 200; Murphy, *Diplomat Among Warriors,* 93–94; Philippe Burrin, *France under the Germans: Collaboration and Compromise,* trans. Janet Lloyd (New York: New Press, 1993), 124; Hervé Coutau-Bégarie and Claude Huan, *Darlan* (Paris: Fayard, 1989), 454–63.

17. Aglion, *Roosevelt and de Gaulle,* 57–64; Viorst, *Hostile Allies,* 79; Murphy, *Diplomat Among Warriors,* 109–11; Kenneth Pendar, *Adventure in Diplomacy: Our French Dilemma* (New York: Da Capo, 1976), 76, 84–86; Langer, *Our Vichy Gamble,* 226–33; Général Charles Mast, *Histoire d'une Rébellion, Alger, 8 novembre 1942* (Paris: Plon, 1969), 50–53; Robert Gildea, *Fighters in the Shadows: A New History of the French Resistance* (Cambridge, Mass.: Belknap Press, 2015), 246–47.

18. Viorst, *Hostile Allies,* 88, 90–93, 106–7; Aglion, *Roosevelt and de Gaulle,* 111–12; de Gaulle, *Complete War Memoirs,* 312–13; Mark W. Clark, *Calculated Risk* (New York: Harper and Row, 1950), 36–37.

19. Langer, *Our Vichy Gamble,* 277–80, 288–89; Churchill, *Second World War,* 4:432–36; Clark, *Calculated Risk,* 53, 57; Harry C. Butcher, *My Three Years with Eisenhower* (New York: Simon and Schuster, 1946), 97; Viorst, *Hostile Allies,* 96–97; Dwight D. Eisenhower, *Crusade in Europe* (New York: Doubleday, 1948), 81, 83–84; Leahy, *I Was There,* 116; Aglion, *Roosevelt and de Gaulle,* 136; Gildea, *Fighters,* 126.

20. Clark, *Calculated Risk,* 68, 70–71, 80–81; Bernard Pujo, *Juin, Maréchal de France* (Paris: Albin Michel, 1988), 106–7; Alphonse Juin, *Mémoires,* vol. 1 (Paris: A. Fayard, 1959), 68; Murphy, *Diplomat Among Warriors,* 116–22; Henri Giraud, *Un Seul But, la Victoire, Alger 1942–1944* (Paris: R. Julliard, 1949), 17–20; Mast, *Histoire,* 27–28, 38–39, 85, 98, 102, 107, 110–11; Gildea, *Fighters,* 246–47.

21. Aglion, *Roosevelt and de Gaulle,* 111; de Gaulle, *Complete War Memoirs,* 348–49; Langer, *Our Vichy Gamble,* 164–65, 295–97, 301, 303. The OSS may have overestimated the strength of support for de Gaulle within France: Allan Mitchell reports that significant support for de Gaulle within France appeared only after the Allies seized North Africa. See Allan Mitchell, *Nazi Paris: The History of an Occupation, 1940–1944* (New York: Berghahn, 2008), 93–94, 98.

22. Eisenhower, *Crusade,* 99–101; Giraud, *Un Seul But,* 23–25.

23. Mast, *Histoire,* 79, 84; Juin, *Mémoires,* 1:74, 78–82, 85–86, 88; Coutau-Bégarie and Huan, *Darlan,* 586–90; Pendar, *Adventure in Diplomacy,* 111–16; Pujo, *Juin,* 116–17. The British attack on Mers-el-Kébir and Dakar probably provide sufficient explanation for the aggressiveness of the French navy. Why the air force would have been so hostile to the Allies is open to debate, but General Mast noted the reluctance of air force officers to join in the pro-Allied French military underground—only three officers joined. See Mast, *Histoire,* 77–78.

24. Pujo, *Juin,* 121. This is a loose translation of: "Alors, mon général, qu'est-ce que c'est que toutes ces conneries!"

25. Juin, *Mémoires,* 1:89–90, 94–96; Giraud, *Un Seul But,* 35, 38–39; Butcher, *My Three Years,* 181–82, 184; Clark, *Calculated Risk,* 105, 108–10, 116–17; Murphy, *Diplomat Among Warriors,* 135–39; Pujo, *Juin,* 122–23.

26. Péréon, *L'image de la France dans la Presse américaine,* 252–53.

27. Griffiths, *Pétain,* 311–15; de Gaulle, *Complete War Memoirs,* 357.

28. Butcher, *My Three Years,* 181–82, 184; Clark, *Calculated Risk,* 105, 116–17; Juin, *Mémoires,* 1:96–97, 107; Murphy, *Diplomat Among Warriors,* 135–39; Giraud, *Un Seul But,* 41–42; Viorst, *Hostile Allies,* 120–21.

29. *Chicago Tribune,* 11 November 1942; Macmillan, *Blast of War,* 211; Aglion, *Roosevelt and de Gaulle,* 134–35; de Gaulle, *Complete War Memoirs,* 354–55; de Gaulle, *The Speeches of General de Gaulle,* 2:61, 69; Hull, *Memoirs,* 2:1196; Jean Raymond Tournoux, *Pétain et la France: la Seconde Guerre mondiale* (Paris: Plon, 1980), 409; Viorst, *Hostile Allies,* 122–23; Péréon, *L'image de la France dans la Presse américaine,* 284–88.

30. Aglion, *Roosevelt and de Gaulle,* 136–38; Coutau-Bégarie and Huan, *Darlan,* 665–67; Hull, *Memoirs,* 2:1198–1200; Viorst, *Hostile Allies,* 99, 123; Churchill, *Second World War,* 4:631–36; de Gaulle, *Complete War Memoirs,* 357; Jackson, *A Certain Idea of France,* 248–49.

31. Eisenhower, *Crusade,* 115; de Gaulle, *Complete War Memoirs,* 353–54; Macmillan, *Blast of War,* 210–12; Harry Coles and Albert Weinberg, *Civil Affairs: Soldiers Become Governors* (Washington, D.C.: U.S. Army Center of Military History, 2004), 34–37.

32. De Gaulle, *Complete War Memoirs,* 358; Juin, *Mémoires,* 1:112–14. Boisson was much despised by de Gaulle for forcefully opposing the Anglo-Free French invasion of Dakar in 1940; Bergeret had been the head of the French Air Force.

33. Macmillan, *Blast of War,* 232, 294–95; Eisenhower, *Crusade,* 129; Murphy, *Diplomat Among Warriors,* 145–46; Butcher, *My Three Years,* 225, 230, 232–36. Pro-Allied putschists of 8 November 1942 remained in prisons in North Africa until February 1943: see Gildea, *Fighters,* 256. Langer, *Our Vichy Gamble,* 315–19, quotes from a September presidential directive placing Murphy in charge of Civil Affairs and assigning him ultimate civil authority in French North Africa. As that assignment was buried in a pile of other directives, it is understandable that his responsibility for CA came as a surprise to Murphy in November.

34. Murphy, *Diplomat Among Warriors,* 163, 166–69, 171–72; Churchill, *Second World War,* 4:680–82, 693–94.

35. Murphy, *Diplomat Among Warriors,* 174–76; Robert E. Sherwood, *Roosevelt and Hopkins: An Intimate History* (New York: Harper Brothers, 1948), 683–84; Macmillan, *Blast of War,* 253–54.

36. *FRUS* 1943, 2:139–41, Murphy to Roosevelt and Hull, 7 June, 1943; 145–46, Roosevelt to

Eisenhower, 10 June 1943; Jean Monnet, *Memoirs* (New York: Doubleday, 1978), 191–95, 197–201; Murphy, *Diplomat Among Warriors*, 179–80; Funk, 124–28; Gildea, *Fighters*, 280–82; Jackson, *A Certain Idea of France*, 262–75.

37. Giraud, *Un Seul But*, 281–82, 286–87; de Gaulle, *Complete War Memoirs*, 472–73; Monnet, 186; Macmillan, *Blast of War*, 290–94; Murphy, *Diplomat Among Warriors*, 180–82; Gildea, *Fighters*, 283. The fascinating story of how de Gaulle outmaneuvered Giraud is told in Funk, *passim*.

38. Henri Amouroux, *La grande Histoire des Français après l'Occupation*, vol. 7 (Paris: Robert Laffont, 1985), 124–30; Richard Vinen, *The Unfree French: Life under the Occupation* (New Haven, Conn.: Yale Univ. Press, 2006), 321; de Gaulle, *Complete War Memoirs*, 505–6; Giraud, *Un Seul But*, 270–76. The U.S. had promised safe passage to Peyrouton and was trying to fulfill its promise. Macmillan points out that Boisson had been governor-general of West Africa when British sailors held in captivity were subjected to inhumane treatment. However, Cooper—"ambassador" to the CFLN—states that Churchill also wanted the Vichy administrators freed (*Old Men*, 318).

39. *FRUS* 1943, 2:184–86, various memos, August 1943; 188, *aide memoire*, Hull, 30 August 1943; de Gaulle, *Complete War Memoirs*, 430.

40. Régine Torrent, *La France américaine: Controverses de la Libération* (Brussels: Editions Racine, 2004), 148–50, 175; Forrest C. Pogue, *The Supreme Command* (Washington, D.C.: Office of the Chief of Military History, Deptartment of the Army, 1954), 142–43; *FRUS*, 1943, 2:188–92, Edwin Wilson, Algiers, memo of conversation with de Gaulle, 10 November 1943; NARA RG 331, SHAEF/G-5/652, box 12, Accord of 14 December 1943 between UK and CFLN; ANF F1a 3006, ordonnance declaring state of siege in France by Emmanuel d'Astier, Comm. Int. and André Le Troquet, Min. de Guerre, 29 February 1944.

41. Pogue, *The Supreme Command*, 144–46; Butcher, *My Three Years*, 512; Robertson, *When Roosevelt Planned*, 107; de Gaulle, *Complete War Memoirs*, 509; *FRUS* 1944, 3:660–65, 29, Chapin to Hull, March 1944; Alfred Chandler, ed. *The Papers of Dwight D. Eisenhower*, vol. 3, *The War Years* (Baltimore: Johns Hopkins Univ. Press, 1970), Eisenhower to Marshall, 21 March 1944; Coles and Weinberg, *Civil Affairs*, 666–70.

42. ANF F1a 3304, Accords Franco-American, March 1944; ADBdR 6 S 10/10, Ordonnance du CFLN, Algiers, 4 April 1944 (on AFA); NARA RG 331, SHAEF/G-5/2, box 12, "Draft No. 5," "Arrangements for Civil Administration and Jurisdiction in French Territory Liberated by an Allied Expeditionary Force," n.d. (attached cover letter suggests May 1944). Torrent, *France américaine*, 168–69, points out the craftiness of Monnet.

43. *FRUS* 1944, 3:696, Hull to Chapin, 2 June 1944.

2. THE AIR WAR IN FRANCE

1. Richard Overy, *The Bombing War: Europe, 1939-1945* (London: Allen Lane, 2013), 560–61; Claudia Baldoli and Andrew Knapp, *Forgotten Blitzes: France and Italy under Allied Air Attack, 1940–1945* (London: Continuum, 2012), 2. Baldoli and Knapp, *Forgotten Blitzes*, relates that the Allies unleashed eight times as many tons of bombs on France as the Germans dropped (74,172 tons, including V weapons) on the United Kingdom, 1940–1945.

2. Wesley F. Craven and James L. Cate, eds. *The Army Air Forces in World War II* (Chicago: Univ. of Chicago Press, 1948–1951), 1:662–64; Eddy Florentin, *Quand les Alliés bombardaient la France* (Paris: Perrin, 1997), 87–92.

3. Florentin, *Quand les Alliés*, 161–64; Baldoli and Knapp, *Forgotten Blitzes*, 194; Overy, *Bombing War*, 560.

4. Craven and Cate, *Army Air Forces*, 2:246–51; Eric Alary et al., *Les Français au quotidien, 1939–1949* (Paris: Perrin, 2006), 510.

5. Craven and Cate, *Army Air Forces*, 2:244; Florentin, *Quand les Alliés*, 140–41, 144, 146–51; Baldoli and Knapp, *Forgotten Blitzes*, 115; Robert Gildea, *Marianne in Chains: Daily Life in the Heart of France during the German Occupation* (New York: Metropolitan Books, 2004), 292; Jean-Luc Leleu et al., *La France pendant la Seconde Guerre Mondiale* (Paris: Fayard and le Ministère de la Défense, 2010), 244.

6. NARA RG 331, 93A SHAEF PWD, Decimal File 381–884.5; Florentin, *Quand les Alliés*, 140, 149; Baldoli and Knapp, *Forgotten Blitzes*, 42.

7. Jacques Fiérain, "D'Une Guerre A L'Autre" and "Nantes Depuis La Libération," in *Histoire de Nantes*, ed. Paul Bois (Toulouse: Privat, 1977); Alary et al., *Les Français*, 511; Florentin, *Quand les Alliés*, 249–58. Overy, *Bombing War*, 560–61, citing Ren. Gén. reports of the era, reports 1,282 dead from the two raids. Régine Torrent, *La France américaine: Controverses de la Libération* (Brussels: Editions Racine, 2004), 53, cites different police reports to Vichy on popular opinion in Nantes.

8. Gildea, *Marianne in Chains*, 291–94; Baldoli and Knapp, *Forgotten Blitzes*, 193; Craven and Cate, *Army Air Forces*, 2:240, states that French resentment was widespread and proportional to the number of French casualties; Florentin, *Quand les Alliés*, 67, 71–74, 76; Elizabeth Wiskemann, *The Europe I Saw* (New York: Saint Martin's Press, 1968), 184, 194; Alary et al., *Les Français*, 514. Torrent, *La France américaine*, 22–34, posits that Vichy propaganda met with mixed results, but by and large the French public accepted French casualties as an inevitable part of the war.

9. Florentin, *Quand les Alliés*, 103, 130–32; Craven and Cate, *Army Air Forces*, 2:239–40, 247; Stephen Bourque, *Beyond the Beach: The Allied War Against France* (Annapolis, Md.: Naval Institute Press, 2018), 106–7.

10. Alary et al., *Les Français*, 509; Baldoli and Knapp, *Forgotten Blitzes*, 195–97; Armand Idrac, *My Normandy: A Teenager Lives through World War II*, trans. Joanne Silver (Wayne, Penn.: Beach Lloyd Publishers, 2005), 27; André Maurois, *Memoirs*, trans. Denver Lindley (New York: Harper and Row, 1970), 262–65; André Maurois, *Rouen Dévasté* (Fontaine-le-Bourg: Le Pucheux, 2004); Torrent, *La France américaine*, 30; Simon Kitson, "Criminals or Liberators? French Public Opinion and the Allied Bombing of France, 1940–1945," in *Bombing, States, and Peoples in Western Europe, 1940–1945*, ed. Claudia Baldoli, Andrew Knapp, and Richard Overy (London: Continuum, 2011), 279, 284, 286–87, 290. Régine Torrent found public opinion turned negative in the spring of 1944 (*La France américaine*, 39).

11. ADA SC 4102, comm. police, Romilly-sur-Seine, to Préf., 3 September 1943; Police Commissioner, Troyes, to Préf., 6, 8, 9 September 1943; order of Generalmajor von Kirchbach, 1 November 1943; Sturmfuhrer Hellenthal to Préf., 2 November 1943; ADMM WM 1525, comm. police, Pont-à-Mousson, to Préf., 3 July 1944. Baldoli and Knapp found similar sentiments about dead airmen around northern France (*Forgotten Blitzes*, 210), as did Kitson ("Criminals or Liberators?"

282). Kitson also concluded that crowds of French people in the streets, often cheering Allied pilots, contributed to increased civilian casualties ("Criminals or Liberators?" 280).

12. ADMM WM 1525, mayor, Bouillonville, to Préf. with attached testaments of Jean Muller, Hélène Blanvolet, and Roger Granger, 16 January 1946; mayor, Flirey, to Préf., 20 January 1946; mayor, Laneuveville-devant-Nancy, to Préf., 25 January 1946; Baldoli and Knapp, *Forgotten Blitzes*, 212.

13. Agnès Humbert, *Résistance: A Woman's Journal of Struggle and Defiance in Occupied France*, trans. Barbara Mellor (New York: Bloomsbury, 2008), 7, 21; Julian Jackson, *France: The Dark Years, 1940–1944* (Oxford: Oxford Univ. Press, 2001), 409; Florentin, *Quand les Alliés*, 613. There is a large and growing number of works devoted to the French resistance networks that helped downed Allied airmen return to Britain and the war. See, for example, Sherri Greene Ottis, *Silent Heroes: Downed Airmen and the French Underground* (Lexington: Univ. Press of Kentucky, 2001).

14. NARA RG 498, UD 186, box 899, Eugene François d'Hallendre, recommendation for Medal of Freedom with bronze palm, 17 September 1946; Lucienne d'Hallendre, recommendation for Medal of Freedom with bronze palm, 17 September 1946; Mathurin Branchoux, recommendation for Medal of Freedom with silver palm, 18 July 1946.

15. NARA, RG 498, UD 186, box 899, Paul Campinchi, recommendation for Medal of Freedom with gold palm, 4 March 1946; Marie Rose Zerling, recommendation for silver palm, 18 May 1946; Marie Wiame, recommendation for gold palm, 18 February 1946; Ottis, *Silent Heroes*, 147, 150–51.

16. Florentin, *Quand les Alliés*, 613.

17. Craven and Cate, *Army Air Forces*, 3:149, 159; Florentin, *Quand les Alliés*, 369–71; Bourque, *Beyond the Beach*, 194; Louis S. Rehr and Carleton R. Rehr, *Marauder, Memoir of a B-26 Pilot in Europe in World War II* (Jefferson, N.C.: McFarland, 2004), 37, 42, 50, 54; John Keegan, *Six Armies in Normandy, from D-Day to the Liberation of Paris* (New York: Penguin, 1983), 155–57. Bourque, *Beyond the Beach*, 170, 185–86, 188–90, emphasizes that medium bombers and fighter-bombers were effective when pilots were trained to bomb, but most were not and thus were wildly inaccurate.

18. Winston S. Churchill, *The Second World War* (Boston: Houghton Mifflin, 1951), 5:527–30; David Eisenhower, *Eisenhower: At War 1943–1945* (New York: Vintage, 1987), 192, 229–30; Harry Butcher, *My Three Years with Eisenhower* (New York: Simon and Schuster, 1946), 522–23, 525–26, 535, 543; Florentin, *Quand les Alliés*, 263, 370, 464–65; Alfred Chandler, ed., *The Papers of Dwight D. Eisenhower*, vol. 3, *The War Years* (Baltimore: Johns Hopkins Univ. Press, 1970), 1842–45, Eisenhower to Churchill, 2 May 1944; Bourque, *Beyond the Beach*, 160.

19. Craven and Cate, *Army Air Forces*, 3:151–54; Robert Aron, *Histoire de la Libération de la France, Juin 1944–Mai 1945* (Paris: Librairie Arthème Fayard, 1959), 352, 354; Florentin, *Quand les Alliés*, 203–4, 262, 371–72.

20. Craven and Cate, *Army Air Forces*, 3:157–59; Florentin, *Quand les Alliés*, 443–45; Bourque, *Beyond the Beach*, 184–85.

21. Florentin, *Quand les Alliés*, 445, 451, 456–60; Bourque, *Beyond the Beach*, 185–94, 204. Bourque reports between 160 and 400 *rouennais* perished that week under Allied bombs (page 194).

22. Craven and Cate, *Army Air Forces*, 3:156; Florentin, *Quand les Alliés*, 498–99, 518–19; NARA RG 331, 93A, SHAEF, Psychological Warfare Division, box 103, contains many leaflets dropped by Allied airmen over France.

23. NARA RG 331, 93A, SHAEF, Psychological Warfare Division, box 103, leaflet.

24. Florentin, *Quand les Alliés*, 488–89, 527.

25. Ibid., 466, 471–73, 476, 485, 490–92, 499, 508–9; NARA RG 331, 93A, SHAEF, Psychological Warfare Division, box 103, leaflets.

26. Florentin, *Quand les Alliés*, 481–84; ADMM, WM 468, Liste des faits de guerre survenues dans la région de Vosges; Meurthe-et-Moselle, 20 avril–20 mai 1944; région de Nancy, 24 mai–25 juin 1944; Nicole H. Taflinger, *Season of Suffering: Coming of Age in Occupied France, 1940–45* (Pullman: Washington State Univ. Press, 2010), 97; Dwight D. Eisenhower, *Crusade in Europe* (New York: Doubleday, 1948), 233.

27. Churchill, *Second World War*, 5:715; ADA SC 4102, gendarme report, Troyes, 4 May 1944; Pref., Troyes, report, 5 May 1944; Ren. Gén. report, Troyes, 9 May 1944; Sous-Préf., Bar-sur-Aube, to Min. Int., 21 July 1944; ADA NA 10011, ms., "4 Mai 1944, Le Bombardement du Camp de Mailly"; Florentin, *Quand les Alliés*, 558, reports that 42 Lancasters were lost in the raid on Mailly, but gives no source or further comment. Bourque, *Beyond the Beach*, 141.

28. Craven and Cate, *Army Air Forces*, 3:155; Florentin, *Quand les Alliés*, 280–81, 284, 524, 541; Overy, *Bombing War*, 575.

29. Florentin, *Quand les Alliés*, 526–35, 609, 612; Baldoli and Knapp, *Forgotten Blitzes*, 234, 246n62.

30. Bourque, *Beyond the Beach*, 138–48.

31. Florentin, *Quand les Alliés*, 447–48, 515–16, 543; Bourque, *Beyond the Beach*, 256–57.

32. Craven and Cate, *Army Air Forces*, 3:494–98; NARA RG 331, 93A SHAEF PWD, box 102 and 103. I reviewed around 40 pamphlets dropped on France and found the propaganda light-handed and saw nothing obviously untrue.

33. NARA RG 331 93A SHAEF Decimal File 381–884.5, PWD, box 26, "Experiences and Attitudes of thirty-three Organization Todt Workers"; Baldoli and Knapp, *Forgotten Blitzes*, 129, 215; Idrac, *My Normandy*, 27; Xavier de Guerpel, *1939–1945: Une Certaine Vie de Château au Bocage Normand* (Conde-sur-Noireau: Editions Ch. Corlet, 1973), 172–73.

34. Torrent, *France américaine*, 30–34; FRUS 1944, 3:699–700, Murphy, Algiers to State, 4 June 1944; Bourque, *Beyond the Beach*, 193–94, 197–98; Kitson, "Criminals or Liberators?" 292, came to the same conclusions as Baldoli and Knapp about French stoic acceptance of the destruction caused by Allied bombings: it was accepted when accurate and understood.

35. United States, Department of the Army, *Army Battle Casualties and Nonbattle Deaths in World War II, Final Report* (Washington, D.C.: Office of the Comptroller of the Army, 1953), 92–93; Florentin, *Quand les Alliés*, 587, 614; Baldoli and Knapp, *Forgotten Blitzes*, 261; Overy, *Bombing War*, 561–62; 574; Leleu, *France*, 245; ADMM, WM 468, Liste des faits de guerre survenues dans la région de Meurthe-et-Moselle, 20 avril–20 mai 1944; my colleague Jérôme Leclerc in Nancy tracked down the first name of Gilles Mouilleron.

3. NORMANDY

1. Harry L. Coles and Albert K. Weinberg, *Civil Affairs: Soldiers Become Governors* (Washington, D.C.: U.S. Army Center of Military History, 2004), 11–12. The best treatment of Civil Affairs

that I have found is in Régine Torrent, *La France américaine: Controverses de la Libération* (Brussels: Editions Racine, 2004), 101–52.

2. Françoise Passera and Jean Quellien, *Les Civils dans la Bataille de Normandie* (Bayeux: OREP Editions, 2014), 13–15; Mary Louise Roberts, *D-Day Through French Eyes, Normandy 1944* (Chicago: Univ. of Chicago Press, 2014), 35–38.

3. Harry C. Butcher, *My Three Years with Eisenhower* (New York: Simon and Schuster, 1946), 580; ANF F1a 4005, mayor, Ste. Mère-Eglise, to comm. rép., n.d. [15 July 1944, date of attached cover letter from F. Coulet to P. Koenig]; Roberts, *D-Day*, 38–47, 57.

4. Dwight D. Eisenhower, *Crusade in Europe* (New York: Doubleday, 1948), 256–58; Eddy Florentin, *Quand les Alliés bombardaient la France* (Paris: Perrin, 1997), 561–63; Stephen Alan Bourque, *Beyond the Beach: The Allied War Against France* (Annapolis, Md.: Naval Institute Press, 2018), 232–33.

5. James A. Huston, *Across the Face of France: Liberation and Recovery 1944–63* (West Lafayette, Ind.: Purdue University Studies, 1963), 54–59; Passera and Quellien, *Les Civils*, 43; Richard Overy, *The Bombing War: Europe, 1939–1945* (London: Allen Lane, 2013), 578.

6. Huston, *Across the Face of France*, 59, 61; Wesley F. Craven and James L. Cate, eds., *The Army Air Forces in World War II*, vol. 3 (Chicago: Univ. of Chicago Press, 1951), 193; Florentin, *Quand les Alliés*, 566–67, 72; Passera and Quellien, *Les Civils*, 21, 30, 42, 99; Bourque, *Beyond the Beach*, 235, 245–48; Roberts, *D-Day*, 85.

7. Xavier de Guerpel, *1939–1945: Une Certaine Vie de Château au Bocage Normand* (Conde-sur-Noireau: Editions Ch. Corlet, 1973), 84; 174–77, 183; NARA RG 331, 93A, SHAEF, PWD, "A Survey of attitudes of Normans to Allied Landings," 21 August 1944; Military History Institute (MHI), Veterans Surveys, 1st Inf. Div., 16th Inf. Reg., box 1, Captain William T. Dillon.

8. ADMM, WM 468, Préf., Bar-le-Duc, to Min. Int., 26 July 1944; Sous-Préf., Lunéville to Préf., 29 June 1944.

9. ADMM, WM 468, gendarme reports, Nancy, 17 August 1944; Toul, 14 August 1944; ADMM WM 1520, comm. police, Nancy, 8 August 1944; ADA SC 4102, gendarme reports, Troyes, Bar-sur-Seine, Nogent, August 1944; Robert Capa, *Slightly Out of Focus* (New York: Holt, 1947), 163; William Dreux, *No Bridges Blown* (South Bend, Ind.: Univ. of Notre Dame Press, 1971), 145; NARA RG 331/ 97, box 116, "German Atrocities," binder four, report of Captain Perry Miller; Claudia Baldoli and Andrew Knapp, *Forgotten Blitzes: France and Italy under Allied Air Attack, 1940–1945* (London: Continuum, 2012), 235; Jean-Luc Leleu et al., *La France pendant la Seconde Guerre Mondiale* (Paris: Fayard and le Ministère de la Défense, 2010), 175, 177. Seven hours after the FFI destroyed the bridge at Bar-sur-Seine, two French trains stopped on both sides of the gap to allow the passengers from one train to walk across a temporary wooden bridge, which replaced the blown rail bridge, to a second train waiting on the other side. Six Allied fighter planes attacked the trains, demolishing both locomotives and five passenger cars, and killing three French women and two men outside the train; nine more were injured, three of them gravely.

10. Marie-Louise Osmont, *The Normandy Diary of Marie-Louise Osmont: 1940–1944*, trans. George L. Newman (New York: Random House, 1994), 25, 33, 37; ANF F1a 4006, gendarme reports, Carentan, 6 and 7 June, 18 July 1944; Caen, 27 July, 2 August 1944; F1a 4005, gendarme reports, Ste. Mère-Eglise, 6 July 1944; Bayeux, 10 July and 22 June 1944. This dossier contains many reports such as these.

11. Passera and Quellien, *Les Civils*, 132; de Guerpel, *Une Certaine Vie*, 183–87; Roberts, *D-Day*, 63–64.

12. MHI, Veterans Surveys, 29th Inf. Div., box 2, Captain John K. Slingluff, 175th Inf. Reg.; ANF F1a 4005, Coulet to Koenig, 20 June 1944; Passera and Quellien, *Les Civils*, 70–71, 73–75, 78; Omar N. Bradley, *A Soldier's Story* (New York: Holt, 1951), 283; Eisenhower, *Crusade in Europe*, 232, 270.

13. Florentin, *Quand les Alliés*, 566, 607; *New York Times*, 20 June 1944; de Guerpel, *Une Certaine Vie*, 85; Passera and Quellien, *Les Civils*, 161–62; Bourque, *Beyond the Beach*, 249; ANF F1a 4006, Coulet to Koenig, report on visit to Avranches, 4 August 1944; MHI, Hansen Diary, 1 July 1944; Crane Brinton, "Letters from Liberated France," *French Historical Studies* 2, no. 1 (1961): 4.

14. Dreux, *No Bridges Blown*, 200–201; Max Hastings, *Overlord: D-Day and the Battle for Normandy* (New York: Simon and Schuster, 1984), 258–59; ANF F1a 4006, Coulet to Koenig, 4 August 1944; Nelson Douglas Lankford, ed., *OSS Against the Reich: The World War II Diaries of Colonel David K. Bruce* (Kent, Ohio: Kent State Univ. Press, 1991), 138, 143; Passera and Quellien, *Les Civils*, 148, 219; Peter Schrijvers, *The Crash of Ruin: American Combat Soldiers in Europe during World War II* (New York: New York Univ. Press, 1998), 158–60.

15. Hastings, *Overlord*, 261, 286; Schrijvers, *Crash of Ruin*, 159–60.

16. MHI, Hansen Diary, 12 June 1944; Huston, *Across the Face of France*, 68; Passera and Quellien, *Les Civils*, 234; NARA RG 331, 93A, SHAEF, PWD, "A Survey of attitudes of Normans to Allied Landings," 21 August 1944; Lankford, *OSS Against the Reich*, 187; Simon Kitson, "Criminals or Liberators? French Public Opinion and the Allied Bombing of France, 1940–1945," in *Bombing, States, and Peoples in Western Europe, 1940–1945*, ed. Claudia Baldoli, Andrew Knapp, and Richard Overy (London: Continuum, 2011), 292.

17. Bradley, *A Soldier's Story*, 293–94; MHI, Maginnis Papers, box 1, clippings, *Worcester Daily Telegram*, 26 June 1944; *Boston Daily Globe*, 9 August 1944; John J. Maginnis and Robert A. Hart, ed., *Military Government Journal: Normandy to Berlin* (Amherst: Univ. of Massachusetts Press, 1971), 5–6, 15.

18. MHI, Maginnis Papers, box 1, Log, 11–13 June 1944; Maginnis and Hart, *Military Government Journal*, 9–12; Edwin P. Hoyt, *The GI's War: The Story of American Soldiers in Europe in World War II* (New York: McGraw Hill, 1988), 409. Passera and Quellien, *Les Civils*, report that Mayor Caillard and the others were killed on 6 June.

19. Maginnis Log, 14, 15 June; NARA RG 331, SHAEF /G-5/62/2, box 5, 21st Army Group Reports, Lieutenant Colonel Omer V. Claiborne, Chief Currency Section, report, n.d.

20. Maginnis Log, 16–18 June, 1944; Maginnis and Hart, *Military Government Journal*, 14–19; ANF F1a 4005, Coulet to Koenig, 27 June 1944.

21. Maginnis Log, 23–25 June, 4, 13, 23, 28 July, 1 August 1944; Maginnis and Hart, *Military Government Journal*, 27–29.

22. Maginnis Log, 16–22 June 1944, 1944; Maginnis and Hart, *Military Government Journal*, 21; ANF F1a 4004, Arreté No. 7, 16 June 1944; de Guerpel, *Une Certaine Vie*, 232, 234.

23. Maginnis Log, 23, 25, 26 June 1944; David L. Cohn, *This Is the Story* (Boston: Houghton Mifflin, 1947), 91–92.

24. Maginnis Log, 18–22 June, 31 July 1944; Maginnis and Hart, *Military Government Journal*, 17, 20–21, 24–25.

25. Osmont, *Normandy Diary*, 48–51, 59–60, 75–76, 83, 99; de Guerpel, *Une Certaine Vie*, 236.

26. Maginnis Log, 21, 22, 26 June, 8, 17, 19, 28 July, 5 August 1944.

27. Maginnis Log, 16, 21, 22, 26 June, 6, 7, 8, 11, 17, 19 July 1944.

28. Maginnis Log, 22–23 June 1944; ANF F1a 4005, Coulet to Koenig, 20 June 1944; Roland G. Ruppenthal, *Logistical Support of the Armies*, 2 vols. (Washington, D.C.: U.S. Army Center of Military History, 1953), 1:433.

4. THE FREE FRENCH GOVERNMENT IN NORMANDY

1. François Coulet, *Vertu des Temps difficiles* (Paris: Plon, 1967), 215, 220; Charles de Gaulle, *The Complete War Memoirs of Charles de Gaulle,* trans. Jonathan Griffin and Richard Howard, 3 vols. (New York: Da Capo, [1984]), 2:554; Forrest C. Pogue, *George C. Marshall: Organizer of Victory, 1943–1945* (New York: Viking, 1973), 400–403, 458–59; George McJimsey, ed., *Documentary History of the Franklin D. Roosevelt Presidency,* vol. 47, *Establishing Civil Government in Occupied Europe* ([Bethesda, Md.]: University Publications of America, 2001), 114–16. Charles Robertson, *When Roosevelt Planned to Govern France* (Amherst: Univ. of Massachusetts Press, 2011), offers an excellent discussion of Roosevelt's preference for AMGOT and Eisenhower's ardent desire to avoid it. Régine Torrent, *La France américaine: Controverses de la Libération* (Brussels: Editions Racine, 2004), 75–221, also offers an excellent and comprehensive discussion of the controversies swirling around AMGOT. Duff Cooper's memoirs reveal British frustration with Roosevelt over questions of French sovereignty; Duff Cooper, *Old Men Forget: The Autobiography of Duff Cooper* (New York: Dutton, 1954), 324–30.

2. Harry C. Butcher, *My Three Years with Eisenhower* (New York: Simon and Schuster, 1946), 241, 513, 540; Jean Lacouture, *De Gaulle,* vol. 1, trans. Patrick O'Brian (New York: Norton, 1990), 513, 517; Robert Aron, *Histoire de la Libération de La France, Juin 1944–Mai 1945* (Paris: Libraire Arthème Fayard, 1959), 62–64; Robertson, *When Roosevelt Planned,* 112–13; ANF F1a 3304, March 1944 Franco-American Accords Signed in Algiers; Coulet, *Vertu,* 219–20; Torrent, *France américaine,* 142–43, 145, 148–49, 152–53, 175–77; Cooper, *Old Men Forget,* 331.

3. NARA RG 331, SHAEF G-5/30/06/, box 64, Lieutenant Colonel D. R. Ellias, report on British zone, 9–12 June 1944; Nelson Douglass Lankford, ed., *OSS Against the Reich: The World War II Diaries of Colonel David K. Bruce* (Kent, Ohio: Kent State Univ. Press, 1991), 72.

4. Lacouture, *De Gaulle,* 1:528–30; Coulet, *Vertu,* 228–32; Robertson, *When Roosevelt Planned,* 151; Alan Moorehead, *Eclipse* (New York: Harper and Row, 1968), 116–17; Aron, *Histoire de la Libération,* 76, 78–79; NARA RG 331, SHAEF G-5/30/06/, box 64, Lieutenant Colonel D. R. Ellias, report on British zone, 9–12 June 1944. Colonel Bruce noticed (page 87) that photos of Pétain still hung in "place of honor in some homes we have visited" in late June, but the residents still expressed great enthusiasm about their liberation.

5. Coulet, *Virtu,* 73, 81, 159–60; Lacouture, *De Gaulle,* 1:264, 293, 305; Aron, *Histoire de la Libération,* 87–90; Torrent, *France américaine,* 216–17; NARA RG 331, SHAEF/G-5/30/06, box 64, Lieutenant Colonel D. R. Ellias, report, 9–12 June 1944; minutes of weekly staff conference, G-5 Div., 13 June 1944; SHAEF/G-5/676, box 14, Proclamation of D. Eisenhower, n.d.; SHAEF/G-5/2/10 Financial Reports, box 5, report, no author, 22/25 June 1944; ANF F1a 4006, Coulet to Comm. délégué de Finance, 5 August 1944.

6. ANF F1a 4005, Coulet to Koenig, 18, 27 June, 10, 13 July 1944; F1a 4004, Arrêtés, 16–17 June 1944; No. 32, 30 June 1944; Sous-Pref. Bayeux, Circulaire No. 4, n.d. [June 1944]; NARA RG 331, SHAEF/G-5/30/06/, box 64, minutes of weekly G-5 staff conference, 29 June, 13 July 1944. The French paid their own troops in North Africa (Marcel Vigneras, *Rearming the French* [Washington, D.C.: Office of the Chief of Military History, Department of the Army, 1957], 217). NARA RG 498, First Army HQ, G-5, box 2950, Reports from Major W. D. Shepard, Royal Art., Fiscal Section, 2–6 July 1944; Coulet, *Vertu*, 226.

7. NARA RG 498, First Army HQ, G-5, box 2950, Major W. D. Shepard, Royal Art., Fiscal Section, reports, 2–6 July 1944; RG 331, SHAEF/G-5/62/2, box 5, 21st Army Group Reports, Lieutenant Colonel Omer V. Claiborne, Chief Currency Section, report, n.d.; SHAEF/G-5/2/10 Financial Reports, box 5, report, no author, 22/25 June 1944; ANF F1a 4005, Coulet to Koenig, 27 June, 3, 6, 13 July 1944; agreement between Coulet and Allies, Bayeux, 27 June 1944; Dir. Banque de France to Laroque, 8 July 1944; F1a 4004, Arrêté No. 33, 1 July 1944; F1a 3304, réunion des délégués régionaux d'Aide des Forces Alliées (AFA), 6–8 January 1945; NARA RG 331, SHAEF HQ files, box 1, Financial-France, report, 1 October 1945; Coulet, *Vertu*, 221, 244. In fact, the G-5 officer was mistaken: he deposited nine boxes of supplemental francs and 51 boxes of Bank of France notes in Cherbourg, see ANF F1a 4005, Dir. Banque de France, Cherbourg, to Coulet, 8 July 1944.

8. ANF F1a 4005, poster signed by Mayor Paul Renault, Cherbourg, 19 June 1944; Coulet to Koenig, 10 July 1944; Dir. Banque de France, Cherbourg, to Coulet, 8 July 1944; NARA RG 331, SHAEF/30/06, box 64, minutes of weekly G-5 staff conference, 29 June 1944.

9. ANF F1a 4005, Coulet to Koenig, 20, 23, 24, 27 June 1944; NARA RG 331, SHAEF/G-5/2/10 Financial Reports, box 5, report, no author, 22/25 June 1944; Coulet, *Vertu*, 222, 252; Torrent, *France américaine*, 193–94.

10. ANF F1a 4005, Coulet to Koenig, report, 31 July 1944; Coulet to Comm. Intérior Tixier, 9 July 1944; NARA RG 331, SHAEF/G-5/2/10 Financial Reports, box 5, report, no author, 22/25 June 1944; Coulet, *Vertu*, 237, 251.

11. Coulet, *Vertu*, 239–44; McJimsey, *Documentary History*, 182–83, memorandum [to FDR], no author, 4 July 1944; *New York Herald Tribune*, 16 June 1944; *Boston Globe*, 18 June 1944; Robertson, *When Roosevelt Planned*, 180–84. The Allies set up no AMGOT in Sardinia, which was administered by Italians. French Second Lieutenant Paul Fouchet reported to Algiers in 1943 that the AMGOT in Sicily was very light-handed and that all administration was run by Italians with minimal supervision by the Allied military. See Torrent, *France américaine*, 150–51.

12. Robertson, *When Roosevelt Planned*, 160–61; Coulet, *Vertu*, 246–48; Harry L. Coles and Albert K. Weinberg, *Civil Affairs: Soldiers Become Governors* (Washington, D.C.: U.S. Army Center of Military History, 2004), 709–10, gives a summary of Lewis's version. Aron, *Histoire de la Libération*, 93–94, gives the fist-pounding version.

13. ANF F1a 4005, Coulet to Koenig, 20 June 1944; Coulet, *Vertu*, 248.

14. Coulet, *Vertu*, 234–36, 249–50.

15. ANF F1a 4005, Coulet to Koenig, 3 July 1944; NARA RG 331, SHAEF, G-5, box 64, minutes of weekly G-5 staff conference, 4, 11 July 1944; RG 498, First Army HQ, G-5, box 2950, Operations Report, A1A1 Detachment, 7 July 1944.

16. ANF F1a 4005, Coulet to Koenig, 11 July 1944 (Coulet referred to Lévy as "Jean" rather than

Jacques), 25 July 1944; F1a 4006, Coulet to Comm. Interior, 6 August 1944; NARA RG 498, First Army HQ, G-5, box 2950, Operations Report, A1A1 Detachment, 8 August 1944.

17. NARA RG 331, SHAEF, G-5, box 64, minutes of weekly G-5 staff conference, 6, 11, 13, 20 July 1944; box 5 Captain Roger A. McShea, report, 22 August 1944; ANF F1a 4006, minutes, meeting of SHAEF representatives and French officials concerned with civilian supplies, and agreement, 31 July 1944.

18. ANF F1a 4006, Garnier-Thenon, weekly report, Section Travail, 29 July 1944.

19. Ibid.

20. Ibid.; ANF F1a 4006, Coulet to Brigadier General Robbins, 21st Army Group, 31 July 1944; Coulet to Comm. de Travail, with accord with Allies on hiring and paying workers, 10 August 1944; Garnier-Thenon, report on Manche, 8 August 1944.

21. ANF F1a 4006, Coulet to Koenig, report on visits to Granville and Avranches, 4 August 1944; F1a 4005, Coulet to Koenig, report on visit to Manche, 31 July 1944; Coulet, *Vertu,* 252.

22. ANF F1a 4006, Laroque to Koenig, report on Rennes, 13 August 1944; Coulet to Koenig, 17 August 1944.

5. LIBERATED CHERBOURG

1. Dwight D. Eisenhower, *Crusade in Europe* (New York: Doubleday, 1948), 217, 234, 240.

2. Wesley F. Craven and James L. Cate, eds., *The Army Air Forces in World War II,* vol. 3 (Chicago: Univ. of Chicago Press, 1951), 199–201; Gabrielle M. Maddaloni, "Liberation and Franco-American Relations in Post-War Cherbourg" (Master's thesis, Fort Leavenworth, Kansas, U.S. Army Command and General Staff College, 2008), 21–27; Omar N. Bradley, *A Soldier's Story* (New York: Holt, 1951), 307–8, 312; Max Hastings, *Overlord: D-Day and the Battle for Normandy* (New York: Simon and Schuster, 1984), 163–65; Charles C. Wertenbaker, *Invasion!* (New York: Appleton Century, 1944), 133–48; MHI, James Alexander Crothers Papers, box 2, "Port of Cherbourg"; Harry C. Butcher, *My Three Years with Eisenhower* (New York: Simon and Schuster, 1946), 599.

3. Edwin P. Hoyt, *The GI's War: The Story of American Soldiers in Europe in World War II* (New York: McGraw Hill, 1988), 425; MHI, Crothers Papers, "Port of Cherbourg"; Butcher, *My Three Years with Eisenhower,* 598–99; NARA RG 498, First Army HQ, First European Civil Affairs Regiment, box 2951, Public Safety Activities in Cherbourg, 14 August 1944; Daily Report, Public Safety Section, 4 July 1944.

4. Hastings, *Overlord,* 165; Robert Capa, *Slightly Out of Focus* (New York: Holt, 1947); Butcher, *My Three Years with Eisenhower,* 597–98.

5. NARA RG 498, First Army HQ, First European Civil Affairs Regiment, box 2951, Report of Economic Section, 2 July 1944; Lieutenant Colonel Joseph Hensel, Report on the Civil Defense of Cherbourg, 25 July 1944; Report on Public Safety Activities in Cherbourg, 14 August 1944; Operations Report, 8 August 1944; Report of Major W. C. Henderson, Relief Section, 20 July 1944; ANF F1a 4005, Captain G. M. Lambert, French Army liaison officer, "Rapport sur la situation à Cherbourg," 18 June 1944; Coulet to Min. Int., 30 July 1944; Wertenbaker, *Invasion!,* 134.

6. NARA RG 331, SHAEF, G-5, box 64, Major E. J. Boulton, report on U.S. zone, 11 June 1944;

minutes of weekly staff conference, 1, 16 August 1944; RG 498, First Army HQ, G-5, box 2950, report on Public Safety, 14 August 1944; Operations Report, CA, 8 August 1944.

7. MHI, Potter Papers, "Engineer Memoirs," 39; MHI, Crothers Papers, "Port of Cherbourg," 10; Butcher, *My Three Years with Eisenhower,* 598–99. Maddaloni, "Liberation and Franco-American Relations," provides a detailed discussion of the efforts necessary to clear the harbor (57–63).

8. Richard D. Courtney, *Normandy to the Bulge: An American Infantry GI in Europe During World War II* (Carbondale: Southern Illinois Univ. Press, 1997), 23; Butcher, *My Three Years with Eisenhower,* 600.

9. MHI, Crothers Papers, "Port of Cherbourg," 8–11; MHI, Potter Papers, "Engineer Memoirs," 38; Hilary Footitt, *War and Liberation in France: Living with the Liberators* (New York: Palgrave Macmillan, 2004), 74–75.

10. NARA RG 498, First Army HQ, G-5, box 2950, Operations Report, CA, 8 August 1944; Report on Electrical Services; "Draft," 1 August 1944; box 2951, Report Public Health, Captain J. Basora-Defillo, 2 July 1944.

11. NARA RG 498, First Army HQ, G-5, box 2950, Captain Westervelt, Report on Communications Services, 1 August 1944.

12. NARA RG 498, First Army HQ, G-5, box 2950, Report on Public Safety, 14 August 1944.

13. NARA RG 498, First Army HQ, G-5, box 2950, Operations Report, A1A1 Detachment, 8 August 1944; Report of Major W. C. Henderson, Relief Section, 8, 10 July 1944; Report on Relief and Welfare, 16 August 1944; NARA RG 498, First Army HQ, G-5, box 2951, Dr. Bonnel, Rapport sur l'état de la Ville de Cherbourg, 10 July 1944; Report Public Health, Captain J. Basora-Defillo, 2 July 1944; ANF F1a 4006, Colonel Wayne R. Allen, Chairman Gen. Purchasing Bd., ETO, to Colonel Laroque, Bayeux, 16 August 1944.

14. NARA RG 331, 93A SHAEF PWD, Decimal File 381–884.5, box 26, "Experiences and Attitudes of thirty-three Organization Todt Workers"; SHAEF, G-5, box 64, Major E. J. Boulton, report, 11 June 1944; minutes of weekly staff conference, G-5 Div., 25 July 1944; NARA RG 498, First Army HQ, G-5, box 2950, Major W. C. Henderson, Relief Section, 6, 16 July 1944; Report on Relief and Welfare, 16 August 1944, NARA RG 498, First Army HQ, G-5, box 2951, Report of Economic Section, 2 July 1944; ANF F1a 4006, Garnier-Thenon, weekly report of "Section Travail," 29 July 1944.

15. NARA, RG 498, First Army HQ, G-5, box 2950, Lieutenant B. A. Wilcocks, Reports of Transportation Section, 15, 25 July 1944; Operations Report, CA, 8 August 1944; Report on Relief and Welfare of Cherbourg, 16 August 1944; NARA, RG 498, First Army HQ, G-5, box 2951, Report from Supply Section, 2 July 1944.

16. NARA, RG 498, First Army HQ, G-5, box 2950, Report on Relief and Welfare, 16 August 1944. Despite the poor living conditions of the refugees, French officials still blamed the insect infestation on foreign Todt workers in the city. See NARA, RG 498, First Army HQ, G-5, box 2951, Dr. Bonnel, Rapport sur l'etat de la Ville de Cherbourg, 10 July 1944.

17. NARA, RG 498, First Army HQ, G-5, box 2950, Report on Relief and Welfare, 16 August 1944; Major Henderson, reports 4, 7, 10, 24 July 1944. All mail leaving Cherbourg for Germany had to be read by Army censors to ensure that sensitive information did not get into German hands.

18. NARA, RG 498, First Army HQ, G-5, box 2951, Report of Economic Section, 2 July 1944; NARA, RG 498, First Army HQ, G-5, box 2950, Report on Relief and Welfare, 16 August 1944; MHI, Hansen Diary, 1 July 1944; ANF F1a 4006, Garnier-Thenon, weekly report of "Section Travail," 29 July 1944.

19. NARA, RG 498, First Army HQ, G-5, box 2950, report of Relief Section, 7–10 July 1944; NARA, RG 498, First Army HQ, G-5, box 2951, Public Safety Activities in Cherbourg, 14 August 1944; RG 331, SHAEF, G-5/2, box 47, Report Displaced Persons Branch, 7 September 1944; Armand Idrac, *My Normandy: A Teenager Lives through World War II*, trans. Joanne Silver (Wayne, Pa.: Beach Lloyd, 2005), 53–54.

20. NARA, RG 498, First Army HQ, G-5, box 2951, HQ, Reports, Transportation Section, July–August 1944.

21. NARA, RG 498, First Army HQ, G-5, box 2951, HQ Detachment, CA Regiment, report, Lieutenant B.A. Wilcocks and Lieutenant Colonel Edward J. Gully, n.d. [circa 4 August 1944]; Public Safety Activities in Cherbourg, 14 August 1944; Footitt, *War and Liberation*, 71–72.

22. MHI, Crothers Papers, "Port of Cherbourg,"; ADBdR 6 S 10/10, SHAEF memo, 18 July 1944; NARA, RG 498, First Army HQ, G-5, box 2951, Reports of the Transportation Section, 4 July, 4 August 1944.

23. NARA, RG 498, First Army HQ, G-5, box 2950, Operations Reports, CA, 7 July 1944; Footitt, *War and Liberation*, 73.

24. NARA, RG 498, First Army HQ, G-5, box 2950, Operations Report, CA, 8 August 1944; ANF F1a 4005, Coulet to Koenig, 24 June, 1 July 1944.

25. NARA, RG 498, First Army HQ, G-5, box 2951, Report on Public Safety, 14 August 1944; Report of Major B. J. Scheinman, CA Legal Section, 9 August 1944; RG 498, First Army HQ, G-5, box 2950, Operations Report, CA, 8 August 1944; Capa, *Slightly Out of Focus*, 165.

26. NARA, RG 498, First Army HQ, G-5, box 2951, Dr. Bonnel, Rapport sur l'état de la Ville de Cherbourg, 10 July 1944; Report on Public Safety Activities in Cherbourg, 14 August 1944; Report, Major W.J.H. Palfrey, Public Safety Officer, 28 July 1944; Maddaloni, "Liberation and Franco-American Relations," 77–79; David L. Cohn, *This Is the Story* (Boston: Houghton Mifflin, 1947), 95; Marie-Louise Osmont, *The Normandy Diary of Marie-Louise Osmont: 1940–1944*, trans. George L. Newman (New York: Random House, 1994), 11–12, 17.

27. NARA, RG 498, First Army HQ, G-5, box 2950, Operations Reports, CA, 3–6 July 1944; Footitt, *War and Liberation*, 88; ANF F1a 4004, Arreté No. 11, 17 June 1944; F1a 4005, Coulet to Koenig, 27 June 1944. Coulet never saw the supposed American newssheet and was even unsure of its title.

28. NARA, RG 498, First Army HQ, G-5, box 2950, Operations Report, A1A1 Detachment, 8 August 1944; ANF F1a 4006, Coulet to Comm. Interior, 6 August 1944.

29. NARA, RG 498, First Army HQ, G-5, box 2951, Lieutenant Roland Cote, QMC, report, 11 August 1944; Report of Captain Harry Proctor, Supply Section, 22 July, 1, 4 August 1944; MHI, Crothers Papers, "Port of Cherbourg," 17.

30. NARA, RG 498, First Army HQ, G-5, box 2951, reports of Naval Liaison, 2, 3, 4, 10, 19, 20, 22, 26, 27, 31 July, 3 August 1944.

31. MHI, Crothers Papers, "Port of Cherbourg," 10–17.

32. NARA, RG 498, First Army HQ, G-5, box 2951, Lieutenant Roland Cote, QMC, report, 11 August 1944; Maddaloni, "Liberation and Franco-American Relations," 80–85; Footitt, *War and Liberation*, 81–84.

6. LIFE DURING WARTIME IN NORMANDY AFTER D-DAY

1. Xavier de Guerpel, *1939–1945: Une Certaine Vie de Château au Bocage Normand* (Conde-sur-Noireau: Editions Ch. Corlet, 1973), 182, 191, 200–201, 210–11; Françoise Passera and Jean Quellien, *Les Civils dans la Bataille de Normandie* (Bayeux: OREP Editions, 2014), 82, 84.

2. ANF F1a 4005, Coulet to Koenig, "visit to Caen," 11 July 1944; "situation in Caen," 18 July 1944. On Caen, see Michelin Guide, *Normandy* (Clermont-Ferrand: Michelin et Cie., 1974), 56–59.

3. ANF, ibid.; Passera and Quellien, *Les Civils*, 108–9.

4. Passera and Quellien, *Les Civils*, 90–92, 110–11.

5. Ibid., 100, 118.

6. ANF F1a 4005, Coulet to Koenig, reports, 18 and 27 July 1944.

7. ANF F1a 4005, Coulet to Koenig, report, 31 July 1944.

8. ANF F1a 4005, Coulet to Koenig, "visit to la Manche," 31 July 1944; Coulet to Koenig, 20, 23, 27 June 1944; F1a 4006, Délégué aux Réfugiés, weekly report, 28 July 1944.

9. NARA RG 331, SHAEF, G-5, box 64, report Major E. J. Boulton, 11 June 1944; minutes of weekly G-5 staff conference, 29 June, 4, 11, 13, 20 July 1944; ANF F1a 4006, Délégué aux Réfugiés, weekly report, 28 July 1944.

10. NARA RG 331, SHAEF, G-5, box 64, report Major E. J. Boulton, 10–11 June 1944; minutes of weekly G-5 staff conference, 11, 25 July 1944; MHI, Hansen Diary, 9 June 1944; ANF F1a 4005, Coulet to Koenig, 20, 23 June 1944; F1a 4006, Délégué aux Refugies, weekly reports, 4 and 11 August 1944; Nelson Douglass Lankford, ed., *OSS Against the Reich: The World War II Diaries of Colonel David K. Bruce* (Kent, Ohio: Kent State Univ. Press, 1991), 144.

11. Max Hastings, *Overlord; D-Day and the Battle for Normandy* (New York: Simon and Schuster, 1984), 253–56; Edwin P. Hoyt, *The GI's War: The Story of American Soldiers in Europe in World War II* (New York: McGraw Hill, 1988), 443; Robert Capa, *Slightly Out of Focus* (New York: Holt, 1947), 163.

12. ANF F1a 4006, Délégué aux Réfugiés, weekly report, 4 August 1944; NARA RG 331, SHAEF, G-5, box 64, minutes of weekly G-5 staff conference, 20 July 1944.

13. NARA RG 498, HQ ETO, Provost Marshal, box 4340, Normandy Base Section, graphs and charts; NARA RG 498, First Army HQ, G-5, box 2950, report on Relief and Welfare, 16 August 1944; RG 331, SHAEF, G-5, box 64, minutes of weekly G-5 staff conference, 20 July 1944, contains the 100,000-ton figure for Red Cross donations: 3 tons of clothing per refugee in France in July 1944! RG 331, SHAEF, G-5/2, box 54, report of W.H.G. Giblin, 6 November 1944; RG 498, First Army HQ, G-5, box 2951, reports from Relief Section, 7 and 8 July 1944; ANF F1a 4006, Délégué aux Refugies weekly report, 11 August 1944; Délégué aux Refugies to Coulet, 15 August 1944.

14. NARA RG 498, First Army HQ, G-5, box 2951, reports from Relief Section, 7, 8, and 10 July 1944.

15. NARA, RG 498, First Army HQ, G-5, box 2951, daily report from Relief Section, 9, 10, 12, 14 July, 4, 16 August 1944; ANF F1a 4006, Délégué aux Réfugiés, weekly report, 18 August 1944.

16. ANF F1a 4006, Délégué aux Réfugiés, weekly report, 18 August 1944; NARA RG 331, SHAEF, G-5, box 47, report of Captain Henry Parkman Jr., 18 January 1945; NARA RG 331, SHAEF, G-5, box 64, minutes of weekly G-5 staff conference, 16 Aug.1944; NARA RG 498, First Army HQ, G-5, box 2931, Public Safety Activities in Cherbourg, 14 August 1944.

17. ANF F1a 4005, Coulet to Koenig, 23 June 1944; NARA RG 331, SHAEF, G-5, box 64, Major E. J. Boulton, report, 11 June 1944; minutes of weekly G-5 staff conference, 29 June, 4, 11, 13 July 1944; Roland G. Ruppenthal, *Logistical Support of the Armies,* vol. 1 (Washington, D.C.: U.S. Army Center of Military History, 1953), 1:441–42; Jean Quellien, *La Bataille de Normandie, 6 Juin–25 Août* (Paris: Tallendier, 2014), 169; Régine Torrent, *La France américaine: Controverses de la Libération* (Brussels: Editions Racine, 2004), 245–46.

18. NARA RG 331, SHAEF, G-5, box 64, Major E. J. Boulton, report on U.S. zone, 11 June 1944; minutes of weekly G-5 staff conference, 29 June, 13, 20 July, 1, 16 August 1944; SHAEF, G-5/2, box 47, report Displaced Persons Branch, 7 September 1944; Passera and Quellien, *Les Civils,* 235.

19. NARA RG 331, SHAEF, G-5/2, box 47, report Displaced Persons Branch, 7 September 1944.

20. NARA RG 331, SHAEF, G-5/2, box 12, Colonel Bruce Easley, AG, to Supply and Economics Branch of SHAEF, 19 November 1944; ANF F1a 4006, Délégué aux Réfugiés to Coulet, 18 August 1944.

7. THE U.S. ARMY MEETS THE FRENCH FORCES OF THE INTERIOR

1. Charles de Gaulle, *The Complete War Memoirs of Charles de Gaulle,* trans. Jonathan Griffin and Richard Howard, 3 vols. (New York: Da Capo, [1984]), 2:592–93; Harry Butcher, *My Three Years with Eisenhower* (New York: Simon and Schuster, 1946), 526; Dwight D. Eisenhower, *Crusade in Europe* (New York: Doubleday, 1948), 247–48; Robert Gildea, *Fighters in the Shadows: A New History of the French Resistance* (Cambridge, Mass.: Belknap Press, 2015), 127, 223, 331, 336–39. Gildea offers an insightful discussion of the debates and infighting within the AS (263–77).

2. H. Roderick Kedward, "STO et maquis," in *La France des Années noires,* vol. 2, *De l'Occupation à la Libération,* ed. Jean-Pierre Azéma and François Bédarida (Paris: Editions du Seuil, 2000), 309–24; Olivier Wieviorka, *The French Resistance,* trans. Jane Marie Todd (Cambridge Mass.: Harvard Univ. Press, 2016), 346; Gildea, *Fighters,* 255–56, 297.

3. Robert Aron, *Histoire de la Libération de La France, Juin 1944–Mai 1945* (Paris: Librairie Arthème Fayard, 1959), 180; Eddy Florentin, *Quand les Alliés bombardaient la France* (Paris: Perrin, 1997), 605; Gildea, *Fighters,* 327.

4. Gildea, *Fighters,* 47–48, 334–35, 337–38; J. E. Kaufmann and H. W. Kaufmann, *G.I. Joe in France: From Normandy to Berchtesgaden* (Westport, Conn.: Praeger, 2008), 182; S. J. Lewis, *Jedburgh Team Operations in Support of the 12th Army Group, August 1944* (Fort Leavenworth, Kans.: Combat Studies Institute, 1991), x; Marcel Vigneras, *Rearming the French* (Washington, D.C.: Office of the Chief of Military History, Department of the Army, 1957), 304–5; Claude Delasselle, Joel Drogland, Frédéric Gand, Thierry Roblin, and Jean Rolley, *Un Département dans la Guerre 1939–1945: Occupation, Collaboration et Résistance dans l'Yonne* (Paris: Editions Tirésias, 2006), 463–66, 468, 470, 484; Benjamin Jones, *Eisenhower's Guerrillas: The Jedburghs, the Maquis, and the Liberation*

of France (New York: Oxford Univ. Press, 2016), 192–93; Gildea, *Fighters*, 332; Wieviorka, *The French Resistance*, 350.

5. Charles R. Codman, *Drive* (Boston: Little, Brown, 1957), 161; Patrick K. O'Donnell, *Dog Company* (Boston: Da Capo Press, 2012), 142; Lewis, *Jedburgh*, x; MHI, Hansen Diary, 1 July 1944; Omar N. Bradley, *A Soldier's Story* (New York: Holt, 1951), 365; Jones, *Eisenhower's Guerrillas*, 175–76, 187, 195–96.

6. William Dreux, *No Bridges Blown* (South Bend, Ind.: Univ. of Notre Dame Press, 1971), 135–39, 177–79, 191–94, 230–31, 246, 251, 259–61, 274–75; Robert Capa, *Slightly Out of Focus* (New York: Holt, 1947), 163–64.

7. Dreux, *No Bridges Blown*, 230; Capa, *Slightly Out of Focus*, 164–65; Nelson Douglass Lankford, ed., *OSS Against the Reich: The World War II Diaries of Colonel David K. Bruce* (Kent, Ohio: Kent State Univ. Press, 1991), 156.

8. MHI, Veterans Surveys, 29th Inf. Div., box 1, First Lieutenant Donald L. Van Roosen, 115th Inf. Reg.; box 2, CWO 3 William G. Gideon, 175th Inf. Reg.; box 3, John J. Somers, T/5, 111th Field Artillery Battalion; 2nd Infantry Division, box 1, Corporal Leon E. Grijalva; Private Raymond E. Konrad; T-4 Ivan Mack; T-4 Sam Nuckolles; Sergeant John B. Savard; Staff Sergeant Robert T. Thompson; John B. Savard, "My Life Until Now: The Story of a Boy Growing Up in the Thirties"; MHI, Hansen Diary, 28 August 1944.

9. MHI, Veterans Surveys, 4th Inf. Div., box 1, Colonel Norborne P. Gatling, 12th Inf. Reg., AT Company; 1st Inf. Div., 16th Inf. Reg., box 1, Lieutenant Colonel John B. Beach.

10. Codman, *Drive*, 194–95; MHI, Veterans Surveys, 1st Inf. Div., 26th Inf. Reg., box 1, PFC James T. Lingg; 16th Inf. Reg., box 1, Captain William T. Dillon.

11. NARA RG 498, UD 186, box 900, Escape and Evasion Citations, Major [French Army] Marius Vanneyre, Recommendation for a Bronze Medal of Freedom, 12 July 1946.

12. MHI, Veterans Surveys, 4th Inf. Div., box 1, Colonel Norborne P. Gatling, 12th Inf. Reg., AT Company; 2nd Inf. Div., box 1, Private Raymond E. Konrad; Dreux, *No Bridges Blown*, 216–17, 231; John Maginnis and Robert Hart, ed., *Military Government Journal: Normandy to Berlin* (Amherst: Univ. of Massachusetts Press, 1971), 106.

13. Robert Gildea, *Marianne in Chains: Daily Life in the Heart of France during the German Occupation* (New York: Metropolitan Books, 2004), 324, and French historian Luc Capdevila, cited in Gildea, *Marianne in Chains*, 462n24; Gildea, *Fighters*, 225–26; MHI, Veterans Surveys, 1st Inf. Div., box 2, Sergeant Leroy N. Stewart; 29th Inf. Div., box 1, Major Robert Earl Henne, 115th Inf. Reg; 175th Inf. Reg., CIC, box 2, First Lieutenant William C. Frodsham Jr.; 4th Inf. Div., box 1, PFC Frank T. Beutel, HQ Intell. and Recce; Peter Schrijvers, *The Crash of Ruin: American Combat Soldiers in Europe during World War II* (New York: New York Univ. Press, 1998), 151–53.

14. Dreux, *No Bridges Blown*, 229, 260–62, 274–75; *Stars and Stripes* (Besançon, edition), 15 September 1944; ADY 1222 W 38, Ren. Gén., Auxerre, to Comm. Rép., Dijon: "Circulaire No. 67," December 1944. Robert Aron's *Histoire de la Libération de La France* (1959), is strongly Gaullist and stands out among works that emphasize the role of the French and FFI in particular in liberating France.

15. *Stars and Stripes* (Besançon edition), 19 September 1944; *Chicago Tribune*, 19 September 1944; MHI, Hansen Diary, 15 September 1944; Jones, *Eisenhower's Guerrillas*, 230–31, 234–35.

16. NARA RG 338, Third Army, Inspector General Section, Reports and Investigations, July 1944–November 1944, box 2, Hemingway Investigation, testimony of Ernest Hemingway, 6 October 1944.

17. Ibid.

18. NARA RG 338, Third Army, Inspector General Section, Reports and Investigations, July 1944–November 1944, box 2, Hemingway Investigation, interview of Colonel David K. E. Bruce, 10 October 1944; Lankford, ed., *OSS Against the Reich*, 161–64.

19. France, Armée, Division blindée, 2. *La 2e [i.e. deuxième] d. b., Général Leclerc, Combattants et Combats en France, présentés par un Groupe d'Officiers et d'Hommes de la Division* (Paris: Arts et métiers graphiques, 1945), 45–46; Bruce interview; Lankford, ed., *OSS Against the Reich*, 168–70.

20. See Vigneras, *Rearming the French*, 305, for French government estimates of FFI dead. This number may represent a liberal estimate, and in any event it is almost impossible to distinguish FFI from "*fusillés*" or others killed by the Germans in the murderous chaos of the summer of 1944.

21. Pierre Bécamps, *Libération de Bordeaux* (Paris: Hachette, 1974), 104; Wieviorka, *The French Resistance*, 375; MHI, Hansen Diary, 15, 16, 18 September 1944; Edwin P. Hoyt, *The GI's War: The Story of American Soldiers in Europe in World War II* (New York: McGraw Hill, 1988), 488; MHI, Herman H. Pohl Papers, box 1, "News Briefs," 7 August 1944; de Gaulle, *The Complete War Memoirs*, 3:849–51; Rick Atkinson, *The Guns at Last Light: The War in Western Europe, 1944–1945* (New York: Holt, 2013), 152. Many of the German troops holed up in the Atlantic pockets were axillary troops and not first-rate Wehrmacht.

22. Vigneras, *Rearming the French*, 305; Jones, *Eisenhower's Guerrillas*, 204–5; ANF F1a 3304, comm. rép., Rennes, reports, 16 November, 1 December 1944.

23. ANF F1a 3304, comm. rép., Rennes, reports, 1, 16 December 1944; F1a 3006, Préf., Var, to comm. rép., Marseille, 26 December 1944; F1a 3305, Ren. Gén., Marseille, report, 15 February 1945; ADBdR 149 W 182, Fiche, HQ Delbase, note, n.d. [probably December 1944]; Ren. Gén., Marseille, to comm. rép., 22 February, 14 March 1945; de Gaulle, *The Complete War Memoirs*, 3:680–81. Commissioner Gorgeu, in Rennes, had been the Radical (center-left) mayor of Brest before the war.

24. Régine Torrent concludes that the FFI wore out their welcome among the French even faster than American GIs did (in October 1944), in Régine Torrent, *La France américaine: Controverses de la Libération* (Brussels: Editions Racine, 2004), 227–28.

8. SURVIVING THE BREAKOUT

1. ADA SC 4102, gendarme reports, Bar-sur-Seine, 2 August 1944; ADMM WM 468, comm. police, Nancy, to Préf., 2 August 1944; Claude Delasselle, Joel Drogland, Frédéric Gand, Thierry Roblin, and Jean Rolley, *Un Département dans la Guerre, 1939–1945: Occupation, Collaboration et Résistance dans l'Yonne* (Paris: Editions Tirésias, 2006), 480–83.

2. ADA SC 4102, gendarme tele. reports, Nogent-sur-Seine, 7, 8 August 1944; gendarme tele. report, Pont- Ste.-Marie, 7 August 1944; ADMM WM 468, gendarme tele. report, Nancy, 8 August 1944.

3. ADA SC 4102, gendarme report, follow-up report, and comm. police report, Troyes, 4 August 1944.

4. ADMM WM 468, gendarme reports, Nancy, 8, 10, 12, 17 August 1944; comm. police, Nancy to Préf., 2 August 1944; Préf., Bar-le-Duc, to Min. Int., 12 August 1944; gendarme report, Bar-le-Duc, 12 August 1944; ADA SC 4102, gendarme report, Bar-sur-Seine, 10 August 1944.

5. ADMM WM 468, gendarme report, Longwy, 14 August 1944; Préf., Bar-le-Duc to Min. Int., 12 August 1944; ADA SC 4102, gendarme tele. report, Bouilly, 7 August 1944; gendarme report, Bar-sur-Seine, 10 August 1944.

6. Louis S. Rehr and Carleton R. Rehr, *Marauder: Memoir of a B-26 Pilot in Europe in World War II* (Jefferson, N.C.: McFarland, 2004), 73; ADMM WM 468, Civil Defense, Nancy, to Préf., 26 August 1944; phone messages received by gendarmes, Neuves-Maisons, 26 August 1944; Nelson Douglas Lankford, ed., *OSS Against the Reich: The World War II Diaries of Colonel David K. Bruce* (Kent, Ohio: Kent State Univ. Press, 1991), 167.

7. ADMM WM 468, "Avis Important" attached to gendarme report, Nancy, 22 September 1942; ADMM WM 1525, Mayor, Coincourt, to Préf., 14 January 1946.

8. ADMM WM 468, Sous-Préf., Lunéville, reports to Préf., 28 August 1944; gendarme, Lunéville, multiple reports and tele. messages to Préf., 28 August 1944; gendarme, Thiaucourt, to Préf., 28 August 1944; tele. messages received at Gendarmerie, Nancy, 29 August 1944.

9. Benjamin Jones, *Eisenhower's Guerrillas: The Jedburghs, the Maquis, and the Liberation of France* (New York: Oxford Univ. Press, 2016), 197–99; NARA RG 331/97, box 115, German atrocities, Police report of Pierre Seite, Saint-Pol-de-Léon, n.d.

10. ADA SC 4273, report by Ren. Gén., Troyes, "La Libération du Département," 19–21, 52; Françoise Passera and Jean Quellien, *Les Civils dans la Bataille de Normandie* (Bayeux: OREP Editions, 2014), 220–22.

11. Edwin P. Hoyt, *The GI's War: The Story of American Soldiers in Europe in World War II* (New York: McGraw Hill, 1988), 454.

12. ADA SC 4273, Ren. Gén., "La Liberation du Département," 80–81; Charles C. Wertenbaker, *Invasion!* (New York: Appleton Century, 1944), 177; Alan Moorehead, *Eclipse* (New York: Harper and Row, 1968), 114; Richard Tobin, *Invasion Journal* (New York: Dutton, 1944), 142–43; Pierre Maillaud, *Over to France*, trans. Francis Cowper (London: Oxford Univ. Press, 1946), 103–4; Sartre quoted in Henri Amouroux, *La grande Histoire des Français après l'Occupation*, vol. 8 (Paris: Robert Laffont, 1988), 533; Fabrice Virgili, *Shorn Women: Gender and Punishment in Liberation France*, trans. John Flower (London: Berg, 2002), 97.

13. John J. Maginnis and Robert A. Hart, eds., *Military Government Journal: Normandy to Berlin* (Amherst: Univ. of Massachusetts Press, 1971), 98.

14. NARA RG 331, SHAEF, G-5, box 64, Major E. J. Boulton, report, 11 June 1944; minutes of weekly G-5 staff conference, 29 June 1944; Moorehead, *Eclipse*, 112; Hoyt, *The GI's War*, 391; MHI, Hansen Diary, 9, 10 June 1944; Lankford, ed., *OSS Against the Reich*, 96; Patrick K. O'Donnell, *Dog Company* (Boston: Da Capo, 2012), 137; MHI, Veterans Surveys, 29th Div., box 2, Captain John K. Slingluff.

15. ANF F1a 4005, comm. police, Bayeux, to comm. general, 22 June 1944; police interviews with Jeanne Cardet and Mayor Pagny, 23 June 1944; Inspector of Primary Education, Bayeux, to comm. rép., 24 June 1944; Richard Vinen, *The Unfree French: Life under the Occupation* (New Haven, Conn.: Yale Univ. Press, 2006), 160.

16. Delasselle et al., *Un Département dans la Guerre*, 475, 484, 491, 502–3; ADA SC 4273, Ren.

Gén. report, "La Libération du Département," 55–61; SC 4102, compte rendu, Gendarmerie commander, Troyes, 29 August, 3 September 1944; SC 24642 B, Préf., Troyes to CA, inviting Americans to attend a ceremony honoring "les fusillés" [the shot] of the Aube, 31 October 1944; ADY 1222 W 11, Ren. Gén., Auxerre, note, 29 August 1944.

17. Delasselle et al., *Un Département dans la Guerre,* 516–19; ADY 1222 W 38, comm. police, Migennes, "list des tondues à Migennes," 10 September 1944; ADA SC 4273, "La Libération du Département," 80–81; ADY 319, Ren. Gén, Migennes, report, 6 November 1944; Virgili, *Shorn Women,* 53–57, 113, 116–19, 129–31.

18. ADY 1222 W 38, comm. police, Sens, 28 August 1944; Delasselle et al., *Un Département dans la Guerre,* 484.

19. ADY 1 W 319, comm. police, Joigny, 7 September 1944; Ren. Gén., Migennes, report, 6 November 1944; gendarme report, 4 November 1944; 2me Bureau, 8me Military region, report, 2 November 1944; Delasselle et al., *Un Département dans la Guerre,* 520–21. Membership in Colonel de la Rocque's PSF was cited by many in the wake of the liberation as exoneration or damnation depending on circumstances and point of view of the commenter. In Chanard's case, prewar membership presumably casts suspicion upon his political motives.

20. ANF F1a 4006, P. Larocque to Koenig on situation in Rennes, 13 August 1944; ADY 1 W 324, Dir. of Ravit. Gén., Yonne, to Commandant of FFI, Auxerre, 1 September 1944.

21. NARA RG 331, SHAEF, G-5, box 64, minutes of weekly G-5 staff conference, 20 October 1944; box 12, memo from Major General John T. Lewis, Head of Mission to France, to Eisenhower, 3 December 1944.

22. ADY 1222 W 11, Ren. Gén., Auxerre, notes, 29 August, 6 September 1944; Maginnis and Hart, eds., *Military Government Journal,* 118.

23. ADY 1 W 324, Arrêté de Comm. Guerre [Diethelm], n.d.; ADA SC 39175, notice, Préf., Troyes, 29 August 1944; Charles-Louis Foulon, *Le Pouvoir en Province à la Libération: les Commissaires de la République, 1943–1946* (Paris: Fondation nationale des sciences politiques, Armand Colin,1975), 219–21; Marcel Vigneras, *Rearming the French* (Washington, D.C.: Office of the Chief of Military History, Department of the Army, 1957), 319; Françis-Louis Closon, *Commissaire de la République du Général de Gaulle: Lille, Septembre 1944–Mars 1946* (Paris: Julliard, 1980), 83–88; Maginnis and Hart, *Military Government Journal,* 111, 128–29, 135, 150–51. Robert Gildea portrays de Gaulle's overt hostility toward the FFI and FTP in Robert Gildea, *Fighters in the Shadows: A New History of the French Resistance* (Cambridge, Mass.: Belknap Press, 2015), 410–12.

24. Vigneras, *Rearming the French,* 320; de Gaulle, *The Complete War Memoirs,* 3:677–88; ANF F1a 3304, Haas-Picard to Captain Bloch, 18 October 1944, with attached list of armaments and equipment requested from Lend-Lease.

9. LORRAINE AND ALSACE

1. Michael Marrus and Robert Paxton, *Vichy France and the Jews* (New York: Schocken, 1983), 7; Richard Vinen, *The Unfree French: Life under the Occupation* (New Haven, Conn.: Yale Univ. Press, 2006), 39, 105; Thomas Johnston Laub, *After the Fall: German Policy in Occupied France, 1940–1944* (New York: Oxford Univ. Press, 2010), 47. Trying to determine even an approximate

number of French who served in the German military is a frustrating enterprise, as different sources, including French government ones, give widely varying figures. One memo produced by a French official in charge of trying to pry loose from the Soviet grip French citizens held as POWs in the USSR lamented that "180,000 families in Alsace-Lorraine live in anxiety because they do not know the fate of their sons enrolled in the German military or auxiliary forces." And that number reflects only the number missing and unaccounted for. See ANF F1a 3303, memo, Autorité Alliée de Contrôle Comité de Coordination, 3 October 1945. Préf., Haute Marne [sic] to Min. Int., 18 August 1945, complained that 22,978 men from his department had served in the Wehrmacht and only 2,859 had come home by August 1945! And these numbers were *"bien inférieure à la réalité."*

2. Fernand l'Huillier, "Sur la Nazification de l'Alsace," *Revue d'Histoire de la Deuxième Guerre mondiale* 30, no. 120 (October 1980): 66; NARA RG 331 93A, SHAEF, PWD, Captain G. Curtis, "Interview with Alsatian who served in the German Army and escaped in 1944," 5 October 1944; MHI, John J. Maginnis Papers, Maginnis Diary, 26 June 1944.

3. ANF F1a 3303, note, n.d., "Situation des Alsaciens et des Lorrains faits Prisonniers par les Armées Alliée"; Colonel Alden Sibley, COS, SHAEF to French COS for National Defense, Paris, 14 October 1944; Séance du Comité de Défense nationale, 17 October 1944; C. de Gaulle to For. Min., 21 October 1944; F1a 3306, Min. Int. to Haas-Picard, 4 January 1945; Sérvice Central de Alsace-Lorraine to Min. Int., 15 May 1945. F1a 3303 contains scores of memos on the subject of the fate of Frenchmen who served in the German military.

4. NARA RG 331/ 97, box 116, German Atrocities, Narration of events in Mussidan, Dordogne, 11 June 1944; atrocities at Couvonges, 2 September 1944; ANF F1a 4006, comm. police, Coutances, report, 8 August 1944; Benjamin Jones, *Eisenhower's Guerrillas: The Jedburghs, the Maquis, and the Liberation of France* (New York: Oxford Univ. Press, 2016), 239. French serving in the SS could have been volunteers from anywhere in France or conscripts from the eastern provinces. Ever-shifting Nazi policies over recruitment into the SS and the Wehrmacht could have landed French conscripts into the SS.

5. ADMM WM 1525, Mayor, Jarny, to Préf., 14 January 1946; Mayor, Epiez-sur-Chiers, to Préf., 10 January 1946; Préf. to Mayor Armaucourt, 24 January 1946; Paul Druaux, Aboncourt-en-Vosges, statement, 24 January 1946.

6. Edwin P. Hoyt, *The GI's War: The Story of American Soldiers in Europe in World War II* (New York: McGraw Hill, 1988), 484; Richard D. Courtney, *Normandy to the Bulge: An American Infantry GI in Europe During World War II* (Carbondale: Southern Illinois Univ. Press, 1997), 36–37.

7. ADMM WM 1525, Ren. Gén., Nancy, reports, 1 and 2 September 1944; James A. Huston, *Across the Face of France: Liberation and Recovery 1944–63* (West Lafayette, Ind.: Purdue University Studies, 1963), 167–70; Hugh M. Cole, *The Lorraine Campaign* (Washington, D.C.: U.S. Army Center of Military History, 2007), 93–96; Pierre Barrel and Jean-Claude Bonnefont in Michel Parisse, *Histoire de Nancy* (Toulouse: Privat, 1978), 452; Gilbert Grandval and A. Jean Collin, *Libération de l'Est de la France* (Paris: Hachette, 1974), 190–92.

8. S. J. Lewis, *Jedburgh Team Operations in Support of the 12th Army Group, August 1944* (Fort Leavenworth, Kans.: Combat Studies Institute, 1991), 48–50, 54–59; Jones, *Eisenhower's Guerrillas,* 253–58.

9. MHI, Veterans Surveys, 4th Inf. Div., box 1, Colonel Norborne P. Gatling, 12th Inf. Reg., AT Company; NARA RG 338, Third Army, Inspector General Section, Reports and Investigations,

July–November 1944, box 3, Looting by American Troops of Haboudange, France, 13–15 November 1944; ADMM WM 1521, Comm. Central, Nancy, to Dir. Police, 21 October 1944; Courtney, *Normandy to the Bulge*, 38. French people in the region of Nancy and throughout the Meurthe-et Moselle speak French and not a German dialect, which in Lorraine is heard only north and east of Metz. See also l'Huillier, "Sur la Nazification de l'Alsace," 59–68, on Alsatians' and Lorrainers' response to German annexation.

10. NARA RG 338, Third Army, Inspector General Section, Reports and Investigations, July 1944–November 1944, box 3, Looting by American Troops of Raucourt [sic], France, 13–15 November 1944; *Stars and Stripes* (Strasbourg edition), 12 December 1944; *Stars and Stripes* (Nancy edition), 7 February 1945; ANF F1a 3304, Préf., Metz, report, 15 December 1944.

11. ADMM WM 1521, Sous-Préf., Lunéville, to Préf., Nancy, 2 October 1944; Ren. Gén., Nancy, 4 November 1944; Sous-Préf., Toul, to Préf., Nancy, 6 November 1944; Sous-Préf., Pont-à-Mousson, to Préf., 20 November 1944.

12. ADMM WM 1521, comm. police, Nancy, 28 September 1944; gendarme report, Nancy, 26 September 1944.

13. ANF F1a 3304, Comm. Rép. P. Chailley-Bert to Haas-Picard, 16 November 1944.

14. ADMM WM 1521, Ren. Gén., Pont-à-Mousson, 6 November 1944; ANF F1a 3304, Comm. Rép. P. Chailley-Bert to Haas-Picard, 16 November 1944.

15. NARA RG 338, Third Army, Inspector General Section, Reports and Investigations, July 1944–November 1944, box 3, Looting by American Troops of Haboudange, 17 December–2 January 1945.

16. Ibid.

17. NARA RG 338, Third Army, Inspector General Section, Reports and Investigations, July 1944–November 1944, box 3, Looting by American Troops of Haboudange, 17 December–2 January 1945, M. Goy, Laxou, to comm. rép., Nancy, 25 November 1944. Max Hastings discusses looting and theft by GIs in Germany in *Armageddon: The Battle for Germany, 1944–1945* (New York: Knopf, 2004), 429–31.

18. NARA RG 338, Third Army, Inspector General Section, Reports and Investigations, July 1944–November 1944, box 3, Looting by American Troops of Raucourt [sic], France, 13–15 November 1944, comm. rép., Nancy, to General Patton, 10 December 1944; Hugh M. Cole, *The Lorraine Campaign*, 350. Map XXVIII reveals that Haboudange lay on the sector border between the 35th and 26th Divisions, which delayed the arrival of CIC and CA officers, who ended up coming from the 26th Division.

19. NARA RG 338, Third Army, Inspector General Section, Reports and Investigations, July 1944–November 1944, box 3, Looting by American Troops of Raucourt [sic], France, 13–15 November 1944, comm. rép., Nancy, to General Patton, 10 December 1944.

20. ANF F1a 3305, Chailley-Bert to Haas-Picard, "extrait d'un rapport sur la situation en Moselle," 17 December 1944.

21. ANF F1a 3305, Ren. Gén., Paris, to Haas-Picard, 3 January 1945; MHI, Hansen Diary, 3 August 1944.

22. Courtney, *Normandy to the Bulge*, 41–42; ADMM WM 1521, special delegation from Maxéville to Préf., 16 April 1945.

23. NARA RG 338, Third Army, Inspector General Section, Reports and Investigations, July 1944–November 1944, box 2, Investigation of alleged loss, destruction or looting of property at L'Ecole des Beaux-Arts, Nancy, 25 November 1944.

24. ADMM WM 1521, Ren. Gén. to Sous-Préf., 21 February 1945.

25. ANF F1a 3304, Comm. Rép. de Relations Interalliées [Coulet] to SHAEF, 5 November 1944; minutes of meeting of delegates from all ministries having relations with the allies, 30 October 1944, 1 February 1945; Préf., Nancy, report, 15 December 1944; F1a 3305, extraits du comm. police, Nancy, 16 December 1944; Nicole H. Taflinger, *Season of Suffering: Coming of Age in Occupied France, 1940–45* (Pullman: Washington State Univ. Press, 2010), 125–26.

26. Charles de Gaulle, *The Complete War Memoirs of Charles de Gaulle,* trans. Jonathan Griffin and Richard Howard, 3 vols. (New York: Da Capo, [1984]), 3:831–39; Alphonse Juin, *Mémoires,* 2 vols. (Paris: A. Fayard, 1959), 2:78–86; Dwight D. Eisenhower, *Crusade in Europe* (New York: Doubleday, 1948), 362–63; Winston Churchill, *The Second World War,* 6 vols. (Boston: Houghton Mifflin, 1950), 6:281; Harry Butcher, *My Three Years with Eisenhower* (New York: Simon and Schuster, 1946), 738; Franklin L. Gurley, "Politique contre Stratégie: La Défense de Strasbourg en décembre 1944," *Guerres mondiales et Conflits contemporains,* no. 166 (April 1992): 89–114, offers an excellent discussion of the affair and reports that Churchill uttered only five cryptic words during the meeting, "Strasbourg, that is the point."

27. ANF F1a 3303, comm. rép., Strasbourg, to Min. Int., 6 January 1945; Council of Ministers, Paris, notes, 9 January 1945; comm. police, Strasbourg, telegram to Min. Int., and reply, 10 January 1945; ADMM WM 1525, Ren. Gén., Nancy, report, 8 January 1945; *Stars and Stripes* (Nancy edition), 25, 26 January, 20 March 1945; NARA RG 331, SHAEF, G-5, box 47, Captain Henry Parkman Jr., report, 18 January 1945.

10. ENDURING WARTIME IN LORRAINE

1. There were 2,337,228 Normans in 1936 (in 4,435 square miles) versus 3,085,381 Alsatians and Lorrainers (in 7,622 square miles).

2. As previously noted, the population of Alsace and Lorraine was more disturbed by the Nazis, and the total number of French residents reduced. Casualty figures are from United States, Department of the Army, *Army Battle Casualties and Nonbattle Deaths in World War II: Final Report* (Washington, D.C.: Office of the Comptroller of the Army, 1953), 32, 92–93.

3. ADMM WM 1523, Préf. to Colonel McKay, 20 September 1944; WM 1518, Liberation reports, Fréménil, Hablainville, Merviller, Veho, n.d. [1945]; ANF F1a 3303, Préf., Haut-Rhin, Colmar, to Min. Int., 18 April 1945; ADMM WM 1521, gendarme, Champeneux, report, 9 October 1944.

4. ADMM WM 1521, report, no author [probably the mayor of Morville], Pont-à-Mousson, 20 November 1944.

5. ADMM WM 1523, comm. police, Pont-à-Mousson, 6 November 1944; ADMM WM 468, Sous-Préf., Lunéville to Préf., Nancy, 30 August 1944; WM 1525, Ren. Gén., Nancy, reports, 9 and 12 September 1944; comm. police, Nancy, reports, 10, 11, 12, 17 September 1944; Nicole H. Taflinger, *Season of Suffering: Coming of Age in Occupied France, 1940–45* (Pullman: Washington State

Univ. Press, 2010), 109–11; Gilbert Grandval and A. Jean Collin, *Libération de l'Est de la France* (Paris: Hachette, 1974), 196.

6. ADMM WM 1515, Ren. Gén., Nancy, 24 September 1944; comm, police, Nancy, 20 September, 10, 11, 24 October 1944; Sous-Pref, Lunéville, to Préf., 10 October 1944; Sous- Préf., Briey, to Préf., 12 October 1944; pres. délégué mun. council, Malzéville to Préf., 23 October 1944; Grandval and Collin, *Libération de l'Est de la France*, 188.

7. ADMM WM 1521, Ren. Gén., Nancy, 6 November 1944; WM 1525, Ren. Gén., Nancy, 12 September 1944; *La Liberté Retrouvée: La Libération de la Meurthe-et-Moselle* (Nancy: Conseil Générale de la Meurthe-et-Moselle, 2005), 22.

8. Nelson Douglas Lankford, ed., *OSS Against the Reich: The World War II Diaries of Colonel David K. Bruce* (Kent, Ohio: Kent State Univ. Press, 1991), 196; ADMM WM 1525, Ren. Gén. to Préf., Nancy, 20 September 1944; gendarme reports, Nancy, 22 September, 12 and 14 December 1944; Asst. Engineer, Ponts et Chaussée, to Préf., Nancy, 2 October 1944; Préf., Nancy, to Min. of Pub. Works, Paris, 20 October 1944; comm. police to Préf., Nancy, 29 October, 4 November 1944.

9. ADMM WM 1525, Sous-Préf., Briey to Préf., 22 November, 20 December 1944; Ren. Gén., Nancy, 26 December 1944; comm. police, Pont-à-Mousson, 28 December 1944; comm. police, Nancy, 20 January 1945; ADY 1 W 319 contains many reports of mysterious lights and flares in the Yonne over a period of many months right up to VE Day.

10. ADY 1 W 324, Etat Major, 3eme Bureau, Region Militaire, Dijon, note, 31 August 1944; gendarme, Tonnerre, report, 17 November 1944; ADY 1 W 319, gendarme, Auxerre, reports, 14 December 1944, 8 January 1945.

11. ADBdR 149 W 182, Colonel Mamier, Delta Base, to Commandante French Milt. Region XV, 23 December 1944; ADA SC 4260, Sûreté nationale Bulletin Quotidien d'Informations, 17, 20 December 1944; ADMM WM 1525, Ren. Gén., Nancy, 26 December 1944; Jacques Nobécourt, *Hitler's Last Gamble: The Battle of the Ardennes*, trans. R. H. Berry (London: Chatto and Windus, 1967), 206, 208–10, 251–52; Paul Jankowsky, *Communism and Collaboration; Simon Sabiani and Politics in Marseille, 1919–1944* (New Haven, Conn.: Yale Univ. Press, 1989), 138; Henri Amouroux, *La grande Histoire des Français après l'Occupation* (Paris: Robert Laffont, 1993), 10:342–44; Harry C. Butcher, *My Three Years with Eisenhower* (New York: Simon and Schuster, 1946), 724; Charles R. Codman, *Drive* (Boston: Little, Brown, 1957), 233.

12. ADMM WM 1525, Sous-Préf., Briey to Préf., 22 November 1944; ADA SC 4260, Sûreté nationale Bulletin Quotidien d'Informations, 26, 27, 29 December 1944; ANF F1a 3304, Préf., Châlons-sur-Marne, report, 9 January 1945; F1a 3306, General Pleas Rogers, HQ COMZ to Min. Int., 2 January 1945; ADY 1 W 319, gendarme, Fontainebleau, report, 14 January 1945; Frances DeBra Brown, *An Army in Skirts: The World War II Letters of Frances DeBra* (Indianapolis: Indiana Historical Society Press, 2008), 145.

13. ADMM WM 1525, comm. police, Pont-à-Mousson, 28 December 1944; comm. police, Nancy, 20 January 1945; ADA SC 24642 B, Melvin J. Stickney, CIC, memo, 11 April 1945; ADY 1 W 319, gendarme, Chassy, report, 26 February 1945; gendarme, Auxerre, report, 4, 6 March 1945; ANF F1a 3261, comm. rép., Bordeaux, report, 1 March 1945; ADMM 358, Secretaire Général pour la Police, Nancy, to Min. Int., summary of arrests for 1945; Hilary Footitt, *War and Liberation in France: Living with the Liberators* (New York: Palgrave Macmillan, 2004), 155.

11. AMERICANS IN LIBERATED PARIS

1. MHI, Hansen Diary, 13 August 1944; Rick Atkinson, *The Guns at Last Light: The War in Western Europe, 1944–1945* (New York: Holt, 2013), 236.

2. NARA RG 331 SHAEF, G-5, box 64, minutes of weekly G-5 staff conference, 10 August 1944; memo, Major General Leven C. Allen, HQ 21st Army Group, 22 August 1944; William F. Ross and Charles F. Romanus, *The Quartermaster Corps: Operations in the War against Germany* (Washington, D.C.: U.S. Army Center of Military History, 2004), 538–39; Charles de Gaulle, *The Complete War Memoirs of Charles de Gaulle,* trans. Jonathan Griffin and Richard Howard, 3 vols. (New York: Da Capo, [1984]), 2:640–41.

3. NARA RG 331, SHAEF G-5, box 64, Daily Journal, HQ Paris, 1st Euro. CA Reg., 26 August 1944; Edwin P. Hoyt, *The GI's War: The Story of American Soldiers in Europe in World War II* (New York: McGraw Hill, 1988), 480.

4. Hoyt, *The GI's War,* 480–81; MHI, Hansen Diary, 28, 31 August, 8 September 1944.

5. Nelson Douglass Lankford, ed., *OSS Against the Reich: The World War II Diaries of Colonel David K. Bruce* (Kent, Ohio: Kent State Univ. Press, 1991), 178–79; MHI, Hansen Diary, 31 August 1944; NARA RG 331, SHAEF G-5, box 64, Daily Journal, HQ, Paris, 26, 27, 28 August 1944; memo from Eisenhower, SHAEF, n.d.

6. NARA RG 331 SHAEF, G-5, box 64, Bruce McDaniel, report on Relief for Paris, 17 April 1945; report, "Paris Supply Situation," 29 August 1944; memo, Eisenhower, SHAEF, to Combined Chiefs, n.d. [soon after 24 August 1944]; Jean-Luc Leleu, Françoise Passera, and Jean Quellien, *La France pendant la Seconde Guerre Mondiale* (Paris: Fayard and le Ministère de la Défense, 2010), 269; Allan Mitchell, *Nazi Paris: The History of an Occupation, 1940–1944* (New York: Berghahn, 2008), 111, 114, 144.

7. MHI, Hansen Diary, 23 September 1944; Dwight D. Eisenhower, *Crusade in Europe* (New York: Doubleday, 1948), 296–97; NARA RG 331 SHAEF, G-5, box 64, minutes of weekly G-5 staff conference, 10 August 1944; memos, Colonel Homer Jones to SHAEF, 9 and 26 September 1944.

8. NARA RG 331 SHAEF, G-5, box 64, memo, Colonel Homer Jones to SHAEF, 9 November 1944; memo from Commissariat of Supply, Paris, to Colonel Black, 7 December 1944; resume of cross-channel tele. conversation between Colonel Sherman and Colonel Howland, 28 August 1944; memo, Colonel Bruce Easley Jr. to SHAEF, 19 December 1944; minutes of meeting "Critical Supply Situation in Paris," 19 January 1945; Bruce McDaniel, report on Relief for Paris, 23 December 1944, 17 April 1945; MHI, Hansen Diary, 23 September 1944.

9. NARA RG 331 SHAEF, G-5, box 64, memo, Colonel Homer Jones to SHAEF, 26 September 1944; memo, Colonel H. C. Nolen, 25 November 1944; NARA RG 331 decimal file 385, entry 87, box 28, memo, Brigadier General Robert A. McClure, chief PWD, "Supplies," 11 September 1944; Bruce McDaniel, report on Relief of Paris, 17 April 1945; Janet Flanner, *Paris Journal, 1944–1965* (New York: Atheneum, 1965), 3–6; Abbott Joseph Liebling, *Normandy Revisited* (New York: Simon and Schuster, 1958), 220; Gertrude Stein, *Wars I Have Seen* (London: Batsford, 1945), 173.

10. Roland G. Ruppenthal, *Logistical Support of the Armies,* 2 vols. (Washington, D.C.: U.S. Army Center of Military History, 1953), 2:31–32; MHI, Hansen Diary, 7, 22 September 1944; Lankford, ed., *OSS Against the Reich,* 179.

11. Ruppenthal *Logistical Support of the Armies*, 2:497; MHI, Betty M. Olson Papers, ms., 74; Stein, *Wars I Have Seen*, 173; NARA RG 498, ETO, IGO Reports, box 4666, report of visit to Paris leave center, April 1945.

12. Ruppenthal, *Logistical Support of the Armies*, 2:497; MHI, Olson Papers, ms., 6, 23 January 1945; Frances DeBra Brown, *An Army in Skirts: The World War II Letters of Frances DeBra* (Indianapolis: Indiana Historical Society Press, 2008), 216; NARA RG 498, ETO, IGO Reports, box 4666, report of visit to Paris Leave Center, 1 April 1945; box 4339, Investigation of broadcast by Herbert Clark on 15 February 1945.

13. NARA RG 498, ETO, IGO Reports, box 4666, report of visit to Paris Leave Center, 1 April 1945.

14. NARA RG 498, Ninth Army HQ, box 2947, report, 1 February 1945; ADY 1 W 328, comm. rép. to Préf., 17 January 1945; comm. rép. circular to mayors, 23 February 1945. The LVF (Légion des voluntaires français contre le bolchevisme) was a small expeditionary force raised to fight alongside the SS in Russia.

15. MHI, Olson Papers, ms., 47–48, 52, 58, letters, 10 January 1945; Brown, *Army in Skirts*, vii–iii, 121–22, 124, 128–29, 131, 140.

16. MHI, Olson Papers, ms., 52–58, 63–65, 74, 91, letters, 1, 27 October 1944; Brown, *Army in Skirts*, 124–25, 131, 135, 153, 197.

17. William S. Triplet, *A Colonel in the Armored Divisions: A Memoir, 1941–1945* (Columbia: Univ. of Missouri Press, 2001), 115; MHI, Olson Papers, ms., 70, letters to parents, 1, 27 October, 2, 12 December 1944, 3, 16 January 1945; Brown, *Army in Skirts*, 122, 124, 126, 128, 134, 158; NARA RG 331, SHAEF, G-5, box 64, memo, Dwight D. Eisenhower to Combined Chiefs, n.d. [shortly after 24 August 1944]; MHI, Hansen Diary, 31 August 1944.

18. Donald Harrison, ed., *From the Letters of Robert S. Gerdy, 1942–1945: A Personal Record of World War II* (Philadelphia: Dorance, 1969), 243–48, 257, 267, 275; Brown, *Army in Skirts*, 197.

19. MHI, Veterans Surveys, 2nd Inf. Div., box 1, John Savard, "My Life Until Now: The Story of a Boy Growing Up in the Thirties."

20. Brown, *Army in Skirts*, 123, 153, 157, 165, 198.

21. Anthonly Beevor and Artemis Cooper, *Paris After the Liberation, 1944–1949* (New York: Doubleday, 1994), 78; MHI, Olson Papers, ms., 47–48, 91, letters, 16, 30 December 1944; Brown, *Army in Skirts*, 132, 135, 137, 146, 150, 152, 158–59, 163.

22. Jean Galtier-Boissière, *Mon Journal depuis La Libération* (Paris: La Jeune Parque, 1945), 36; Harrison, ed., *From the Letters of Robert S. Gerdy*, 246; MHI, Olson Papers, ms., 434, 439, 445, 477, letters, 5, 29 January 1945; Brown, *Army in Skirts*, 132, 152. Gerdy saw American films with French subtitles in November 1944.

23. MHI, Olson Papers, ms., 10, 11, 15, 18, 78, letters, 27 January, 8 February 1945; NARA RG 331, G-5, box 64, memo, Colonel H. C. Nolen to SHAEF, 25 November 1944; memo, Colonel Bruce Easley Jr. to SHAEF, 19 December 1944; minutes of meeting "Critical Supply Situation in Paris" 19 January 1945; Bruce McDaniel, report on Relief for Paris, 17 April 1945; box 62, Min. Ind. Prod., Paris, to SHAEF, Versailles, 2 February 1945; Triplet, *Colonel in the Armored Divisions*, 117.

24. Harrison, ed., *From the Letters of Robert S. Gerdy*, 277–78, 279–80.

25. *Stars and Stripes* (Nice edition), 27 March 1945.

26. MHI, Olson Papers, letters, 23 January, 8 March, 15 April 1945; Harrison, ed., *From the Letters of Robert S. Gerdy,* 297; Régine Torrent, *La France américaine: Controverses de la Libération* (Brussels: Editions Racine, 2004), 279.

27. Hans A. Schmitt, *An Ordinary Life in Extraordinary Times, 1933–1946* (Baton Rouge: Louisiana Univ. Press, 1989), 199–201. Schmitt was born half-Jewish in Frankfurt, escaped Germany to England, and landed in the United States at 17 in 1938 to attend college.

28. Harrison, ed., *From the Letters of Robert S. Gerdy,* 290, 299, 293–308. Gerdy had been posted to London for eight months. Brown, *Army in Skirts,* 139, 165, 173, 178, 201.

29. ANF F1a 3303, *Le Franc-Tireur,* 30 June 1945, and unidentified press cutting; Torrent, *France américaine,* 282–83.

CONCLUSIONS: THE LIBERATORS AND THE LIBERATED

1. See Thomas Laub, *After the Fall: German Policy in Occupied France, 1940–1944* (New York: Oxford Univ. Press, 2010); Philippe Burrin, *France under the Germans: Collaboration and Compromise,* trans. Janet Lloyd (New York: New Press, 1993); Richard Vinen, *The Unfree French: Life under the Occupation* (New Haven, Conn.: Yale Univ. Press, 2006); and Allan Mitchell, *Nazi Paris: The History of an Occupation, 1940–1944* (New York: Berghahn, 2008).

2. Historians such as Robert Aron, offered a Gaullist version of the heroic FFI in his influential *Histoire de la Libération de La France, Juin 1944–Mai 1945* (Paris: Librairie Arthème Fayard, 1959). Recently, historian Olivier Wieviorka has proffered an excellent discussion of the protean narratives of the war years in *Divided Memory: French Recollections of World War II from the Liberation to the Present,* trans. George Holoch (Stanford, Calif.: Stanford Univ. Press, 2012), and his own version of the resistance in *The French Resistance* (Cambridge Mass.: Harvard Univ. Press, 2016). The latter work is well complemented by Robert Gildea, *Fighters in the Shadows: A New History of the French Resistance* (Cambridge, Mass.: Belknap Press, 2015).

3. Stephen Alan Bourque offers an informative discussion of debates among the Allies about the bombing strategy in *Beyond the Beach: The Allied War Against France* (Annapolis, Md.: Naval Institute Press, 2018), 46–51.

4. Ibid., 185, 188–90, 260–61, discusses the inaccuracy of light and medium bombers.

5. Claudia Baldoli and Andrew Knapp, *Forgotten Blitzes: France and Italy under Allied Air Attack, 1940–1945* (London: Continuum, 2012), 236, 261; Jean Quellien in Jean-Luc Leleu, Françoise Passera, and Jean Quellien, *La France pendant la Seconde Guerre Mondiale* (Paris: Fayard and le Ministère de la Défense, 2010), 262–65; Danièle Voldman in Leleu et al., *La France pendant la Seconde Guerre Mondiale,* 266. Simon Kitson, "Criminals or Liberators? French Public Opinion and The Allied Bombing of France, 1940–1945," in *Bombing, States, and Peoples in Western Europe, 1940–1945,* ed. Claudia Baldoli, Andrew Knapp, and Richard Overy (London: Continuum, 2011), 291–92. Around 90,000 civilians were deported from France to concentration camps. Around 75,000 were Jews, of which about 25,000 were French. The balance were Jews who had sought refuge in France before 1940. About 3,000 French Jews returned to France in 1945. I came across no document produced by the GPRF protesting the number of French civilian deaths caused by

Allied actions. Andrew Knapp and Richard Overy note numerous diplomatic protests by the CFLN against inaccurate Allied bombing during the war in Baldoli and Knapp, *Forgotten Blitzes*, 235–36, and Richard Overy, *The Bombing War: Europe, 1939–1945* (London: Allen Lane, 2013), 575. I am using Quellien's estimates of dead FFI here and not the 24,000 reported in Marcel Vigneras, *Rearming the French* (Washington, D.C.: Office of the Chief of Military History, Department of the Army, 1957), 305.

6. Eddy Florentin, *Quand les Alliés bombardaient la France* (Paris: Perrin, 1997), 587; Overy, *The Bombing War*, 581, Régine Torrent, *La France américaine: Controverses de la Libération* (Brussels: Editions Racine, 2004), 225.

7. Forrest C. Pogue, *George C. Marshall: Organizer of Victory, 1943–1945* (New York: Viking, 1973), 543; Florentin, *Quand les Alliés*, 614; Eisenhower, *Crusade in Europe*, 467–68; United States, Department of the Army, *Army Battle Casualties and Nonbattle Deaths in World War II, Final Report* (Washington, D.C.: Office of the Comptroller of the Army, 1953), 32–33, 92–93. The U.S. Eighth Air Force lost 5,129 bombers and around 44,000 aviators in combat or in accidents, so the United States also had a conception of acceptable losses in order to achieve victory. Of course, not all were lost over France. The RAF lost another 10,321 bombers and 55,500 aviators—also a total figure for all of Europe and North Africa, and not just over France. Hence, almost 100,000 Allied aviators lost their lives in the war; that was the price paid, whether willingly or not. *Final Report* breaks down casualties by campaign, but it does not separate losses in Belgium and the Rhineland from those incurred in France. Therefore, arriving at statistics for losses in France requires creativity. The European Theater excluded Italy.

8. Florentin, *Quand les Alliés*, 605–9, 612–13.

9. For French historians who promote the myth of AMGOT, see Henri Michel, *The Second World War*, trans. Douglas Parmee (New York: Praeger, 1975), 2:663–64; Jean Lacouture, *De Gaulle*, trans. Patrick O'Brian (New York: Norton, 1990), 1:502–4. Lacouture relates that the only alternatives to American recognition of de Gaulle's regime in France were AMGOT or a continuation of Vichy. Even the highly respected Michel claims that the U.S. Army deposed officials appointed by de Gaulle's delegates and reinstated Vichy officials; I found no evidence that ever happened. Olivier Wieviorka, in *Normandy: The Landings to the Liberation of Paris*, trans. M. B. DeBevoise (Cambridge, Mass.: Belknap Press, 2008), 300–22, gives a reasoned and deeply informed discussion of AMGOT and Allied recognition of de Gaulle. Régine Torrent provides a comprehensive and well reasoned examination of AMGOT in *France américaine*, 75–221; however, she claims that FDR never said he *would* install AMGOT, only that he *could* (218–19).

10. Torrent, *France américaine*, 241–46, 255, asserts that the French generally blamed the Allies for shortages that became acute in the fall of 1944.

BIBLIOGRAPHY

PRIMARY SOURCES

Manuscripts and Archives

National Archives, College Park, Maryland
Record Group 331, SHAEF
  G-5
  Psychological Warfare Department
  German Atrocities
  General Staff Secretariat, Numeric Files
  HQ Files
Record Group 338, Operations
  Third Army, Inspector General Section, Reports and Investigations
Record Group 498, HQ ETO
  recommendations for decorations for French citizens
  Courts Martial
  Inspector General Office
  Provost Marshal
  Judge Advocate General
  First Army HQ, G-5

U.S. Army Military History Institute, Carlisle Barracks, Pennsylvania
James Alexander Crothers Papers
Chester B. Hansen Papers
John J. Maginnis Papers
Betty M. Olson Papers
Herman Pohl Papers
William E. Potter Papers
Veterans Surveys
  1st, 2nd, 4th, and 29th Infantry Divisions

Archives nationales, Pierrefitte-sur-Seine, France
F1a 3261
F1a 3303, 3306
F1a 4004–4006

Archives départementales de l'Aube
NA 10011
SC 4102
SC 4259, 4260, 4273
SC 24642 B
SC 39175

Archives départementales des Bouches-du-Rhône
6 S 10/10
149 W 182

Archives départementales de Meurthe-et-Moselle
WM 358
WM 468
WM 1518, 1520, 1521, 1523, 1525, 1533

Archives départementales de l'Yonne
1 W 319, 324, 328
1222 W 11
1222 W 38

Published Documents

Chandler, Alfred D., ed. *The Papers of Dwight D. Eisenhower*. Vols. 3 and 4, *The War Years*. Baltimore: Johns Hopkins Univ. Press, 1970.

McJimsey, George, ed. *Documentary History of the Franklin D. Roosevelt Presidency*. Vol. 47, *Establishing Civil Government in Occupied Europe*. [Bethesda, Md.]: University Publications of America, 2001.

U.S. Department of State. *Foreign Relations of the United States*. Vols. 2–4. Washington D.C.: Department of State, 1943, 1944, 1945.

Memoirs and Contemporary Works

Aglion, Raoul. *Roosevelt and de Gaulle: Allies in Conflict: A Personal Memoir*. New York: Free Press, 1988.

Bradley, Omar N. *A Soldier's Story.* New York: Holt, 1951.

Brinton, Crane. "Letters from Liberated France." *French Historical Studies* 2, nos. 1 and 2 (1961): 1–27, 131–56.

Brown, Frances DeBra. *An Army in Skirts: The World War II Letters of Frances DeBra.* Indianapolis: Indiana Historical Society Press, 2008.

Butcher, Harry C. *My Three Years with Eisenhower.* New York: Simon and Schuster, 1946.

Capa, Robert. *Slightly Out of Focus.* New York: Holt, 1947.

Churchill, Winston S. *The Second World War.* 6 vols. Boston: Houghton Mifflin, 1949–1950.

Clark, Mark W. *Calculated Risk.* New York: Harper and Row, 1950.

Closon, Françis-Louis. *Commissaire de la République du Général de Gaulle: Lille, Septembre 1944–Mars 1946.* Paris: Juillard, 1980.

Codman, Charles R. *Drive.* Boston: Little, Brown, 1957.

Cohn, David L. *This Is the Story.* Boston: Houghton Mifflin, 1947.

Cooper, Duff. *Old Men Forget: The Autobiography of Duff Cooper.* New York: Dutton, 1954.

Coulet, François. *Vertu des Temps difficiles.* Paris: Plon, 1967.

Courtney, Richard D. *Normandy to the Bulge: An American Infantry GI in Europe During World War II.* Carbondale: Southern Illinois Univ. Press, 1997.

Dreux, William B., *No Bridges Blown.* South Bend, Ind.: Univ. of Notre Dame Press, 1971.

Eisenhower, Dwight D. *Crusade in Europe.* New York: Doubleday, 1948.

Flanner, Janet. *Paris Journal, 1944–1965.* New York: Atheneum, 1965.

Foulon, Charles-Louis. *Le Pouvoir en Province à la Libération: les Commissaires de la République, 1943–1946.* Paris: Fondation nationale des sciences politiques, Armand Colin, 1975.

France, Armée, Division blindée, 2. *La 2e [i.e. deuxième] d. b., Général Leclerc, Combattants et Combats en France, présentés par un Groupe d'Officiers et d'Hommes de la Division.* Paris: Arts et métiers graphiques, 1945.

Galtier-Boissière, Jean. *Mon Journal depuis La Libération.* Paris: La Jeune Parque, 1945.

de Gaulle, Charles. *The Complete War Memoirs of Charles de Gaulle,* translated by Jonathan Griffin and Richard Howard. 3 vols. New York: Da Capo, 1984.

———. *Mémoires de Guerre: L'Unité, 1942–1944.* Paris: Plon, n.d.

———. *The Speeches of Charles de Gaulle,* translated by Sheila Mathieu and W. G. Corp. 2 vols. London: Oxford Univ. Press, 1943.

Giraud, Henri. *Un Seul But, la Victoire, Alger 1942–1944.* Paris: R. Julliard, 1949.

Grandval, Gilbert, and A. Jean Collin. *Libération de l'Est de la France.* Paris: Hachette, 1974.

de Guerpel, Xavier. *1939–1945: Une Certaine Vie de Château au Bocage Normand.* Conde-sur-Noireau: Editions Ch. Corlet, 1973.

Harrison, Donald, ed. *From the Letters of Robert S. Gerdy, 1942–1945: A Personal Record of World War II.* Philadelphia: Dorance, 1969.

Hull, Cordell. *The Memoirs of Cordell Hull.* 2 vols. New York: Macmillan, 1948.

Humbert, Agnès. *Résistance: A Woman's Journal of Struggle and Defiance in Occupied France,* translated by Barbara Mellor. New York: Bloomsbury, 2008.

Idrac, Armand. *My Normandy: A Teenager Lives through World War II,* translated by Jo-anne Silver. Wayne, Pa.: Beach Lloyd, 2005.

Juin, Alphonse. *Mémoires.* 2 vols. Paris: A. Fayard, 1959.

de Kérillis, Henri. *I Accuse de Gaulle.* New York: Harcourt, Brace, 1946.

Lankford, Nelson Douglas, ed. *OSS Against the Reich: The World War II Diaries of Colonel David K. Bruce.* Kent, Ohio: Kent State Univ. Press, 1991.

Leahy, William D. *I Was There: The Personal Story of the Chief of Staff to Presidents Roosevelt and Truman.* New York: Whittlesey House, 1950.

Liebling, Abbott Joseph. *Normandy Revisited.* New York: Simon and Schuster, 1958.

Macmillan, Harold. *The Blast of War, 1939–1945.* London: Macmillan, 1967.

Maginnis, John J., and Robert A. Hart, eds. *Military Government Journal: Normandy to Berlin.* Amherst: Univ. of Massachusetts Press, 1971.

Maillaud, Pierre (Pierre Bourdan). *Over to France,* translated by Francis Cowper. London: Oxford Univ. Press, 1946.

Mast, Général Charles. *Histoire d'une Rébellion, Alger, 8 novembre 1942.* Paris: Plon, 1969.

Maurois, André. *Memoirs,* translated by Denver Lindley. New York: Harper and Row, 1970.

———. *Rouen Dévasté.* Fontaine-le-Bourg: Le Pucheux, 2004.

Mendès-France, Pierre. *The Pursuit of Freedom.* London: Longmans, Green, 1956.

Monnet, Jean. *Memoirs,* translated by Richard Mayne. New York: Doubleday, 1978.

Moorehead, Alan. *Eclipse.* New York: Harper and Row, 1968.

Murphy, Robert. *Diplomat Among Warriors.* New York: Doubleday, 1964.

Osmont, Marie-Louise. *The Normandy Diary of Marie-Louise Osmont: 1940–1944,* translated by George L. Newman. New York: Random House, 1994.

Pendar, Kenneth Whittemore. *Adventure in Diplomacy: Our French Dilemma.* New York: Da Capo, 1976.

Rehr, Louis S., and Carleton R. Rehr. *Marauder: Memoir of a B-26 Pilot in Europe in World War II.* Jefferson, N.C.: McFarland, 2004.

Schmitt, Hans A. *An Ordinary Life in Extraordinary Times, 1933–1946.* Baton Rouge: Louisiana Univ. Press, 1989.

Stein, Gertrude. *Wars I Have Seen.* London: Batsford, 1945.

Taflinger, Nicole H. *Season of Suffering: Coming of Age in Occupied France, 1940–45.* Pullman: Washington State Univ. Press, 2010.

Tobin, Richard L. *Invasion Journal.* New York: Dutton, 1944.

Triplet, William S. *A Colonel in the Armored Divisions: A Memoir, 1941–1945.* Columbia: Univ. of Missouri Press, 2001.

Weygand, Maxime. *Recalled to Service: The Memoirs of General Maxime Weygand*, translated by E. W. Dickes. London: Heinemann, 1952.

Wertenbaker, Charles C. *Invasion!* New York: Appleton Century, 1944.

Wiskemann, Elizabeth. *The Europe I Saw.* New York: St. Martin's Press, 1968.

Periodicals

Boston Globe
Chicago Tribune
New York Herald Tribune
Stars and Stripes

SECONDARY SOURCES

Alary, Eric, Bénédicte Vergez-Chaignon, and Gilles Gauvin. *Les Français au quotidien, 1939–1949*. Paris: Perrin, 2006.

Amouroux, Henri. *La grande Histoire des Français après l'Occupation*. 10 vols. Paris: Robert Laffont, 1976–1993.

Aron, Robert. *Histoire de la Libération de La France, Juin 1944–Mai 1945*. Paris: Libraire Arthème Fayard, 1959.

Atkinson, Rick. *The Guns at Last Light: The War in Western Europe, 1944–1945*. New York: Holt, 2013.

Azéma, Jean-Pierre, and François Bédarida, eds. *La France des Années noires*. Vol. 2, *De l'Occupation à la Libération*. Paris: Editions du Seuil, 2000.

Baldoli, Claudia, and Andrew Knapp. *Forgotten Blitzes: France and Italy under Allied Air Attack, 1940–1945*. London: Continuum, 2012.

Baldoli, Claudia, Andrew Knapp, and Richard Overy, eds. *Bombing, States and Peoples in Western Europe, 1940–1945*. London: Continuum, 2011.

Bécamps, Pierre. *Libération de Bordeaux*. Paris: Hachette, 1974.

Beevor, Anthony, and Artemis Cooper. *Paris After the Liberation, 1944–1949*. New York: Doubleday, 1994.

Bois, Paul, ed. *Histoire de Nantes*. Toulouse: Privat, 1977.

Bourque, Stephen Alan. *Beyond the Beach: The Allied War Against France*. Annapolis, Md.: Naval Institute Press, 2018.

Burrin, Philippe. *France under the Germans: Collaboration and Compromise*, translated by Janet Lloyd. New York: New Press, 1993.

Cole, Hugh M. *The Lorraine Campaign*. Washington, D.C.: U.S. Army Center of Military History, 2007.

Coles, Harry L., and Albert K. Weinberg. *Civil Affairs: Soldiers Become Governors*. Washington, D.C.: U.S. Army Center of Military History, 2004.

Coutau Bégarie, Hervé, and Claude Huan. *Darlan*. Paris: Fayard, 1989.

Craven, Wesley F., and James L. Cate, eds. *The Army Air Forces in World War II*, vols. 1–3, Chicago: Univ. of Chicago Press, 1948–1951.

Delasselle, Claude, Joel Drogland, Frédéric Gand, Thierry Roblin, and Jean Rolley. *Un Département dans la Guerre 1939–1945: Occupation, Collaboration et Résistance dans l'Yonne*. Paris: Editions Tirésias, 2006.

Donnison, Frank, S.V. *Civil Affairs and Military Government North-West Europe, 1944–1946*. London: Her Majesty's Stationary Office, 1961.

Eisenhower, David. *Eisenhower: At War 1943–1945*. New York: Vintage, 1987.

Etienne, Jean-Louis. *La République Restaurée: Les Pouvoirs et l'Opinion à la Libération en Meurthe-et-Moselle*. Nancy: Archives de Meurthe-et-Moselle, 1995.

Florentin, Eddy. *Quand les Alliés bombardaient la France*. Paris: Perrin, 1997.

Footitt, Hilary. *War and Liberation in France: Living with the Liberators*. New York: Palgrave Macmillan, 2004.

Fuller, Robert L. *The Struggle for Cooperation: Liberated France and the American Military, 1944–1946*. Lexington: Univ. Press of Kentucky, 2019.

Funk, Arthur L. *Charles de Gaulle: The Crucial Years, 1943–1944*. Norman: Univ. of Oklahoma Press, 1959.

Gildea, Robert. *Fighters in the Shadows: A New History of the French Resistance*. Cambridge, Mass.: Belknap Press, 2015.

———. *Marianne in Chains: Daily Life in the Heart of France during the German Occupation*. New York: Metropolitan Books, 2004.

Giraud, Henri-Christian. *De Gaulle et les communistes*. 2 vols. Paris: Albin Michel, 1988–1989.

Griffiths, Richard. *Pétain: A Biography of Marshal Philippe Pétain of Vichy*. Garden City, New York: Doubleday, 1972.

Gurley, Franklin L. "Politique contre Stratégie: La Défense de Strasbourg en décembre 1944." *Guerres mondiales et Conflits contemporains*, no. 166 (April 1992): 89–114.

Hastings, Max. *Armageddon: The Battle for Germany, 1944–1945*. New York: Knopf, 2004.

———. *Overlord: D-Day and the Battle for Normandy*. New York: Simon and Schuster, 1984.

Hitchcock, William I. *The Bitter Road to Freedom: A New History of the Liberation of Europe*. New York: Free Press, 2008.

Hood, Ronald Chalmers. *Royal Republicans: The French Naval Dynasties between the World Wars*. Baton Rouge: Louisiana State Univ. Press, 1985.

Hoyt, Edwin P. *The GI's War: The Story of American Soldiers in Europe in World War II*. New York: McGraw Hill, 1988.

l'Huillier, Fernand. "Sur la Nazification de l'Alsace." *Revue d'Histoire de la Deuxième Guerre mondiale* 30, no. 120 (October 1980): 59–68.

Hurstfield, Julian G. *America and the French Nation, 1939–1945*. Chapel Hill: Univ. of North Carolina Press, 1986.

Huston, James A. *Across the Face of France: Liberation and Recovery 1944–63*. West Lafayette, Ind.: Purdue University Studies, 1963.

Jackson, Julian. *A Certain Idea of France: The Life of Charles de Gaulle*. N.p.: Allen Lane, 2018.

———. *France: The Dark Years, 1940–1944*. Oxford: Oxford Univ. Press, 2001.

Jankowski, Paul. *Communism and Collaboration: Simon Sabiani and Politics in Marseille, 1919–1944*. New Haven, Conn.: Yale Univ. Press, 1989.

Jones, Benjamin F. *Eisenhower's Guerrillas: The Jedburghs, the Maquis, and the Liberation of France*. New York: Oxford Univ. Press, 2016.

Kaufmann, J. E., and H. W. Kaufmann. *G.I. Joe in France: From Normandy to Berchtesgaden*. Westport, Conn.: Praeger, 2008.

Keegan, John. *Six Armies in Normandy, from D-Day to the Liberation of Paris*. New York: Penguin, 1983.

Kitson, Simon. "Criminals or Liberators? French Public Opinion and the Allied Bombing of France, 1940–1945." In *Bombing, States, and Peoples in Western Europe, 1940–1945*, edited by Claudia Baldoli, Andrew Knapp, and Richard Overy. London: Continuum, 2011.

Lacouture, Jean. *De Gaulle*, translated by Patrick O'Brian. 2 vols. New York: Norton, 1990.

La Liberté Retrouvée: La Libération de la Meurthe-et-Moselle. Nancy: Conseil Générale de la Meurthe-et-Moselle, 2005.

Langer, William L. *Our Vichy Gamble*. New York: Norton, 1966.

Laub, Thomas Johnston. *After the Fall: German Policy in Occupied France, 1940–1944*. New York: Oxford Univ. Press, 2010.

Leleu, Jean-Luc, Françoise Passera, and Jean Quellien. *La France pendant la Seconde Guerre Mondiale*. Paris: Fayard and le Ministère de la Défense, 2010.

Lewis, S. J. *Jedburgh Team Operations in Support of the 12th Army Group, August 1944*. Fort Leavenworth, Kans.: Combat Studies Institute, 1991.

Lilly, J. Robert. *Taken by Force: Rape and American GIs in Europe during World War II*. Basingstoke, UK: Palgrave Macmillan, 2007.

Maguire, G. E. *Anglo-American Policy Towards the Free French*. New York: St. Martin's Press, 1995.

MacDonald, Charles B. *The Mighty Endeavor: American Armed Forces in the European Theater in World War II*. New York: Oxford Univ. Press, 1969.

Maddaloni, Gabrielle M. "Liberation and Franco-American Relations in Post-War Cherbourg." Master's thesis, Fort Leavenworth, Kansas, U.S. Army Command and General Staff College, 2008.

Marrus, Michael R. *The Unwanted: European Refugees in the Twentieth Century*. New York: Oxford Univ. Press, 1985.

Marrus, Michael R., and Robert O. Paxton. *Vichy France and the Jews*. New York: Schocken, 1983.

Maule, Henry. *Out of the Sand: The Epic Story of General Leclerc and the Fighting Free French*. London: Odhams, 1966.

Michel, Henri. *Histoire de la France Libre*. Paris: Presses Universitaires de France, 1972.

———. *The Second World War*, translated by Douglas Parmee. 2 vols. New York: Praeger, 1975.

Michelin Guide. *Normandy*. Clermont-Ferrand: Michelin et Cie., 1974.

Mitchell, Allan. *Nazi Paris: The History of an Occupation, 1940–1944*. New York: Berghahn, 2008.

Neiberg, Michael. *The Blood of Free Men: The Liberation of Paris, 1944*. New York: Basic, 2012.

Nobécourt, Jacques. *Hitler's Last Gamble: The Battle of the Ardennes*, translated by R. H. Berry. London: Chatto and Windus, 1967.

O'Donnell, Patrick K. *Dog Company*. Boston: Da Capo, 2012.

Ottis, Sherri Greene. *Silent Heroes: Downed Airmen and the French Underground*. Lexington: Univ. Press of Kentucky, 2001.

Ousby, Ian. *Occupation: The Ordeal of France, 1940–1944*. London: John Murray, 1997.

Overy, Richard. *The Bombing War: Europe, 1939–1945*. London: Allen Lane, 2013.

Parisse, Michel. *Histoire de Nancy*. Toulouse: Privat, 1978.

Passera, Françoise, and Jean Quellien. *Les Civils dans la Bataille de Normandie*. Bayeux: OREP Editions, 2014.

Paxton, Robert O. *Vichy France: Old Guard and New Order, 1940–1944*. New York: Columbia Univ. Press, 1972.

Péréon, Yves-Marie. *L'image de la France dans la Presse américaine, 1936–1947*. Brussels: Peter Lang, 2011.

Pogue, Forrest C. *George C. Marshall: Organizer of Victory, 1943–1945*. New York: Viking, 1973.

———. *The Supreme Command*. Washington, D.C.: Office of the Chief of Military History, Deptartment of the Army, 1954.

Pujo, Bernard. *Juin, Maréchal de France*. Paris: Albin Michel, 1988.

Quellien, Jean. *La Bataille de Normandie, 6 Juin–25 Août*. Paris: Tallendier, 2014.

Reynolds, David. *Rich Relations: The American Occupation of Britain, 1942–1945*. New York: Random House, 1995.

Roberts, Mary Louise. *D-Day Through French Eyes, Normandy 1944*. Chicago: Univ. of Chicago Press, 2014.

Robertson, Charles L. *When Roosevelt Planned to Govern France*. Amherst: Univ. of Massachusetts Press, 2011.

Ross, William F., and Charles F. Romanus. *The Quartermaster Corps: Operations in the War against Germany*. Washington, D.C.: U.S. Army Center of Military History, 2004.

Ruppenthal, Roland G. *Logistical Support of the Armies.* 2 vols. Washington, D.C.: U.S. Army Center of Military History, 1953.

Schrijvers, Peter. *The Crash of Ruin: American Combat Soldiers in Europe during World War II.* New York: New York Univ. Press, 1998.

———. *Liberators: The Allies and Belgian Society, 1944–1945.* Cambridge: Cambridge Univ. Press, 2009.

Sherwood, Robert E. *Roosevelt and Hopkins: An Intimate History.* New York: Harper Brothers, 1948.

Sweets, John F. *Choices in Vichy France: The French under Nazi Occupation.* New York: Oxford Univ. Press, 1986.

———. "La Police et la Population dans la France de Vichy: une Étude de Cas Conforme et Fidèle." *Guerres mondiales et Conflits contemporains,* no. 155 (July 1989): 63–73.

Torrent, Régine. *La France américaine: Controverses de la Libération.* Brussels: Editions Racine, 2004.

Tournoux, Jean Raymond. *Pétain et la France: la Seconde Guerre mondiale.* Paris: Plon, 1980.

United States, Department of the Army. *Army Battle Casualties and Nonbattle Deaths in World War II, Final Report.* Washington, D.C.: Office of the Comptroller of the Army, 1953.

Van Creveld, Martin. *Supplying War: Logistics from Wallenstein to Patton.* Cambridge: Cambridge Univ. Press, 1977.

Vigneras, Marcel. *Rearming the French.* Washington, D.C.: Office of the Chief of Military History, Department of the Army, 1957.

Vinen, Richard. *The Unfree French: Life under the Occupation.* New Haven, Conn.: Yale Univ. Press, 2006.

Viorst, Milton. *Hostile Allies: FDR and Charles de Gaulle.* New York: Macmillan, 1965.

Virgili, Fabrice. *Shorn Women: Gender and Punishment in Liberation France,* translated by John Flower. London: Berg, 2002.

Weigley, Russell F. *Eisenhower's Lieutenants: The Campaign of France and Germany.* Bloomington: Indiana Univ. Press, 1981.

Wieviorka, Olivier. *Divided Memory: French Recollections of World War II from the Liberation to the Present,* translated by George Holoch. Stanford, Calif.: Stanford Univ. Press, 2012.

———. *The French Resistance,* translated by Jane Marie Todd. Cambridge, Mass.: Harvard Univ. Press, 2016.

———. *Normandy: The Landings to the Liberation of Paris,* translated by M. B. DeBevoise. Cambridge, Mass.: Belknap Press, 2008.

INDEX